W9-ABP-351

ENGLAND IN EGYPT

ENGLAND IN EGYPT

BY

VISCOUNT MILNER

NEW YORK
Howard Fertig
1970

First published in 1892 by Edward Arnold Ltd.
13th edition 1920 [here reprinted]

HOWARD FERTIG, INC. EDITION 1970
Published by arrangement with Edward Arnold Ltd.

Library of Congress Catalog Card Number: 68:9624

PRINTED IN THE UNITED STATES OF AMERICA
BY NOBLE OFFSET PRINTERS, INC.

PREFACE

TO THE THIRTEENTH EDITION

FIRST published in 1892, 'England in Egypt' has passed through a number of editions. In none of these was the text in any way altered, though an appendix to the sixth edition, by the late Sir Clinton Dawkins, and another to the eleventh edition, by the late Sir Eldon Gorst, brought the narrative of events contained in the original work up to 1904.

I always expected that the twelfth edition, which appeared in 1915, would be the last. And indeed for some years past the demand for the book has, very naturally, fallen off. But recent events have led to a revival of interest in the political relations of Great Britain and Egypt, of which this volume was the first to give the British public a connected account. And though, since its first appearance, other works, notably Lord Cromer's monumental 'Modern Egypt,' have given later and fuller information, attention has now once more been directed to 'England in Egypt,' and at the urgent request of my publisher I have consented to the issue of the present, the thirteenth, edition of a work that is now nearly thirty years old.

In doing so I have again abstained from altering a single word of the original text or trying to modify the views expressed in it by the light of subsequent events. Even if I had time to venture on so hazardous an experiment, I doubt whether it would be of any advantage to my readers. 'England in Egypt,' when first written, was the expression of recent and vivid experience, and whatever value it possesses as a historical document might be seriously impaired by an attempt to 'bring it up to date.' Moreover, with all its imperfections, there is nothing in the book which I have any desire to recant. Many and great changes, mostly for the better, have come over Egypt in the last thirty years, but these changes have been, in the main, only the natural and desired result of the policy which 'England in Egypt' was written to explain. That policy, the policy initiated and for many years directed by Cromer, had for its object the establishment in Egypt of 'an order of things,' to quote the words of Lord Granville, which 'should possess the elements of stability and progress.' Whatever view may be taken of the condition of Egypt to-day, there can be no doubt that 'the elements of stability and progress' are incomparably stronger than they were when we first took her in hand. On the material side, Egypt, from being an impoverished and almost bankrupt country, has become a prosperous and wealthy one. And if here, as elsewhere, moral and social progress has lagged behind material development, yet even in these respects Egypt has gone up many degrees in the scale of civilization. At the present moment the question of the future political status of Egypt has once more become a burning one. This is not the place to discuss that grave and complex problem. But there is one reflection with regard to it which can hardly fail to occur to any reader of 'England in Egypt.' That it should be possible to contemplate so large a measure of independence as is now proposed for Egypt, is surely the most striking tribute to the efficacy of Great Britain's reforming work.

Strangely enough, the view has been expressed in some quarters that any relaxation of British control over the administration of Egypt would be an abandonment of the objects which we have hitherto been pursuing in that country. Nothing could be further from the truth. The establishment of Egypt as an independent state in intimate alliance with Great Britain, so far from being a reversal of the policy with which we set out, would be the consummation of it. Unless all our past declarations have been insincere, and all our professions hypocritical, this is the goal to which our efforts have always been directed. It may, indeed, be argued that the goal has not been reached, that Egypt is not yet strong enough to stand on her own feet, that the proposed changes in her constitution are premature and will end in failure. Such arguments are entitled to respectful consideration. But what cannot be maintained, with any regard for historical accuracy, is that those changes, in themselves, are not absolutely in accordance with the constantly declared policy of Great Britain. That we should attempt them at all, is evidence at once of our good faith and of our confidence in the soundness of the work which we have been doing in Egypt for the last eight and thirty years. If the attempt is successful, we shall have put the crown on one of the most remarkable enterprises ever undertaken by one nation for the regeneration of another.

October 15, 1920.

PREFACE

TO THE FIRST EDITION

THE following book is the result of my experience and my inquiries during a residence of several years in Egypt. When I began writing it, eight months ago, I never contemplated leaving Egypt immediately. I counted on several years, during which I could complete my studies and give them an adequate literary form. Unexpectedly recalled to England, and confronted at once with new and arduous duties, I had to answer the question, whether I should abandon my work, put it aside in the hope of finishing it gradually in leisure moments, or give it to the world at once, in however defective a shape. I could not bring myself to abandon it, for it seemed to me, with all its shortcomings, to have some value and interest, especially at the present time. I saw great danger in postponing it; for not only might the leisure necessary for its completion never come to me, but my writing would certainly lose some of the force which attaches to the record of experiences that are still recent and vivid. So I decided to bring out my book at once in the best form that hurry and stress of other business would allow me to give to it. Freshness and timeliness would, I hoped, atone for the lack of completeness and finish. Whether my decision was a wise one, it is not for me to say. But I have felt bound, out of respect for my readers, to offer some explanation for the evident hastiness of the work, and the consequent omissions in substance and imperfections in style—of which no one can be more conscious than the author.

A. M.

LONDON,
November, 1892.

CONTENTS

NOTE.

THE spelling of Arabic words has caused me great difficulty, with which every scholar will sympathize. Finally, I decided that in a book of this kind any elaborate principle of transliteration was out of place. So I have followed, to the best of my ability, the simple phonetic system recommended by the Royal Geographical Society, the main rules of which are that the vowels have the same value as in Italian, and the consonants the same value as in English. and that a single accent (') is used, where necessary, to denote the syllable on which the stress of pronunciation falls.

ENGLAND IN EGYPT

CHAPTER I.

INTRODUCTORY: THE LAND OF PARADOX.

MORE than two thousand years ago, the Father of History, in his comprehensive survey of the then known world, singled out Egypt as pre-eminently the land of wonders. 'I speak at length about Egypt,' he says, 'because it contains more marvellous things than any other country, things too strange for words.' To the miracles of its rainless climate and all-begetting river, to the mysterious monuments of human power and perseverance towering since the remotest ages over its inexhaustibly fertile plain, Egypt added, in its history and institutions, in the character and customs of its inhabitants, other marvels not less unique. No country upon earth could vie with it in idiosyncrasy or in interest. And this is the case even at the present day. In the world as known to Herodotus, Egypt, though fallen from its ancient grandeur, still filled a considerable space. Now it is a mere speck on the map. In wealth, in power, in population, in intelligence, it has dwindled to insignificance. But its pre-eminence in interest stands unimpaired.

The fascination of its primeval monuments remains, and every year an increasing crowd of pilgrims comes from all quarters of the earth to do them homage. The annual miracle of the Nile flood remains, more deeply impressive perhaps to the few strangers who are privileged to witness it than all the tombs and all the temples. And as in its physical singularity, as in its stupendous antiquities, so in the life and habits of its people, and in the form—yes, nowadays above all, in the form of its government—Egypt is still, like the Egypt of Herodotus, the chosen home of what is strange and unexampled and paradoxical. Conqueror after conqueror has swept over the land. Dynasty has supplanted dynasty. There have been centuries of political chaos, from which the wonder is that anything at all has escaped. Paganism has given way to Christianity, Christianity to Islam. Yet amid countless changes, the country retains one unchanging attribute. Alike in its greatness and in its impotence, in prosperity and in ruin; whether split up among a number of petty rulers, or united under one gigantic despotism; whether prostrate before the fantastic images of a thousand gods, or plunged in fanatical devotion to a Divine Unity of which any image is a desecration, Egypt, altered in so many aspects, remains unalterably, eternally abnormal. This genius for eccentricity is something that no change can exorcise. Paradox seems rooted in the soil.

Nowhere in the world will you find a peasantry whose daily life presents so many elements of the odd and picturesque as the fellahin of Egypt. Nowhere do East and West jostle each other in such startling contrast or with more grotesque results. And nowhere, surely nowhere, is civilized government carried on under more incredible conditions. The monstrosities of the Political Constitution of Egypt as it exists to-day may be the latest, but they are certainly not the least of the wonderful things, 'too strange for words,' of which, in the moral as in the physical order, the Nile valley has from time immemorial been so prolific.

'The women of Egypt,' says Herodotus, 'are employed in trade and business, while the men stay at home to spin and weave. Other nations in weaving throw the woof up the warp, but an Egyptian throws it down. In other countries sons are constrained to make provision for their parents; in Egypt it is not the sons, but the daughters. In other countries the priests of the gods wear hair; in Egypt they are shaved. In other countries the dwellings of men are separated from those of beasts; in Egypt man and beast live together. Other nations fasten their ropes and hooks to the outside of their sails, but the Egyptians to the inside. The Greeks write and read from left to right, but the Egyptians from right to left.' And so on, through a long tale of peculiarities, some superficial and some essential, not a few of which cannot here be quoted with any respect for the delicacy of modern taste. But long as the tale is, it would be easy to match it by a list of the anomalies, the intricacies, and the shams with which the Political System of Egypt, in its latest development, positively bristles.

This is a matter on which I speak with feeling, and with no slight experience. Among the thousands of travellers who annually visit Egypt for health, amusement, or instruction, there are, say, one per cent.—but that nowadays is no inconsiderable number—who, despite the attraction of the ancient monuments of the country and the striking features which characterize its present life, have still some interest to spare for the social and economic conditions, on which the welfare of its picturesque inhabitants depends, and for the strange political experiment, unique in history, of which it is at this moment the scene. To not a few of these inquirers it has been my humble duty to try and explain how the machine worked—or did not work. Where they happened to be quite new to the subject, I have a vivid recollection of the look of strained attention, passing through blank bewilderment to ultimate despair, with which they followed my well-meant efforts to guide them amidst the labyrinth of jarring interests, conflicting authorities, and hopelessly disintegrated sovereignty. That painful result was no fault of theirs, nor was it, as I hope subsequent pages may show, altogether the fault of the expositor. It is not given to mortal intelligence to master at one blow the complexities of Turkish suzerainty and foreign treaty rights; to realize the various powers of interference and obstruction possessed by Consuls and Consuls-General, by Commissioners of the Public Debt, and other 'Mixed Administrations'; to distinguish English officers who are English from English officers who are Egyptian, foreign judges of the International Courts from foreign judges of the Native Courts; to follow the writhings of the Egyptian Government in its struggle to escape from the fine meshes of the Capitulations; to appreciate precisely what laws that Government can make with the consent of only six Powers, and for what laws it requires the consent of no less than fourteen. Yet these are only some of the incidents of that strange phantasmagoria which makes Egyptian politics to-day so worthy a counterpart, in respect of the odd and the contradictory, to the customs of the ancient Egyptians, as they appeared to the astonished eye of the great Greek historian.

Imagine a people the most docile and good-tempered in the world in the grip of a religion the most intolerant and fanatical. Imagine this people and this faith, congenial in nothing but their conservatism, flung into the maelstrom of European restlessness and innovation. Imagine a country full of turbulent foreigners, whom its police cannot arrest except *flagrante delicto*, and whom its courts cannot try except for the most insignificant offences. Imagine the Government of this country unable to legislate for these foreigners without the consent of a dozen distant Powers, most of them indifferent and some ill-disposed. Imagine it carrying on its principal business in a foreign tongue, which yet is not the tongue of the predominant foreign race. Imagine it struggling to meet the clamorous growing needs of to-day with a Budget rigorously fixed according to the minimum requirements of the day before yesterday. Imagine the decrees of this Government liable to be set at naught by courts of its own creation. Imagine its policy really inspired and directed by the Envoy of a foreign state, who in theory is only one—and not even the *doyen*—of a large number of such Envoys, and the chief administrative power really wielded by a man, who in theory is a mere 'Adviser without executive functions.' Yes, imagine all these things, and then realize that they are no 'Mikado'-like invention of comic opera, no nightmare of some constitutional theorist with a disordered brain, but prosaic, solid fact—an unvarnished picture of the political Egypt of to-day. And yet if one of the now extinct race of political philosophers, who used to amuse themselves with framing ideal polities, had gone out of his mind, and if in that madness, with all his theories mixed up and all his principles topsy-turvy, he had evolved a model constitution, the result might have been something like this. It surely could not have been anything more apparently irrational, anything at first sight more incompatible with the most elementary kind of decent government, to say nothing of development and progress.

E pur si muove. For in the Land of Paradox grapes *do* grow from thorns and figs from thistles. If the conditions, under which the government of Egypt has to be carried on, seem like a nightmare, the revival of the country during the last few years, under and in spite of these conditions, is almost worthy of a fairy tale. Here, again, the spirit of the eccentric and the improbable, which seems inseparable from all things Egyptian, has rollicked in a new surprise.

The task which Great Britain found upon her hands after Tel-el-Kebir was to all appearance one of the most thankless rôles ever thrust upon an unwilling actor. Unpromising enough in any case, it seemed perfectly hopeless, when once we had shrunk from a radical solution of the difficulty, and had determined just to make the best of the anomalous situation we found existing, and to which our arrival superadded a new anomaly. Yet the result has been beyond all human expectation. Egypt is far enough off even now from anything like an ideal standard of civilization or administrative excellence; but the difference between Egypt now and Egypt in the latter days of Ismail is as the difference between light and darkness. Look where you will—at the army, at finance, at agriculture, at the administration of justice, at the everyday life of the people and their relations to their rulers—it is always the same tale of revival, of promise, of a slowly developing faith in the existence of such a thing as equity, of a nascent—if only just nascent—spirit of self-reliance and improvement. And this in the place of almost general ruin and depression, of a total distrust in the possibility of just government, and a rooted belief in administrative corruption as the natural and invariable rule of human society. That seems a remarkable revolution to have taken place in ten years. It is doubtful whether, in any part of the world, the same period can show anything like the same tale of progress. The most absurd experiment in human government has been productive of one of the most remarkable harvests of human improvement.

In this contrast lies the romance of Egyptian history during the past decade. It is not the nature of the work done which is exceptional or worth writing about; still less the methods by which it has been done. They have been ordinary enough. They have consisted in the application of a reasonable amount of common-sense and common honesty to a country ruined by the absence of both. What is extraordinary, unique, and remarkable, what is worth recording and driving home, is not the work done, but the difficulties under which it has been done, difficulties which at first sight might have seemed to make any progress at all impossible. An increasing number of people in this country now take an interest and feel a pride in the progress of Egypt under British influence, but even now it is only very few who realize what the nature of that progress is, against what obstacles it has had to contend, and what are the conditions necessary for its continuance.

The object of the present volume is to make these matters clearer. The next three chapters (II., III., IV.) contain an analysis of the special difficulties, under which the work of reform has had to be carried on in Egypt during the past decade. The two following chapters (V. and VI.) give a brief historical sketch of the development of that work. The five succeeding chapters (VII.-XI.) describe some of its more important details. The three final chapters (XII.-XIV.) are devoted to a consideration of the influences, foreign or native, which have been favourable or unfavourable to the work, and of the prospects of its progress in the future.

It is impossible to write on such a subject without occasionally expressing opinions; but most distinctly my object is not to propound my personal opinions—a matter of very small moment. It is to give an accurate sketch of a most complicated problem, a true account of an interesting piece of history. I have not worried the reader by quoting authorities, but I have spared no pains to verify every statement, either by reference to published records, or by careful consultation of men intimately acquainted with the work of the several departments of government. Mistakes there may be, but they are assuredly not due to a desire to twist or conceal facts in favour of any particular view, however strongly I may hold it. If the facts will not support it, perish the view! *Magis amica veritas.* My aim is not to influence, but to inform—not polemical, but didactic.

Didactic! If ever a writer damned himself at the very outset, I would seem to have done so by using that word. But I am reassured by the inexorcisable quality of interest attaching to everything Egyptian. Didactic is generally synonymous with dull, but Egypt and dulness are incompatible ideas. Indeed, it is one of the pitfalls of the Egyptian administrator, that serious things constantly wear such comic aspects. He is so frequently reminded of Offenbach, that it is difficult for him to realize that he is not playing in Opéra Bouffe, but making history.

Take, for instance, the 'firman' incident of 1892. It was important that the new Khedive should receive a firman from the Sultan confirming his authority, very important that he should receive one couched in proper terms. Jurists might contend that, with or without a formal investiture, Abbas II. was *de jure* as well as *de facto* Khedive of Egypt from the moment of his father's death. But the fact remained that, in the eyes of a great portion of the population, the Khedive was only half a Khedive until he had obtained the special and personal recognition of the Sultan, not merely by telegram, but in the solemn traditional form. The protracted negotiations over the despatch and the contents of the firman were therefore political business of a really serious kind. But their external aspect was ludicrous in the extreme.

For weeks the quidnuncs of Cairo—and their name is legion, and they are the most feather-brained members of their genus that can be found in all the world—were electrified by a constant succession of conflicting reports as to the whereabouts and the tenor of the much-expected document. It had started. It had not started. It had received orders to start. It really would have started, but the caligraphy had at the last moment been found to be defective, and the Sultan, who was very particular about caligraphy in papers of this importance, had commanded it to be written over again. And so on *ad infinitum*, every fresh move being underlined by the suggestion of some dark diplomatic manœuvre, till quiet people began to regard the firman as a sort of Mrs. Harris, and the British fleet, which had been sent to salute its arrival, steamed off and left it to come or stay away as it pleased. And then, and not till then, it really had started, but only to encounter on its way those British men-of-war, the honour of whose escort the Turkish Envoy seemed so anxious to avoid, and to be greeted on its arrival at Alexandria by the presumably unwelcome compliment of their exultant salute. So the great State Document did come at last, but by the time of its coming not the gravest diplomatist in Cairo could hear the word 'firman' without some twitching of the corners of the mouth.

But even then the comedy was not over; the second and the third acts were still to come. No sooner had the firman reached Cairo than dark rumours began to spread abroad that this momentous document, which it had taken so much time and trouble to procure, was after all not everything that it ought to be. As a matter of fact, and as all the world now knows, these rumours were true. The firman had been 'doctored,' and it required all the promptitude and firmness of the British Consul-General in Cairo, and all the efforts of British and pro-British diplomacy elsewhere, to get the error put right. That again was important business, but I am not now concerned with the substance of the business, but with its humorous externals. The firman had come, but it was in a bag, and nobody dare open that bag, lest the contents should prove a disagreeable surprise. The solemn bearer, a Turkish dignitary of the highest rank and most tremendous achievements, was appealed to, to reassure the anxious Egyptian Government as to the purport of the fateful instrument. With eloquent expressions of infinite regret, the Envoy declared himself unable to satisfy this apparently modest request. He was a soldier, he said, and not a politician; it was not for him to inquire into the intentions of his august Imperial Majesty, but only to see that the document containing the expression of those intentions was safely delivered to the person for whom it was destined. Yes; that was all very well, but might he not nevertheless be acquainted with the substance of the document? No; he deeply regretted that he was not. Had he not been furnished with a copy of it? No; a copy had indeed been prepared for him, but it was unfortunately late in delivery, and he could not delay the hour of his departure.

Nothing could exceed the absurdity of this *impasse*. And there things might have remained to this day and hour—the grave ambassador bowing over his bag, and its equally grave consignee declining to open it—had not the activity of the diplomatists behind the scenes finally found a way out of the difficulty. As a result of their exertions, a curtly worded telegram was hastily despatched to the Khedive by the Porte. This informal message modified in an essential particular the terms of the carefully drafted firman, and gave back ungraciously with the left hand what it had been sought deliberately to abstract with the right. And then at last the bag could be opened, and with much pomp and circumstance the firman—a gorgeous parchment—was read before assembled Cairo, on the steps of Abdin Palace. And so, at the same place and hour, was the telegram—a flimsy little piece of paper. Yet so perfect was the command of countenance possessed by all the actors in the splendid ceremony, that no uninitiated witness would for one moment have suspected the substantial contradiction, or even noticed the formal incongruity, of the two documents.

There still remained a farcical afterpiece connected with the payment of fees for this colossal comedy. These fees had been carefully stipulated beforehand by the Porte, were magnanimously refused on the spot by its Envoy, but had, nevertheless, some weeks afterwards to be quietly sent to Constantinople. For the stately Turkish Government, even in that moment of highest dudgeon and proudest reserve, was not insensible to the charm of six thousand pounds of ready money.

If I have dwelt at seemingly disproportionate length upon this singular incident, the reason is, not that I overrate its individual importance, but that the element of the serio-comic, of which it is such a brilliant instance, plays so constant and conspicuous a part in the drama of Egyptian politics. It is one of the paradoxes of which that drama is full, that things must not be taken otherwise than seriously because they are superficially ridiculous. It is this curious combination of external absurdity and deep underlying importance which gives its peculiar piquancy to the whole Egyptian problem.

Whether I shall succeed in rendering that problem clear and intelligible, the following chapters must show; but I hardly believe that any want of skill on my part can be sufficiently great to render it uninteresting. The Egyptian question of to-day has many sides, and can be viewed in many aspects. Perhaps there are hardly two people in the world who would entirely agree in their statement of it; but there are at least two things which may be asserted with regard to it without fear of contradiction. It has one radical defect —that it is never simple; it has one ineradicable charm —that it is never commonplace.

CHAPTER II.

RESTORING ORDER.

On September 13, 1882, the British army, under Sir Garnet Wolseley, stormed the earthworks of Tel-el-Kebir, and with one brilliant dash scattered to the winds the forces and the hopes of 'Ahmed Arabi, the Egyptian.' Nine-tenths at least of the so-called 'rebel' army were only too delighted at the opportunity of throwing away their arms and their uniforms, of donning once more with all haste their 'galabias' of blue cotton and returning to the unconstrained life and patient labour in their beloved fields, which were so much more congenial to them than the duties and the dangers of military service. The next day, September 14, two squadrons of British cavalry reached Cairo. They had ridden straight across the desert, some forty miles, and both men and horses were nearly dead from fatigue, yet the citadel and city, though occupied by a strong body of Arabi's troops, surrendered without a show of resistance. The 'rebellion' was at an end. Our business in Egypt seemed already all but finished.

How ironical, as we look back upon it over the ten past years of ceaseless and still far from completed effort, appears now that confident anticipation of an early end to our intervention! We had gone to Egypt professedly with no other object than to 'restore order,' nor can there be the smallest doubt of the absolute *bona fides* of that profession. It is not surprising if certain foreign critics, judging our intentions by our acts, regarded our armed interference as the much-desired result for which Great Britain had long been scheming, and which her previous hesitations had been deliberately calculated to render necessary. Nor have subsequent events failed to add plausibility to this insinuation. The theory is ingenious, yet never was ingenious cynicism more utterly wide of the truth. No one who remembers the character of the British Government of that day, or the profound distaste of foreign enterprise which animated the bulk of its followers, can doubt for one moment that Mr. Gladstone's Ministry was sincerely anxious to avoid any fresh interference in the affairs of Egypt, much more the tremendous step of military occupation. But the English Government and people were swept along in spite of themselves by the current of events. First the desire to humour France and keep in step with the forward policy of M. Gambetta, then the fearfully rapid spread of popular and religious excitement in Egypt, brought about a situation in which the cult of *laissez faire* was no longer possible even to its most faithful votaries.

Here was a country, the very centre of the world, the great highway of nations, a country which during the last half-century had been becoming ever more and more an appanage of Europe, in which thousands of European lives and millions of European capital were at stake, and in which of all European nations Great Britain was, by virtue of its enormous direct trade and still more enormous transit trade, the most deeply interested. And this country, which the common efforts and sacrifices of all the Powers had just dragged from the verge of bankruptcy, was now threatened, not with bankruptcy merely, but with a reign of blank barbarism. I know that many people held at that time, a few perhaps hold even now, that the fears which were excited by the massacres of Alexandria and Tanta, and by the general dissolution of Egyptian society in the early summer of 1882, were exaggerated. But subsequent experience has proved to absolute demonstration that this was not the case. So far from being exaggerated, the fears which were universal at that moment perhaps fell even short of the danger which was actually impending. In any case, the state of disorder already reached was of the extremest gravity. European property was no longer safe; European blood, including that of a number of our own countrymen, had already been shed. There was every symptom of further violence, not only to all Europeans, but to all Christians.

Face to face with this frightful emergency, the English Government looked to the European Concert; it looked to Turkey; it looked in the last resort to combined action with France, to avert the otherwise inevitable duty of independent interference. But the flame of anarchy spread too fast for the slow movements of diplomacy. No one else was ready or willing to strike at once. So at the very last moment the country which, after all, had the greatest interest at stake, the country which, by virtue of its position outside Continental complications, had least to risk by acting, and which, owing to its command of the sea, was best able to act quickly, was *nolens volens* obliged to bell the cat. And when at last we had overcome our conscientious, if ill-timed hesitancy, our action was beyond all anticipation prompt and effective. Let it always be remembered that Great Britain did save Egypt from anarchy, and all European nations interested in Egypt from incalculable losses in blood and treasure, to say nothing of the deep dishonour which those losses, foreseen and yet unhindered, would have brought on civilized mankind.

It is no part of my purpose to justify Great Britain's intervention in 1882. This book is concerned with the consequences of that intervention, not with the intervention itself. But there is one theory in connection with it (a page in the ever-fascinating volume of speculations about what might have been, if something had not been done that was done) to which it may be well to devote a brief consideration. I refer to the theory that, if there had been no foreign intervention, if Egypt had been left to herself to work out her own salvation, the Arabist movement would have ended in substituting a new and better order for that which it sought to destroy. Personally I do not think that, even if such a consummation had been possible, the civilized world would have been justified in tolerating the appalling amount of destruction—destruction of many precious and invaluable things as well as of much inveterate evil—which would have been inevitable in the process. But I go further, and maintain confidently that such a consummation was never in the range of possibility at all. The Arabist movement possessed great destructive force, but it had not within itself the elements necessary for the construction of anything enduring.

The assertion just made does not imply any wholesale condemnation of Arabi and his associates. It is possible to approve their aims, and yet to disbelieve entirely in their capacity to carry them out. Their objects, or rather their first objects (for as the movement grew its spirit rapidly deteriorated), were neither unreasonable nor blameworthy. It was natural that the non-Turkish officers of the Egyptian army should resent the constant preference shown for their fellow-officers belonging to the narrow Turkish oligarchy, which has so little claim to the affection of the Egyptian people. It was natural that, when this agitation, originating in a mere fight between opposing military coteries, had swollen to the dimensions of a 'National movement,' it should direct its attention and its attacks towards the gross abuses arising out of the privileged position of foreigners. These abuses, redounding as they do to the profit of the worst sort of Europeans and quasi-European Levantines, are even now, as we shall have plenty of occasion to see hereafter, one of the severest of the plagues of Egypt. But in the latter days of Ismail they had grown to perfectly frightful proportions. The European concession-hunter and loan-monger, the Greek publican and pawnbroker, the Jewish and Syrian money-lender and land-grabber, who could always with ease obtain the 'protection' of some European Power, had battened on the Egyptian Treasury and the poor Egyptian cultivator to an almost incredible extent. In a very great measure, then, there was reason in this onslaught upon European privilege, and even in the ominous and misleading watch-cry of 'Egypt for the Egyptians.'

But Egypt is too delicate and too complicated a problem for the application of any 'cry,' any of those crude generalities dear to the heart of demagogues. The indiscriminate condemnation of Europeans and European influence included not only all that was worst, but all that was best in Egypt, not only the evil cohorts of trickery, usury, and oppression, but all the most powerful instruments of reform, education, and progress. If the abuse of European privilege is the bane of Egypt, European influence of the legitimate kind is the mainspring of improvement. European usury has gone near to ruin the country, but of European capital, wisely applied, it stands in quite peculiar need. The exclusion of Europeans, ay, and even of the more detested but still useful Eastern Christians and Jews, who also have their necessary place in Egyptian society, would have meant the exclusion of half the wealth, and of far more than half the intelligence and enterprise, to say nothing of all the reforming energy and initiative which the country possessed.

And this crusade was got up at the very moment when the better European influences were steadily triumphing over the worse, and when, under the beneficent guidance of the Dual Control, the country was gradually entering upon the path of pure, economical, and equitable administration. But how could absolutely uneducated men like Arabi and his associates be expected to make these fine distinctions? How, even if they apprehended them themselves, could they have brought them home to the fanatical schoolmen and ignorant peasants who were their warmest supporters? As a matter of fact, the Arabist movement passed with frightful rapidity from a protest against the abuse of European influence to an attack upon that influence in every form; and it was passing at the moment when it was arrested into an attack not only upon everything European, but upon everything Christian. The ever-smouldering hatred of Moslem for Copt had been stirred into flame, and in another month the half-million and upwards of native Christians of Egypt, including many of its richest and most intelligent inhabitants, would have gone the way of their hated rivals, the Syrians, and have swelled the list of the proscribed.

It is not to be supposed that Arabi, or even his abler associate and evil genius, Mahmud Sami, ever intended or approved these excesses of the revolution, of which they were the originators and remained to the last the nominal chiefs. It was not, we may be sure, their programme to regenerate society on the ruins of all its most capable and progressive elements, whether native or foreign. They were like the magician's apprentice who could evoke genii, yet could not control them when evoked. But can it for one moment be believed that the unaided forces of poverty and fanaticism, stimulated by a smarting sense of past oppression, and uncontrollable even by their original leaders, would have succeeded in establishing the strong popular government, of which certain visionaries had the vanity to dream?

How far the National party was from such a goal is shown by the intrigues with the Sultan, the nervous clutching at Turkish aid, which form such a curious feature in the later developments of Arabi's policy. The first idea, and one of the soundest, at the bottom of the National movement, was the desire to root up the upas-tree of Turkish predominance. And yet, before that movement had achieved anything positive, its leader, tossed about like a rudderless boat in the storm which he had raised, was seeking to propitiate Constantinople. Can there be a more conclusive proof that he was wholly powerless to carry out his own programme; that the revolution, left to itself, would not have resulted in a new and better order, but only, after a fearfully destructive reign of terror, in a new and severer form of the old slavery? The last state of the house would have been worse than the first, while everything valuable in it would have been smashed to pieces in order to arrive at that dismal conclusion.

No; the objects which the Egyptian National party had in view—the original and sound objects—were not to be achieved by the feeble agitators who led, or by the ignorant populace who composed it. They were destined, by one of the strangest ironies of fate, to be slowly realized under the auspices of the foreign invaders who so unceremoniously extinguished Arabi and all his works. Many of England's reforms in the Nile valley are in the direction of the ideal which the National party had at heart. The only effective Arabists Egypt has ever known are some of the British officials in the Egyptian service.

But to return to our famous policy of 'restoring order,' or, as the more official version put it, 'restoring the authority of the Khedive.' It is clear that this was not merely our professed, but our true and only object. Yet we were very far at the time from realizing all that it implied. The restoration of authority may be an easy or a difficult, a short or a very protracted business, according to the nature of the circumstances which have caused authority to be upset. Power, however strong and well established, is liable to accidents. A mob may temporarily possess itself of a quarter of the most civilized city. A rebellion having little real root in popular feeling may, as in 1745, achieve a local and temporary success, even against an essentially sound and mighty government. In such cases the restoration of authority is a comparatively simple matter. When once the police have got the better of the mob, when once the rebel army has been defeated, everything returns rapidly, and almost of itself, to its original condition. But the case is very different where the collapse of authority comes from within; where its overthrow is due, not to the strength or suddenness of the attack, but to inherent weakness; where the riot, the rebellion, or whatever the proximate cause of disaster may be, is not the real cause, but merely one of the results, merely an acute symptom, of a deep-seated malady. Those who would 'restore order' after such a collapse cannot content themselves with the removal of the symptom. They must go deeper and seek to cure the disease.

Such was the case of Egypt after the tremendous breakdown, of which Arabi and his mutinous soldiers were the instruments, but inner rottenness of long standing the real cause. The system of government which had been bowled over like a ninepin by the feeble arms of Arabi and his associates, weakest though far from worst of rebels, could not be 'restored' by simply being re-erected. No doubt the inhabitants of the Nile valley are the most easily governed people in the world; yet even in the Nile valley government must rest on some force, material or moral—on popular consent or on obedient bayonets, or, at very least, on that strange prestige, the 'divinity that doth hedge a king,' which, especially in the East, sometimes preserves for many years a despotism from which all real vitality has departed. But the government of Egypt which Arabi upset had possessed none of these indispensable supports. The native ruling class was vicious and incapable. The country teemed with officials, but few, very few of them were men. Tyrannous to the weak, they quailed before the slightest threat of lawlessness on the part of the strong. And from strong and weak alike they readily accepted bribes, to pervert justice or neglect duty.

Nor was the administration as much strengthened as it ought to have been by the large brigade of foreigners who had been imported into it. They were often ill-chosen, and even when honest and capable they lacked influence. While their numbers excited native complaint, they were unable, under the then existing conditions, to effect such an amount of improvement as would have justified their presence, and gradually allayed the discontent arising from their introduction. The needs of the public Treasury, loaded with a gigantic debt, were such that the administration, which had to raise enormous taxes to provide for those needs, could not in any case have been popular. But when to grievous necessary taxation were added the still greater burdens resulting from official incompetence, injustice, and corruption, there resulted a degree of misery and oppression which even in the patient East could not but engender a spirit of revolt.

The Government was thus clearly devoid of one great possible mainstay of authority—popular support, or acquiescence. But how was it off for material force? The army was recruited from the poorest and most oppressed section of the people, and was shamefully ill-used into the bargain. Its officers, who were themselves partly taken from the peasant class, had been in arrears of pay for years, and when the financial embarrassments of the State necessitated the dismissal of a large number of them, they were allowed to go without either the back-pay or the pension to which they were entitled. Such treatment infallibly bred disloyalty. Had the army at least been justly dealt with, and consequently trustworthy, the Government might have despised the sufferings of a deeply wronged but most submissive people. As the case actually stood, the army itself was the chief source of danger.

There remained, then, only prestige. But the personal prestige of the Khedive, at one time enormous, had greatly declined in the years preceding 1882. Ismail, indeed, had been all-powerful, and even when in his later years, owing to his impecuniosity and bad faith, and the growing interference of the European Powers which his misgovernment necessitated, real power was slipping from his grasp, he still managed to maintain the semblance and the terror of it. Foreign Envoys might bully, or foreign residents begin to laugh at him, but there were very few natives, and they men of exceptional courage and character, who did not quail before him to the very latest day of his reign. But his better son was in a very different position. He succeeded to weakness, and with all his excellent qualities, qualities which at a later date and under fairer auspices were of untold value to his country, Tewfik Pasha was not the man to restore by his own unaided personality that awe of the Khedivial name, which circumstances

The mere fact of its existence impaired the power by weakening the prestige of the native Government, and, on the other hand, the Control itself lacked material support. Had time been granted, it might have ended by creating for the Government a new source of strength in the prosperity and contentment of the people; but before its beneficent influence had had time to be recognised, the smash came.

Looking back now, with the wisdom derived from subsequent experience, it is easy to see that the Control experiment was foredoomed to failure. So great an interference with native authority, however necessary for the rescue of the country, was not justified, if the interfering Powers were not prepared to give the weakened native Government effective material assistance, until such time as the prosperity and contentment, which the new system would have created in the long-run, had made that assistance superfluous. Had this been done, the revolution, with all its destructive consequences and the resulting necessity of British intervention, might possibly have been avoided. But, be that as it may, the interrupted work of the Dual Control was now to be taken up under more favourable auspices, shielded and stimulated by the protecting presence of British power.

This, then, and no less than this, was meant by 'restoring order.' It meant reforming the Egyptian administration root and branch. Nay, it meant more. For what was the good of recasting the system, if it were left to be worked by officials of the old type, animated by the old spirit? 'Men, not measures,' is a good watch-word anywhere, but to no country is it more profoundly applicable than to Egypt. Our task, therefore, included something more than new principles and new methods. It ultimately involved new men. It involved 'the education of the people to know, and therefore to expect, orderly and honest government—the education of a body of rulers capable of supplying it.'*

* 'Britain's Work in Egypt.' Edinburgh: T. and A. Constable, 1892.

CHAPTER III.

THE VEILED PROTECTORATE.

SUCH was the nature of the task we undertook. But its grim immensity dawned very slowly on the British Government and the British people. In fact, it is pretty evident, to judge from many utterances which appear about Egypt even now, that a considerable section of the public have not realized it up to the present day. Was it well that we began in ignorance of what lay before us? It is possible that, had we foreseen the extent of the liabilities we were incurring, we might never have put our hand to the plough. That would have been a misfortune for Egypt. Whether it would have been in the long-run any real relief to England, I must leave my readers to judge when they have heard me out. But, on the other hand, it is certain that, if we had understood from the beginning the extent of the enterprise on which we were embarking, and had nevertheless persisted in it, much time would have been saved, and many blunders would have been avoided. Our failure to grasp the situation from the first, the uncertainty of our aims, the consequent tentativeness and vacillation of our policy—these have all along been a heavy drag upon the work of reform in Egypt. If, in spite of all, we have attained a large measure of success, that result has been due to the characteristic tenacity of the race, to the business-like way in which certain Englishmen on the spot set about the duty nearest them without looking to right or left. It has been due to the practical instinct which, under the teaching of experience, has led them, and especially one of them, to work out for himself and his country some sort of coherent and definite line of action amid the bewilderment of hot fits and cold fits at home, of alternate orders to advance and retreat, of some things rashly begun, and others unwisely neglected. But more of this hereafter.

Let me recall to the mind of my readers the position of affairs in Egypt in the autumn of 1882. We were in absolute possession of the country. We had smashed the *de facto* Government, and the Government *de jure* was a phantom. There was for the moment no authority but that of our army, no law but our will. That something had to be done to clear up this situation was evident, but what? Were we to elect for the right of might and to annex the country? Our previous declarations rendered such a course difficult, but, even had it been easy, the majority of Englishmen were profoundly averse to it. Were we to proclaim a Protectorate, permanent or temporary? That would have been less difficult, and at the time certainly nine-tenths of the world expected such a denouement. I shrewdly suspect that, if the chancelleries of the Continent were to give up their secrets, it would be found that most of the Powers were at heart in favour of it. The Europeans in Egypt, just saved by the skin of their teeth, were for the moment almost to a man of the same mind. As late as April 4, 1883, two thousand six hundred of the European inhabitants of Alexandria and other towns, representing almost all the European wealth and enterprise of the country, and including not only Greeks, Italians, Germans, and Austrians, but even some Frenchmen, presented a petition to Lord Dufferin, praying that the British Occupation might be permanent. At the same time, a similar desire was expressed in a memorandum from the American Missionary Society, perhaps the most widely spread and most beneficent of all the foreign agencies engaged in the diffusion of education on the banks of the Nile. There is no doubt, either that the establishment of a Protectorate would at that time have been most popular with almost all the resident foreigners, or that our refusal to establish it subsequently converted into enemies many of those who at first would have enthusiastically welcomed us.

It is true that even the proclamation of a Protectorate would have been very little in keeping with the professions under cover of which we sent out our military expedition. But the fulfilment of the professions made by a nation in the act of going to war is not in common human practice—whatever ought to be the case in an ideal world—apt to be rigidly exacted of the same nation at the moment of victory. In the heat and flurry of a resort to arms, and under the natural impulse to justify so extreme a measure, much is always promised, which, even if intended, it is afterwards found impossible to perform; and such non-performance is, within reasonable limits, readily condoned by the public opinion of mankind. It would no doubt be invidious for Great Britain to proclaim a Protectorate over Egypt to-day. But it is not so much the declarations we made before our victory as their constant reiteration ever since, which constitutes the obstacle. At the end of 1882, such a step was not only almost universally expected; it would have been generally welcome. The British Government, however—and it is fair to remember that in this respect it only reflected the unmistakable trend of public feeling—shrank from so bold a course. 'He that wills the end must will the means' is good logic, but it is not the logic which, in questions of imperial policy, has as yet commended itself to the British people.

If, then, we were not going to annex, and not going to protect, what were we going to do? Our policy, as far as we had one, was laid down in the able and memorable despatch which Lord Granville addressed to the Great Powers on January 3, 1883. 'Although for the present,' says that document, 'a British force remains in Egypt for the preservation of public tranquillity, Her Majesty's Government are desirous of withdrawing it as soon as the state of the country and the organization of proper means for the maintenance of the Khedive's authority will admit of it. In the meantime, the position in which Her Majesty's Government are placed towards His Highness *imposes upon them the duty of giving advice with the object of securing that the order of things to be established shall be of a satisfactory character, and possess the elements of stability and progress.*'

It is worth while to look closely at this famous declaration. In it the Government of Great Britain announced its object: 'the establishment of an order of things possessing the elements of stability and progress.' What that meant we have seen, though at the time when he used the phrase, Lord Granville could perhaps hardly have been expected to see it. But the British Government at the same time indicated the means which it meant to employ to attain that object. It was to be obtained by 'giving advice'—charming euphemism of the best Granvillian brand. For the advice of an armed man in possession of your property is apt to be something more than a mere recommendation; it is an order. And so Lord Granville himself very vigorously interpreted the term 'advice' on the first important occasion on which the Khedive and his Ministers seemed disinclined to listen to their English counsellors. 'I hardly need point out,' he wrote to Sir Evelyn Baring, on January 4, 1884, 'that in important questions, where the administration and safety of Egypt are at stake, it is indispensable that Her Majesty's Government should, so long as the provisional occupation of the country by English troops continues, be assured that the advice which, after full consideration of the views of the Egyptian Government, they may feel it their duty to tender to the Khedive, should be followed. It should be made clear to the Egyptian Ministers and Governors of provinces, that the responsibility which for the time rests on England obliges Her Majesty's Government to insist on the adoption of the policy which they recommend, and that it will be necessary that those Ministers and Governors who do not follow this course should cease to hold their offices.' That, at any rate, was plain speaking.

It is true that we have not always insisted with this amount of energy on the acceptance of our advice, even in important matters. Moreover, there has never been any understanding between Great Britain and Egypt, or even any clear idea in the minds of British statesmen themselves, as to the limits within which our right of giving authoritative advice should be exercised. The same matter has been treated by us at one time as within the sphere of our influence, and at another time as without it. Certain unlucky questions seem destined to be permanently half in and half out. But, however that might be, the mere liability to have advice offered to it, which on certain occasions it would be bound to accept, was sufficient to place the Egyptian Government in a state of tutelage. Thus we did after all establish a Protectorate in Egypt, but not a complete or legitimate one. On the contrary, it was a Protectorate which we would not avow ourselves, and therefore could not call upon others to recognise. It was a veiled Protectorate of uncertain extent and indefinite duration for the accomplishment of a difficult and distant object.

It is far from being my intention to criticise this policy, much less to condemn it. The longest way round may be the shortest way home, and it is possible that the course adopted by England may be found ultimately to have certain advantages, which the more direct and less irritating method of declaring a regular Protectorate, permanent or temporary, would not have possessed. All I wish to point out now is, how the attainment of our object of setting up a stable order of things—complicated enough in any case—was rendered enormously more complicated by our preference for an incomplete and informal over a thorough-going and proclaimed Protectorate. That preference would have increased our difficulties in any country. It increased them a hundred-fold in a country so abnormal as Egypt, the independence of which was already subject to restrictions of many kinds. I fear I must expand at some little length both of the above propositions.

And first as to the relations existing between the English and Egyptian Governments, regarded apart from the international shackles previously imposed upon the latter. To understand the delicacy of these relations, it is necessary to analyze the methods by which British influence in Egypt is exercised. There are three points to be considered: the British troops, the British Consul-General, and the British officials in the Egyptian service. The position of each of these presents anomalies which would be impossible anywhere except in paradoxical Egypt.

The British troops have, of course, no sort of status in the country. They are not the soldiers of the Khedive, or foreign soldiers invited by the Khedive. They are not the soldiers of the protecting Power, since there is in theory no protecting Power. In theory their presence is an accident, and their character that of simple visitors. At the present moment they are no longer, from the military point of view, of vital importance, for their numbers have been repeatedly reduced, and for several years past they have not exceeded, and do not now exceed, three thousand men. It is true that their presence relieves a certain portion of the Egyptian army from duties it would otherwise have to perform, and that, if the British troops were altogether withdrawn, the number of Egyptian soldiers might have to be somewhat increased. But its value as part of the defensive forces of the country does not, of course, constitute the real importance and meaning of the British Army of Occupation. It is as the outward and visible sign of the predominance of British influence, of the special interest taken by Great Britain in the affairs of Egypt, that that army is such an important element in the present situation. Its moral effect is out of all proportion to its actual strength. The presence of a single British regiment lends a weight they would not otherwise possess to the counsels of the British Consul-General. Take the troops away, and you must either run the risk of a decline of British influence, which would imperil the work of reform, or devise, for a time at least, some new and equivalent support for that influence—a problem not perhaps impossible, but certainly difficult of solution.

We now come to the British 'Agent and Consul-General.'* That functionary is, like any other British Minister at a foreign Court, the authorized exponent of the views and wishes of the English Government to the Government of Egypt. His position, unlike that of our troops, is a normal and legitimate one; but, if normal in form, it is even more anomalous in substance than any other part of this strange piece of political mechanism. Formally only one of more than a dozen consuls-general, and possessing no higher attribute or authority than any of his colleagues, he is in reality, as the exponent of the wishes of what is in reality the protecting Power, the ultimate authority in the country in all those matters—and they are a varying number—which the protecting Power chooses for the moment to regard as calling for the exercise of its control. He is the real, but unproclaimed, arbiter over an administrative area of fluctuating dimensions—no easy position to fill with effectiveness and without offence. Nor has that position been rendered easier by the fact that, on two occasions since the Occupation, the Consul-General has been superseded, in a greater or less degree, by Envoys Extraordinary. From November, 1882, to May, 1883, the responsibility for the direction of Egyptian affairs was practically transferred from the Consul-General (Sir E. Malet) to Lord Dufferin. From November, 1885, to December, 1887, that responsibility was divided between the then Consul-General, Sir Evelyn Baring, and Sir Henry Drummond Wolff.†

* The full title of Sir Evelyn Baring (Lord Cromer) is 'Minister Plenipotentiary and Consul-General.' Some of his colleagues, notably the Frenchman, have the same rank. The rest are only 'Consuls-General,' but with the additional appellation of 'diplomatic agents,' which indeed best represents their true character, as their functions are rather diplomatic than consular.

† If I do not here refer to the mission of Lord Northbrook in September and October, 1884, it is because that mission was too short, and of too special a character, to be regarded as a serious invasion upon the authority of the Consul-General.

It remains to consider the British officials in the Egyptian service. There were a good many of these before the days of the Occupation, and there are not so many more now; but, of course, the Occupation and its consequences have entirely altered their position and influence. Here, again, we must distinguish between fiction and fact. In theory, the British officials of the Khedive are just like his other officials, the servants of an absolute master, as liable as his other servants to be overruled or dismissed. They are with few exceptions not even the heads of their respective services, but under the orders of native Ministers. But though this is their formal position, and though the form is most rigorously observed by the British officials themselves, no Egyptian for a moment forgets that these men—his colleagues, in some instance his subordinates—are citizens of the State which holds Egypt in the hollow of its hand. Their advice is not like ordinary advice. Their dismissal is not to be lightly thought of; in fact, without exceptionally valid reasons, it is not to be thought of at all.

A further anomaly arises from the relation of these British Egyptian officials to the British Consul-General. In theory, again, he has no more to do with them than the representative of any foreign Power has to do with the servants of the Government to which he is accredited. But, as a matter of fact, the Consul-General is engaged in superintending a certain work of internal reform. He is, to that extent, a part of the Government of Egypt, and these men are practically his principal instruments. Conceal the fact as you please, be as careful as you please that the British officials shall abide by the strictest official decorum, and shall try to forget that they are anything but ordinary members of the Egyptian Administration; yet it is but human nature that in moments of especial difficulty they should turn to their Consul-General for guidance and support.

Is it necessary, in view of these facts, to explain any further how the indefiniteness of British authority, and the irregular methods by which it is exercised, inevitably increase the friction which must in any case arise between two Governments standing to one another in the relations of guardian and ward? The position of the Egyptian Ministers and higher officials is under the circumstances necessarily a trying one. It is hard for them to know what they may do and what they may not; where counsels tendered to them are suggestions, and where they are commands. It is hard for them to feel any cordiality towards members of the same service who may, at a given moment, be appealing for counsel to an outside authority. Where they are themselves at heart cordially with us, their position, though difficult, may not be intolerable; but where they are at heart opposed to the policy we may be pursuing, or only half convinced of its wisdom, it is too much to expect that they should contentedly accept the responsibility, and even bear the odium, which that policy may in a particular instance excite among the majority of their countrymen, while all the time they feel it is not their own.

Moreover, the situation is one which offers every encouragement to that tendency to intrigue, which is the besetting vice of all Eastern statesmen. The Khedive, after all, is the ruler of the country, and it is he who must ultimately decide whether a particular measure shall or shall not be adopted. If he can be induced to turn a deaf ear to the proposals of the British Agent, the latter is checkmated. The idea of playing off his Sovereign against his foreign taskmaster is thus one which lies very near to an irritated Egyptian Premier. And it has more than once been adopted, though never with success. Moreover, there is always the last hope, that the British Agent himself may be going beyond his instructions, and that, if the British Government can only be got at, it may be induced to disavow him. In at least one memorable instance, to which I shall have to refer presently, this card was actually played, and played with great boldness, though the result was discomfiture. Such are the rocks on which successive Egyptian Ministries, that of Sherif, of Nubar, of Riaz, have split.

Try to find out from any Egyptian who is hostile to England—not a fool or a fanatic, but a reasoning opponent—what is the cause of his hostility, and you will probably discover that it comes to this—that he does not know where he is with us. He would like best that we should go away. Failing this, he would be content if we were to take over entirely the government of the country. But why we should hang on worrying him, as he considers it, without doing any good to ourselves, is more than he can fathom. 'If you want us to walk in our fashion, why don't you leave us alone; if you want us to walk in yours, then govern us and have done with it.' No doubt this is a superficial point of view. No doubt an Englishman, wishing to defend the policy of his country, has an answer and a good one. 'We could not let you continue in the old paths,' he might reply, 'because they were a proved failure. Had you had the capacity and the character to keep things straight, there would have been no insolvency, no revolution, no necessity for our interference. But, on the other hand, we English don't want to stay in your country for ever. We don't despair of your learning to manage decently your own affairs. If we were to go away to-morrow, you would not succeed in doing so, because you have not yet shaken off the old traditions. You still require a deal of training in a better school. But, at the same time, if we were to take the government of the country entirely out of your hands, you would never learn to do better. You need to be shown what to do, but you also need to practise doing it. You need energy, initiative, self-reliance. How could you ever develop them if we were to keep you absolutely in leading-strings?' And the reply is good, but it is a hard saying to our imaginary Egyptian grumbler. He may not be able to formulate a rejoinder to it, but if he could analyze his own feelings he might express them thus: 'I am an Oriental, and I want to be a master or to have a master. I am prepared to be your humble, obedient servant, or I am prepared, quite prepared, to do without you. But I don't understand divided responsibility or limited freedom of action. Your kind consideration in letting me have my own way at times—just when it happens to suit you—does not make me feel a bit more free, but only a great deal more uncomfortable.'

I am reminded in this connection of an incident which it would be better to relate without mentioning names. It was the case of a certain nomination which happened to be very important from the point of view of pure administration, but to which the Native Minister, who was asked to make it, and who was a man of strong character though rather narrow intelligence, was for some reason or other violently opposed. It is not often that the British Consul-General in Cairo interferes about particular nominations, but in this case the stake was considerable, and he felt bound to carry his man. The appointment was suggested, in the first instance, in the most gentle and least offensive manner; but the Minister was not to be appeased by such conciliatory tactics. He flew into a passion, declared he would never consent, and threatened resignation. When he found that the suggestion, though not pressed with excessive vehemence, was not withdrawn, he left no stone unturned to prevent its acceptance. He delayed, he intrigued, he raised side-issues, he tried to drag the Khedive into the quarrel, and to set him and the British Consul-General by the ears. At last the patience of the latter began to give out, and he had it intimated to the recalcitrant Minister that this was a question about which the British Government would stand no further trifling. The bearer of the message expected an explosion, but not a bit of it. 'Eh bien,' said the imperious old gentleman, with a shrug of the shoulders; 'si c'est un ordre, je n'ai plus rien à dire.' And the thing was done. His despotic disposition could understand an order, but what he could not tolerate was good advice which was contrary to his own inclinations.

There is a world of instruction in that little episode. It would have been easier, so much easier, to push through our work of reform if we had seen our way to adopt from the first a more uniformly decided tone. Far from exciting opposition, such an attitude would have quelled it. 'The masterful hand of a resident,' to use the famous phrase of Lord Dufferin, 'would soon have bent everything to his will.' It was not the same thing for a quasi-resident disguised under the garb of a mere Diplomatic Agent. No doubt the friction between Englishmen and natives is at present vastly less than it was at the beginning. Years of common work are producing a better mutual understanding. The irksomeness of a false situation has been mitigated by wont and habit, the political, like the human, body gradually accustoming itself to the most unsuitable clothes. It has been minimized by the skill and patience of the extraordinary man who for nine years has been the interpreter of Great Britain's will to Egypt, and among whose great qualities the power of distinguishing big things from small, and of not fussing about the latter, is perhaps one of the most remarkable. But a difficulty it still remains, and will remain, and one that ought constantly to be borne in mind in judging our efforts to carry out our appointed task of establishing 'an order of things which should have the elements of stability and progress.'

CHAPTER IV.

INTERNATIONAL FETTERS.

THE obstacles to progress, which I have thus far been considering, are such as we should have had to encounter even if the country, of which we were temporarily taking charge, had been an independent one. But Egypt was very far from being an independent country. She is a vassal State, bound by the obligations of her suzerain, and, over and above her vassalage to Turkey and its consequences, she is under an international tutelage in respect of her finances, which has no parallel in the world. It remains, therefore, to examine the various restrictions on the freedom of action of the Egyptian Government, arising from the circumstances just referred to—restrictions which existed prior to our occupation, but of which, by adopting the policy of a veiled rather than an avowed Protectorate, we doomed Egypt and ourselves to feel the full inconvenience.

Egypt is a part of the Ottoman Empire. The power of the Khedive is an emanation from the power of the Sultan, but it is an emanation of the most ample kind. The great Firman of June, 1873, which sums up, with certain additions, the attributes of sovereignty bestowed on the Khedive by all previous acts, confirms to the ruler of Egypt, subject to the payment of an annual tribute of 750,000 Turkish pounds,* the absolute control of the internal administration and finances of that

* About £675,000 sterling.

country; it empowers him to conclude commercial conventions with foreign Powers as long as such conventions do not infringe the political treaties of the Porte; it allows him to raise loans, and to keep up as large an army as may be necessary for purposes of defence, as well as to build ships of war other than ironclads. It acknowledges his right to coin money in the Sultan's name. It declares the Khediviate hereditary in the family of Ismail Pasha, according to the law of primogeniture. No delegation of sovereign power, short of its absolute abandonment, could well have been more complete. It is true that the later firman of August, 1879, which appointed Tewfik Pasha after the deposition of Ismail, modified in two important particulars the provisions of the firman of 1873. It deprived the Khedive of the right of raising loans without the consent of the Sultan, and of keeping up, in time of peace, an army of more than eighteen thousand men. But with these exceptions the Khedive remained absolute within the limits of the provinces assigned to him, which comprised not only Egypt proper, but the vast and ill-defined territories known by the name of the Sudan.

The Sultan had given to his representative on the throne of Egypt with no sparing hand, but he could not give what he had not got. He could not liberate his vassal from the existing restrictions upon his own sovereign authority. The international obligations of Turkey remained binding upon Egypt, and among them the remarkable series of treaties known as the 'Capitulations,' the earliest of which date back to the fifteenth and sixteenth centuries, and which limit in so singular a manner the sovereign power of the Sultan within his own dominions. The history of these treaties is a very interesting one, but it would take us too far afield to enter upon it here. The first Capitulations were, strictly speaking, not so much treaties as concessions. The Sultans of those days neither regarded the rulers of the Christian states of the West as equals to be treated with, nor was their principal aim to obtain reciprocal advantages in exchange for the privileges they granted. Their primary object was to make it possible for Christians to reside and trade in the territories of the Porte, by protecting them against the ill-usage to which, as defenceless strangers of an alien faith, they would otherwise have been exposed. The omnipotent despots, who granted the first Capitulations, would have smiled at the thought, that the favours they were almost contemptuously conferring could ever become a serious source of weakness or embarrassment to their successors.

Yet so it has come to pass. While Turkey has dwindled, the foreigners within her borders have become stronger. The need of the Capitulations has diminished, but their advantages have been claimed and conceded to one European nation after another, and extended, rather than curtailed, in these successive concessions.* But even if they had not been so extended, those advantages would have a very different import to-day from that which they possessed at the time when they were granted. It was one thing for the absolute ruler of one of the mightiest of existing empires to give up, of his own free grace, some portion of his sovereign power for the benefit of a handful of foreign traders, whose distant and, at that time, comparatively weak Governments were little likely to exact a very strict execution of the rights thus bestowed. The immense preponderance of material power on the one side quite excluded the possibility of any inconvenient exercise, much less abuse, of legal privilege on the other. But it is quite another thing when that same empire, enfeebled and declining, finds itself face to face with a large number of foreign residents armed with privileges, which amount to a complete right of extra-territoriality, and which their Governments—no longer inferior suitors, but dangerous rivals, or necessary protectors—are determined to see respected to the full.

* At the present moment the nations possessing Capitulations with Turkey are the following: In Europe—France, Italy, England, Germany, Austria, Russia, Holland, Spain, Sweden, Denmark, Belgium, Portugal, and Greece; and in the New World—the United States and Brazil.

Of all the privileges conferred upon foreigners by the Capitulations, by far the most important, in these days, are those of immunity from taxation, excepting customs-duties (and, in the case of foreigners owning real property, land-tax), of inviolability of domicile, and of exemption from the jurisdiction of the local courts. The latter privilege is, however, neither complete nor uniform. The extent of it varies considerably in the different treaties, and has varied even more largely in practice at different times. The subject is one of continual dispute between the representatives of the Powers and the Ottoman authorities, and the results of the struggle may differ according to the degree of insistence on the part of the particular Power interested, or the degree of regard which the Porte is at a given moment disposed to show to it.

In no part of the Ottoman Empire have the privileges granted by the Capitulations received so wide, and indeed abusive, an extension as in Egypt. Claims have been made and admitted, and practices have sprung up and acquired the sanction of use and precedent, which, in many cases, are not only not justified by the treaties, but actually contrary to their express provisions. The fact is that, in their constant efforts to extend the limits of their privileges, foreigners* have obtained from the weakness or mistaken liberality of the rulers of Egypt concessions which were not to be wrung from the stronger and more conservative Government of Turkey.

Thus in Egypt it is a matter of well-established usage that a foreigner committing a criminal offence† is tried by his consul; or, if his consul is not competent, by the competent court in his own country. In Egypt, too, the principle of inviolability of domicile has been interpreted in a manner which not only makes the arrest of

* By 'foreigners,' in this and the following pages, I mean the citizens or protected subjects of countries having Capitulations with Turkey, just as, for the sake of brevity, I use the term 'the Powers' to designate these countries themselves.

† Except very trifling offences, which, as we shall see hereafter, may now be tried by the Mixed Tribunals.

criminals difficult, but places the greatest obstacles in the way of the Government in its attempt to obtain proof of breaches of the law. Before a foreigner's domicile can be entered—and his domicile is taken to include all his premises—his consul or some representative of his consulate must be present. But in hundreds of cases the consul takes good care to be out of the way, until the incriminating articles—the stolen goods, or the contraband tobacco, or hasheesh, or whatever else they may be—have been carefully removed. Indeed, on the subject of contraband alone, a whole chapter might be written, full of instances in which the revenue has been defrauded by virtue of the Capitulations. A foreign ship in an Egyptian port is as inviolable as a foreigner's house on land. There have been innumerable cases in which a vessel, known to contain contraband, has had to be watched day and night for many days together by the coastguards, until a consular agent could be got hold of in whose presence they might board her. When the indispensable official has at last arrived, the ship has simply put to sea, only to return and play the same game over again in a more convenient spot, until she has finally succeeded in landing her cargo.

Another common instance of the abuse of the Capitulations is that of a foreign criminal, or gang of criminals, taking refuge upon the premises of another foreigner of different nationality. Here at least two consular agents are necessary before the police can act—one to legalize the infraction of domicile, the other to legalize the arrest. But if the criminals themselves are of different nationalities, three, four, or even more consulates may have to be represented. Now, it is difficult enough to get a single consulate to move; to obtain the timely co-operation of two or more of them is next door to an impossibility.

And the difficulty of arresting a criminal is not greater than that of ensuring his proper punishment when arrested. It is a serious evil, in any case, that foreign criminals should not be amenable to the courts of the land, even where natives or the native Government are the victims of their criminality. But the nuisance becomes intolerable where the foreign authority, which is substituted for those courts, allows itself to be biassed in favour of the criminal because he is a fellow-countryman. An English miscreant, if handed over to his consular authority, is pretty certain to meet with the punishment he deserves. The English consular jurisdiction in Egypt extends to all crimes, and the consuls are, in their capacity of judges, little disposed to show leniency to their fellow-countrymen. But other consular courts have either a more limited jurisdiction, or, even when competent to deal with every sort of offence, are liable to be overruled by courts of appeal in their own country. Such courts of appeal are in most cases obliged to decide upon depositions without hearing or seeing the witnesses, and are naturally ignorant of local conditions. They are thus hardly in a position to form a good judgment, even if their disposition is excellent.

But, unfortunately, the impartiality of foreign judges trying their own countrymen for offences committed against Egyptians is not always unimpeachable; and this is especially the case with the judges of that foreign nationality which is most numerously represented in Egypt—the Greek. Instances are frequent—they are, perhaps, less common than they used to be, but they are far too common still—in which Greek criminals—thieves, forgers, even murderers—have been handed over to their consul, and have either been allowed to escape before trial, or have been acquitted in the teeth of the evidence, or, if condemned in Egypt, have appealed with success to a lenient court at Athens. Ruffians of the worst description, whom it had been difficult to arrest, and even more difficult to get convicted, have thus returned to Egypt after an incredibly short sentence to resume their old career of crime. Can it be wondered at, under these circumstances, that the Greeks are notorious throughout the country for truculent defiance of authority, for violence, and for lawlessness?

It would be hard to exaggerate the amount of injustice, or the hideous administrative confusion, arising from this state of things. But the immunity often accorded to criminals is not the most serious, though it is the most sensational, evil resulting from the abuse of the Capitulations. Of more far-reaching consequence are the obstacles they interpose to every kind of administrative reform, and to the general march of progress. Where would the growth of civilization be without the power of creating new offences? Step by step, as the development of the public conscience condemns certain acts as immoral, or experience shows them to be injurious to the general interest, the legislature follows and makes them punishable. But the Capitulations oppose a solid barrier to this process, alike as regards the suppression of vice and the repression of nuisances. Whether it be a question of public morals—such as the closing of gambling hells and houses of ill-fame, or the control of the sale of intoxicating liquors—or a question of public convenience—such as the preservation of a canal bank, or the enforcement of the most essential sanitary rules—the same difficulty presents itself. From the prevention of false coining to the regulation of a cabstand, it is always the old story. No doubt the Government is free to make the necessary laws, but as long as the penalties contained in them are not applicable to foreigners, what is the use? It would simply be giving a profitable monopoly of lawlessness to the foreigner at the expense of the Egyptian; and in matters of this kind it is precisely the low-class foreigners, with whom the country swarms, who are the principal offenders. It is they who are the false coiners, who keep the gambling hells, the liquor shops, the disorderly houses; it is they who build upon canal banks, or throw their refuse into the public streets. The Egyptian courts cannot try them, nor is it certain that their own courts, even if willing, would be competent to do so, for the offences in question are offences by virtue of Egyptian municipal law. But foreigners have the right to be tried not only by their own courts, but by their own laws; and in any particular case the offence which the foreigner has committed against Egyptian municipal law may perhaps not be an offence against the municipal law of his own country. The penal code of that country may possibly have no provision applicable to the case.

In order that an Egyptian municipal law may apply to foreigners, it must in every case have been enacted with the approval of all the Powers. But the approval of fourteen or fifteen separate Governments is not an easy thing to obtain, even for the most reasonable proposal. The matter might be simpler if the proposal were certain to be judged on its merits; but it is ten to one that it will not be thus judged in all the quarters to which it is necessary to apply. One or other of the Powers may be biassed by the clamour which its subjects on Egyptian soil are sure to raise against any infringement of their privileges, however just and necessary. The Minister who has to deal with the case may be afraid of attacks in Parliament, on the score of sacrificing his countrymen abroad; or the Power in question may just then be seeking some favour from the Egyptian Government, and be tempted to make its consent to the proposed law depend upon the granting of that favour; or it may withhold its consent simply from ill-humour at the political situation in Egypt. And since English influence has been paramount in the Nile Valley, there is at least one Government which can generally be reckoned upon to be in such a condition of ill-humour. But the refusal of a single Power is sufficient to nullify the consent of all the rest. Innumerable are the embarrassments of a weak country like Egypt, when circumstances have deprived it of one of the most essential attributes of sovereignty.

It would not be fair to omit the brighter side of the picture. The state of the Criminal Law as regards foreigners remains deplorable. But in the great domain of Civil Law the anarchy resulting from the Capitulations had, even before 1882, begun to give way to legality and order. This happy result was due to the institution in February, 1876, of the International or 'Mixed' Tribunals.* Previous to the establishment of these tribunals,

* The 'Mixed Tribunals' were established, in the first instance, for five years. They were renewed for successive periods of one

all suits against foreigners had to be brought before their respective consular courts, and these courts, as we have seen, are often animated by anything but a judicial spirit. But when the foreigner himself had an action to bring, he entirely declined to go before the Native Courts. Alleging that no justice could be had in that quarter, he would appeal to the Consul-General of his country to get his claim settled by diplomatic action. This was more particularly the case when his claim was against the Egyptian Government, and such claims were legion. Nor would it be possible to give any idea of the unscrupulousness with which foreign Diplomatic Agents, especially during the reign of Ismail, used their influence to obtain from poor weak Egypt the payment of even the most preposterous demands.

The great object of securing a concession in those days was, not to carry on a useful enterprise, but to invent some excuse for throwing it up, and then to come down upon the Government for compensation. Moreover, almost any loss which befell a foreigner, or any injury which he sustained, even if due entirely to accident or to his own fault, was made the occasion for demanding an indemnity. If his property was stolen, the Government was to blame for not keeping sufficient police. If his boat ran ashore in the Nile, the Government was to blame for not dredging the river. 'Please shut that window,' Ismail Pasha is related to have said to one of his attendants during an interview with some European concessionaire, 'for if this gentleman catches cold it will cost me £10,000.' And this was hardly an exaggeration. When the Mixed Tribunals came into existence, there were £40,000,000 of foreign claims outstanding against the Government! What the real amount of injury which they represented was may be judged from the fact that in one case, where 30,000,000 francs had been demanded, the Mixed Courts awarded the plaintiff £1,000.

---

year from February 1, 1881, 1882, and 1883; and again for periods of five years from February 1, 1884, and February 1, 1889.

Indeed, Egypt in the sixties and seventies was the happy hunting-ground of financiers and promoters of the shadiest description. Industrial and commercial enterprise might or might not be profitable to the persons undertaking it. But the man who was lucky enough to have a case against the Government could regard his fortune as assured. The same ruler, who could with impunity perpetrate acts of gross perfidy and injustice towards his native subjects, was himself mercilessly tricked and plundered by the foreign vampires that found such a congenial home upon Egyptian soil. It has often been said of Ismail that he liked to be cheated, that he had a positive partiality for rogues, even when they exercised their roguery at his expense. Whether it was owing to this idiosyncrasy, or simply owing to a sense of his own weakness, it is certain that he bore the extortion of European adventurers with remarkable patience, and consoled himself under it by a plentiful exercise of his gift of humorous cynicism.

But all this was no fun for the country, which had to pay the piper. Fortunately for Egypt, it also became intolerable to the Europeans themselves. The better class of residents and merchants found that the difficulty of obtaining justice, which arose from the multitude of petty and conflicting jurisdictions, far outweighed any advantages they might derive from being themselves amenable only to their own consuls. The Egyptian Government was thus encouraged to propose, and after eight years of weary negotiation enabled to carry, with the consent of all the Powers,* a law creating a single strong international jurisdiction, to supersede for the great majority of civil cases the existing consular courts. The new tribunals were made exclusively competent to try all suits in which the plaintiff and defendant were of different nationalities—that is to say, all suits between

* See, for the names of these, the list given on p. 38, note. All the countries there mentioned took part in the establishment of the Mixed Tribunals except Brazil, which, having no subjects, no interests, and no Diplomatic Agent in Egypt, is left out of account in the international arrangement of Egyptian affairs.

natives and foreigners as well as between foreigners not belonging to the same country—and they were authorized to deal with actions concerning real estate, even between persons of the same nationality.* Only cases of personal status, such as questions of marriage, inheritance, etc., were excluded from their jurisdiction. But in criminal matters it was confined to offences committed by the personnel of the tribunals in the discharge of their official duties, to offences committed against the tribunals, such as contempt of court or forcible opposition to the execution of judicial decisions, and to breaches of certain petty police regulations ('*contraventions de simple police*').

The composition of the Tribunals was partly native and partly foreign, but the foreigners were everywhere in a majority—in the proportion of four to three in the Courts of First Instance, and of seven to four in the Court of Appeal. Among the foreign judges, the United States and all the European Powers, except Spain and Portugal, which, however, have subsequently contributed members to the Courts, were represented.† The honorary presidency of each court was reserved for an Egyptian subject, but the vice-president, who was the real acting chief, was in every case a foreigner. To the Austrian, Lapenna, the first president of the Court of Appeal, a jurist of eminence and a man of the highest character, belongs the memorable honour of having been the first to direct the young institution in the right path. The circumstance is worth recording, for Austria is one of the Powers which, like our own country, has been very honourably represented in Egypt, and her influence on

* It has been much debated whether the provision giving the Mixed Tribunals jurisdiction in suits about real property, 'between persons of the same nationality,' applied to the case of an action between two natives. The Court of Appeal has lately decided that it does not. Nevertheless, natives do often, by mutual agreement, bring their differences about real estate before the Mixed Tribunals.

† The composition of the International Tribunals has undergone various changes in the sixteen years of their existence, but not of a kind to alter their character in any material respect.

Egyptian affairs has almost always been exercised in a beneficent direction.

As has been stated, the creation of the Mixed Tribunals was only possible after prolonged and difficult negotiations. Great Britain, though not at that time occupying the same position of prominence in Egyptian affairs as has since fallen to her, was favourable and helpful from the first. But several of the other Powers required a great deal of convincing and coaxing, while France manifested throughout a reluctance, amounting almost to deliberate obstruction, which was only overcome at the last moment by an unwontedly energetic and resolute attitude on the part of Egypt. The credit of having been the first to give an effective form to the conception of international justice for Egypt, and of bearing the burden and heat of the struggle for its establishment, belongs to Nubar Pasha. But for his far-sightedness, dexterity, and persistence, the new courts would probably never have seen the light, and his successful efforts for their introduction have earned for him a claim to the lasting gratitude of Egypt as well as to the respect of the civilized world. Whatever the failings of his character, whatever the subsequent errors of his policy, this great achievement will and ought to be remembered in his honour, when all the rest is long forgotten.

The struggle was hard, but the prize was worth fighting for. The Mixed Tribunals have now been working for upwards of sixteen years. Opinions differ greatly about their merits, but no impartial judge will question that, on the balance of advantages and disadvantages, they have been of enormous benefit to Egypt. Their members have not always been well chosen. Their code and procedure are not in all respects particularly suitable to the condition of the country. Their judgments have in many instances suffered from personal and political bias. But not only has their jurisdiction been an immense improvement on the state of things which preceded it, but they have set Egypt a new standard of equity, and have familiarized the public mind with the spectacle, previously unknown, of judicial method, impartiality, and incorruptibility.*

But while the creation of the Mixed Tribunals certainly tended to improve the administration of justice, it evidently did not simplify the political constitution of Egypt. The tribunals were a new stronghold of foreign influence, a new surrender of the sovereign rights of the Native Government. They might nominally be the Courts of the Khedive, who appointed their foreign members, although on the proposal of the Powers. But they were in reality foreign Courts deriving their authority from outside, and they have not hesitated to exercise that authority against the Native Government, whenever they thought it right to do so. Add to this, that they naturally enjoy an amount of influence and respect which could not attach to the numerous petty tribunals for which they were substituted. Judicially far better, they are at the same time politically far more formidable than the authorities whom they have supplanted.

Something remains to be said of the third and perhaps the unfairest of the three great privileges belonging to foreigners in Egypt under the Capitulations—I mean that of exemption from all direct taxes excepting the land tax. This immunity was not inequitable, in view of the condition of the Mussulman East, at the time when it was first granted. Aliens in a semi-barbarous country, in a country of different manners and of a hostile religion, occupying in almost all respects a position of marked inferiority as compared with its native inhabitants, the European residents in the Ottoman Empire during the sixteenth century were fairly entitled to escape from some of the burdens of citizenship, where they were admitted to so few of its advantages. But in Egypt at the present day—whatever may be the case in other parts of the Ottoman dominions—foreigners enjoy all

* I am well aware that there have been judges of the Mixed Courts whose incorruptibility was not above suspicion. Grave scandals have occasionally occurred. But such cases are very exceptional.

the benefits of government in as great a degree as natives, and perhaps even in a greater. There is no reason whatever why they should not bear their share of the expenditure of the State from which they derive their full share of advantage. And the equal distribution of public burdens as between foreigners and natives has of late years been a question not only of equity but of necessity. It was no theoretical love of equality merely, but the urgent wants of the Treasury, which led the British Government, from the first moment of the Occupation, to plead earnestly with the other Powers for their consent to the taxation of foreigners on the same footing as Egyptians. The small success which has attended ten years of effort in this direction is the most eloquent comment on the obstacles which the international servitude of Egypt often places in the way of reforms that are as irresistible on grounds of justice as they are necessary for the good administration of the country.

The three principal taxes to which in 1882 natives were, and foreigners were not, subject, were the house tax, the license tax ('patente'), and the stamp duties. After more than a year of pleading and discussion, where no argument was possible, the consent of the Powers was obtained to a decree applying the house tax to everybody. But the decree turned out to be unworkable. The safeguards for the protection of foreigners which had been inserted in it were such, that by simply not electing representatives to the Commissions of Assessment and Revision, on which the presence of a certain number of them was necessary, the European residents were able to make the law a dead letter. The decree passed in March, 1884, had accordingly to be suspended in November of the same year. This was the position of affairs when the Convention of London was signed in the spring of 1885. On that occasion the six Great Powers unanimously declared that they would accept a new decree for the house tax, modified so as to dispense with the presence of foreigners on the Assessment and Revision Commissions, if the foreigners should continue obdurate. But it is one thing to approve in principle and another to facilitate in practice. It took a whole year more before a workable decree could be devised for applying the house tax to foreigners, and it was not till 1887 that foreigners actually paid the tax. The receipts under this head of revenue then immediately jumped up from £45,000 to £110,000 a year, and they have gone on increasing since. Thus the four years' delay had cost the Egyptian Government upwards of £200,000, and that at the direst crisis of its financial fortunes, when a second bankruptcy appeared almost inevitable.

The declaration of the Great Powers about the house tax was accompanied by a pledge that they 'would accept the application to their subjects, in the same manner as to natives, of the stamp tax and the license tax, and would engage to undertake immediately, in concert with the Egyptian Government, the study of the draft laws establishing these two taxes.' As soon therefore as the house tax was secured, the Egyptian Government turned its attention to the license tax. The difficulties thrown in the way were innumerable, but after infinite worry a decree extending this tax also to foreigners was accepted by the Powers and promulgated. This was in March, 1891, six years after the approval of that extension in principle by the terms of the London Convention. But the child of so much labour was destined to have a very short existence. The tax was a light one, yet so loud was the outcry raised against it by the European population, and so likely did it appear that the execution of the decree would lead to serious trouble with some of the very Governments which had accepted it, notably those of France and Greece, that within less than a year it was thought better to abandon the measure altogether. In January, 1892, the license tax was therefore given up both for natives and Europeans, for the Egyptian Government could hardly have faced the odium of maintaining it for natives alone, when they had during so many years been protesting against the iniquity of such a distinction. And so the net result of all the fighting, worry and waste of time, and of all the abuse which the unlucky Egyptian authorities have had to encounter for their endeavour to equalize the incidence of this tax, is that the tax has been lost to them altogether. Under these circumstances they are not likely to feel much encouraged to repeat the same experiment with regard to the third of the disputed imposts, namely, the stamp duties. The equalization of the incidence of the stamp duties may be regarded as postponed to the Greek Kalends.

A government which cannot legislate for, and cannot tax, the strangers resident in its dominions—especially when those strangers form, by virtue of their numbers, wealth, and influence, a very important section of the community—is lamentably shorn of its due measure of authority and of respect. But this weakness in the position of Egypt, springing from the Capitulations, has been greatly enhanced by the further disabilities and restrictions which she has brought upon herself by her unfortunate financial career. There is no country in the world to the position of which a policy of profuse expenditure and reckless borrowing was more ill-suited. Other states which have plunged in the same direction —though perhaps none ever went to such lengths—could at least fall back, in the last resort, on the desperate remedy of repudiation. But Egypt had no such *ultima ratio* open to her. She was not independent in this respect, like Costa Rica or Honduras. The Government might defraud its native creditors, but it was impossible to think of adopting a similar simple policy in the case of foreigners. European influence in the country was far too strong, the indebtedness of Egypt to more than one great European nation was far too deep, to allow Ismail Pasha to shake off the burden of his enormous loans, or even to lighten that burden, without the concurrence of the Powers.

At the same time it was evident, towards the close of Ismail's reign, that the unlightened burden was more than Egypt could by any possibility carry. The Powers, therefore, were forced to come to the rescue. They had, after all, no object in allowing Egypt to be plunged further and further into the slough of insolvency. On the contrary, the general dissolution of Egyptian society, in which such insolvency threatened to result, would have been very awkward for them all. And so, after five years of abortive, or incomplete, efforts to find a solution, an all-round arrangement was ultimately arrived at, and embodied in the famous Law of Liquidation, of July, 1880, by which Egypt compounded with her creditors on terms dictated to her by the Powers, but which they in return made binding upon all their subjects.* Egypt emerged from the crisis with the interest on her debt immensely reduced, and able once more to meet her liabilities, but tied hand and foot, unable to move, almost unable to breathe, without the consent of Europe.

A complete account of the desperate struggles of Ismail to escape the financial bondage which he saw impending, but which was not consummated till after his deposition, and of the successive steps by which the finances of Egypt were brought under international control, would fill a volume by itself. It is not my business to enter here upon that long and complicated history. But I must try to sum up its net result, as it affected the freedom of action of the Egyptian Government at the date of the British Occupation, and, with numerous but unessential modifications, still affects it to-day. The two main elements in the financial vassalage of Egypt are the powers of the International Commission of the Debt and the limits set to administrative expenditure by the Law of Liquidation.

* The Law of Liquidation was promulgated after having received the sanction of the six Great Powers only, but it is binding on the citizens of all the countries which have the benefit of the Capitulations. In order to avoid any difficulties which might be raised by the smaller Powers, and at the same time to save the waste of time which would have resulted from applying separately to them all, the six Powers agreed to bring the decree under the notice (*porter à la connaissance*) of the other States concerned. This was a diplomatic way of saying that they would guarantee its acceptance. And so it came to pass ; and ever since it has been the practice to regard the assent of the six Powers as sufficient to give the force of law—as against all the world—to any decree dealing with the Egyptian debt, or with the relations of Egypt and her creditors. For other decrees affecting the rights of foreigners all the fourteen Powers have still to be consulted.

The 'Caisse de la Dette,' or, as it is called in Egypt, simply the 'Caisse,' is an institution which, from comparatively small beginnings, has grown to be an important and ubiquitous factor in the government of the country. It is one more *imperium in imperio*, another wheel—it would be hard to say the how-manieth—to the coach of Egyptian administration. The Caisse was first constituted by the decree of May 2, 1876, and consisted at the outset of only three members, a Frenchman, an Austrian, and an Italian. An Englishman was added in 1877, and in 1885 Germany and Russia demanded, and obtained, the right to be represented. The Commission, therefore, now consists of six members, but their functions and position are very different from those of the original board.

In the beginning, the Commissioners were little more than receivers of certain revenues, which had been specially assigned to the service of the Debt. They were representatives, not so much of the Powers as of the creditors, the British Government refusing, in the first instance, even to go the length of proposing a British Commissioner. At present they may be described, not only as receivers of revenue on behalf of the creditors, but as guardians acting on behalf of the Powers, to watch over the execution of the complicated series of agreements—decrees, conventions, declarations, protocols—which constitute, in their totality, the international compact regulating the finances of Egypt. In that capacity they even possess a certain legislative power, and many decrees recite, in their preamble, the adhesion of the Caisse to the provisions, or some of the provisions, which they contain. The Commissioners of the Caisse are, indeed, appointed by the Khedive, and are, technically, Egyptian officials. But in reality they are almost as much foreign representatives as the Consuls-General themselves. Their dignity is little less, their importance in the administrative work of the country even greater, than that of the majority of those functionaries.

Does the Egyptian Government wish to adopt any

general measure for the relief of taxation? It must have the approval of the Caisse, for such a reduction will of course affect the receipts of the provinces specially assigned to the bondholders, and those revenues cannot be reduced without the consent of the Commissioners. Does it wish to raise a fresh loan, even for the most legitimate purposes—such as the commutation of pensions, or the construction of irrigation works, which will augment the revenue? Here, again, it must have the Caisse with it, before it can as much as begin to collect the whole series of other necessary consents—that of Turkey, and that of the six Great Powers. And when the loan is approved, and the money raised, it is once more the Caisse which will be charged with the disbursement of it, and with the duty of seeing that it is applied to the specified objects.

But over and above their positive functions, the Commissioners of the Caisse exercise a wide, though not easily definable, influence upon the financial policy of the country. Occupying a position of special trust, possessing a special knowledge of the details of a most complex situation, they are the natural advisers of their respective Governments on all questions of a financial character, which the Egyptian Government may be obliged to submit to the approval of the Powers. To them was entrusted the task of elaborating, in conjunction with that Government, the details of the unfortunate license tax already referred to. Their advice has been sought and followed with regard to such important issues as the abolition of the Corvée, or the conversion of the Privileged Debt. Moreover, the Egyptian Government themselves often seek the counsel, and invite the co-operation, of the Commissioners in matters lying quite outside the strict limits of their functions. And this partly because of the real capacity and helpfulness of some of the Commissioners, and partly from policy. For it is a matter of immense importance to the persons who have to carry on the daily work of the Egyptian administration whether the Caisse is or is not in a good temper. It may make all the difference between limping along somehow and coming to an absolute standstill.

But the powers of interference possessed by the Caisse cannot be fully understood without a glance at the extremely peculiar financial system embodied in the Law of Liquidation. The Powers, as we have seen, stepped in to save Egypt from bankruptcy, but in return they put her into a strait-waistcoat of the severest kind. The Revenues of the State were divided into two nearly equal parts, of which one was to go to the Caisse for the benefit of the bond-holders, and the other to the Government to defray the expenses of administration. There were thus practically two Budgets, but the principles applied to them were very different. If the Budget of the Caisse showed a deficit, the Government was bound to make good that deficit, whereas if the Caisse had a surplus, however large, the Government had no right to share it. On the other hand, if the Government had a deficit, the Caisse could not be called upon to make up the deficiency, while, if the Government had a surplus, the Caisse had certain contingent claims thereon. This was bad enough, but this was not all. For the Caisse might have a claim on an imaginary surplus of the Government which did not really exist at all. This sounds nonsensical, but in matters Egyptian it would be rash indeed to take no account of a thing because it sounded nonsensical. That is rather a reason why it should exist. And, as a matter of fact, this particular arrangement, though in my humble opinion unwise, was not so absurd as it looks at first sight. The explanation of it is, that the Law of Liquidation fixed an ideal figure for the national expenditure—a sum which, in the opinion of the Powers, Egypt ought not to go beyond. If the revenues of the Government exceeded this ideal figure, then the Government was to be regarded as having a surplus, no matter what its real expenditure might have been; and on that surplus the Caisse might, under certain circumstances, have a claim.

These provisions of the Law of Liquidation have

been somewhat altered by the Convention of London* concluded in March, 1885, which I shall have to explain at some length hereafter, and will therefore not dwell upon now. The one thing to notice here—and it is a matter of capital interest—is the first appearance on the scene of the Limit of Expenditure—the fixed sum which it was held that Egypt ought not to exceed, and which she was in any case to be regarded as not exceeding. The Limit of Expenditure is the essence of the Law of Liquidation, and it is a canon of Egyptian finance which, though often modified in details, has been preserved in substance ever since. It is the keystone of the whole system, and it is of more than purely financial, it is of first-rate administrative and political importance.

But all that concerns us here is its bearing on the position of the Caisse. It is evident that the moment you distribute the financial resources of a State, not according to its actual expenditure, but according to what it is supposed that it ought to spend, mere questions of account attain an importance which in the nature of things does not properly belong to them. Thus it may, under certain circumstances, make an enormous difference to the Government of Egypt whether items of expenditure, which it has actually incurred, can or cannot be brought under the head of 'authorized' expenditure. If they can be so brought, the Government is allowed to defray them out of its available revenues. If they cannot, they must be defrayed—Heaven knows how!—while the money which might have covered them is all the time flowing into the coffers of the Caisse. Finance is an important part of politics all the world over, but Egypt is the only country I am acquainted with where

* By the term 'Convention of London,' which frequently occurs in this book, I mean not only the Convention itself, but the Declaration of even date, together with the Khedivial Decree of July 27, 1885, a draft of which was annexed to, and the provisions of which were sanctioned by, the Declaration. All these together constitute one international arrangement, modifying the Law of Liquidation, and having the same sanction as that law.

not only Finance but Accounts are politics. And on all disputed questions of account the Caisse, with the Powers behind it, has the whip hand.

I cannot leave this portion of my subject without some mention—it shall be of the briefest—of the three 'Mixed Administrations'—the Railway Board, the Commission of the Daira, and the Commission of the Domains. Each of these bodies consists of three members—an Englishman, a Frenchman, and an Egyptian—and enjoys a sort of quasi-independence conferred by decrees which, as they form a part of the general settlement between Egypt and her creditors, are practically unalterable without the consent of the Powers.

The Railway Board, which dates from 1876, was called into existence as an additional protection to the bond-holders, the receipts of the railways being one of the principal revenues set aside for the payment of the coupon. It does its work well enough, but there is no longer any conceivable ground why it should occupy a special position outside the regular Civil Service. It would be just as reasonable to have a special international commission for the administration of the customs, or for that of each of the provinces of Behera, Gharbía, Menufía, and Siút, the receipts of which, no less than those of the railways, are pledged to the creditors and paid direct to the Caisse de la Dette.

The Daira and Domains Commissions are even more superfluous. They date from 1877 and 1878 respectively, and each of them administers a vast property of several hundred thousand acres, consisting of estates that once belonged to the Khedive or the Khedivial family, but which are now mortgaged to the holders of the Daira and Domains loans. Undoubtedly the better course would be to sell these lands, redeem the respective debts, as far as possible, with the proceeds of the sales, and create, in exchange for the unredeemed portion of each of them, an equivalent amount of Privileged or Unified Stock. The general debt of Egypt would thus be somewhat increased; but, on the other hand, two costly and needless administrations would be economized, and the lands would get back into the hands of the native cultivators, who are best able to turn them to good account. Moreover, the Budget would be relieved of a heavy annual charge in respect of the deficit on the Daira and Domains accounts, which arises from the inadequacy of the net revenue of these properties to meet the interest on the loans to which they were respectively pledged. It is true that the Daira lands have for the last two years, under the able management of Mr. Hamilton Lang and M. Gay Lussac, not only escaped a deficit, but actually yielded a surplus, an event hitherto unheard of in their history. But the Domains Commission has never yet succeeded in making its estates pay anything like the interest on the Domains loan. Its annual deficit varies between £100,000 and £200,000 a year, and is a terrible drain on the general purse.

Yet the chances of getting rid of the incubus are decidedly remote. France has always shown a peculiar tenderness for the Daira and Domains administrations, and especially for the latter, which it regards as a stronghold of French influence in the country. As a matter of fact, it does not really promote French influence to saddle Egypt with a number of superfluous French officials. But this truth is apparently not recognised at the Quai d'Orsay. Any way, France made it a special condition of her assent to the conversion of the Privileged Debt in 1890 that not more than £300,000 worth of either the Domains or the Daira lands should be sold in any one year up to 1905, so that it will take thirteen years from 1892 to get rid of either of the Commissions. Until the expiration of that period they must just be looked upon as part of the international top-hamper which Egypt has to carry, and be borne with such patience as may be.

So much for the legal limitations, various and complex, upon the freedom of action of the Egyptian Government. But there are moral limitations no less substantial, if less easy to define. We have seen the extent to which the principle of Internationalism has entrenched itself in the Nile Valley. International

Courts judge the Khedive's subjects, and may condemn his Ministers. International agreements limit his power of borrowing, and dictate to him what he may spend. In many instances he cannot make a law or issue a police order without international sanction. Nominally the vassal of the Sultan, who yet exercises little control over the administration, and whose remaining influence is religious rather than political, the Khedive is practically the vassal of Europe, and especially of the Great Powers. This fact, carefully concealed in matters of form, but still ever present to the minds of men, inevitably gives to the representatives of the Powers an authority and influence very different from that of ordinary diplomatic agents. It is difficult for any of them, even the humblest, to avoid occasionally slipping into the rôle of Mentor, and if he does, it is perfectly inadmissible to treat him otherwise than with deference. For an offended Agent may mean an offended Power, and an offended Power may mean the indefinite postponement of some useful or necessary measure.

May I add, without indiscretion, that some of these gentlemen are the touchiest of mankind, and that their touchiness extends, by a sort of contagion, to most of the foreign officials in the country, the English not entirely excepted? And inasmuch as Egypt abounds in anomalous officials, and is, moreover, by a sort of fatality, peculiarly productive of anomalous situations of every kind, the result is embarrassing in the extreme. As I look back upon my residence in Egypt, I seem to see one long vista of questions of etiquette, and especially of precedence, as alarming in their possible consequences as they were utterly ludicrous in themselves. If there is one dignitary in the world who deserves the indulgent sympathy of all humane men, it is the Grand Master of Ceremonies to His Highness the Khedive.

I fear I have been explaining at tedious length, but I am sadly conscious how difficult it must be, despite all explanations, for a reader not acquainted with Egypt to realize what difficulties beset the everyday business of government—to say nothing of any large scheme of improvement and reform—in consequence of the countless international fetters by which Egypt is bound, the forts and blockhouses of European privilege with which the country is studded. Wherever you turn there is some obstruction in your path. Do you want to clear out a cesspool, to prevent the sale of noxious drugs, to suppress a seditious or immoral print, you are pulled up by the Capitulations. Do you want to carry out some big work of public utility, to dig a main canal, or to drain a city, you are pulled up by the Law of Liquidation. You cannot borrow without the consent of Turkey; you cannot draw upon the Reserve Fund without the consent of the Caisse; you cannot exceed the Limit of Expenditure without the consent of the Powers. Do you, impeded and hampered on every side, finally lose patience and break through, for however good an object, the finest mesh of the net which binds you, or lay a finger on even the most trivial European privilege, you have a Consul-General down upon you at once. Nay, more; you may have the British Government down upon you, because your action may have brought upon its head the remonstrances of a foreign ambassador, and you may be spoiling some big hand in the general game of foreign politics by your tiresome little Egyptian difficulty. And all the while the foreign papers in Egypt are howling at you for not suppressing nuisances which foreign privilege does not allow you to touch, and for not devoting to public improvements money which international conventions do not allow you to spend. And all the while the natives are grumbling, and with far more reason, because they are not protected against foreign encroachment, and because their money is not set free to be spent upon the objects which they have at heart. And their complaints are naturally directed against their English guides. 'You are constantly interfering with our affairs,' they say, 'and ordering us to do this and to leave the other undone. But when it is a question of compelling foreigners to make some sacrifice for the general good, you do not seem to be equally courageous. Bully us yourselves if you must, but at least defend us in return against the bullying of others. It is too much that we should suffer the restraints without enjoying the advantages of a state of dependence.'

Nor is the answer to these complaints altogether easy. It is certain that, if we had grasped the Egyptian nettle boldly, if we had proclaimed from the first our intention of exercising, even for a time, that authority which, as a matter of fact, we do exercise, we could have made the situation not only much more endurable for the Egyptians, but much easier for ourselves. Had we seen our way to declaring even a temporary Protectorate, we might have suspended the Capitulations, if we could not have got rid of them altogether, as France has done in Tunis. Had we been willing to guarantee the debt or a portion of the debt, not only could the interest have been at once reduced and the financial burdens of the country enormously lightened, but Europe would no doubt have agreed to free the Egyptian Government from the network of restrictions which had been imposed upon it for the protection of the bond-holders. In order to have Great Britain as surety for their bond, the creditors would have abandoned with alacrity all these minor safeguards.

I have said before, and I repeat, that I am not criticising Great Britain's policy. I repeat that the line adopted, the line of minimizing what we were doing, of avoiding radical solutions and of living from hand to mouth, may have certain ultimate advantages. But there can be no doubt that it enormously complicated the immediate problem. Here we were engaged upon the task of building up order in a country where government had utterly collapsed, and which was singularly poor in native governing capacity. And we were to build it up without adopting any clearly defined position or exercising any definite authority, by means of advice, of influence, of a peculiar and irritating kind of diplomatic pressure. And that pressure had to be brought to bear upon native rulers, who to a great extent were not in sympathy with us, and even when in sympathy, were not free, but fettered by restrictions of the most various kinds —ancient restrictions arising from Egypt's vassalage to Turkey, and modern restrictions which were the result of her unfortunate financial history. Surely the situation was one that presented quite unexampled difficulties. It will be my endeavour in the succeeding chapters to indicate how those difficulties were met.

CHAPTER V.

THE YEARS OF GLOOM.

BEFORE advancing any further, I am compelled to trouble the reader with a few words of explanation as to the exact nature of the ground which we are about to traverse. If, for the moment, I proceed on historical lines, it must not be thought that I am attempting to write a regular history of Egypt since Tel-el-Kebir. Such a history will no doubt appear in due time, and it ought to be a very interesting book. The aim of the present volume is simply to give a general idea of the work of economic and political regeneration at present in progress in Egypt. But as even this modest structure can hardly be erected without a historical framework, however slender, the present and the following chapter must be devoted to a sketch of the salient features of Egyptian history since 1882. Such an outline will render more intelligible the subsequent examination, item by item, of the most important branches of the work of reform.

The beginning of all things, so far as that work is concerned, was the special mission to Egypt of Lord Dufferin, at that time British Ambassador in Constantinople. Lord Dufferin arrived in Cairo early in November, 1882. Not two months had elapsed since the defeat of Arabi, yet Egyptian affairs were already getting into a considerable tangle. With masterly skill the newcomer extricated the Egyptian and British Governments from the mess into which they had drifted over the trial of the rebel leaders. With equal resolution and promptitude he quashed the unfortunate experiment of scraping together a foreign police-force from the most diverse quarters—from Anatolia, from Epirus, and even from Austria and Switzerland. The new Albanian guardians of the peace, who had already distinguished themselves by causing a riot in the streets of Alexandria, were disbanded. The process of recruiting in Geneva and other cities, which had been regarded with favour by the local authorities of those towns as a happy means of getting rid of some of their least desirable citizens, was summarily put a stop to. Having thus cleared the ground, our Envoy proceeded to lay down the general lines on which Egypt was to be restored to order and prosperity, and endowed, if possible, with the capacity of self-development.

The policy of Lord Dufferin has been put on record by his own hand in a series of despatches, too good to be buried in a Blue Book, of which that of February 6, 1883, is the most comprehensive and elaborate. It is impossible for anyone well acquainted with Egypt to read those despatches without admiration. Their writer's mastery of the subject is extraordinary. Behind all his formal civility to the misleading catchwords, the impractical ideals, which he felt bound to treat with respect, there is a manly grasp of fact, and a clear appreciation of the essential needs of Egypt, and of the true remedies for her distress. No man knew better than Lord Dufferin that it was not paper constitutions, even of the most approved pattern, not emancipating decrees, even if glowing with the spirit of modern Liberalism, not courts or codes hastily copied from those of Western Europe, which could restore the prosperity of Egypt and give her inhabitants either bread or justice. It was the slow disagreeable work of reforming in detail, in the performance of their daily duties, the several branches of the administration, until order should gradually be evolved from chaos, and until, under competent guides armed with adequate authority, native officials should gradually acquire the habit of energy, equity, self-reliance and method.

All this Lord Dufferin realized, but his manner of presenting the case was hardly calculated to make others realize it. He said enough to save his own reputation for clear-sightedness, but not enough to impart to those whom it concerned the full knowledge which he himself possessed. To anyone who looks closely and critically at his words, the whole truth is there—the hard actual facts, as well as the possibilities of a better future. But for all that the general effect was likely to be delusive. The stream of his sanguine eloquence might well sweep away the reader in imagination past the rocks and shallows—which are all marked, but without being emphasized—to a welcome goal seemingly near, but really most difficult of attainment.

There were not wanting at the time critics who, comparing his unobtrusive notes of warning with his general hopefulness of tone, roundly accused Lord Dufferin of writing with his tongue in his cheek, of not believing in his own forecast or his own prescription. Against this imputation he himself warmly, and no doubt sincerely, protested; and up to a point his protest was entirely justified. He was right in not despairing of the ultimate independence of Egypt; he was right in the direction which he strove to give to reforming effort. But, on the other hand, he certainly glossed over the deep-rooted obstacles which his scheme of reform was bound to encounter, and, above all, the length of time which would be required to accomplish it. His rose-coloured picture of an Egypt 'untrammelled by external importunity, though aided by sympathetic advice and assistance,' of the Egyptians governing themselves on civilized principles 'without an irritating and exasperating display of authority' on our part, though 'under the uncompromising ægis of our friendship,' was exactly suited to hit the prevailing taste both in Egypt and Great Britain. It flattered the self-importance and the shallow Liberalism of the Pashas, always ready to sympathize with reforms until they begin to come home to them in the shape of harder work, diminished license, and fewer opportunities of self-enrichment. It was no less grateful to the British people in their honest desire to play the part of guide, philosopher, and friend to the people of Egypt, but to play it cheap; and at the same time it concealed from both parties the disagreeable side of the business—from the Egyptians the long period of irksome control and training through which they would have to pass on their road to a civilized independence, from the English the corresponding period of close attention to the affairs of Egypt, and the effort, anxiety, and risk which such attention involved.

It was perhaps owing to this dexterous manipulation of light and shade that Lord Dufferin, besides doing a large amount of excellent work in Egypt, succeeded in leaving the country a popular man. During the six months of his stay, a substantial beginning had been made in the reconstruction of the army. The use of the kurbash had been prohibited by law, and vigorous steps had been taken to prevent that prohibition from remaining a dead letter. The civil and criminal Codes, which were a necessary preliminary to the establishment of reformed Native Tribunals, had been completed. The Khedivial Government had undertaken to call in experts from India to look after the Irrigation Department. The modest and sensible scheme of Representative Institutions elaborated by Lord Dufferin had been promulgated by Khedivial decree. On all hands there was real progress, but the appearance of progress was even greater than the reality. The native authorities were delighted with themselves, and in an excellent good humour with the British Envoy. When he left the country in May, 1883, it was amid a shower of mutual congratulations. The fair vision of a reformed and autonomous Egypt seemed, after all, not to be so very difficult to realize.

It is quite evident that such hopes were destined in any case to prove premature. But there is something singularly dramatic in the rapidity and completeness of the disappointment which awaited them. Fate dealt very hardly with the optimistic forecasts of the Dufferin epoch. It was certainly an unusual combination of misfortunes that a country, still staggering under the wounds inflicted on it by a recent revolution, should be visited within six months, first by a devastating epidemic, and then by a tremendous military disaster. Yet such was the destiny of Egypt in the summer and autumn of 1883.

The severe invasion of the cholera, which swept over the country in June and July of that year, revealed in the most startling manner the utter rottenness of the internal administration. The frightfully insanitary condition of the towns and villages, the absence of any kind of preparation, the scarcity of hospitals, and the still more fatal scarcity of properly trained doctors, combined to render the visitation a particularly severe one. But all these evils were greatly aggravated by the phenomenal helplessness of the native officials in face of this sudden emergency. Their task was not complicated by any widespread panic on the part of the population. Mussulman fatalism preserves the bulk of the Egyptian people from the blind terror, almost amounting to madness, which the approach of pestilence is apt to inspire among the Christian inhabitants of the Nile Valley, and especially among those of Levantine or Southern European origin. On this occasion the Khedive himself set the example of fearlessness and contempt for death, and that example was followed, in a greater or less degree, by every section of his Mohammedan subjects. There was no want of courage, and there was no want of good-will; but there was a most lamentable display of administrative incapacity. Except here and there, where some Anglo-Egyptian or English functionary, like General Stephenson, then commanding the Army of Occupation in Cairo, boldly took matters into his own hands, disorganization reigned supreme.

But the epidemic of cholera, devastating as it was, had nothing like the same far-reaching consequences as the second great calamity which befell Egypt in 1883—the annihilation of General Hicks's army in Kordofan. Yet, if the effects of that defeat were terrible, they were not more appalling than its causes. I do not refer to the worthlessness of the old Egyptian Army. That had already been proved to demonstration. A new and greater revelation was that of the incompetence of the Egyptian Government to take any intelligent resolution on a question at once so vital and so clear as that of the Sudan. If the cholera had broken down the rank and file of the administration, the Sudan crisis revealed the absence of all power of direction at its head. Seldom if ever has a disaster been more wantonly courted than the destruction of Hicks. The Egyptian Government held in its hands all the evidence that reasonable men could desire of the hopeless inadequacy of Hicks's forces to accomplish the task which they were sent to perform. Yet that did not prevent it from sending them. It was the simplest arithmetical theorem that Egypt, loaded with debt and with a new deficit staring her in the face, could not afford to reconquer the more distant regions of the Sudan. Yet that did not prevent the Government from squandering upon an attempt to reconquer them a sum of money, admittedly inadequate for the purpose, but which, if wisely applied, would have sufficed to save the nearer and more important provinces which had not yet fallen into the hands of the rebels.

How came Great Britain to allow Egypt to engage upon a course at once so futile and so perilous? The answer is a curious piece of political psychology. The British Government had from the first taken up the position that it was 'not responsible for the affairs of the Sudan.' It followed as a logical consequence that, whatever follies the Egyptian Government might commit in that quarter, Great Britain was bound not to interfere to prevent them. And to this theory we clung with extraordinary tenacity during all the time that the Hicks disaster was in course of preparation. General Hicks was in the habit of sending despatches to the Egyptian Government through Sir E. Malet, the British Consul-General. These despatches, despite the forced hopefulness of certain phrases, teemed with indications of the desperate nature of the venture he was about to make. But Sir E. Malet was under the strictest orders to hand them over to the Egyptian Government without attempting to influence its decision. His rôle in the matter, as he was specially instructed to declare, was that of a mere postman. Over and over again the Egyptian Government was informed that it could do just as it liked in all matters connected with the Sudan; that it might keep it or give it up, withdraw its troops, or reinforce them. The matter was one about which Great Britain had simply nothing to say.

The faith in the power of phrases to alter facts has never been more strangely manifested than in this idea, that we could shake off our virtual responsibility for the policy of Egypt in the Sudan by an official disclaimer. To separate the inseparable is unfortunately beyond the power of diplomatic declarations, however precise and emphatic. We were by our own express admission, as well as by the plain and palpable circumstances of the case, responsible for the stability of the Egyptian Government. But the Sudan was still an integral part of the Khedive's dominions. Its retention involved, even under normal conditions, a loss of £200,000 a year to the Egyptian Treasury. If things got worse, there was no saying what proportions that loss might assume. There were forty thousand Egyptian troops in the country, yet they had not succeeded in coping with the Mahdi. If the flame of rebellion could not be quenched, there was no saying how far it might spread. It was possible to hold, that the best course for Egypt was to try and cut the Sudan adrift altogether, withdrawing her troops while it was yet time, and concentrating all her efforts upon the defence of her own frontier. But it was not possible to hold, that the course she might pursue with regard to the Sudan was otherwise than of urgent and vital importance to herself. The very existence of Egypt might depend upon the proper handling of a question concerning which we, the temporary guardians of the country, were declaring that we had no responsibility!

The theory of our limited liability for the management of the affairs of Egypt is one that has played a great part in the history of the last ten years. Its genesis is not difficult to explain. As has been already shown, we plunged into the business of setting Egypt on her legs without any conception of the extent or the difficulty of the task. As the magnitude of our undertaking began to reveal itself to us, we strove by every means in our power to limit our obligations, and to narrow the field of our interference. We felt that we were bound to see Egypt out of trouble in vital issues, but that in all other things she had better look after herself. And in certain cases this principle has not proved a bad one. When we had our hands too full, and were doing everything badly because trying to do everything at once, it was a prudent policy to concentrate our scattered energies, and to direct our whole attention to a few essential points. But the success of such a course depends entirely upon a right judgment as to what is essential at a given time. And our judgment on that question was never more hopelessly at fault, than when we averted our eyes from what was going on in the Sudan and hugged ourselves with the fiction that we were not responsible for the action of the Egyptian Government in that region. It was this fiction which destroyed Hicks and his ten thousand men.

We met with a tremendous punishment. The country, which we had vainly dreamed to exclude from the sphere of our responsibilities, was destined to become the old Man of the Sea to the British Sinbad. Millions of pounds had to be spent, thousands of lives to be sacrificed before we could extricate ourselves from the consequences of our original neglect.

General Hicks's doomed army started from Khartum on September 9, 1883. 'The troops,' in the words of the brave but ill-starred O'Donovan, who accompanied the expedition, 'scarcely deserved the name of soldiers, so little were they acquainted with even the most elementary principles of the military art.' 'I am writing this,' he wrote in the course of the march, 'under circumstances which bring me almost as near to death as it is possible to be without being absolutely under sentence of execution or in the throes of some deadly malady . . . in company with cravens that you expect to see run at every moment and leave you behind to face the worst . . . to die with a lance-head as big as a shovel through you.' On September 24, the expedition left the Nile at El Duem, one hundred miles above Khartum, and struck westward into the hostile wastes of Kordofan. And therewith the curtain fell upon it, and with it upon Egyptian rule in the Sudan. Hicks's objective was the town of El Obeid, at that time the headquarters of the Mahdi, but he never arrived there. After marching some two hundred miles along dubious routes, and amid constant skirmishing, the Egyptian troops, with their line of communications cut off, and surrounded by overwhelming numbers of a daring and savage enemy, were annihilated in a great battle fought on November 5, at Shekan, when they had got within some two days' journey of their goal. Very few escaped to tell the story. It was not till a long time afterwards that a connected account of the disaster was supplied by one of the handful of survivors.

But if the details were long in coming to hand, the main fact became known with all the proverbial rapidity of evil things. Before the end of November, everybody in Cairo was aware that Egypt's last desperate venture for the recovery of her fast-dissolving empire had ended in a supreme catastrophe. Yet even then the gravity of the situation seemed not to dawn upon the Egyptian Government. After as before the defeat of Hicks, they kept playing with the question of the Sudan. The idea of abandoning it was intensely unpopular, and they could not make up their minds to accept the bitter necessity, which yet was palpable to every clear-sighted observer. Just as, before the despatch of Hicks, the logic of facts imperiously demanded withdrawal from the outlying provinces and concentration at Khartum for the defence of the rest, so now the same logic pointed with equal clearness to withdrawal from the whole country and concentration at Wadi Halfa for the defence of Egypt. But there is nothing which a Turk finds harder than to recognise a defeat, even in order to avoid a worse one. Prompt resolution is never his strong point, least of all the resolution to accept an unpleasant truth and to act unhesitatingly upon it. Had the Egyptian Ministry been left to themselves, there is no saying what new disasters their reluctance to look facts in the face might not have brought upon their country.

Good fortune willed that they should not be left to themselves. The moment was one which called aloud for clear insight and resolute will, and, by a happy coincidence, there had just appeared on the Egyptian stage a man who possessed both those qualities in an exceptional degree. On September 11, two days after Hicks's army started from Khartum, Sir Evelyn Baring, returning to Egypt after an absence of three years, had entered upon the duties of British Consul-General. We may imagine what must have been his feelings, if during the succeeding months he devoted some portion of his time to reading the correspondence relative to Hicks's expedition—which had now irrevocably started—and noting therein the certain presages of that calamity, for which he could now do nothing but wait. Nor is it possible to help wondering whether, if he had been at the helm some months sooner, that expedition would ever have been allowed to set out. But be that as it may, when the blow had once fallen, he had no hesitation as to the line to be pursued. Sir Evelyn Baring is a man of a decided mind. His view may be right or it may be wrong, but it is always definite, and he is always determined to push it through. In this instance, his view was that Egypt could by no possibility retain the Sudan, and that, this being so, her only wise course was to cut it adrift at once and altogether, and keep every man and every shilling that remained to her for the defence of her own frontier. And the British Government unhesitatingly adopted the advice of its representative. Throwing to the winds its previous attitude of indifference, it instructed Sir Evelyn to inform the Egyptian Cabinet that the Sudan must be abandoned with all possible promptitude, and that any Minister who would not fall in with this programme must go. Thus did we ourselves give the lie direct to our long-cherished theory that the policy of Egypt with regard to the Sudan was no business of ours.

Undoubtedly the decision was a right one. In saying that, do not let me be supposed to argue that the possession of the Sudan, or at least of a considerable portion of it, is not important, and may not even in the long-run be necessary, to the welfare of Egypt. But a man who is in the extremest straits does well to give up even an essential part of his establishment, rather than go altogether into bankruptcy. A hardly pressed garrison may find it necessary to abandon even the most important outposts in order to preserve its citadel. The fact that Egypt gave up the Sudan, when she simply had not the strength to hold it, is no reason why she should not recover it, or part of it, when she once more has the strength. Nor can any blame attach to those who took upon themselves the odious, but necessary, duty of throwing overboard a valuable cargo which, if retained, was bound to sink the ship. On the contrary, it is to them that the credit of having saved Egypt principally belongs.

When it became apparent that the British Government was determined to insist on the abandonment of the Sudan, Sherif Pasha, who had been Prime Minister since the restoration of the Khedive's authority in September, 1882, immediately resigned. For a moment it seemed doubtful whether anyone could be found to take his place. There were at that time only three great luminaries in the Egyptian political firmament—Sherif Pasha, Riaz Pasha, and Nubar Pasha. Sherif had gone.* Riaz, who had been Minister of the Interior under Sherif, but had retired because he was not allowed to hang Arabi, could not be induced to fill the vacant place. There remained then only Nubar, the ablest, but also the most adaptable, of the trio. With much apparent hesitation, and not, perhaps, without some real

* Sherif Pasha never returned to power. He died during the Ministry of his successor, in April, 1887.

reluctance, this statesman finally consented to take over the reins of government, and on January 8, 1884, a new Ministry was formed, with Nubar as its head, and with retirement from the Sudan as the first article of its programme.

The eighteen months succeeding the accession of Nubar Pasha to office were the most critical period in the history of our dealings with Egypt. The old proverb that it never rains but it pours has seldom appeared so true. Everything—yes, absolutely everything—seemed bent upon going wrong at one and the same time. Alike in military matters, in diplomacy, and in politics, Great Britain was simply haunted by the Egyptian Question. Nor was the position in Egypt itself ever more uncomfortable, whether for the protectors or the protected.

This was the epoch of all that desperate fighting in the Sudan, which will ever fill a memorable page in the annals of the British Army. In February, 1884, General Baker, at the head of a rabble of so-called 'gendarmerie,' converted for the moment into soldiers, was ignominiously routed in an attempt to relieve Tokar. At the time of Baker's defeat General Gordon was already far on his famous journey to Khartum. Then followed in quick succession the first English expedition to Suakin, the loss of Berber, the Nile campaign, the fall of Khartum, the second Suakin expedition, and our final abandonment of the whole business, culminating in the withdrawal of the British troops from Dongola in June, 1885.

The story of the Sudan campaign is one of almost mythic grandeur. In its richness of adventure and surprise, in the extraordinary variety of its difficulties and dangers—the vast physical obstacles to be overcome, the daring and incalculable enemy to be encountered—above all, in the dramatic completeness of our final failure, there has been nothing equal to it in recent times. But it is no duty of mine to recall that sad though fascinating tale of suffering and of heroism. The extraordinary refinement of blundering which made our action the ridicule of the world; the splendid acts of gallantry which redeemed our blunders; the hand-to-hand fights of Homeric intensity, which are brought to mind by the mention of Abu Klea and Abu Kru, of Tamai, or of 'MacNeill's *Zariba*'; the lofty tragedy associated for ever with the name of Khartum—all these are too deeply impressed upon the memory of Englishmen to need any celebration here. And if the broad outlines of the story are matter of common knowledge, its details have quite recently been presented to the public in the completest possible form by Major Wingate in his standard work on 'Mahdiism and the Egyptian Sudan.'* No man could possibly have been better fitted to perform that task. A practical soldier, with long and varied experience of Sudanese warfare, Major Wingate has also been for a number of years the chief of the Intelligence Department of the Egyptian Army. Knowing the language and the people, he has amassed and digested an amount of information which was not within the reach of any other man, and has presented it in a form which may safely be regarded as final. It would be idle on my part to detain the reader by a repetition of any portion of the events which have already been made the subject of so full and conclusive a chronicle.

Neither is it my intention to enter into the history of those diplomatic embarrassments which, in an equal or greater degree than our entanglement in the Sudan, tended to render the situation of England with regard to Egypt delicate and even dangerous. In her attempts to loosen the financial fetters which were strangling Egypt, to settle the question of the Suez Canal, and to come to some amicable understanding with the other Powers as to her own position in the Nile Valley, Great Britain was doomed to encounter the resolute hostility of France, while she had at that time, with the exception of Italy, no single friend in the councils of Europe. The consequence was a series of harassing negotiations, which did indeed, for a wonder, ultimately result in a tolerable arrangement of Egyptian finances, but left everything

* London: Macmillan and Co.

else *in statu quo*. The abortive agreement between England and France with reference to the Canal in the summer of 1884; the contemporaneous and equally abortive Conference on the financial question; the Northbrook mission of the following autumn, with its awkward consequences; the resumption of negotiations in the beginning of 1885, and the Convention resulting from it —these are not incidents which, for our present purpose, need more than a passing mention. Their permanent effects, so far as they had any, will be noted in later chapters. Their details are now of interest only to diplomatists, and an adequate discussion of them would be quite out of keeping with the proportions of the present work.

But if we are not immediately concerned either with the war in the Sudan or with the negotiations simultaneously going on in London and elsewhere in reference to the affairs of Egypt, there is one respect in which both the one and the other have an important bearing on our subject. I refer to the reflex action of these disturbing influences upon the position of Englishmen in Egypt. Never before or since has that position been a more difficult one than in 1884 and 1885. Never has the friction between the British officials and their Egyptian colleagues been more severe. Never has British control been more unpopular, alike with the foreign and the native inhabitants of the country. And to a large extent, without doubt, that tension and that unpopularity were due to the causes just mentioned. The abandonment of the Sudan had been extremely unwelcome to all classes of the population. The subsequent errors of our policy were not calculated to inspire respect either for our wisdom or our resolution. The obvious fact that we were getting into hot water with other nations over the Egyptian Question excited the hopes of our enemies, while it damped the spirits and enfeebled the support of our few well-wishers.

If there is one thing essential to the success of our work in Egypt, it is the tranquillity of the public mind, a belief in the fixity of our intentions and the permanence of the reforms which we have instituted. There is no truer remark in the great report of Lord Dufferin already referred to, full though it be of ingenious observations, than the sentence in which he says, 'unless they are convinced that we intend to shield and foster the system we have established, it will be in vain to expect the timid politicians of the East to identify themselves with its existence.' The power, and not only the power, but even the popularity of England in Egypt has always varied in proportion to the degree of general belief in the permanence of English control. But during the period of which I am speaking that belief was very feeble. There was no conviction of the permanence of anything. There was no general feeling of tranquillity, but, on the contrary, perpetual unsettlement, incessant alarms from without, incessant rumours of change within —all eagerly seized upon and exaggerated by the European, and especially the French, press, which, thanks to the Capitulations, was entirely beyond the control of the Government.

Those external influences, though they certainly aggravated, did not alone cause our growing troubles. The illusions of the Dufferin epoch had by this time vanished into thin air. The period of disenchantment and dissatisfaction, which was sure to come when the native officials began to feel the irksomeness of our control, was now full upon us. The essence of Lord Dufferin's system—and it was the only possible system if there was to be any effective reform in Egypt—was to put a certain number of Englishmen into high posts in the various administrations, and to trust to their influence to get things gradually into order. But it soon became apparent that that influence, if it was to be of any use, involved pressure. The native functionaries were beginning to find out that they could no longer, as in old times, do just as they pleased. Of course the bad ones—and I fear they were the majority —detested the restrictions upon their power, which they had been accustomed to use for purposes of personal profit. But even the good ones were unhappy. All their old notions were upset; all their old habits had to be altered. And the process was naturally a very trying one, especially at the outset. An eminent writer has said that there is no pain like that of a new idea. If this be so, the existence of an Egyptian official at that time must have been one long succession of pangs.

The sense of discomfort and the spirit of resentment were not confined to the officials. These feelings were almost universal among natives of the upper class. To some extent, no doubt, the hostility of that class was due to a patriotic dislike to foreign interference. But there are probably few countries in which patriotic sentiment counts for less than it does in Egypt. What really angered the Pashas was the loss of their former authority. To be rich in Egypt in old times was to be, within your own sphere, an autocrat. Once conciliate the officials—no difficult matter in most cases—and your course was clear. But with English influence at headquarters, and with English inspectors going about the country, it was no longer so easy to escape the restraints of a regular administration of the law.

Those restraints were now making themselves felt in many directions, but in none were they more disagreeable to the great land-owners—and every rich native is a land-owner—than in the regulation of the water-supply. Of all their old privileges, the most valuable was that of taking water from the public canals how they pleased, when they pleased, and in whatever quantity they pleased. But the Public Works Department was the first in which English influence became supreme, and the first manifestation of that influence was a rigorous control of the distribution of water. The odium excited by that control among the most powerful natives was, in the beginning, very great. At the present day it is probable that the general improvement of the irrigation system, by which no one has profited more than they, has fully consoled them for the loss of their old unjust advantages. But seven or eight years ago that loss was fresh and keenly felt, while the compensating benefits were still in the future.

And if the upper classes had reasons of their own for disliking British influence, the bulk of the people were no less discontented, though from a very different cause. They were suffering from the reaction of disappointment which followed the grand Nationalist debauch of 1882. If there is one thing absolutely certain, it is that the great majority of the Egyptian nation, and especially the peasantry, have benefited enormously by our presence in the country. For the few, the new system has meant loss as well as gain: for the many, it is all pure gain. At no previous period of his history has the fellah lived under a government so careful to promote his interests or to protect his rights. But no conceivable government, however friendly to him, could possibly have fulfilled the hopes excited in his breast during the months of revolution. In time, no doubt, he would learn to contrast the new administration with the old, much to the advantage of the former. For the moment, the comparison lay, not between one administration and another, but between the hard facts of any settled government and the wild dreams of a brief period of license. And the fellah had a special reason for regretting that interlude of anarchy. He was heavily in debt. His creditors were almost entirely Christians—Greeks, Syrians, or Copts. During the days of Arabi the Greeks and Syrians had mostly fled. The Copts, who remained, were much too frightened to think of asserting their rights. But now they were all back again, and insisting upon the fulfilment of the fellah's obligations. The Government might protect him against illegal exactions; it was powerless, even if it had been willing, to relieve him from his legal debts. For the restoration of order meant the re-establishment of the authority of the Mixed Courts. And these courts would insist upon the payment in full of debts due to foreigners, even if the Government should desire to effect a composition. Thus rich and poor alike were, for different reasons, ill-affected towards the new régime.

But how about the foreign residents? They, at least, it might have been supposed, would be grateful to us for the restoration of order, and eager to second our efforts for the improvement of the system of government. As a matter of fact, the great majority of them met those efforts with nothing but unintelligent criticism and sullen obstruction. The effusive thankfulness with which they had greeted our arrival was soon exhausted, while the irritation which they felt at our tendency to support the natives against foreign encroachment was a permanent source of bitterness.

The Europeans in Alexandria had a special grievance on account of the delay in the payment of the indemnities for the damages caused by the bombardment and subsequent conflagration. But apart from this particular cause of ill-humour, the European community generally was deeply disappointed at the continued stagnation of business. When the British forces first occupied Egypt, and the foreigners who had fled during the rebellion flocked back, there was a general impression that, under the ægis of a civilized government, enterprise would at once take a new start, and the country would rapidly attain a degree of prosperity such as it had never yet known. But the expected revival did not come, and the consequent disappointment was not the less severe because it was essentially unreasonable. It was no fault of ours that Egypt could not recover at a bound from the consequences of the financial profligacy of the reign of Ismail, and from the damage caused by the rebellion. The embarrassments of the Exchequer, inherited from the old régime, were a heavy drag upon the well-being of the people. It was impossible, while taxation was strained to its utmost limit, and while, in spite of enormous taxation, the State seemed unable to meet its liabilities, that the country as a whole should be prosperous. Moreover, the depleted condition of the Treasury during the last few years had entailed a neglect of those great Public Works, the proper maintenance of which is the first condition of the wealth of Egypt. The country is rich, but it is rich by artificial means. Without an elaborate canal system it might become a desert. With that canal system neglected and in disorder, it is not rich but poor. The restoration of national solvency, and such an arrangement of the finances as would allow of the necessary sums being devoted to Public Works, were thus essential conditions of the return of prosperity, and these conditions could not be attained in a moment. They depended upon an agreement between the Great Powers, and it was not till nearly three years after our occupation that such an arrangement was arrived at.

No doubt the slowness of the revival of business was due, in some degree, to the public uncertainty as to the ultimate intentions of Great Britain. This unfavourable influence continues to militate against the prosperity of the country even at the present day. Foreign capital is still shy of Egypt ; it remembers the upset of 1882, and it hesitates to embark in a quarter where, under uncontrolled native administration in the future, a similar upset might again be possible. That fear is wearing off with the lapse of years, and with the growth of the impression, at present largely prevalent, that Great Britain intends by some means or other to keep a controlling hand upon Egypt. But, though the feeling of insecurity is nowadays much diminished, it has not entirely disappeared. And at the time of which I am speaking it was still at its height.

There were other and less creditable causes of foreign discontent. British influence could not at once revive trade, or compensate Egypt for the loss of an important market in the Sudan. But it did from the outset, and with ever-increasing effectiveness, tend to diminish other sources of profit, which were of a less legitimate character. Europeans had earned much money in Egypt in the days of Ismail. Some of it was made by honest enterprise in developing the resources of the country. But a great deal was made by jobbery, by usury, and by positive fraud—at the expense of the Government or of the people. To that sort of money-making the new spirit now being breathed into the administration was necessarily fatal. A volume might be written on this subject. I will confine myself to illustrating my meaning by the development of a single but most important point.

I have said that the peasantry were in debt, and that their creditors were mostly Europeans. I have shown why we could not give them relief from existing debts. Yet, in the long-run, we could give them something better. We could cut at the root of the principal causes which made their indebtedness so great, and its terms so oppressive. The fellah had for years past been driven to borrowing, and to borrowing on ruinous conditions, by the Government itself. The tax-gatherer had paved the way for the usurer. It was not the amount of taxation, crushing as in many cases it was, which did the mischief. It was above all the irregular, cruel, and arbitrary manner in which the taxes were collected. The fellah was seldom sure of the amount which would be demanded of him. He was never sure of the moment when the demand would be made. That moment might, as likely as not, be the very one at which he was least able to pay. Called upon to find ready money while his crops were still in the ground, he was simply driven into the arms of the money-lender. His choice lay between so many blows of the kurbash and the acceptance of the usurer's terms, however onerous. Under these circumstances, money was borrowed at as much as 60 per cent. per annum. Worse than that, it was often obtained by the sale of the growing crops, which were estimated for the purpose of the advance at half or less than half their value. This state of things was bad enough, and it was pretty general; but the ruin of the cultivator was consummated in many instances by positive collusion with the usurer on the part of corrupt officials. The latter would demand the payment of taxes by the peasant, who was already in debt, at the very time when the interest on his debt was due. If he had any cash at all, the authorities were bound to get it. When the usurer came after them, nothing was left to the fellah but to surrender his land and cattle, or to renew his bond on still more ruinous terms. He was, in fact, entirely at the mercy of the lender.

It is evident that, under these circumstances, the small foreign capitalist without a conscience enjoyed in Egypt opportunities of making a fortune which probably could not be rivalled anywhere else in the world. It is equally evident that with the introduction of—I do not say an absolutely just and perfect—but a more or less sane and equitable method of collecting taxes, a method which sought to secure the dues of the State at the least instead of the greatest cost to the cultivator, these opportunities of speedy money-making were vastly reduced. And then the usurers began to howl about the decay of prosperity. The clamour of disappointed greed and defeated dishonesty augmented the general chorus of complaint at the slackness of business, and at the disappearance of all those signs of exuberant but fictitious prosperity, which were characteristic of the epoch of rapid, unsound development under Ismail Pasha.

With all these influences working against them, with the native officials hostile or bewildered, and the native magnates angry and rebellious, with a dejected population and a cantankerous foreign colony, and with the shadow of our diplomatic difficulties and of our grand fiasco in the Sudan deepening the general gloom, the position of the English in Egypt in 1884 and 1885 was trying in the extreme. The Anglo-Egyptian functionaries were new to their work; their objects were misunderstood; they had not the material means of relieving one-half of the evils which they saw and deplored. The British Consul-General was bombarded with suggestions which presupposed a free hand and an overflowing exchequer, while in fact he was directing a manacled government, with bankruptcy staring it in the face. And to add a final touch to all our troubles, the British nation was at that moment in one of its most unreasonable moods on the subject of Egypt. The violence of partisan controversy obscured every issue. Public opinion was fickle, impatient, wholly uninformed. It needed a back as broad as that of Sir Evelyn Baring to bear the accumulated weight of all the work, worry, and misconstruction which attended that hard, uphill struggle to improve administration while preserving solvency.

I have spoken repeatedly of the British officials in Egypt. It will be convenient at this point to note the number, position, and principal names of the Englishmen and Scotchmen—for Scotland had an important share in the business—who were at that time in the service of the Khedive. Even prior to 1882, a number of our countrymen had been employed in high administrative posts. Apart from the Caisse de la Dette and the 'Mixed Administrations,'* there was Mr. Caillard, the Director-General of Customs; Mr. Halton, the Post-Master-General; and Mr. (now Sir Gerald) Fitzgerald, the Director-General of Accounts. But after the Occupation, both the number and the power of the British officials was very greatly increased. In the main the new appointments followed the lines laid down by Lord Dufferin; that is to say, Englishmen were placed in virtual command of these departments, the immediate strengthening of which seemed essential to the revival of the country. Those departments were the Army, Finance, Public Works, Police, and to some extent Justice. To the Army the Khedive appointed twenty-seven English officers, the chief of them being Sir Evelyn Wood, who was nominated Sirdar or Commander-in-Chief. The Police were placed under General Baker, with three or four Englishmen immediately under him. The Irrigation Department was entrusted to Colonel (now Sir Colin) Scott-Moncrieff, and when he was, after six months, promoted to the post of Under-Secretary of State for Public Works, his place as Inspector-General was taken by Colonel Ross, another Anglo-Indian. Two more engineers from India were appointed inspectors of circles of irrigation, and the number subsequently grew to four. In the Department of Justice, England was represented by a Procureur-Général, or, as we should say, Attorney-General, attached to the new Native Courts, which came into existence in

* See p. 57.

the beginning of 1884. The first occupant of this post was a distinguished Indian Judge, Sir Benson Maxwell.

Most important of all, but also most difficult to explain, is the position we took up in the Ministry of Finance. Financial troubles had been the cause of Egypt's breakdown and the origin of foreign interference in the country. For any effective control over Egyptian affairs, the first and most necessary step was to get a firm grip of the Finance Department, upon which all depended. For three years before Tel-el-Kebir this department had been in the joint occupation of England and France, subject, of course, to those international restrictions on which I have already dwelt at sufficient length. Masters of the Finance Ministry, the English and French Controllers initiated a work of reform which extended far beyond their immediate province, though it sprang directly from an intelligent appreciation of the reasons of Egypt's financial collapse. If that reform cut deeply into the internal administration of the country, the fact was due, not to any roving spirit of philanthropy on the part of the Controllers, but to the absolute necessity of keeping a tight hand upon the provincial officials, if the peasantry were not to be plundered and the Treasury ruined by the falling off of the land-tax—the mainstay of the revenue.

Having started with the object of balancing the Budget, the Controllers were thus on the highroad to governing the country. But, as we have seen, the Control failed from the want of material force behind it. When it became a question of supporting the Controllers against the Arabists, England and France could not agree as to the means to be employed. Finally, France backed out of the business, and England was left alone to re-establish European control over the finances of Egypt. And having re-established it alone, she naturally claimed to conduct it alone. No one could possibly contest the justice of this demand, even if there had not been other excellent arguments for substituting the single-minded action of a single Power for the constant friction of two jealous rivals. And, as a matter of fact,

France only protested, and did not even protest very vehemently, when at the close of the year 1882 England induced the Egyptian Government to abolish the two Controllers, and to substitute for them a single 'Financial Adviser,' who under the circumstances was naturally an Englishman.

The Financial Adviser is the corner-stone of English influence inside the Egyptian Administration. His functions were only gradually defined, and for the most part by negatives, but in practice he soon acquired a generally recognised and very wide authority. It was agreed at the beginning that he was not to be an executive officer, but that, on the other hand, all executive officers were to give him any information he might require. He was to have a seat on the Council of Ministers, but without a vote; in this respect he inherited a right which had appertained to the Controllers. At a later stage, when some discussion arose as to the amount of attention to be paid to the recommendations of the Financial Adviser, the English Government laid it down that 'no financial decision should be taken without his consent,' and this interpretation was never called in question by the Egyptian Government. But seeing that most important acts of government involve some financial question, the position of a man having a veto on any financial measure is very nearly that of the Tribune of the People in ancient Rome, who had a veto on everything; and a man who has a veto on everything is master of the situation. When, moreover, the person who is already master of the situation by virtue of his functions, also happens to be a citizen of the State which is in military occupation of the country, there is no need to dwell at tedious length upon the magnitude of his powers. The thing speaks for itself.

And the importance of the rôle of Financial Adviser, great in any case, certainly lost nothing in the hands of the persons to whom that rôle was successively entrusted. Sir Auckland Colvin, the first occupant of the office, who had previously been one of the two Controllers, was a strong man. His successor, Sir Edgar

Vincent, though only twenty-six years old at the time of his appointment in November, 1883, was not only a strong man, but one whose natural inclination, encouraged by success, has always led him to play a decidedly forward game. And he needed all his qualities, for the task before him was one of exceptional difficulty. If Egypt was to be permanently improved, the first condition was to make her solvent. And to ensure solvency it was necessary to pinch and screw in a manner which for the time being retarded improvement. Parsimony, however necessary, was bound to be unpopular. But no fear of unpopularity ever shook Vincent in his conviction of the priority of financial over all other considerations, and, firmly supported by the British Consul-General, he succeeded in establishing the principle that to make both ends meet was the first and the great commandment. It was fortunate for the Financial Adviser that he possessed a charm and finesse which softened as far as was possible the inevitable harshness of such a policy. By these means he succeeded for a time in conciliating even Nubar Pasha, though that statesman detested what he called Vincent's 'fiscality.' It is true that the friendly relations which at first existed between the two men were afterwards disturbed, but that is a subject to which I must return later on.

There was one point, and one point only, on which even the severe financiers who controlled the destinies of Egypt were disposed to admit an exception to their great principle of economy. The necessity of large expenditure on Public Works was, for the reasons already explained, too imperious, even in the interests of the Treasury itself, to be ignored by any sagacious person. The Finance Ministry, while turning a deaf ear to other claims, showed from the first a certain leniency to the demands which were made upon it in the name of Irrigation. And its comparative generosity in this respect was not abused. The shrewd and practical Scotchman, who was seated at the Ministry of Public Works, certainly made the most of his available money.

Baring, Vincent, Moncrieff—these were the men who

bore the burden and heat of those early days of stress, and who deserve the chief credit for the ultimate unexpected success of our unpromising experiment in the civil government of Egypt. There were others who contributed largely to the result, and in future chapters we shall come across many of them. For the moment these three names may suffice.

Though the men I have just mentioned were the most important, they were not, for a certain time at least, the most conspicuous of our countrymen in Egypt. The sensational figure of Anglo-Egyptian politics in their most critical phase was not Baring, or Vincent, or Moncrieff, but Clifford Lloyd. The whole of the Clifford Lloyd episode is interesting, not only from the striking personality of its hero, but from the illustration which it affords alike of the wavering character of British policy and of the great ever-recurring point of conflict between Egyptian Ministers and their English advisers. Mr. Clifford Lloyd's appointment was in itself a departure from our original programme. It was no part of Lord Dufferin's scheme to entrust Englishmen with the management of the Interior, except in so far as such management was implied in the control of the finances, of irrigation, and of the police. But six months' experience showed, that simply to leave the Interior alone was a policy not easy to adhere to. The incessant complaints of official tyranny, and especially of the illegal use of the kurbash, the hideous abuses brought to light in the prisons, the filthy condition of the towns and villages, and, above all, the hopeless breakdown of the administration during the cholera, combined to convince everybody interested in Egypt that something must be done. Only nobody knew exactly what. Under such circumstances the usual English remedy—and it is often not a bad one—is to seize upon the first strong man who can be found and give him full powers to do what he pleases. 'We don't know what we want you to do, but go and do something,' were practically the instructions with which Mr. Lloyd, who had gained a considerable reputation for strength and courage as a resident magistrate in Ireland, was sent to Egypt in September, 1883, as 'Director-General of Reforms.' The vagueness of the title was appropriate. No vaguer mission was ever entrusted to any human being.

But if the mission was vague, not so the missionary. There is reason to believe that Mr. Lloyd, who had never previously been in Egypt, made up his mind as to everything that ought to be done within the first month after his arrival. No doubt it was easier for him to do so, because of the very glaring character of some of the existing evils. The overcrowding of the prisons, for instance, the use of torture to obtain evidence, the fouling of the canals which in Egypt supply the only drinking water—all these were monstrosities too flagrant to admit of any but one opinion. And to reform all these Mr. Lloyd set to work with the tremendous energy and directness which constituted the strength of his character. But that strong character had its faults, and they were on the same large scale as its merits. His enthusiasm for reform was undoubted. His power of work, and of making others work, was marvellous. His manner carried way, on first acquaintance, even the least impressionable people. But he was deficient in judgment and circumspection. He was inclined to rush everything. He had not the least sympathy or patience with men of opposite opinions and character to himself. These were defects peculiarly unsuited to a situation of great delicacy, in which strength itself might be a weakness unless coupled with a certain amount of tact. Mr. Lloyd, to put it plainly, was the proverbial bull in a china shop.

It would serve no good purpose to revive the memory of all the conflicts of which Mr. Lloyd was the exciting cause, and in which his objects were generally right and his methods generally wrong. What the great native functionaries principally complained of was his tendency to pass over their heads and deal directly with the provincial officials. Egyptian Ministers have by long habit become resigned to the presence of European advisers at their elbows in Cairo and Alexandria. What they dislike is to see these Europeans going out into the provinces. They do not so much object to taking orders themselves, if it is clearly understood that they alone are entitled to give orders to their subordinates. 'Tell us what you want done,' they say to their foreign monitors, 'and we will take care that your wishes are carried out; but do not attempt to see to their execution yourselves.'

Evidently there is much to be said for this view of the case, and I should be the last to maintain that Englishmen have in all instances adequately recognised the force of it. But there is another side to the question. In no country more than in Egypt is it necessary not merely to give orders, but to keep a sharp look-out that they are obeyed. If you had thoroughly trustworthy and competent agents, you might be content to confine yourself to a general direction at headquarters. But it would be impossible to maintain that the provincial officials are, still less that they were, generally trustworthy and competent.

No doubt the only ultimate solution is to improve the quality of these officials. But that is a work of time, like all radical reforms in Egypt, or elsewhere. In order to effect such improvement you must choose carefully the men whom you appoint—a duty which in old times was shamefully neglected; but you must also, for a time at any rate, look after them when appointed. Without a certain amount of English inspection, the provincial administration would never have made any progress. Nor does the presence of inspectors in the provinces necessarily undermine either the authority of the Ministers at headquarters, whose intelligence officers they are, or that of the local officials. There are not wanting instances, in which Englishmen acting in this capacity (and I am thinking especially of the Inspectors of Irrigation), have after awhile got on thoroughly well with the provincial governors, and come to be regarded by them as friends and helpmates, and not as spies and intruders.

The more or less permanent antagonism, which I have

been seeking to explain, was never so acute as during the brief period of Mr. Lloyd's activity in Egypt. It culminated in the bitter personal feud between him and Nubar Pasha. When the latter took office, under the circumstances already stated, in January, 1884, Mr. Lloyd had just been three months in the country, but the stir he had already caused was considerable. It is doubtful whether the new Prime Minister can ever have relished the prospect of having so strong-willed and ubiquitous a coadjutor. But at the first moment of his accession to power he and Mr. Lloyd were the best of friends. There is extant a report from the latter—which in view of subsequent events it is impossible to read without a smile—in which he hails the Nubar Ministry as the beginning of a new and better era. Animated by this spirit of confidence, Mr. Lloyd was easily persuaded to resign his roving commission as 'Director-General of Reforms,' and to accept instead the Under-Secretaryship of State for the Interior. The suggestion was entirely in accordance with Nubar's conscientious conviction of the necessity of preserving the official hierarchy from outside interference, and of assigning to inevitable Englishmen definite posts within its ranks. Was it, or was it not, also inspired by the belief that Mr. Lloyd, who was a bad man of business, would break his neck sooner in a high administrative office than he would as a free-lance with no red tape to get entangled in? If it was, the calculation was a shrewd one. Mr. Lloyd lost no time in falling foul of his immediate chief, the Minister of the Interior. A little while longer and he was at loggerheads with nearly all the Ministers. I can well believe that traps were laid for him, and that a man—who, had he been the most conciliatory of his species, would still have been detested for his zeal and single-mindedness—was deliberately baited in order to tempt him to destruction. But, be that as it may, the amount of friction was enormous, and by the month of April things had come to such a pass that Nubar Pasha was threatening to resign, unless the British Government would agree to recall Mr. Lloyd.

The great bone of contention was the reorganization of the police. Mr. Lloyd's plan was to place them, in all matters of discipline, entirely under the orders of their own officers. But the native idea of government is that of strict one-man rule in each locality. That all the officials in a district, whatever their character, should be absolutely under the Mamur, and all the officials in a province absolutely under the Mudir, appears to Egyptian eyes an essential postulate of discipline and order. The proposal to remove the local police in any respect from the direct control of the Mamurs and Mudirs was loudly declared to be subversive of all authority. An increase of crime—so ran the argument—would inevitably follow. It followed. Nubar Pasha was evidently determined at all costs to get rid of Mr. Lloyd; and he was in a strong position to have his way if he insisted on it, for Nubar was at that moment the necessary man. Great Britain was growing increasingly anxious to interfere no more than she could possibly help with the government of Egypt. That being the case, it was indispensable to have an Egyptian Ministry possessing a certain amount of authority. With Sherif and Riaz out of the hunt, Nubar was the only man whose presence at the head of a Cabinet could save it from being derided as a set of puppets; and in order to have a Nubar Cabinet we were bound to humour Nubar.

To make his position worse, and, indeed, to make it finally hopeless, Mr. Lloyd chose the moment, when he was already engaged in a desperate struggle with Nubar and his colleagues, to come to violent blows with one of his own countrymen—Sir Benson Maxwell. The spectacle of two Englishmen, both occupying high posts and doing similar work, engaged in bitter and public conflict with one another was the reverse of edifying. Nubar Pasha saw his chance. Of course, he backed Sir Benson Maxwell against Mr. Lloyd; but in the long-run he made use of the opportunity to rid himself triumphantly of them both. By the middle of 1884 Mr. Lloyd had disappeared from the Ministry of the Interior, and Sir Benson Maxwell from the Ministry of

Justice. They returned to England to fight out their battle in the columns of the *Times*, and neither of them was replaced.* An attempt was, indeed, made to fill the void, caused by the disappearance of Mr. Lloyd from the internal administration, by the appointment of two English Inspectors-General. But in view of the determined opposition of Nubar Pasha the plan was dropped.

The blow to English influence was severe, and it took a long time to recover from it. How was it that Great Britain ever submitted to such a defeat? The answer has already been partially indicated. The cause of our surrender must be sought in the lassitude and disgust with the whole Egyptian imbroglio, which was coming over the British nation and Government, and in the tremendous overwork of Sir Evelyn Baring. To run the whole administration of Egypt, under such unfavourable conditions, with so much opposition from every side, and with no authority for coping with that opposition except the weight of personal influence, was more than could be expected of any man. At the decisive moment of the Clifford-Lloyd crisis Sir Evelyn was in London, endeavouring to find a way out of the financial embarrassments, which daily grew more threatening, and which, till the conclusion of the London Convention in the spring of the following year, would have been alone sufficient to absorb all his attention. When, later in the year, he returned to Egypt, it was with the fixed intention—perhaps even with positive instructions—to take in sail, and confine himself exclusively to those problems which were of irresistible urgency.

As Great Britain was determined not to take over the government of Egypt, it seemed necessary, even at some risk, to make large concessions to native ideas, and to leave a wide field for the independent action of native statesmen. There were some questions so critical that it was impossible to turn away from them. The defence

* Mr. Lloyd had no English successor. Sir Benson Maxwell's place remained vacant for six months, and was then filled, for one year only, by Sir Raymond West.

of the frontier, the regulation of the finances, the safe-guarding of the water-supply—these were matters which could not possibly be allowed to take their chance. But there was a disposition to leave everything else hence-forward to native management. Nubar, the author of the Mixed Tribunals, was a great authority on judicial reform; let him look after the working of the new Native Courts himself. He was intensely jealous of our interference in the interior; let him provide for internal security in his own fashion.

The experiment was not destined to prove a success. All the problems on which we turned our backs in 1884 have had to be taken up again since; all the positions from which we retreated then have had to be re-occupied. But, under the circumstances, retreat was inevitable. We had undertaken more than we could do with such energy as we were able or willing to bring to bear on the work. It is a complete delusion to believe that the finances of Egypt, or any single department of the Government, can be put into permanently sound order without grappling with the administration as a whole. But it was not a delusion to think, in 1884, that one or two burning questions might—nay, under the circumstances, must—be dealt with before we could afford to turn to the rest. It might have been better if we could have driven all our coaches abreast, but, under the circumstances, no other course was open to us than to try and take them through the defile one by one.

Meantime misfortune still pursued us, even on the narrower lines on which we had now decided to operate. The negotiations between the Powers for the settlement of the financial question having, for the time being, broken down, Lord Northbrook came to Egypt as High Commissioner, in September, 1884, to see what could be done on the spot. On his advice the Egyptian Government decided to burst its fetters, and to instruct the Mudirs of the Assigned Provinces, as well as the heads of the Customs and the Railway Administration, to pay the balance of their receipts for the current half-year (which closed on October 25) direct to the Treasury, instead of to the Caisse de la Dette. This step was a plain violation of the existing decrees regulating the relations of Egypt with her creditors, which had received the assent of the Powers. The justification for so extreme a measure was, of course, nothing less than absolute necessity. Moreover, the Caisse had already money enough to pay the forthcoming coupons on the debt. The sums intercepted would simply have gone to swell the Sinking Fund. It was absurd that Egypt should be devoting large amounts to the reduction of her Funded Debt when she was at the same time obliged to borrow on short loans at a much higher rate of interest, and, even with such borrowing, could not meet her current expenses. The alternative to drawing upon the Assigned Revenues was to suspend the payment of the tribute to Turkey—which would have given rise to fresh trouble of the gravest kind—or to mulct the Government officials—which would have thrown the whole administration into disorder. Moreover, at the abortive Conference in London all the Powers had admitted, in principle, the necessity of suspending the Sinking Fund, although they had not been able to agree to any definite scheme.

Such were the arguments, and they were strong ones, with which the Egyptian Finance Minister, in a letter addressed to the Commissioners of the Debt, on September 28, defended his illegal action. And the British Government did its best to justify that action to the other Great Powers, its associates in the guardianship of the financial arrangements of Egypt. But the answer was everywhere unfavourable. Even admitting—so we were told—that a suspension of the Sinking Fund was inevitable, this arbitrary manner of carrying it out struck at the root of what was in substance an international bargain, and was calculated to destroy credit in the good faith of the Egyptian Government. This was the language held to the British Ambassadors at Berlin and Vienna, no less than at Paris, and it was impossible to ignore the force of such objections.

On September 25, 1884, the Consuls-General of

France, Germany, Russia, and Austria addressed identical notes to the Egyptian Government protesting against its action with regard to the Assigned Revenues. The protest was couched in very stiff terms. Italy, faithful to her attitude of friendliness to Great Britain, did not act with the other Powers. But she also protested, though in milder language. Worse than that, the Commissioners of the Caisse, on October 4, obtained a writ from the Mixed Tribunals summoning the Prime Minister and the Minister of Finance to answer for the order given by them to the heads of the Assigned Administrations, and the latter for having obeyed that order.

In view of this threatening aspect of affairs, the Egyptian Government, acting under British advice, adopted a very propitiatory attitude. It bowed the neck to the smiter, explained piteously that, if it had sinned, it had only done so under the gravest compulsion, and pointed out that the regular payment of the Assigned Revenues to the Caisse had already been resumed. Nevertheless, the action before the Mixed Tribunals went on, and on December 18 the Court of First Instance condemned the Government. The latter appealed, not so much in the hope of reversing the decision as in order to gain time. For the negotiations between the Great Powers for the resettlement of Egyptian financial affairs had now been resumed, and by means of a variety of concessions Great Britain at last succeeded in getting them all to agree to a workable arrangement. This arrangement was embodied in the Convention of London, the provisions of which form the fundamental canon of Egyptian finance up to the present day.* With the signature of that Convention by the six Powers and by Turkey on March 18, 1885, the dispute between the Caisse and the Egyptian Government ceased to have any further practical importance, and it was agreed that the appeal should not come on for hearing. But the whole episode, and especially the judgment pronounced by the Court of

* See p. 185 and following pages.

First Instance, was a severe blow to the Government, and was little calculated to increase its confidence in, or affection for, its British advisers.

Another awkward incident which occurred about the same time was connected with the suppression of a scurrilous French newspaper, the *Bosphore Egyptien*. I entirely despair of being able to convey to my readers any idea of the unbridled license in which some foreign journals in Egypt, and the *Bosphore* above all others, are accustomed to indulge when criticising the conduct of the Government or the persons of its principal members. Our own countrymen have been from the first the special butt of malicious sarcasm or downright blackguardly invective on the part of the *Bosphore*, but with true British stolidity they have, as a rule, taken no notice of these attacks. But the more sensitive native authorities are less disposed to submit to them with patience. Nubar Pasha in particular has always had a strong opinion as to the degree in which the abuse of the freedom of the press is calculated to aggravate the difficulty of governing an Oriental population. He was especially uneasy on this score during the time when the public mind in Egypt was deeply agitated by the sensational events in the Sudan. Throughout this critical period, the *Bosphore Egyptien* amused itself by publishing every kind of lie that was calculated to excite alarm or provoke disturbance. Hence on February 29, 1884, the Government, in the exercise of its undoubted right, issued a decree suppressing the paper. But the editors of the *Bosphore* took not the smallest notice. They simply became more violent and more mendacious. For thirteen months the Government put up with this open defiance of its authority. But when at the beginning of April, 1885, the *Bosphore* published a pretended proclamation of the Mahdi inciting to rebellion in Egypt, and on the day following, as if to leave no doubt of the malignity of its intentions, reproduced that document in an Arabic translation, the cup of endurance overflowed. Nubar Pasha informed the French Consul in Cairo that the Government had instructed the police to close the printing establishment from which the *Bosphore* was issued, and invited him, according to the usual practice, to send a delegate to be present at the execution of the order. The Consul referred the matter to his Consul-General, and the latter at once protested. He declared that, so far from allowing the Consul to give any countenance to the proposed measure, he would himself send a member of his own staff expressly to resist it. In spite of this opposition, however, the establishment in question was entered by the police on April 8, and the printing press was seized.

The act excited a perfect storm of fury among the French inhabitants in Egypt, which found its echo in Paris. The French Foreign Minister demanded reparation, alleging that the domicile of a French subject had been illegally violated, and a French diplomatic agent ill-treated by the police. The fiction of the ill-treatment of the diplomatic agent was soon exploded. But on the other point France had technically a valid ground of complaint. It was part of the bad luck, which seemed at this time to dog the steps of the Egyptian Government, that even in a case like this, where it was absolutely right in substance, it had fallen into an error of form. The establishment which had been closed proved to be a general printing business, and the house in which it was located to be inhabited by several foreigners. The act of entering it without the concurrence of the consular authority was thus clearly a violation of the sacredness of domicile assured by the Capitulations.

It is evident that, if the printing-office could not be entered without the concurrence of the Consul, the Consul was able, by refusing that concurrence, practically to deprive the Government of its undoubted right to suppress a seditious paper. But that is just one of the many instances in which the fundamental powers inherent in every Government are nullified in Egypt by the anomalous privileges of Europeans. According to the text of the treaties, France, the aggressor, was in the right, and the injured and much-enduring Egyptian

Government in the wrong. And so poor Nubar Pasha had once more to eat humble pie. The British Foreign Office was at this time very anxious to propitiate France in respect of Egyptian affairs. It accordingly advised the Egyptian Premier to allow the printing establishment to be reopened, and himself to make a formal visit of apology to the French Consul-General. And Nubar Pasha took the advice, but he was deeply chagrined by this fresh humiliation. No doubt Great Britain would not have gone so far on the road of concession, if France had not given an informal undertaking that the *Bosphore* should only reappear *pro formâ*, and that she would agree to a Press Law giving the Egyptian Government, for the future, some effective control over the excesses of foreign journalistic criticism. Both those promises have been broken.

Up to this point our dealings with the affairs of Egypt had certainly not been an unqualified success. For two years we had been in the hottest of hot water. Our unpopularity was excessive. The taunts and jeers of our enemies were loud and incessant. But he laughs best who laughs last. The work of England in Egypt was, after all, not destined to end in failure and derision. Even in those years of gloom there were not wanting hopeful signs to anyone who looked below the surface. Behind all the political worries and muddles a great deal of good work was quietly going on. The foundations of reform were being solidly laid in more than one direction. The Public Accounts had been got into thorough order, and the old abuses in the collection of the land tax completely suppressed. A Commercial Treaty had been concluded with Greece, which for the first time enabled the Government to deal effectively with smugglers, and which proved of great importance in augmenting the Customs Revenue. The work of the irrigation engineers was already telling in a much more regular supply of water and a consequent increase in the crops. The hardships of the Corvée system had been greatly mitigated. In the humble duties assigned to it in the Nile campaign, the despised Egyptian army had shown soldier-like qualities, with which at the outset hardly anyone had been willing to credit it. Thus on many sides there was steady, unobtrusive progress, although the great visible results were yet to come.

What the country now needed was time for the good seed sown to ripen. It needed persistence on the part of its rulers in the work of internal reform. And as regards its external relations it needed a little wholesome neglect. Egypt had for some time past had more attention paid to her by the outside world than was at all for her advantage. She had been the football of English politics, an overworked pawn in the game of international rivalries. With English parties quarrelling over her on the one hand, and the Powers quarrelling over her on the other, it was difficult for the country to enjoy that repose which, now that it had been started on the right road, was so necessary to its progress.

But during the course of the year 1885 a number of events combined to procure this much-needed period of tranquillity. The war in the Sudan, except so far as the defence of the frontier was concerned, was brought to a close. The London Convention ensured a respite from immediate financial embarrassments, besides providing fresh funds for necessary public works, and for the payment of the Alexandria Indemnities, that fertile source of foreign enmity and interference. Nor was it only financial relief which the London Convention afforded. That invaluable agreement had also an important political side. For it was one of the conditions on which Egypt was allowed to make a temporary reduction in the interest on her debt, that, if payment in full could not be resumed at the end of two years, a fresh International Commission, similar to that which had prepared the Law of Liquidation, should be appointed to make an exhaustive inquiry into the financial condition of the country. And as at that time hardly anybody believed that Egypt would be able to resume payment in full, an opportunity of re-opening the whole Egyptian question at no distant date seemed assured. With such a prospect before them, even the parties most opposed to the continuance of the existing régime in Egypt were disposed to possess their souls in patience for a little while. Moreover, in Great Britain itself the Irish Question began more and more to absorb public attention, and political busybodies were content to leave Egypt alone.

The period of respite thus afforded was invaluable. It gave the country and its temporary rulers their first fair chance. Freed from the embarrassing amount of attention which they had hitherto received, freed from the angry clamour of unpaid claimants, and from the daily anxiety how to make both ends meet, furnished for the first time with the means of providing for the most urgent material needs of the country, they were able to pursue their business with a certain amount of ease of mind, and with a certain healthy latitude of action. And they made a splendid use of their opportunity. When, after some years, general attention began once more to be directed to the affairs of Egypt, a very different picture presented itself from that state of public penury, and of popular despondency and discontent, which marks the history of the first troublous years succeeding the British Occupation.

CHAPTER VI.

THE BREAK IN THE CLOUDS.

THE affairs of Egypt during the three years after Tel-el-Kebir are recorded in no less than ninety-eight Blue Books. For the subsequent seven years the number of Blue Books is only thirty-four, and of these more than two-thirds are concerned with the first half of the period. The amount of this official literature stands in inverse proportion to the progress of the country. We have seen that the years 1883-85 were years of intense strain, during which the escape of Egypt from her many and importunate troubles still hung in the balance. Since that time she has been marching steadily along the road of improvement. But not until recently has she been marching at a rapid pace. During 1886, 1887, and 1888 the condition of the country, though unquestionably ameliorated, remained in many respects critical. Its financial embarrassments had been greatly relieved, but it was still doubtful whether permanent equilibrium could be attained without a fresh liquidation. It is only in the last two or three years that Egypt has definitely turned the corner and entered upon an era of assured solvency, and even of comparative ease.

And with the advent of financial ease the reforming work of her rulers has received a great impetus. For a long time all that even a purified administration could do was to remove abuses, and to abstain from aggravating the burdens of the people by bad management and injustice. To reduce those burdens, to develop new sources of wealth, or to raise the standard of civilization, was beyond its power. But now a brighter prospect has been opened up. It is true that, if Egypt is to derive all the benefit to which she is entitled from her altered financial position, it will be necessary to give her greater liberty in the matter of expenditure, and to relax still further the international restrictions which prevent the application of the surplus revenue to the improvement of the country. Egypt, after all, is only a big estate with the Government for landlord. And that estate is one which stands in special need of an improving landlord. For many years it was cursed with a wasteful or an impecunious one. Nowadays the material conditions are once more favourable, and there is a new spirit in high places. Only give the Government a reasonable freedom in the use of its resources, and there is no reason why the coming years should not see a further and a vast advance in the material and moral condition of the people.

But I am anticipating. Let me return to the sequence of events in the period now under review. They need not detain us long. The same reason which has reduced the number of the Blue Books enables me to curtail my story. There are few sensational events to record, nor was there, for some time at least, any important new departure in policy. The keynote of the years succeeding the settlement of the financial question by the Convention of London was quiet, useful work along the lines of reform already marked out. In carrying out that work the British functionaries were now destined to meet with more sympathy and co-operation, alike from natives and other Europeans of the better sort, than they had found at the outset. People were beginning to recognise that we had not come to steal the country. They were beginning to feel that, despite many failures and shortcomings, a spirit of equity and method was entering into the conduct of affairs, and that the change was fraught with manifold advantages. Above all, they began to believe that the new order of things had come to stay.

It would be too much to say that the English had grown popular. They are not popular even at the present day. But the intense suspicion and dislike with which they were at one time regarded was decidedly and for ever wearing off. Those elements of Egyptian society which were at heart in favour of honest government acknowledged the advent of what they had long looked for in vain. They would have preferred that the desired boon should have come to them in some other form than that of a foreign occupation. But since the fates had chosen to send it thus, and not otherwise, they were prepared to rally to our side. Better relations, too, were springing up between the British and the native members of the Government service. The Egyptians had learnt to know us, and we had learnt to know Egypt. Moreover, conscientious native officials now felt a sense of security which they had never previously enjoyed. They knew that, if they did what was right, they would be supported against the vindictiveness of powerful private individuals or the caprice of their official chiefs. Intrigue was no longer the chief road to advancement. The faithful discharge of duty was no longer a danger.

It was unfortunate that this better understanding between Englishmen and natives did not extend to the highest Government circles. Between Nubar Pasha on the one hand, and his British coadjutors and the British Consul-General on the other, friction, as the years went on, tended rather to increase than to diminish. It was not that Nubar was out of sympathy with our aims. He is a reformer at heart, and he was much too sagacious not to realize the immense assistance which the presence of the English gave to the cause of reform. But a number of reasons—some personal, some public—combined to render him impatient of our methods. It is evident that the rôle of Egyptian Prime Minister, especially under the present system, is hardly enough to satisfy an eminently able and ambitious man. Now, it is a favourite remark about Nubar Pasha among his own countrymen—who are not generally very forward to recognise one another's merits — that he is 'clever enough to be a great man in any country.' And this is true, and Nubar knows it. Proud of his past achievements, and confident in the infallibility of his own judgment as to what was best for his country, he would under any circumstances have fretted at the advice which, in a hundred instances, Great Britain felt bound to offer him. With every outward show of consideration and gratitude for our admonitions, he resented them in his heart as a sort of slight to his personal dignity. While fully recognising the necessity of British troops, he was doubtful about the utility of the British officials. 'I am in favour of the Occupation,' he has often said, 'but not of the Administrative Occupation.' What he wanted was our support without our guidance.

As a matter of fact he got, from his own point of view, a great deal too much guidance, and he did not get, from any point of view, quite enough support. The chief grievance of the native rulers of Egypt against British policy has always been, that we do not adequately defend them from the importunities of other foreign Powers. If we insist on constituting ourselves their protectors, the least we can do, so they argue, is to afford them protection. They did not ask us to make ourselves their guardians, but, since we have done so unasked, it is at least incumbent on us to discharge the duties appertaining to that character. When we fail in this respect, they feel very much as a fag would feel if his fag-master did not shield him from the bullying of other big boys.

It cannot be denied that Egyptian Ministers have frequently had good cause to complain on this score. And never had any of them better cause than Nubar Pasha, alike in the question of the Press Law, and with regard to the action taken by him, at the direct instigation of Great Britain, in diverting a portion of the Assigned Revenues from the Caisse de la Dette. In both these instances there was the strongest justification for what he did; in both we were really in agreement with him; yet in both we allowed him to meet with a damaging defeat. It is possible that the difficulties of our position were so great that we could not in either case have acted otherwise than we did. But that, Nubar Pasha might well think, was not his affair, but ours. It was for us to look out that we did not get into a position in which we were unable to extend to our involuntary vassals the protection they were entitled to expect from us.

Irritated by recollections of what he no doubt considered our shabby treatment of him in his difficulties with foreign Powers, penetrated by the conviction that Great Britain, while asserting her own authority over his country, was not strong enough to rid it from the curse of 'internationalism,' Nubar grew less and less disposed to act harmoniously with us in the daily work of the administration. Had we in his opinion given adequate support to Egypt in her external relations, he might have looked with less disfavour upon our interference in internal affairs. As it was, his rooted prejudice against the 'Administrative Occupation' became increasingly pronounced.

He even desired to limit the ample executive powers confided to the English inspectors of irrigation. To have yielded to him on this point would have meant disaster. The maintenance of the improvement which had been achieved in the great matter of the water-supply would have been impossible without the ubiquitous energy of these officers. And Sir Colin Scott Moncrieff wisely refused to make any concessions, in this essential question, to the predilections of the Egyptian Premier. Nubar might protest as he pleased against the independent spirit of the inspectors, and their tendency to take the law into their own hands. Sir Colin saw clearly that without considerable liberty of action on their part, without their being allowed in urgent cases to decide for themselves and to give prompt effect to their decisions, the unruly foreigners and despotic Pashas in the provinces would never be got into order. A certain arbitrariness in enforcing the law was better than an unlimited license of breaking it.

But this is a point of view which commends itself with difficulty to the native official mind. The Public Offices at Cairo are full of the most exalted notions of bureaucratic regularity. As long as the files are of adequate dimensions, as long as references are made in the proper quarters, orders given and received by the right people, all the official formalities properly observed, the staff of the Ministries is happy. And not only the staff of the Ministries. This is the system which is dear to the heart of the whole Egyptian bureaucracy, from the vast army of mechanical scribes at its base, to the influential and sometimes highly-cultivated Beys and Pashas at its summit. It keeps them constantly if not too strenuously employed, and it does no harm to anybody. A decree, a circular, an *arrêté ministériel*, an *ordre de service*, a *lettre de rappel*, and all the other favourite products of the Circumlocution Office, have almost come to be regarded as ends in themselves. It is left to the brutal British intruder to worry about the net result of all this clerkly activity, and to make awkward inquiries whether the provisions of the decree, the circular, or whatever it may be, have any existence except on paper.

Now, Nubar Pasha, with all his talent, all his energy, and all his genuine desire to improve the condition of his country, was not free from the rigid administrative formalism which French education seems only to confirm in men of Oriental birth. He was more shocked at things being irregularly done than at their being regularly neglected. Nothing could be less in accordance with the practical spirit of the Public Works Department and its British chiefs. They had to grapple with crying evils, the suppression of which brooked no delay. They could not always stop to go through all the official formalities or to arm themselves with all the regular powers. Hence there was pretty constant material for friction between Nubar and Moncrieff. It is greatly to the credit of both men that, despite the frequent conflicts arising from this fundamental difference, they succeeded in remaining personal friends.

Meantime a fresh cause of difference was growing up

to embitter the relations between Nubar and the English. We have seen how the peculiar circumstances of Egypt gave predominant importance to questions of finance, and involved the supremacy of the Finance Ministry over all other departments of the Government. But Nubar Pasha is not a financier, and he was very little disposed to accept the principle that finance came first and everything else afterwards. He was annoyed by the restrictions placed upon his own freedom of action by the new-born system of Treasury control. Despite his European culture and his liberal sympathies, he is, like every Oriental habituated to high office, something of a despot at heart. He may dilate on the beauty of legality, on the equality of all citizens before the law, on the need of a strict observance of administrative rules. But there is always a reservation in his mind, though he may not avow it, in favour of the indefeasible autocracy of the Head of the State, and of his principal adviser, at least when that adviser happens to be Nubar Pasha. With this principle ingrained in him, he found it irksome and repugnant to be pulled up in anything he wished to do by being told that he could not have the money. And perhaps his repugnance was not lessened by the fact that the financial control which galled him was exercised by a man at least thirty years his junior.

But Vincent had armed himself with a formidable instrument for checking arbitrary expenditure, by the institution of the Committee of Finance. This Committee, which had come into existence early in 1884, consisted at the outset of the Finance Minister, two Englishmen, Vincent and Sir Gerald Fitzgerald; one Austrian, Blum Pasha, who was at that time Under Secretary of State for Finance; and one Frenchman, M. Mazuc. It was a very formidable body. It contained the highest financial authorities in the country, and was representative of all that was most respectable and influential in the European official world. If these men objected to any pension or allowance as contrary to regulations, or protested against any new item of expenditure as extravagant and unnecessary, it was very difficult for the Council of Ministers to override their decisions. The Finance Committee is still a potent engine for maintaining economy and defending the Exchequer against unforeseen charges and unwarrantable claims. It is the great bulwark against jobbery. But nowadays its principles have become so generally recognised, and financial regularity is so much the rule throughout the service, that its work is comparatively light. When first constituted, on the other hand, the Committee was constantly being brought into play, and its control, however salutary, was often bitterly resented by the great officials, including the Prime Minister himself.

Apart from disputes over particular questions of expenditure, there was a radical divergence of view between Vincent and Nubar on the main question of financial policy confronting Egypt at that time. That question, to put it briefly, was this—whether the country could or could not make both ends meet in the long-run on the basis provided by the Convention of London. We have seen that the Convention, besides permanently modifying the Law of Liquidation in a manner favourable to Egyptian interests, had granted certain relief of a temporary character. For two years Egypt was allowed to make a slight reduction of the interest on her debt, but if at the end of that time she could not resume payment in full, there was to be another International Commission.

Alike in the interests of Egypt and of Great Britain, it was highly desirable to avoid such a fresh occasion for the competitive meddling of all the Powers. And Vincent believed that it could be avoided, that Egypt was able on the new basis to pay her way, and to do so, not only for a few years, but for ever. The immediate future was, indeed, a narrow strait, and it might be difficult to steer the vessel through it. But beyond it lay the open sea. For the moment Egypt was still suffering from the accumulated effects of a whole series of disasters —the rebellion, the destruction of Alexandria, the cholera, the loss of the Sudan. But if she could once outlive the consequences of these calamities, then her great natural power of recuperation and the improvement of her Public Works, already sensible, and now about to receive a further impulse from the million provided for this purpose out of the Guaranteed Loan,* would place her definitely beyond the danger of bankruptcy.

If this was a right forecast—and the event has proved that it was—then Egypt could afford to submit even to much hardship, for the time being, in order to attain the great object of permanent solvency. And so Vincent set to work with a vengeance, and by a system of the most rigid economy succeeded in resuming the full payment of interest in 1887. His parsimony gave rise to many murmurs, and as a permanent policy it would no doubt have been mischievous. But temporary parsimony was justifiable in order to rescue the country once for all from the slough of financial embarrassment, and to preserve it from further foreign interference.

Nubar Pasha, however, was out of all sympathy with the policy of necessary parsimony. He detested refusing the credits loudly demanded by the different departments in the name of efficiency and improvement. He detested small savings in salaries and pensions, and a too pedantic attitude towards innocent little jobs. And, on the other hand, he was eager to effect an immediate reduction of the land tax. A humanitarian and a land-owner, he had a double interest in relieving a burden which, while it pressed so heavily on the poor fellah, also took a large slice out of the income of men of his own class. Moreover, such a course would have been popular, while Vincent's plan of clinging to every shilling of revenue, and resisting every additional shilling of expenditure, was evidently much the reverse. And in Nubar's opinion that plan was not only unpopular but useless. He was firmly convinced that Egypt, squeeze as she might, could not in the long-run pull through without a fresh liquidation. If that were so, why should he make himself hated in order to postpone a calamity which was, in any case, inevitable? Was it not better just to let

* See pp. 186, 187.

the smash come, to court that bankruptcy from which, as he wrongly believed, there was no ultimate escaping, in order to have things once for all placed upon an endurable footing? No doubt it would be a nuisance to have all the Powers again putting their fingers into the Egyptian pie. But was it worse, after all, than being perpetually dictated to by the English? Let Egypt, therefore, spend all the money required for good administration; let her reduce excessive taxes; and if, at the end of it all, she could not pay her interest—well, then let there be a new Commission and a new re-settlement of the Debt, and let the country, if necessary, be handed over entirely to the Caisse, or to some other body of international controllers.

It was a short-sighted view. Moreover it was, at bottom, absolutely inconsistent with Nubar's permanent convictions as to the true interests of his country. No man feels more strongly than he, that the first object of an Egyptian statesman must be to save Egypt from becoming a political battle-field for European jealousies. Better a hundred times that she should be subject to the dictation of a single Power, than to the interference of a dozen. Neither would reflection have failed to show him that there was little hope from a fresh International Commission. What the Powers, with the exception of England, most cared about, was the payment of the coupon. If, through Egypt's failure to pay, they had been obliged to take her in hand, it would have been in order to administer her in the interests of the bondholders—and what would then have been the prospect of a reduction of taxation, or of administrative reforms? It was surely the height of folly to snatch at a momentary ease, which led straight to lasting bondage. But Nubar's immediate irritation with the English obscured, for the time at least, his clearness of vision on these wider issues. Under the influence of that irritation, he drifted into an attitude of fixed hostility to the Financial Adviser. And since the British Consul-General, though constantly striving to compose these differences, always ultimately sided with his countryman, Nubar ended by extending to him also the cordial dislike which he had for some time cherished towards Vincent.

During 1887 matters came to something like an open rupture. In the summer of that year Nubar undertook a journey to Europe, ostensibly to make interest for certain measures requiring the assent of the Powers, but really in the hope of inducing the English Government to set Egypt free from what he described as the intolerable domination of the Financial Adviser and the British Consul-General. The English Government, however, stuck to its agents, and his object was defeated.

The period of Nubar's power was now rapidly drawing to a close. For some time he had been falling into general disfavour in Egypt. Perhaps the chief reason for the feeling against him was the growing dissatisfaction with the new Native Tribunals, as well as with the irregular and arbitrary Commissions of Brigandage, which, in respect of a large class of crimes, had been substituted for the Courts. Justice had always been regarded as Nubar's special subject, his strongest point. From the first institution of the new Courts, which was almost coincident with his accession to office, he had claimed, and no one had sought to deny him, the right of being the one man to look after them. In this respect, at any rate, he could not complain of British meddlesomeness. Sir Benson Maxwell had left Egypt in June, 1884. It is true that a new British Procureur-Général, Sir Raymond West, was appointed in January, 1885. But his stay was brief, and in the absence of diplomatic support his recommendations, however sound, might be safely neglected. For reasons already explained, Sir Evelyn Baring had felt obliged to give the administration of justice the go-by and to confine his attention to other matters. Hence Nubar had for several years had an absolutely free hand in all questions of this nature. The Courts were manned from top to bottom with his nominees. When, therefore, complaints of the corruption and incapacity of the judges became general, when nothing was heard on all hands but criticisms of the cumbrous procedure of the courts, of the costliness and delay of litigation, and of the unreliable nature of the results, it was Nubar whom people held responsible.

And the chorus of well-justified discontent was swollen by accusations of a less reasonable but not less damaging kind. It was widely asserted that an undue proportion of the judges were Christians by religion—Syrians or Copts. The statement was not well founded; but it does not require accuracy of statement to play upon religious fanaticism. Nubar has always been vulnerable on the score of his religion. A Christian Premier is necessarily at a disadvantage in Egypt. It is easy to get up an outcry against him as being secretly inimical to the prevalent faith. The unjust clamour about Nubar's alleged partiality to his fellow-Christians gave the finishing touch to the odium into which he had fallen.

But whatever may have been the real cause of the dislike with which Nubar was now generally regarded, he himself loved to attribute it to his connection with the English. However much he might in reality differ with and oppose them, he was, according to his own theory, regarded throughout Egypt as their man. Was it with an idea of purging himself from that taint, that he became more prone than ever to quarrel with the supposed authors of his unpopularity? Early in the year 1888 a decisive issue presented itself. Valentine Baker Pasha, the Head of the Police, had recently died, and Nubar seized the occasion of the vacancy to propose a reorganization of the force, which was framed mainly with the view of getting rid of the English officers. According to this scheme, the Police were to be placed once more entirely under the Mudirs, even for purposes of discipline, and the central office at Cairo was to be abolished. But Sir Evelyn Baring had by this time been forced to recognise the failure of the experiment of leaving the administration of justice entirely in native hands, and he was not in the least disposed to see a further step taken in the same wrong direction. He accordingly insisted that, whatever change might be introduced into the organization of the Police, the chief command should again be entrusted to an Englishman. The consequence was a pitched battle between him and the Prime Minister.

The moment was in many respects an awkward one for Sir Evelyn Baring. Nubar had not always been a great favourite with the Khedive. On more than one occasion during the past four years he had owed his retention in office to the influence of the British Consul-General, who, despite many differences, stuck to him as being the most enlightened and progressive statesman whom the country possessed, and did his best to keep him in the good graces of his master. But at the time when the police question became critical, Nubar had gained a stronger hold upon the Khedive than he had ever previously possessed. The latter was at this juncture greatly perturbed by the presence of his father, the ex-Khedive Ismail, at Constantinople. The Porte, as Tewfik well knew, was implacably hostile to himself. The Sultan had repeatedly tried to get rid of him, and the reappearance of Ismail on the scene appeared to him — and very likely with justice — as a new and threatening move in the game which Turkey was constantly playing for his deposition. But as against Turkish intrigue, Tewfik felt that he could thoroughly rely on Nubar Pasha, and he had a high and well-merited opinion of that statesman's diplomatic skill.

Nubar availed himself of the influence thus gained over his Sovereign to draw the latter into the conflict between himself and Baring. The Khedive was assured that, if only the Egyptian Government took up a sufficiently firm attitude in the matter, the British Government might be induced to throw over its Consul-General. Undeterred by the reverse he had himself sustained in the same quarter some months before, Nubar went so far as to send an emissary to London expressly to complain of Baring's conduct, as tending to reduce the Khedive to a nullity, and to render British influence unpopular. It was a last trump, boldly played, but it failed to win the game. The British Government saw through the manœuvre. It knew its agent too well to suspect him of any leaning to excessive meddlesomeness. It had too much reason to be grateful for the skill and patience with which he had so far steered his way through the maze of Egyptian politics, to dream of sacrificing him. Nubar's emissary met with no better success at the Foreign Office than Nubar himself. A strong hint was given to the ruler of Egypt that, if he expected England to support him against external enemies, he must listen to English advice on vital questions of internal policy. And the warning had its effect. The Khedive saw that, in siding with his Minister, he was running into the very danger from which he had looked to that Minister to preserve him. The fact once realized, his choice was made. The question of the command of the Police was without more delay decided in accordance with the views of Sir Evelyn Baring.

But much more was decided than the command of the Police. Great Britain had again reasserted the principle, first clearly enunciated by Lord Granville with reference to the abandonment of the Sudan, that in important matters British advice must be followed. And she had reasserted it with regard to one of a class of questions which for some years she had been content to treat with comparative neglect. In the Army, in Finance, in Irrigation—the subjects with which, since 1884, we had almost exclusively occupied ourselves—great progress had now been made. It was time to turn once more to other matters which we had abandoned, and in which there had been little or no progress. The ground which had been lost in consequence of the fiasco of Mr. Clifford Lloyd was about to be recovered. The incident just related was the first step towards its recovery.

And, appropriately enough, the Minister who had got rid of Mr. Lloyd was destined himself to disappear with this new departure. Nubar Pasha never got over his defeat on the police question. The Khedive, who was bitterly annoyed at having been led into a false position, had lost all confidence in him, and, of course, Nubar could not expect any longer to have the active support of Sir Evelyn Baring. It is true that his fall did not come at once, and when it did come it was apparently due to a difference between him and the Khedive on some trivial question. But that is what always happens in Egypt. The apparent occasion of any event is pretty certain not to be its real cause. It was not till June, 1888, that Nubar Pasha was dismissed by the Khedive, and then I really forget for what alleged reason. But in reality his fall was decided in the preceding March, when he made his bold bid to get rid of Baring, and came to grief over it.

If I was to deal honestly with my subject, I could not gloss over the growth of the misunderstanding, and the final split, between Nubar and Baring, eminently illustrative as they are of the peculiar difficulties of the problem which I am trying to expound. But I own that I have recorded them with an unwilling pen. No one who knows Nubar Pasha can fail to feel an admiration for his great talents, his thorough culture, his liberal sympathies, or his brilliant gift of expression. Even if he is apt to be 'viewy,' to be carried away by some new idea, without having the patience to probe it to the bottom, or to weigh the objections to it, the fault, though grave, is pardonable in a country where superabundance of ideas is certainly not a besetting sin. Moreover, no one can doubt the sincerity of his desire to do good to Egypt. It is regrettable, if it is not unnatural, that he should have thrown away the unrivalled opportunity of realizing that desire, which the support of Great Britain gave him, through a restless intolerance of the inevitable conditions of such support. Had Nubar, or any other Egyptian statesman, been strong enough to save his country single-handed, there would never have been a Liquidation, a Control, an Arabi, a Tel-el-Kebir. He cannot be excused for his failure to recognise that, since English help was necessary to the salvation of Egypt, he was bound to show a large receptiveness for English ideas.

But do not let us forget the brighter side of our relations with Nubar Pasha. I do not believe that he is personally unfriendly to the English, as they certainly are not unfriendly to him. He has perhaps an excessive contempt for our intelligence. But he has always heartily recognised the honesty of our intentions. No man is more intolerant than he of the popular theory of the Machiavelian character of British policy. If, during his period of office, he fell foul of us over certain questions, on others—and these the most important—he worked heartily with us. In no respect was this co-operation more cordial or more beneficent than in the long struggle for the abolition of the Corvée. There was no subject on which Nubar expended greater energy. It is to his honour that, with all his anxiety for a general reduction of the land tax, he recognised that relief from the Corvée, which was in effect a tax of the severest kind on the poorest class of cultivators, stood first on the list of necessary reforms. If the difficulty of balancing the Budget, and the persistent obstruction of France, prevented his accomplishing all that he desired, he did, at least, reduce by more that one half the number of people annually subject to forced labour, and so paved the way for the complete abolition of this abominable system, which was accomplished within two years after his fall.

Before carrying on this rapid historical survey from the fall of Nubar Pasha to the present day, I must turn aside to notice an important diplomatic episode which belongs to the period of Nubar's Ministry. I refer to the mission of Sir Henry Drummond Wolff to Constantinople and to Egypt. The object of this book is to give an account of the development of Egypt under British influence. It is no part of my purpose to follow the Egyptian Question in its international aspects, except in so far as they bear directly upon the internal progress of the country. But the Wolff mission is of too great importance, from the latter point of view, to be passed over in silence.

The period covered by the episode in question was of nearly two years' duration—from August, 1885, to July, 1887. Sir Henry Drummond Wolff arrived at Constantinople on August 22, 1885, as Envoy Extraordinary and Minister Plenipotentiary to the Sultan 'on a special mission having reference to the affairs of Egypt. The object of Lord Salisbury, at that time Foreign Secretary, was undoubtedly to arrive at such an understanding with Turkey as would allay the intense and growing jealousy of the Porte at our presence in Egypt, and diminish the hostility of France. It was to provide for the maintenance and development of the reforms which we had initiated, while reducing the amount and duration of British interference, and conciliating the other Powers principally interested in Egypt.

In pursuance of that object, Sir Henry signed with the Turkish Foreign Minister on October 24, 1885, a preliminary Convention, which was ratified in the following month by their respective Sovereigns. This Convention provided that an Ottoman and an English High Commissioner should be sent to Egypt, whose business it should be, 'in concert with the Khedive,' to reorganize the Egyptian Army, and to consider what changes might be necessary in the civil administration. The Ottoman High Commissioner was also to take counsel with the Khedive as to the best means of tranquillizing the Sudan by pacific measures, the English Commissioner being kept informed of the course of the negotiations, while any steps decided upon in this direction were to be adopted and executed in agreement with him, 'as forming part of the general settlement of Egyptian affairs.' But by far the most important clause of the Convention was that which stipulated that, as soon as the two High Commissioners should be assured of 'the security of the frontiers and the good working and stability of the Egyptian Government,' they should present reports to their respective Governments, who would then 'consult as to the conclusion of a Convention regulating the withdrawal of the British troops from Egypt in a convenient period.'

The two High Commissioners sent to Egypt under the terms of this Convention were Mukhtar Pasha, on behalf of Turkey, and, on behalf of England, Sir Henry Drummond Wolff himself. Their joint inquiry lasted rather more than a year, at the end of which time

Mukhtar Pasha addressed a long report to the Turkish Government, while Sir Henry Drummond Wolff, who during his stay in Egypt had sent home a series of interesting and valuable reports on a variety of subjects, returned to England in order to give a personal account of his experiences to the British Government. This was at the end of 1886.

As far as the accomplishment of the objects for which they had been sent to Egypt was concerned, the proceedings of the two Commissioners had so far not been very fertile of results. The pacification of the Sudan had not been materially accelerated by the despatch to the frontier of a special envoy from the Khedive, authorized to enter into communication with the insurgent tribes. The discussion as to the organization of the Egyptian Army had consisted simply in the proposal of a perfectly unworkable plan by Mukhtar Pasha, and its rejection by Sir Henry Drummond Wolff. As for the internal administration of Egypt, the inquiries of the two Commissioners had resulted principally in convincing them—and more especially Sir Henry—that there was nothing much the matter with the administration itself, but that the abnormal privileges enjoyed by foreigners under the Capitulations made good government next to impossible. That was true, no doubt; but it was hardly a new light on the situation. It is easy to condemn the Capitulations. The difficulty is to devise a means of getting rid of them.

There still remained the crucial point, namely, the agreement as to the withdrawal of the British troops. This, of course, was all that Turkey really cared about. She had been worrying us on the subject ever since the Occupation, and her efforts had been well seconded by the persistent fretfulness of France. It was in order to try and arrive at some understanding on this thorny question, that Sir Henry Drummond Wolff was once more despatched to Constantinople in January, 1887. Since his first visit to that capital, Lord Rosebery and Lord Iddesleigh had successively presided at the Foreign Office. Now Lord Salisbury was once more Foreign

Secretary. And the instructions which he gave to Sir Henry Drummond Wolff on his return to Constantinople are a landmark in our Egyptian policy no less important than the already quoted despatch of Lord Granville of January 3, 1883, of which, indeed, they constitute the natural development. I make no apology, therefore, for quoting them at some length.

'The Sultan,' so wrote Lord Salisbury on January 15, 1887, 'is pressing the Government of Great Britain to name a date for the evacuation of Egypt, and in that demand he is avowedly encouraged by one, or perhaps two, of the European Powers. Her Majesty's Government have every desire to give him satisfaction upon this point, but they cannot fix even a distant date for evacuation, until they are able to make provision for securing beyond that date the external and internal peace of Egypt. The object which the Powers of Europe have had in view, and which it is not less the desire of Her Majesty's Government to attain, may be generally expressed by the phrase, "The neutralization of Egypt"; but it must be neutralization with an exception designed to maintain the security and permanence of the whole arrangement. The British Government must retain the right to guard and uphold the condition of things which will have been brought about by the military action and large sacrifices of this country. So long as the Government of Egypt maintains its position, and no disorders arise to interfere with the administration of justice or the action of the executive power, it is highly desirable that no soldier belonging to any foreign nation should remain upon the soil of Egypt, except when it may be necessary to make use of the land-passage from one sea to another. Her Majesty's Government would willingly agree that such a stipulation should, whenever the evacuation had taken place, apply to English as much as to any other troops; but it will be necessary to restrict this provision, as far as England is concerned, to periods of tranquillity. England, if she spontaneously and willingly evacuates the country, must retain a treaty-right of intervention if at any time either internal peace or external security should be seriously threatened. There is no danger that a privilege so costly in its character will be used unless the circumstances imperatively demand it.'

The demand that, having restored order and laid the foundations of stable government in Egypt, Great Britain should have a recognised right of defending these works of her creation was certainly not an unreasonable one. And, as we shall see, Turkey, if left to herself, would have accepted it.

At the outset of the fresh negotiations, which now took place at Constantinople, there was a disposition on the part of the British Plenipotentiary to insist that the withdrawal of the British troops should be conditional upon an agreement of all the States concerned to extend the judicial and legislative powers of the Egyptian Government with regard to foreigners. There was, and is, much to be said for such a contention. The position of the European communities in Egypt outside the law is a permanent source of weakness to the Government. With the constant support and protection of a Great Power, it may struggle on successfully in spite of that weakness; but there is undoubted danger of a break-down if such support be withdrawn.

Sir Henry Drummond Wolff, however, did not adhere to this position. As he found that the Turkish negotiators were prepared, though not without a struggle, to accept in principle the right of Great Britain to re-occupy Egypt in case of internal disturbance or external danger, he may have thought that such an arrangement, indicating as it did our continued interest in and determination to uphold the existing order of things, would be a sufficient protection for the Egyptian Government. Moreover, Turkey and Great Britain, if once in agreement, would be in a very strong position to approach the others Powers with a view to obtaining a modification of the Capitulations. Whether or no this was the idea in Sir Henry's mind, an understanding was, after four months of debate, arrived at between him and the Turkish representatives, and embodied in a definite Convention signed by both parties on May 22, 1887.

According to this agreement, the British troops were to be withdrawn from Egypt at the end of three years, unless at that date the appearance of external or internal danger should necessitate the postponement of the evacuation, in which case they were to be withdrawn as soon as the danger had disappeared. Two years after their withdrawal the general supervision exercised by Great Britain over the Egyptian army was to cease. Thenceforward Egypt was to enjoy territorial immunity ('sureté territoriale' are the words used in the authoritative French text, the Sultan having objected to the term 'neutralization'); and, on the ratification of the Convention, the Powers were to be invited to recognise and guarantee the inviolability of Egyptian territory. 'Nevertheless,' the Convention continued (I quote the clauses which at once constituted its essence and caused its failure), 'the Imperial Ottoman Government will make use of its right of occupying Egypt militarily, if there are reasons to fear an invasion from without, or if order and security in the interior were disturbed, or if the Khediviate of Egypt refused to execute its duties towards the sovereign court, or its international obligations.

'On its side the Government of Her Britannic Majesty is authorized by this Convention to send in the abovementioned cases troops into Egypt which will take the measures necessary to remove these dangers. In taking these measures the commanders of these troops will act with all the regard due to the rights of the Sovereign Power.

'The Ottoman troops as well as the British troops will be withdrawn as soon as the causes requiring this intervention shall have ceased.

'If by reason of hindrances the Ottoman Government should not send troops to Egypt, it will send a Commissioner to remain during the period of the sojourn of the British troops with their commander.'*

* This translation of the original French text is not admirable, but I felt bound to quote verbatim.

A further article provided that Great Britain and Turkey should invite first the Great Powers, and then all the others 'who had made or accepted arrangements with the Khediviate of Egypt,' to give their adhesion to the Convention. Annexed to the main document was a declaration by the English Plenipotentiary that, in case during the three years allowed for the withdrawal of the troops any of the great Mediterranean Powers should not have accepted the Convention, Great Britain would regard this state of things as an 'external danger' justifying the postponement of the evacuation. A protocol was likewise annexed, in which Great Britain and Turkey agreed to address the Powers with a view to the establishment in Egypt of 'a local and uniform jurisdiction and legislature' applicable to foreign residents.

Of course, the gist of the whole matter was the recognition by the Sultan of Great Britain's right to reoccupy Egypt in certain cases. It is true that the Sultan reserved to himself a similar right; but since Turkey is never ready in an emergency, this reservation was not of much practical value. Clearly, if there were fresh troubles, it was Great Britain which would have to deal with them. Do not let it be supposed that this was a matter of small importance. If at the beginning of the Arabist movement there had been a single Great Power other than Turkey, with a clear and generally recognised right of intervention, that movement might easily have been kept within bounds. It was the interminable discussion as to what was to be done, and who was to act, which gave time and encouragement to the spirit of rebellion to spread till it became uncontrollable. The right of reoccupation conceded to England by the Convention of 1887 was little likely to be exercised, but the mere knowledge of its existence would have gone far to keep things straight. I do not say for a moment that the right of re-entry is not a very poor substitute for the actual presence of British troops—even a single regiment—in Egypt as a security for the maintenance of order and the progress of reforms. Still, it is a security.

And for that reason, presumably, France, who for the past ten years has given no sign of the smallest interest in the tranquillity or welfare of Egypt, provided she could once get the English out of the country—France, whose one motto in this matter seems to be 'Exeant Angli, ruat cœlum,' put forth every effort to upset the Convention. No sooner did its terms become known than the French Ambassador began to expostulate with the Porte in the most violent and menacing manner. His Russian colleague followed suit. And the two between them so frightened the Sultan that, despite the advice of the Ambassadors of Austria, Germany, and Italy, he could not be induced to ratify the Treaty which his Ministers had signed. For nearly a month after the date fixed, Sir Henry Drummond Wolff was kept kicking his heels at Constantinople, armed with the ratification of the Queen, and ready to exchange it for that of the Sultan. But nothing was done. The continuance of such a situation was clearly incompatible with the dignity of Great Britain, so on July 15, 1887, Sir Henry Drummond Wolff, under orders from Lord Salisbury, finally left Constantinople. No sooner had he gone than the Turkish Ambassador in London was instructed to resume negotiations, but this the British Foreign Minister naturally declined. It was impossible, he declared, to reopen the question at the moment, and he could not bind himself as to the future, though, of course, he 'did not desire to exclude the possibilities of future negotiations.' 'So long,' he added, 'as the Sultan was so much under the influence of other advisers as to repudiate an agreement which he had himself so recently sanctioned, any fresh agreement would obviously be liable to meet with the same fate as the late Convention.'

Thus the negotiations ended in smoke, but they were not without certain consequences in Egypt, both transitory and permanent. As long as they lasted, they exercised an unfavourable and unsettling effect, as indeed do all signs and rumours of change in a country where public opinion is so sensitive, so unbalanced, and so ill-informed as it is in Egypt. But this influence was of a passing character. The permanent element of disturbance, which the Wolff negotiations have left behind them in the Nile Valley, is the presence of the Ottoman High Commissioner.

It was certainly rather hard on poor Egypt, already so rich in conflicting authorities, to have to put up with a fresh meddler in her affairs. Yet such was to be her fate. Sir Henry Drummond Wolff came on a special and limited mission, and went away again. But Mukhtar Pasha, though he came on the same mission, has remained ever since. He has no intelligible attributes. He is not an ambassador, for a sovereign cannot send an ambassador to a portion of his own dominions. The Khedive himself is the representative of the Sultan in Egypt. Neither has Mukhtar any part or lot in the administration of the country. Technically, he is an anomaly; in practice he is the nucleus, often the unwilling nucleus, of the smouldering agitation of Moslem fanaticism or the intrigues of the old Turkish party. His presence is thus a perpetual nuisance, which may at any moment become a danger. Indeed, it actually was a danger at the beginning of 1892, during the brief carnival of seditious excitement which followed the accession of the young Khedive, and which was only quelled by the firm attitude of Sir Evelyn Baring and of the British Government on the question of the Firman.

And if Mukhtar's position is an annoyance to the Egyptian Government, it can hardly be supposed that it is particularly agreeable to himself. He is a straightforward gentleman, as well as a soldier of high distinction. Such a man must surely feel that he is worthy of something better than a place in which he has no work of his own to do, and can hardly help becoming the tool of the underhand and disloyal work of others. No wonder that he himself has often expressed in private his intense anxiety to be recalled. Whether he is kept in Cairo with the deliberate intention of weakening Egypt and annoying England, or whether his retention is simply due to the fact that the Sultan does not want him at home, is one of those mysteries of Turkish diplomacy on which I hesitate to venture an opinion.

But to return to the course of events in Egypt at the point where we left it. Nubar Pasha was dismissed from office in June, 1888. Riaz Pasha, who succeeded him, resigned in May, 1891. Tempting as it is, I will not dilate upon the dramatic contrast in the character of these two lifelong rivals. That contrast has been the theme of every writer on Egyptian politics for the last twenty years. A brilliant sketch of the two statesmen, perhaps a little unfair to Riaz, may be found in Mr. Moberly Bell's 'Khedives and Pashas.' I will assume that my readers are so far acquainted with the two most striking personalities of modern Egyptian history as to know that Nubar is an Armenian Christian, Riaz a Mohammedan by religion, and (whether or not he be of Jewish extraction) a Turk of the Turks by character, education, and sympathy; that the former is a Liberal, the latter a Conservative; that the former is a man of the highest European culture and a perfect master of French, while the latter is intellectually a pure Oriental, and has learnt French too late in life ever to speak it with fluency. Men have been known to question the fortitude of Nubar, but the fortitude of Riaz is unquestionable. Nubar is full of the most modern ideas; Riaz's stock of ideas is limited in amount and mediæval in character. Nubar delights in generalization, but is less happy when he comes to the detail of government. Riaz is a master of detail, and has all the ins-and-outs of Egyptian administration at his fingers' ends. Nubar is witty and epigrammatic. Riaz never said a witty thing in his life, though in his native Arabic he is master of a certain high-pitched eloquence. Nubar is capable of throwing financial considerations to the winds when appealed to on grounds of humanity. Riaz is a rigid economist, and little troubled with humanitarian sentiment. He is not without a certain feeling for the common people, but it is such as a feudal baron of the better sort might have had for the serfs on his estate.

The completeness of the antithesis is extraordinary. And, to heighten the effect of the contrast, it is carried out in the appearance and bearing of the two men no less than in their minds and characters. Nubar is of fine presence, genial manners, and mellifluous speech. Riaz is small and wizened, abrupt and irritable, with a voice which has a tendency to become shrill even under slight provocation. Except in his own house —where his civility is perfect—he is apt to be curt to the verge of rudeness, not only with inferiors but with equals, while he is jealous to exact from all and sundry a respect which he is not always mindful to render.

But if the men themselves are exact opposites, there is a curious similarity in their fortunes. They detest one another; but the impartial historian will record that each, in his own way, has rendered important services to his country. Both of them had much to endure from Ismail Pasha; both of them, at different times, had their work cut out for them in striving, unsuccessfully, to keep that erratic despot from ruining himself and his country. If Nubar may claim the honour of having, by the establishment of the Mixed Courts, laid the foundations of justice, Riaz must be credited with daring opposition to the extravagances of Ismail, and with loyal support given to the Controllers in their struggle to right Egyptian finance. And the experiences of the two men, after the British Occupation, present an even more striking analogy. Each of them in turn sympathized to a certain extent with England's reforming efforts. Each of them worked with us up to a point. But each in his turn fretted at the restraints which co-operation with England imposed upon his own arbitrariness, and ended by quarrelling with our assistance. Before the days of his accession to office Riaz had been known to complain that England did not interfere sufficiently to put things right that were going wrong. But he had not long been Minister before he persuaded himself that she interfered a great deal too much.

So far, then, the cases are parallel. But now we come to a difference. It must be admitted that Riaz had far less excuse for quarrelling with us than his predecessor. When Nubar took office the affairs of Egypt were in an indescribable mess, and for some time after we continued to bungle them in a manner which must have been more than trying to him. Throughout the whole of his administration finances were tight, and he had to incur the odium of a policy of economy which he at heart detested. It is true that during his later years things were decidedly on the mend, but the improvement was not yet generally felt, while the hard measures necessary to ensure it were widely resented. Riaz, on the other hand, succeeded to power under happier auspices. He came, not at a moment of crisis, but at a moment of revival, and throughout his period of office the tide was steadily on the rise. It was his good fortune to see the despised Egyptian Army victorious over the Mahdists, to see the burden of the Debt greatly lightened by a successful Conversion, to see Egypt freed entirely, and presumably for ever, from the curse of the Corvée, to see the land tax reduced by 30 per cent. in the poorest provinces, and, despite that and other reductions of taxation, to see the surplus of revenue over expenditure increase from year to year. And all the time he himself was assiduously kept to the front. Credit was ostentatiously given to him for every success and for every reform.

Had Riaz Pasha been a man of a different temper, he might have been the most popular of Egyptian Premiers. He might have been governing the country to-day, amid general applause, with an almost absolutely free hand, although on the lines of British policy. Certainly no man would have been happier at such a consummation than Sir Evelyn Baring. Much as the British Consul-General has been forced to interfere during all these years, he has invariably sought to interfere as little as possible. His constant object has been that natives should do the work and get the credit, and that, as long as things went decently well, he himself should keep in the background. But all this fair prospect was spoilt by Riaz Pasha's unfortunate genius for making enemies when in power. It is an extraordinary thing how office seems to disagree with him. While he remains a private individual he has always a large following in the country. As a pious Mussulman he has all the strong religious influences on his side. As a large land-owner and excellent agriculturist, intimately acquainted with the daily life, the wants, and the ideas of the people, he knows how to enter into the interests and win the sympathy of the rural sheikhs. But the moment he takes office he becomes unapproachable. He is too nervous for the constant worries of administration, and soon fidgets himself into a fever. Grievances annoy him. Suggestions, even if tendered in the most deferential spirit, are apt to be treated as insults.

It must not be supposed that it was the English only who exercised an irritating effect on Riaz Pasha. He fell foul with remarkable impartiality of foreigners and natives, of the official and of the non-official classes. If anybody, the Syrians and the French were the special objects of his disfavour. It was difficult for him to show the barest justice to a Syrian employé. When the French Agent came to him with any complaint, there was always the risk of an explosion. It is one of the elements of irony, in which the Egyptian situation is so rich, that on more than one occasion foreign representatives, even those belonging to Powers not specially friendly to British policy, complained to their British colleague of the scant courtesy shown to them by the Egyptian Premier. Had any casual stranger dropped in the presence of these gentlemen a remark implying that Egypt was under British control, they would probably have protested against any such assumption. Yet when an Egyptian Minister was rude to them they turned to the British Consul-General to complain, just as a schoolboy might complain to his master of the conduct of one of his fellows. But this by the way.

It took Riaz Pasha some two years to fall out with almost everybody of eminence in Egypt. His administration had been an unbroken series of successes, but despite them all he was now more unpopular than Nubar had ever been. Feeling the ground slipping from under him, he sought to recover himself, as his predecessor had sought, by a stand-up fight with the English. The policy was no more successful on this occasion than on the previous one.

The *cheval de bataille* in the present instance was the question of creating a new English official of high rank, who was to be known as 'Judicial Adviser.' Ever since the last year of Nubar's Ministry we had been compelled to turn our attention more and more to the crying evils connected with the administration of justice. The two greatest of these were the incompetence of the Native Courts, and the arbitrariness of the Commissions of Brigandage. Driven at last to face these new difficulties, Sir Evelyn Baring proceeded by his usual gradual method. Since the retirement of Sir Raymond West native justice had been practically free from all European control. But in October, 1887, a Belgian, M. Legrelle, was appointed Procureur-Général, and was encouraged to make a radical examination of existing abuses. Thus assured of support, M. Legrelle produced, in the course of 1888, a most elaborate report on the working of the Commissions of Brigandage, which showed up the irregularities, the injustice, and the cruelty of these quasi-tribunals in the most startling light. Sir Evelyn Baring now began to press for their abolition. Riaz Pasha, though somewhat reluctant, and professing himself doubtful of the accuracy of the gravest charges brought against the Commissions, ultimately gave way, and in May, 1889, they were suppressed. This was in the early days of Riaz's power, when tension between him and Baring had not yet become serious.

A first great step had thus been taken, but it necessarily involved further measures. The Commissions had been established because the Courts were incompetent to grapple with crime. Evidently the suppression of the former did not, by itself, make the latter less incompetent. On the contrary, the question of improving the Courts presented itself in a more urgent form than before. Baring proposed to strengthen them by increasing the number of the European judges. This time the resistance was more serious, but in the end he again carried his point; and in November, 1889, two additional Englishmen were appointed to the native Court of Appeal, making, in all, three Englishmen and three Belgians.

But to multiply European judges in the Native Courts was only to multiply witnesses to their inefficiency. The more the true state of the case was brought to light, the clearer it became that some radical reform was needed. The British Consul-General therefore urged the temporary appointment of an eminent Indian judge to examine the whole system of native jurisprudence, and to make proposals for its amendment. The suggestion was adopted, and in the spring of 1890 Mr. Scott, a judge of the High Court of Bombay, came to Egypt to advise on the question. He was appointed, in the first instance, for one year.

By the end of 1890 Mr. Scott brought up his report. Without condemning the procedure of the Courts *in toto*, or taking a despondent view of their possible future, he suggested a number of important changes, and, above all, pointed out the necessity of a great improvement in their personnel. It was on the ground of these suggested reforms that Riaz Pasha chose to deliver battle. The Minister of Justice, a puppet in his hands, was pushed into the foreground, and induced to write a memorandum condemning Mr. Scott's proposals root and branch. The animus of the proceeding was evident. The whole question as to whether there should be any reform of justice at all was hanging in the balance. Hence the British Consul-General, under instructions from home, pressed vigorously for the acceptance of Mr. Scott's scheme, and for the permanent appointment of its author to superintend its execution.

Riaz Pasha now sought to involve the Khedive in the dispute, and at first with some appearance of success. But no sooner did the latter realize the gravity of the quarrel in which he was being involved than he drew back, precisely as he had done under similar circumstances in the time of Nubar, and precisely with the same subsequent feeling of resentment against the Minister who had pushed him into an untenable position. Mr. Scott's proposals were therefore accepted, and he himself appointed to a permanent post. Riaz Pasha bowed to the decision, though with a bad grace; but he felt that his power was broken. Just as Nubar was politically dead from the moment when the police question was settled against him, so Riaz was politically dead from the moment of Mr. Scott's appointment. The relations between him and the Khedive became strained, and in May, 1891, he resigned on the plea of ill-health.

The successor of Riaz Pasha was Mustafa Pasha Fehmi, the present Prime Minister. He had served under both Nubar and Riaz—for it is not usual in Egypt, where there are no parties, for a whole Cabinet to be changed with a change of its head—and he has probably more experience of various departments of state than any other Egyptian statesmen. With his accession to power a great, and there is every reason to hope a permanent, change has come over the spirit of the Egyptian Government, especially in its attitude towards ourselves. Mustafa Pasha is the first Egyptian Premier who has been unreservedly in sympathy with the English. It is his firm conviction that Egypt must needs lean on some one of the Great Powers, and that there is no other nation whose protection would be as disinterested as Great Britain's. Never has the co-operation of Englishmen and Egyptians been so cordial as since Mustafa Pasha's succession to office. Never has progress been so general and so rapid.

Without being as strong a man as either of his predecessors, Mustafa Pasha is intelligent, loyal, well-meaning, and well beloved. Indeed, if it were not for the extreme delicacy of his health, he would be an almost ideal Prime Minister under present circumstances. Moreover, his total lack of that imperiousness, which in different degrees had been an attribute of both his predecessors, was particularly appropriate to the conditions existing at the time of his accession to power; for a new factor had now during some years been making itself increasingly felt in Egyptian politics. I allude to the reviving influence of the Khedive himself. For some time before the fall of Riaz, Tewfik Pasha had been steadily growing in popularity and in power. He was more disposed than formerly to take that active part in the work of government which the Constitution of Egypt assigns to the Sovereign. By nature the least despotic of men, he was never likely to exceed the wide rôle by right belonging to him. But he was actually becoming more able and more inclined to fill it.

At the time of Tewfik's death many of the biographies which appeared in the European press represented him as a good-natured puppet, without any hold on the affections of his people or any influence over them. This idea was an anachronism. Such an estimate of his character might have been true at the time of our occupation of the country. Indeed, it could hardly have been otherwise, so crushing up to that date had been the combination of circumstances against him. But of late years better fortune had made him a stronger man. The amelioration which had now set in so decidedly in the condition of the people, the larger harvests, the lighter taxes, the abolition of the Corvée, the diminution of official tyranny and corruption—all these combined to strengthen the position of the Chief of the State. Tewfik Pasha profited by the opportunity which Riaz missed. The bulk of the people, conscious of their improved condition, but not very analytical of its causes, looked for an explanation of their prosperity and for an object of their gratitude, and they found it in the person of the Khedive. The demonstrations of affection with which he was overwhelmed during those journeys in the provinces, of which of late years he had become increasingly fond, could not have been wholly, or even mainly, feigned. There was an unmistakable spontaneity about them; and they helped to give him self-reliance. He felt, and because he felt, he actually was, a greater person than in former days. So untrue is it, that the effect of British policy in Egypt has been to dwarf or undermine the influence of its native rulers.

And if the Khedive himself had now become a power in the country, his character was pre-eminently calculated to preserve him from becoming a dangerous or a disturbing power. He had not the qualities of a conqueror or a creative statesman. He had not the strength of will and perverse fertility of resource which enabled his father to maintain a powerful despotism in spite of general discredit and impending bankruptcy, and to baffle for so long all the efforts of European diplomacy to make him govern on rational principles. Originality and initiative were not Tewfik's strong points. If they had been, he might have been less peculiarly suited to a situation in which his cue was to fall in with and support a policy already traced for him by circumstances, rather than to mark out a policy of his own. But he had tact, patience, dignity, courage, self-possession, a genuine feeling for his people, a real sympathy with the new ideas of just, humane, and progressive government.

But perhaps the most invaluable of all his qualities, under the circumstances of the time, was a certain combination that there was in him of the European and the Oriental. It is interesting to compare him in this respect with his father Ismail, who also combined these opposite elements of character, though in very different proportions. Superficially, Tewfik was far less modern, less European, less civilized than his father. He had hardly ever been out of Egypt. He spoke no European language perfectly. He had not parted with the Mohammedan faith, and he retained at least enough Mohammedan prejudice, as well as acquaintance with the habits and ideas of the people, to get on excellently with the sheikhs and the Ulema,* with the latter of whom Ismail would not so much as pretend to be in any sort of sympathy. But at heart Tewfik was really much more like a constitutional ruler of the Western type than an Oriental despot, while Ismail was a true Oriental despot with a Parisian veneer. Thus Tewfik was able to fall in with the new order of things, without offending the conservative instincts, or even the bigotry of his subjects. He was, in fact, during the later years of his life, an invaluable link between the Europeans and the natives—a heaven-born mediator in that stage of transition through which Egypt was passing. No doubt his rôle was not always compatible with absolute sincerity. He had a habit of agreeing with the man who was speaking to him, though he might just before have agreed with a different speaker in a somewhat different sense. He had a certain tendency to run with the hare and hunt with the hounds. But immense allowance must surely be made for the almost unexampled difficulty of his position. Had he been rigidly sincere, he could hardly have been, to the extent that he was, the man of the situation.

And if his policy seemed occasionally rather tortuous, it nevertheless tended to gain directness and unity as time went on, and as he acquired more confidence in himself and in his surroundings. For several years it was difficult for him to feel sure how he stood with the English. Unable to feel confidence in the certainty of our support, he hesitated to throw in his lot with us. But, as he came to have faith in our steadfastness, he in turn became more steadfast. And that tendency was, doubtless, confirmed by his recognition of, and gratitude for, the benefits which we had bestowed on his country. Very likely he doubted at the outset—and can we wonder at it?—whether English reforms were likely to succeed. But when he saw that good resulted from them, he was prompt to acknowledge it, and to prove the sincerity of his acknowledgment by a greater cordiality of support. He was growing more English in sympathy with every

* See p. 297.

succeeding year. And the more English the ruler of Egypt becomes, the less need is there for that constant interference of English diplomacy, which is, at best, a necessary evil. Had Tewfik Pasha lived another ten years, the Egyptian Question might have passed definitely out of its present still critical phase.

The fates willed it otherwise. Little more than seven months after the last change of Ministry, the Khedive was suddenly cut off in the flower of life. He was a robust-looking man of forty, of regular and most temperate habits—the last person in the world for whom one would have predicted an untimely death. It was at the beginning of January of 1892. For a week we had heard in Cairo that the Khedive, who was at that time residing at the baths of Helwan, some fourteen miles off, was confined to his palace by a slight attack of influenza. Nobody thought anything of it. Suddenly, on the morning of Thursday, the 7th, a report reached the capital that grave complications had set in, and that the Khedive's life was in danger. The Ministers were hastily summoned to Helwan. By seven o'clock the same evening Tewfik Pasha was dead—a victim to the incapacity of his native doctors. Consternation and sorrow were universal. Never was a good and useful life cut off at a more inopportune moment.

It is neither possible as yet to judge, nor would it be proper for me to discuss, how far the present ruler of Egypt is capable of filling the void left by his father's death. Undoubtedly he comes to the throne with far more favourable omens than his predecessor. The net result of the reign of Tewfik Pasha is to leave Egypt more prosperous, and the Khedivial authority more respected than it was. It is not unreasonable to hope that, if the young Khedive—who as far as can be judged inherits his father's virtues with more than his father's strength—can only be given time to acquire the necessary experience, if the course of progressive improvement on which Egypt is now fairly launched be left undisturbed from without, the reign of Abbas II. may fill a bright and memorable page in the book of Egyptian history. But the question of Egypt's future is one which it will be more profitable to discuss when we have finished the examination of her recent progress.

So far I have attempted to describe the general conditions under which the work of reform has been carried out. The succeeding chapters will contain an account of the more salient features of that work in those great departments—the Army, Finance, Public Works, and Justice—in which the task has been at once most important and most difficult.

CHAPTER VII.

THE FELLAH AS SOLDIER.

'MARCHED yesterday morning with three thousand five hundred towards Tokar. . . . On square being only threatened by small force of enemy, certainly less than a thousand strong, *Egyptian troops threw down their arms and ran, allowing themselves to be killed without slightest resistance.* More than two thousand killed. All material lost.'

(Extract from General Baker's telegram, describing his defeat at El Teb, on the road to Tokar, on February 5, 1884.)

'The main body of the dervishes were fifty yards from our front line, and were extending to the right and left to envelop the position. The bulk of their force was directed against the line occupied by the 12th battalion, their attack being pushed home with their usual intrepidity and fearlessness. *The troops, however, stood their ground, and did not yield one inch throughout the line.*'

(Extract from Colonel Holled-Smith's report, describing his victory of Afafit, on the road to Tokar, on February 19, 1891.)

The same attacking enemy—adroit, sudden, and absolutely fearless; the same region of storm-swept desert and treacherous scrub, save that at El Teb the ground was comparatively open, while at Afafit the ambush-sheltering mimosa bushes, ten feet high, came close up to the line of march; the same human material on the side of Egypt—for there was no British soldier, officers excepted, at Afafit, any more than at El Teb—yet how different the result! And this is no accidental contrast.

I could parallel the misconduct of Baker's troops at El Teb by a dozen passages in the despatches recording the series of disgraceful defeats by which, in less than six months, the old Egyptian army lost the whole of the Eastern Sudan. And, similarly, the honourable record of the action at Afafit could be paralleled by many instances of steadiness and gallantry on the part of the new Egyptian army during the recent years of weary frontier warfare about Suakin and Wadi Halfa.

Why does the old army stand almost unequalled in history for cowardice and incapacity? Why has the new army, composed of very much the same elements, so soon achieved an honourable record? It is easy to answer that the difference arises from the fact that the new army has been created by British officers. But that answer only leads to a fresh question. By what magic is it that these men—average British officers for the most part, and no more—have produced such remarkable results? How is it that they have changed the fighting character of a nation in so short a time? To whom is the credit principally due?

There are many who deserve to share the credit, and I believe that those gallant soldiers, who of late years have led the Egyptian forces to victories that have made a certain noise in the world, would be the first to admit that a large portion of it belongs to the men who, in the early days of the army, when everybody ridiculed the idea of the fellahin ever fighting, patiently laid the foundations of all the subsequent success. Perhaps the greatest of their merits was to have believed in the possibility of a native Egyptian army at all. With the miserable collapse of Arabi's large host still fresh in everybody's memory, with reports of the disgraceful and unsoldierlike conduct of the Egyptian troops in the Sudan pouring in from every side, it required a good deal of courage and a good deal of imagination to picture the same class of men standing steady under fire, and even against cold steel, and becoming a terror to their enemies instead of simply being a scourge to the peaceful population whom they were intended to protect.

The problem of the military defence of Egypt, as it presented itself immediately after the British Occupation, was one of the most puzzling it is possible to conceive. One thing only was clear. The existing army was worse than useless. 'The Egyptian army is disbanded,' said the laconic and often-quoted decree of December 20, 1882; and so far at least everybody concerned was cordially unanimous. But what was to take its place? Ninety-nine men out of a hundred would certainly have answered that it could not be a new army composed of the same materials as the old one. It is greatly to the honour of Lord Dufferin that amid the wildest suggestions crowding in upon him, suggestions of Turkish battalions, of mixed European battalions, of every possible combination of riff-raff from all quarters of the globe, he adhered firmly to the principle of entrusting the defence of the country to its own inhabitants. Evidently, if the thing was possible, it was incomparably the best plan. The foreign civilians in Egypt were unruly enough; what would foreign janissaries be likely to be? But, sound as the principle was, its execution might have been very difficult if Lord Dufferin had not been able at that moment to lay his hand upon a man who not only possessed unquestionable military talents and a great experience of war, but was able to rise to the bold conception that even the despised fellah could be turned into a soldier. If it was true that ill-usage had made him a coward, might it not be possible that proper treatment would once more make him a man?

At any rate, Sir Evelyn Wood, to whom the task of creating the new Egyptian army was entrusted, was prepared to try. And he had no difficulty in finding a sufficient number of British officers ready to assist him. I should think few of them ever regretted the enterprise. The Egyptian service, which was at first scoffed at as a career, has proved a road to advancement as good or better than any other in the whole wide field of British empire or influence. Among the twenty-six men originally associated with Sir Evelyn Wood in his bold undertaking are names which have subsequently become as well known as those of Grenfell, Chermside, Hallam Parr, Watson, Wodehouse, Kitchener, and Rundle. British officers have done much for Egypt, but it is equally true that Egypt has done a good deal for them.

And the problem once boldly faced, its difficulties grew less appalling, as difficulties so faced are apt to do. It turned out that the material was not so very bad, after all. No one can pretend that the Egyptian peasant, in his native condition, ranks very high as a fighting animal. Still, looked at with the view of making the best of him, he is not wanting in certain qualities which go a long way in the composition of a soldier. He is, as a rule, healthy, well built, active, easily led, not easily overcome by hardship. Moreover, he is intelligent, docile, and, though wanting in dash, not wanting in a certain fearlessness in the presence of danger. I remember being much struck, during the great fire at Abdin Palace in the summer of 1891, by the extraordinary coolness with which certain of the native firemen stuck to their posts under the most imminent danger of being crushed by the roofs and walls which were tumbling in on all sides of them. It is the same quality which has on various occasions rendered the Egyptian soldier steady and calm under a harassing fire, sufficient to have shaken the nerves of troops who, at a charge or hand-to-hand fight, might be much better than he is. You may call it insensibility to danger if you like, and not true courage. But, call it what you will, it is an extremely valuable quality in war.

An officer of my acquaintance, who is a perfectly impartial critic, and who has had many opportunities of seeing the fellahin fight, declares that behind defences they can be made as good as any troops in the world, while even in the open, if they have only confidence in their leaders, they are fair average soldiers. The fact is, that good leadership is simply everything with Egyptians. The fellah has little individuality or initiative in the field. But he is capable of showing plenty of courage under officers whom he believes in. Witness the various instances—such as the defence of El Obeid, of Senaar, of Kassala, and, above all, of Sinkat—in which soldiers even of the old army, being for a wonder ably commanded, displayed not only a stubborn power of resistance, but daring courage in attack. It is true that the forces engaged on those occasions were not entirely composed of fellahin. But there were many native Egyptians amongst them.

How was it that men, capable of such courage, had yet become a by-word for cowardice? Why would they run away from a mere handful of half-naked Arabs armed with spears, when they had only to stand still and shoot in order to be perfectly safe? The answer must be sought in the treatment to which they had previously been subjected. The fellah, more than most men, requires training to make him a fighter, and he had not had it. More than most men, he is easy to demoralize by bad management, and he had had nothing else. On the one hand, he was never properly taught his business; and, on the other, he was exposed to an amount of degrading ill-usage which would have knocked the manliness out of a Viking. His officers, a miscellaneous crowd, selected on no principle and promoted for anything but merit, were quite unable to keep up real discipline; but, at the same time, they banged their men about in the most cruel and disheartening manner.

The rank and file were wretchedly paid, and the little pay they were entitled to was often intercepted. The officers, who, to do them justice, found their own salary constantly in arrear, recouped themselves by taking the money which ought to have provided the soldiers with food and clothing. There were no sort of arrangements for the comfort of the men. The barracks were filthy beyond description. Provision for the sick and wounded simply did not exist. And, worst of all, perhaps, although there were laws regulating the length of military service, they were, like most other laws in those days of stupid anarchy, completely disregarded. The recruit never knew, when taken from his village, for how many years he might not be kept with the colours. Moreover, he might be sent to the Sudan, which was equivalent to a sentence of perpetual exile, if not of death. No wonder that the conscripts had to be led away in chains, under the blows of the kurbash, and amidst precisely the same violent exhibitions of grief on the part of their relations as usually attend a funeral. No wonder that large numbers of the population were, even in childhood, maimed or blinded, in order that they might escape the terrible fate of having to serve their country. Under such circumstances, what could be more unreasonable than to complain of a want of spirit in the Egyptian soldier? No ingenuity could have devised a system more likely, more certain, to destroy the spirit of any man.

Plainly, the first thing to do was to reverse all this. And it was reversed. The conscription of an army of six thousand men—the number originally fixed by Lord Dufferin—was not a great tax upon a population of six millions, and the men were soon got together. Once enrolled, they found themselves properly fed, clothed, housed. Discipline was strict, but as long as they conducted themselves well, they were absolutely safe from oppression. Their pay was reasonable in amount, and it was never stopped except for misconduct. They were looked after when ill. Indeed, one of the first things which inspired respect and confidence on the part of the soldier in his new officers was the fearless devotion which some of the latter showed in trying to save the lives of their subordinates during the cholera epidemic. The idea of a well-paid officer, who was, of course, expected to think first of his own life and comfort, not only gratuitously exposing himself to danger, but undertaking the most loathsome duties, in order to wrestle with death for the lives of a set of poor peasants, was a new idea to the Egyptian mind. A very great impression was likewise made by the fact that the conscripts were now not only entitled to leave, but regularly allowed to take it. The reappearance of the fellah soldier in his native village, after an absence of a year in barracks—not crawling back, mutilated or smitten by some fatal disease, but simply walking in as a visitor, healthy, well dressed, and with some money in his pocket—was like the vision of a man risen from the dead.

Having thus rapidly won the confidence of their men, the new officers had not much difficulty in knocking them into fair military shape. Here the fellah's quickness, submissiveness, and positive fondness for drill were of the greatest assistance. It is an amusing proof of this predilection, that the soldiers had actually to be prevented from practising their drill in their leisure hours. Not only would a non-commissioned officer get hold of a squad on his own account, whenever an opportunity offered, but it was a common sight to come across a private drilling three or four of his comrades. Within three months of its formation the new army already made a creditable show on parade. Its first recorded review took place on March 31, 1883, and on that occasion its appearance called forth the praises of independent military critics who were present on the ground.

Troops may look well on parade after a few months' drill, and such a smart appearance is of good augury for the future. Yet no man in his senses would dream that so short a time could suffice to make them thorough soldiers, still less to create that very complicated piece of machinery, a fully organized army. To do this is a work of years. But years were in this instance not granted for the completion of the machine before the first serious strain was put upon it. When the new troops were enlisted, it was never contemplated that they should have anything to do with the Sudan. The garrisons already on the spot, reinforced by the remnants of Arabi's beaten army and by some fresh irregular levies, might, it was considered, be left to deal with any trouble in that quarter. Indeed, at that time nobody thought much about the Sudan. But within a year nobody thought much about anything else. The new army had only been some eighteen months under arms when it was called upon to take its share in the effort to stem the rising tide of Mahdiism, which had already covered the greater part of the Sudan, and was threatening to cover Egypt. It was, indeed, decided not to use any portion of the new troops for the relief of Tokar at the time of General Baker's ill-starred expedition in the winter of 1883. But when in the following summer a British force under Lord Wolseley was sent up the Nile to rescue Gordon and the garrisons, Sir Evelyn Wood claimed for his young soldiers the right to take part in the work; and his claim was, after some hesitation, most wisely conceded.

During Lord Wolseley's expedition the Egyptian troops were principally engaged in guarding the long line of communications which extended from Assiut to Korti. In the arduous and often risky work of transport, when the boats containing men and stores had to be dragged for miles against a strong current, or through dangerous rapids, they showed all their best qualities of zeal, obedience, and endurance. Moreover, small detachments, which were actually under fire at Abu Klea and at Kirbekan, behaved with a steadiness which justified the opinion of those who, like Sir Evelyn Wood, believed that a larger share of the actual fighting might safely have been entrusted to the Egyptians.

Whatever grievance there may have been on this score was very soon to be removed. Sir Evelyn Wood, who retired from the position of Sirdar in April, 1885, was not himself destined to lead to victory the troops whom he had trained, and in whose training he had rendered invaluable services, which were perhaps not fully appreciated until after his departure. But when the British army was withdrawn from Dongola in the summer of 1885, a Frontier Field Force was formed under Major-General Grenfell, the new Sirdar, and was composed in about equal numbers of British and Egyptians. And now the morale of the latter was to be put to really severe tests. In the skirmish of Mograkeh, where two hundred of them held a fort against a vastly superior number of dervishes, and in the severe engagement at Ginnis on December 30, 1885, which discomfited the Mahdists in their first serious move upon the frontier of Egypt, the Egyptian soldiers were exposed to the full brunt of battle. It is true that at Ginnis the Frontier Field Force was powerfully reinforced by British troops brought up on purpose to deal a staggering blow to the overweening enemy, still flushed with the exultation of their great victory at Khartum. The chief command was in the hands of Lieut.-General Stephenson, then at the head of the British Army of Occupation. But, for all that, the Egyptians took a substantial part in the fight, and their gallant conduct, coming at a moment when Great Britain was anxiously striving to reduce the number of her troops in Egypt, doubtless contributed to the decision, which was shortly afterwards arrived at, to leave the defence of the frontier in Egyptian hands.

The frontier was now fixed at Wadi Halfa, where it has practically remained to the present day; and by April, 1886, that post was confided entirely to the keeping of the Egyptian army, a British force being, however, for some time longer stationed at Assuan, two hundred miles to the north, in case of emergencies. But this reserve was never called upon for assistance. Its numbers were gradually reduced, and by January, 1888, the last British detachment was withdrawn from that part of the country. Since that time the Egyptian army has proved itself equal to the task of protecting Egypt from the northward pressure of the Sudanese rebels. At Suakin, too, where in 1884 and 1885 such an imposing display of British military force had been considered necessary, Egyptian troops towards the close of the latter year took over the whole defence, and except for a few months in the end of 1888, when, owing to a panic at home, they were quite unnecessarily reinforced by part of the British garrison at Cairo, they have conducted it unaided ever since.

Meanwhile, the extension of the duties of the army had necessitated an increase of its numbers. If its work had been confined to maintaining internal order, and keeping in awe the restless, but really not very formidable, Bedawin on the eastern and western frontiers of Egypt—and this was all for which it was originally intended—the number of six thousand men fixed by Lord Dufferin might have sufficed. But now that it was expected to ward off single-handed the dangerous invasion threatening from the far south, that number was evidently inadequate. At the end of 1883 the infantry still consisted of only eight battalions, recruited exclusively from the fellahin. But in May, 1884, there was raised at Suakin a 9th battalion, composed of Sudanese negroids—the first of the famous black regiments which supply the picturesque and the dashing element in the Egyptian military history of recent times. The experiment of enlisting these blacks proved a great success, and in January, 1886, another battalion of the same kind, the 10th Sudanese, was added to the army. In June of the same year came the 13th Sudanese; in December, 1887, the 11th Sudanese; and, finally, in November, 1888, the 12th Sudanese. That the 13th should come before the 11th and the 12th is a characteristically Egyptian arrangement, but the explanation lies in the fact that there were originally two new fellah regiments which bore the Nos. 11 and 12, but which were suppressed in a fit of economy, and subsequently replaced by the present 11th and 12th, who, like the 9th, 10th, and 13th, are blacks.

A word about the black soldiers. And be it observed that the term 'black' in this connection is not, as it is so often, an exaggeration or a figure of speech. Not even the most sensitive Radical could object to the 9th—13th Sudanese being described as 'black men,' and they themselves are rather proud than otherwise of their own hue of deepest ebony. They are not natives of Egypt, but belong for the most part to the Shillúk and Dinka tribes, who are found on the Upper Nile, from some little distance above Khartum right away to the Equatorial Province. Others come from the west beyond Kordofan, and even from as far as Wadai and Bornu. In build they are not exactly what in Northern countries we should describe as fine men. The Dinka and Shillúk are tall, but slight and narrow-shouldered, with skinny arms and legs. Their lungs are delicate, and great care has to be taken with their clothing, to protect them from catching cold. The men from the western districts are shorter and thicker-set, but even they could not be called robust. But they are all of springy gait and elastic movement, as active as cats, and animated with a real love of fighting, especially of fighting the Arabs of the Sudan, their hereditary enemies and oppressors. In civilization they are far below the inhabitants of Egypt. They are, indeed, mere children, with the thoughtlessness, the waywardness, and the want of foresight of children. But under officers who know how to command their respect and win their affection, they have all a child's docility and devotion.

As soldiers, the blacks are the very reverse of the Egyptians. They are not quick at drill, or fond of it. What they are fond of, and what they shine in, is real battle. It is true they have little sang-froid. They easily get excited, and are hard to hold. The difficulty is to prevent them from firing too fast or charging too soon. At Afafit one of the Sudanese battalions could only be stopped from blazing away at the enemy by their commanding officer going out of the line and passing in front of their rifles. But when it actually comes to close quarters, to charging or receiving a charge, then they have few equals. They have a natural instinct for combat which training may improve, but which it can never beget. In this respect they are immensely superior to the fellahin.

A noticeable fact is the sort of natural *camaraderie* which seems rapidly to spring up between the blacks and Englishmen. The former very easily become attached to their British officers, and those officers, on their side, have a curious kind of fondness for the blacks, which they do not seem to feel in an equal degree for the native Egyptians. This feeling has been known to extend even to the private soldiers of our British regiments, who on more than one occasion have readily fraternized with the Sudanese. These grown-up children, with their light-heartedness, simplicity, and unquestionable pluck, were regarded by Tommy Atkins with half-amused, half-admiring, and inoffensively patronizing affection. The friendship formed between the 79th Highlanders and the 9th Sudanese at the time of the battle of Ginnis is a pleasing case in point. The Highlanders presented their swarthy comrades with a flag which the latter carry along with their regimental colours to this day, and the 9th Sudanese have sometimes been playfully described as the 'second battalion of the Cameron Highlanders.' The curious thing is, that the blacks get on better with the English than they do with the Egyptians, with whom they might naturally be supposed to have so much more in common. Indeed, it is doubtful whether the Sudanese battalions would be manageable without British officers at their head. Hence it has come about that, while of the eight fellah regiments only four have British colonels and majors—the others being entirely officered by natives—the five Sudanese regiments are all under British superior officers. Moreover, in view of the greater difficulty of controlling them in the field, the number of these officers attached to a black battalion is four, while in the Egyptian battalions it is only three.

The addition of this new element greatly strengthened the Egyptian army, and still constitutes its most striking feature as a fighting force. But it is not just to assume, as is sometimes done, that the native Egyptians are of small account in the composition of the army. No doubt the blacks have borne the chief brunt of attack in the majority of engagements. No doubt they are the men whom a commander would most readily pit against the reckless courage of the dervishes. Still, they have not done all the work. The native Egyptians, who have fought steadily beside them in more than one critical struggle, deserve their share of the credit of victory. The truth is, that the two sets of men, with their widely different qualities, form a very strong combination for fighting purposes.

To return to the defence of the frontier. For fully three years the position of the Egyptian garrison at Wadi Halfa was a very anxious one. Wadi Halfa is a fortified camp at the northern extremity of the long desolate defile known as the Batn el Hagar, or 'belly of stones,' through which the Nile works its way in a succession of rapids, with nothing on either hand but ridge upon ridge of tumbled black rock, and beyond it the illimitable desert. At Wadi Halfa, for the first time for many miles, the valley widens out into a broad plain, and on that plain it was wisely decided to await the enemy as they debouched from the wilderness of rock.

The invasion did not take the form of that steady advance in force which was at one time expected. No doubt the Khalifa Abdullah el Taishi who, after the death of the Mahdi in the summer of 1885, had succeeded to supreme power at Khartum, always intended to send a regular army against Egypt. But fortunately he had his hands full in other directions. The tide of dervish attack at the gates of Egypt ebbed and flowed according to the fortunes of the Khalifa in his struggles with the soi-disant adherents of the Senussi in the west, with the Abyssians in the east, and with the numerous rebellions on the part of his own followers, which have threatened, though they have never upset, his power. At the end of 1886, the dervishes for the first time occupied Sarras, a fort in the heart of the Batn el Hagar, some thirty miles south of Wadi Halfa. From this point they harassed the garrison of the latter place and devastated the country all round, cutting down the palm-trees, which are almost its only product. Then they withdrew again for several months, but returned in greater force the following spring. After a severe blow inflicted upon them by the Wadi Halfa garrison, under Colonel Chermside, on April 27, in a brilliant surprise, which was the first unaided victory of the Egyptian troops, the dervishes once more retired, only, however, to return in still larger numbers, and to establish themselves permanently at Sarras towards the end of September. And now followed a long series of desultory raids, not merely in the neighbourhood of Wadi Halfa, but at many points between that place and Assuan, raids which spread terror far and wide among the wretched villagers. The Egyptian troops, though doing their best both by posts established along the river and by gunboats cruising up and down it, found it very difficult to restrain or to punish these forays. Many skirmishes took place, some trifling, others desperate and bloody, like the midnight capture and recapture of the fort of Khor Mussa on August 29, 1888. But though the defence gradually got the better of the attack, especially after the creation of the military Frontier Province under Colonel Wodehouse as governor, nothing decisive occurred. It was in this tedious guerilla warfare that the fighting qualities of the Egyptian army were developed.

Still the expected invasion did not come. It was not till the summer of 1889 that the dervish leader, Wad el Nejumi, goaded by the reproaches of his jealous master, at last made that desperate rush to reach Egypt which he had so long contemplated, but for which he never succeeded in collecting an adequate force. The attempt was a hopeless one from the first. To lead an army of five thousand fighting men, swollen by a crowd of women, children, and camp followers to upwards of twice that number, with inadequate provisions and means of transport, for more than a hundred miles across a waterless desert, only to fight a battle at the end, was a venture which could not possibly succeed against the forces which Egypt now disposed of for purposes of defence. Yet such was the power of Wad el Nejumi's personality, that the bulk of his soldiers followed him with enthusiasm even on this fatal enterprise.

Wad el Nejumi, indeed, is the most heroic figure among all the Arab chieftains of the Sudan war—the Gordon of Mahdiism. It was he who overthrew Hicks. It was he who led the final attack upon Khartum. And he, in the eyes of all the Faithful, was destined to plant the standard of the true Mahdi on the citadel of Cairo. Wild as the dream was, there is no saying that, if he had only had the old Egyptian army to deal with, it might not have been realized.

Nejumi's plan was to avoid Wadi Halfa, by starting

from a point on the western Nile bank opposite Sarras, and striking straight across the desert to Bimban, a place on the river about twenty-five miles north of Assuan. At Bimban he was led to believe that a number of Egyptian rebels would flock to his standard. Till then it was not his intention to offer battle, and he accordingly kept at some little distance from the river, which lay on his right. At the same time he doubtless counted on being able to obtain some provisions, and, above all, water, from the villages along the bank. But here he miscalculated. A flying column, consisting of about half of the Wadi Halfa garrison, under Colonel Wodehouse, dogged his march and kept heading him from the river. When a strong detachment of his army, disobeying his orders, made a push to reach the Nile, they were, after a long day's rough-and-tumble fighting, totally defeated at Argin by Colonel Wodehouse's troops. Still Nejumi pushed resolutely on, despite diminished numbers, despite losses from death and desertion, and the necessity of killing most of the transport animals for want of other food. And the majority of the dervish army never flinched or wavered from their leader. But General Grenfell was now hurrying down from the north with strong reinforcements, and, joining hands with Colonel Wodehouse, he threw himself across Nejumi's line of march at Toski, on August 3, and compelled the Arab leader to give battle.

The dervishes rushed to the attack with their usual splendid bravery, but their end was annihilation. Nejumi himself, almost all his principal captains, and nearly half of his fighting men, were killed. The rest were scattered to the winds, while many died in the attempt to retrace their steps through the arid wilderness. Thus ended one of the most madly daring enterprises in the whole romantic history of the Sudan war. No one can fail to feel a certain admiration for the courage and determination of Nejumi, or for the followers who stuck to him through every trial, and would have sold their lives willingly to preserve his. There is no more touching incident in the history of barbarian warfare than the picture of those stubborn warriors, whom no danger could appal and no hardship subjugate, bursting into tears over the dead body of the chieftain who had led them through intolerable sufferings to certain defeat.

The victory of Toski has had far-reaching consequences. For the two years previous to it the country between Wadi Halfa and Assuan was utterly unsafe. No one ever knew when and where a body of marauding Arabs might not swoop down upon the river bank. The people lived in terror of their lives. The garrisons were constantly on the alert. Now all this region is nearly as quiet as Lower Egypt. A considerable number of tourists go every winter to Wadi Halfa, and Mr. Cook conducts them with an easy mind. A dervish in those parts has become almost as rare a sight as a crocodile. And even for some little distance beyond Wadi Halfa there is a great change. An Egyptian outpost now holds Sarras, and the Egyptian patrols sweep the country for many miles south of it, and seldom see an enemy. The inhabitants, who had all fled before the advance of the dervishes, are gradually returning. On the road between Wadi Halfa and Sarras last winter I saw a number of families, their camels laden with simple domestic utensils or bags of seed, slowly wending their way back to their long-deserted homes.

And what Toski did for the southern frontier the engagement at Afafit in the spring of 1891 has done for the Red Sea Littoral, and for the important district depending on Suakin. Up to the time of that engagement Suakin had for years been practically beleaguered. The siege was carried on with more or less vigour. On one occasion, at the end of 1888, the enemy grew so troublesome, and entrenched themselves so close to the walls of the town, that a large force of Egyptian and British troops were obliged to turn them out at the point of the bayonet. But whether they were threatening Suakin itself, or simply harrying the surrounding country, the dervishes under Osman Digna, who has been the life and soul of the rebellion in this region, were really masters of the situation. The Egyptian governor of the Red Sea Littoral was governor within the walls of Suakin, and no further. And the reason was that the enemy always had a comfortable base of operations in the fertile delta of Tokar. Over and over again the military authorities pointed out that unless this base were captured Suakin would continue in a state of siege, whereas if Tokar were once occupied by Egyptian troops, the whole country for many miles round would be easily restored to tranquillity and to the sovereignty of the Khedive. But so rooted was the objection in England to anything like a fresh forward movement in any portion of the Sudan that it took several years to obtain the consent of the British Government to an advance upon Tokar.

When that advance was at length undertaken, there ensued one short, sharp, and for perhaps ten minutes doubtful, engagement. But the steadiness of the Egyptian soldiers, and the conspicuous gallantry and resource of one or two of the field officers, won the day. Osman Digna suffered a defeat from which he should never recover, and in this portion of the Sudan also there reigns for the present an almost perfect peace, such as has not been known there for nearly ten years.*

I have passed rapidly over the exploits of the Egyptian army. The limits of my space would not allow me to dilate on them, even if I believed more than I do in military history written by civilians. Of greater importance to my subject than the achievements of the army in the past is the question of its trustworthiness and efficiency to carry out, in the present and the future, the objects for which it is maintained. Can it, we may ask, be relied upon to keep the peace within the borders of Egypt, and to protect those borders from attack?

Before proceeding to answer these questions, let me briefly state the present strength of the army. On May 1, 1892, it consisted of fourteen battalions of infantry

* Since these words were written, Osman Digna has reappeared, but the small success attending his latest raid shows how helpless he is without his old base at Tokar.

(eight Egyptian, five Sudanese, and one depot battalion, amounting in all to nearly 10,000 men), ten troops of cavalry (about 800 men), three field batteries and one garrison battalion (about 900 men), one camel corps (300 men), besides staff, military police, medical corps, engineers, transport companies, and so forth. There were 18 field guns, and the total number of guns of position and machine guns was 160. The full establishment was 12,902 officers and men; the actual numbers were 12,547. There has been no material change since then, but I think a small increase is contemplated for 1893. This army, it may be added, costs, roughly speaking, nearly half a million of money, or something less than £40 a man. That is a very different sum from the £130,000 which a high authority estimated eight years ago to be the possible limit of Egypt's military expenditure. But at that time, it must be remembered, the defence of the country was still largely in the hands of British troops.

As far as internal order is concerned, this force would appear amply sufficient. With mere local disturbances or with trouble caused by the Bedawin—the two contingencies which Lord Dufferin contemplated—it is more than able to cope. On the other hand, any general rising like that of 1882 is, under present conditions, hardly conceivable. The Arabist rebellion, it will be remembered, had its origin in the discontent of the army. But the army is now, save for a certain amount of grumbling among the native officers, perfectly contented. The great body of the peasantry only took active part with Arabi tardily and after great incitement, nor had they ever much heart for the business. But at that time their condition was infinitely worse than it is nowadays. An all-round revolt of the fellahin, in their present state of comparative ease and freedom, is not to be thought of. What might happen if the conditions which prevailed in the latter days of Ismail were to return, if the administration were once more to get thoroughly out of hand, and as a consequence the needs of the people were neglected and their burdens increased, it is impossible to predict. But there is no need at present to contemplate any such relapse into misgovernment.

There remains the question of defence against external enemies, a question enormously simplified by the fact that there is in reality only one frontier to be defended. On the north and east, along the Mediterranean, the Suez Canal and the Gulf of Suez, Egypt is no doubt peculiarly liable to maritime attack, while at the Isthmus she might also be invaded by land, as she has been on more than one memorable occasion in her past history. But on these sides Egypt is to-day protected by diplomacy, and if diplomacy did not protect her, it is perfectly certain that no force raised within her own borders ever could. Against a naval invasion by one of the Great Powers, or against a powerful military expedition, European or Turkish, entering by the Isthmus of Suez, no Egyptian army which can be reasonably contemplated would be an effective protection. But if the northern and eastern frontiers can for all practical purposes be left out of account, so can the western. The vast extent of the Libyan Desert puts an invasion of considerable proportions on that side, unless supported from the sea, out of the question.

The rôle of the Egyptian army is thus reduced to the duty of defending Egypt from the south. And here again the problem is of remarkable simplicity. There is only one road of approach from the south practicable for a large army, and that road is narrow and easily defended. I mean the Nile Valley. Moreover, Egypt has on the south-east the great outlying fortress of Suakin. This position is important, not only as deterring an enemy from a possible, though not easily practicable, advance along the Red Sea to Kosseir, whence he might strike across the desert to Kena, but as commanding the route from Berber, the great outlet for the trade of the Sudan. But when you have once garrisoned Suakin, and stationed an adequate force in the Nile Valley, your scheme of defence is completed.

How entirely the idea, that the Egyptian army is

wanted only for external defence, and for external defence on one side, has now been generally accepted, may be seen from the present distribution of the Egyptian forces. When Lord Dufferin contemplated his eight battalions, he stationed them in imagination as follows: three in Cairo, one in Alexandria, and four distributed in other parts of Lower Egypt and Nubia, the vague term 'Nubia' meaning, I suppose, in this instance, the country between Assuan and Halfa. Thus half at least of the whole army, and possibly more, would have been in Lower Egypt. Its actual distribution to-day (1892) is as follows: On the Nile frontier (Assuan, Korosko, Wadi Halfa, and Sarras), seven battalions; at Suakin three battalions (including half a battalion at Tokar); at Cairo and Alexandria three battalions. Thus, nearly three-fourths of the infantry (including all the black troops) are at the two southern points of defence—Suakin and the Nile frontier—while fully half are stationed at the latter. And the other arms are distributed in very much the same proportion. The total numbers are: Frontier, six thousand men; Suakin, two thousand six hundred; Cairo and Alexandria, four thousand. But, then, the four thousand men at Cairo and Alexandria include the depot battalion, the head-quarter staff, and other central establishments. The actual fighting-force in all Lower Egypt is less than three thousand men.

There can be no doubt that, as long as the present purely defensive policy is maintained, the numbers of men stationed on the frontier and at Suakin—men now thoroughly trained, encouraged by past successes, and full of confidence in themselves and their commanders—are more than a match for any enemy who is at all likely to attack them. The insurrectionary movement in the Sudan, whatever its strength may still be within certain limits, is, as an expansive and aggressive force, decidedly on the decline. There is very little probability of another invasion similar to Nejumi's, and still less of its being commanded by another leader like Nejumi. But with an invasion on that scale, even if it came, the

Egyptian army at its present strength is perfectly competent to deal.

There remains a more interesting and a more thorny question, a question continually agitated in Egypt, and to which, however unpopular may be any reference to the subject at present, Englishmen cannot permanently close their eyes. I refer to the re-occupation of the Sudan, or a part of the Sudan. There is probably no point in connection with the much-misunderstood problem of Egypt about which public opinion in this country is enveloped in a deeper cloud of prejudice. Nothing, indeed, could be more natural than the weariness and disgust which came over British feeling as a consequence of the wasted heroism and useless slaughter of the years 1884-85. That attitude of mind fully explains the sense of relief—I might almost say the enthusiasm—with which the decision to withdraw altogether was, at the time, generally welcomed. There were a number of people who even seemed to persuade themselves that, in retiring, and compelling Egypt to retire, from the Sudan, we were performing a peculiarly humane, generous, and Christian act. In reality it is difficult to imagine a subject less suited for moral self-congratulation.

Personally I am convinced that, not only the original decision to abandon the Sudan at the end of 1883, but even the withdrawal of the British troops from Dongola after the Nile expedition in 1885, was fully justified by the circumstances of the case. The defence of both these decisions should, however, be based, not upon their moral loftiness, but upon their material necessity. Great Britain had other matters to attend to, far more urgent than crusading in the Sudan. Without Great Britain, Egypt was much too weak to attempt to hold that country. The effort might have ruined her, but it could have done no possible good to the revolted provinces. Still, while admitting the stern necessity of retreat, and while admiring the sagacity which recognised and the determination which executed it, we must surely feel that that necessity was, from the point of view of humanity, deeply regrettable. It is not a pleasant reflection that the former dominions of Egypt in the Sudan are, perhaps, the only portion of the world where civilization has, during the fifteen years preceding 1892, distinctly retrograded—the one region deliberately given back to barbarism. And it is painful to think that this dark page in Egyptian history belongs to that chapter of it which records the fortunes of Egypt while under the influence of Great Britain.

Fifteen years ago it was as safe to go to Khartum, and even five hundred miles further up the Nile Valley, as it was to go to Wadi Halfa and Sarras. Between Alexandria and Sarras there is perfect security still, but south of Sarras, and thence onward to the Equator, there is now no security whatever. No stranger, certainly no Christian stranger, could be sure of his life for a single day. I do not suppose there is another point in all the world where the line of demarcation between civilization and the most savage barbarism is more sharply marked, and that line is drawn some thousand miles further back than it was in the time of Ismail Pasha.

No doubt the government which existed in the Sudan in Ismail's time was, for the most part, detestably bad, but so was the government of Egypt itself, and for very much the same reasons. In the one country as in the other, order was kept and life was safe; in the one as in the other, the bulk of the population were cruelly oppressed. But then precisely the same influences, which have reformed the government of Egypt, would have sufficed to reform the government of the Sudan; and, bad as the old government of the Sudan was, it now appears mild and beneficent by comparison with the savage tyranny which has succeeded it. Frightful—indeed, almost incredible—are the ravages which war, pestilence, and famine, in their most hideous forms, have wrought during the past ten years in the Upper Valley of the Nile. It is estimated that more than half of the population have perished. The true features of the reign of terror at present established in the Sudan—its cruelty, its bloodthirstiness, and its lust—have lately been revealed to us by an eye-witness of long experience and unquestionable veracity. The reminiscences of Father Ohrwalder, the Austrian priest, who only this year (1892) effected so miraculous an escape from his ten years' captivity in that country, are now before the public. It is impossible for anyone to read the story without a shudder, difficult for an Englishman to read it without a sense of shame.

So far, then, from there being any obligations of honour or humanity to justify the abandonment of the Sudan, honour and humanity alike point to the overthrow of the bloody despotism of the Khalifa as soon as it can be achieved without putting too great a strain on the resources of Egypt. No doubt that time has not yet come. If the Egyptian Government were to be left to itself to-morrow, the recovery of the Sudan is the first thing it would attempt. In that case it would probably fail, and it would certainly involve Egypt in fresh financial difficulties, which might be fatal to her just reviving prosperity. But while an immediate, perhaps even an early, advance upon the Sudan is unadvisable, there can be no doubt that such a movement is not only in the long-run inevitable, but would, if wisely timed and gradually executed, be productive of most desirable results.

For it must not be forgotten that, apart from all questions of sentiment, Egypt has material interests in extending her dominions towards the south, the importance of which cannot be gainsaid. It is not only a question of trade, though the trade in old times was considerable, and would assume large and constantly increasing proportions when order had been restored for a few years. It is a question of security, and the sense of security. There can be no permanent rest for Egypt as long as a reign of explosive barbarism still prevails from Suakin to Darfur, and from Wadi Halfa to Wadelai. The offensive power of that barbarism may wax or wane—it is certainly on the wane at present—but it is always a potential source of incalculable mischiefs. However fireproof a man's own walls, he can hardly be expected to sleep quietly with a fire permanently blazing or smouldering in the neighbouring house.

Moreover, the control of the Nile—at least, up to a point well above the junction of its two great branches—possesses a quite peculiar importance for Egypt. The absence of the old daily reports from Khartum as to the height of the river during the period of its rise is of itself, as any irrigation engineer will tell you, a very serious disadvantage to the country. But there is a graver anxiety behind. The savages of the Sudan may never themselves possess sufficient engineering skill to play tricks with the Nile, but for all that it is an uncomfortable thought that the regular supply of water by the great river, which is to Egypt not a question of convenience and prosperity, but actually of life, must always be exposed to some risk, as long as the upper reaches of that river are not under Egyptian control.

Who can say what might happen, if some day a civilized Power, or a Power commanding civilized skill, were to undertake great engineering works on the Upper Nile, and to divert for the artificial irrigation of that region the water which is essential for the artificial irrigation of Egypt? Such a contingency may seem very remote. I admit that it is very improbable. But before it is laughed out of court, let us consider what would be the feelings of the inhabitants of any ordinary country—our own, for instance—if there were even a remote possibility that the annual rainfall could be materially altered by the action of a foreign Power. Egypt is never likely to feel at ease, the Egyptian Question can never be regarded as even approximately settled, until order is re-established along the Nile Valley to at least a considerable distance beyond Khartum.

And it must not be imagined that the reconquest of the Nile basin will necessarily involve a series of campaigns at all comparable in severity to those which have given the name of the Sudan so ominous a sound in British ears. No doubt the power of the Khalifa will not be upset without at least one severe tussle. It is true that he is now heartily loathed throughout the greater part of the country. His authority is maintained by the great tribe of the Baggara—including the blacks, whom they have enrolled under their standard—and by them alone. But, on the other hand, a well-considered policy of military centralization—for Abdullah El-Taishi is a statesman after his own fashion—has put the Baggara and their black auxiliaries in possession of all the guns and all the ammunition in the whole of the Sudan. Their tyranny over the other tribes has been a cruel and a destructive one, and it has ended in leaving them the only effective military force. At and around Omdurman, which has taken the place of Khartum as the capital of the Sudan, is a powerful army which, though it may be unable to repel attacks upon the more distant provinces of the Khalifa's dominions, would certainly oppose a very formidable resistance to any enemy advancing upon his headquarters.

Fortunately, however, there would be no necessity for Egypt, even if she did attempt the recovery of the Sudan, to grapple at once with the central power of the Khalifa. What would almost certainly be done, on any prudent plan of proceeding, would be, in the first place, to reoccupy Dongola, with or without a simultaneous advance on Abu Hamed. It is quite possible that, with the exercise of a certain amount of diplomacy, the province of Dongola might be recovered without firing a shot. The Danagla and the great warlike tribe of the Jaalin, who lie to the south of them, were the heart and soul of the original rebellion. The Madhi himself was of Dongolese extraction. Wad el Nejumi was a Jaali. But since the leadership of the movement has passed entirely into the hands of the Baggara, and has been abused by them for purposes of self-aggrandisement, the Danagla and the Jaalin are bitterly disaffected. They may hate the Egyptians, but by this time they certainly hate the Baggara more. Were an advance to be made in the first instance only as far as Dongola, it is probable that the inhabitants would content themselves with a mere show of resistance, while it would be a dangerous matter for the Khalifa to send any large number of his myrmidons several hundred miles from their head-quarters, to resist the invading army in a country where, if beaten, they might have the whole population rising against them.

Once established at Dongola, and possibly at Abu Hamed, the Egyptians would not only have recovered a fertile province, which even in old days easily paid its expenses, and which is well capable of supporting an army. They would also occupy inside the Sudan a position certain to form a rallying-point for all the neighbouring tribes that were hostile to the existing tyranny. The prestige of the Khalifa and his Baggara would be greatly impaired by the presence of an Egyptian force within their dominions. Every year there would be more desertion from them to the side of the invaders. And then two alternatives would present themselves to the Khalifa. He must either keep quiet in his own central position and see the outlying provinces fall away from him one after the other, or he must advance to expel the Egyptians from Dongola. If he advanced, he would be likely to meet with the fate which befell Nejumi at Toski. If he did not, it would be for Egypt to choose her own moment for attacking him and striking the decisive blow. She would be in the very advantageous position of being able to postpone her action until she felt absolutely confident that she could afford the necessary force.

Should the policy of recovering the Sudan by the gradual method be ultimately adopted, it would not, with good management, involve any intolerable drain on the finances of Egypt. She need not at any given time undertake more than she could at that time afford. It is, no doubt, improbable that any general would care to attempt the advance on Dongola with a smaller force than four or five thousand men, though, as a matter of fact, so large an army might not be needed. But Dongola once occupied, the large garrison now maintained at Wadi Halfa would not be required at that place; and, though some allowance must be made for the necessity of guarding a longer line of communications, the occupation of Dongola would hardly involve a permament addition of as much as four or five thousand men to the Egyptian army. What additional forces a yet further advance might necessitate, it is vain at this moment, while so many of the circumstances are still conjectural, even to attempt to determine. But, considering the economy of military strength which might be effected in many directions, if the one great danger to Egypt's existence—a hostile barbarous power in the central Sudan—were overcome, it does not seem unreasonable to believe that an army of twenty thousand to twenty-five thousand men would permanently suffice to defend Egypt and the Nile basin, not only up to Khartum, but as far as Fashoda on the White Nile and Sennar on the Blue Nile. And this, together with Kassala, is all that we need at present contemplate, perhaps all that Egypt may ever require. Were she infinitely stronger than she is, great doubt might still be felt as to the wisdom of her seeking to re-establish a straggling empire over the more distant parts of Kordofan, to say nothing of Darfur, the Bahr el Ghazal and Equatoria.

I know that there may be strong opposition to the reconquest of any portion of the Sudan. It will be argued that, if even in old days that country never paid its expenses, Egypt can certainly no longer afford the luxury of so costly a dependency. But the reason why the Sudan was formerly so ruinous to Egypt is, firstly, because she tried to hold too much of it; secondly, because she filled it with a needless swarm of officials, civil and military; and, thirdly, because those officials were utterly bad. If the new Egyptian dominion in the Sudan were to be confined to the Nile basin; if the Government were to content itself with maintaining peace, protecting trade, and keeping a very light hand upon the tribes, left in all their internal affairs to the control of their own chiefs and customs; if, finally, the same securities for honest administration were taken in the Sudan that are now taken in Egypt, there is no reason why the whole of the necessary country should not be governed without loss, and, at the same time, without crushing and irritating the people by excessive taxation. The Sudan could easily support the cost of a moderate garrison, and of a very simple civil administration, while the indirect gain to Egypt from its recovery would be enormous.

There is one possibility bearing on this subject, which, however doubtful and remote, it may be worth while to glance at. British influence is at the present moment predominant at the head waters of the Nile. It may be that, failing to recognise the great importance of Uganda,* we shall abandon our hold on that region. But, if we maintain it, our position there is likely to have important consequences for the future of the Sudan. Immediately to the north of Uganda, and thence onward to the southern limit of the Khalifa's dominions, is a country as rich in first-rate fighting material as any in the world. Tribes of the same character as those who in the Sudanese battalions form the backbone of the Egyptian army, or who, under the name of 'Gehadía,' are so formidable an element in the Khalifa's military strength, will be within the reach and at the disposal of any civilized Power, which has once firmly established itself on the Nyanza Lakes. And, on the other hand, Great Britain is particularly rich in the class of men who can train, control and lead troops, such as these tribes would supply. The negroids of the southern Sudan are a strange mixture of courage and helplessness. Left to themselves, they are powerless. Their backward intelligence, their inability to combine, and their want of leaders have made them at all times an easy prey to the Arab slave raiders, who in mere valour are by no means their superiors. But they will fight splendidly under any leaders who have the gift and habit of command. It has been proved that they make excellent soldiers with British officers at their head. It is certain that, given the choice, they would rather serve anyone than the Baggara Arabs. Some of the best blacks in the Egyptian army are deserters from the other side.

* This passage was written before the recent public controversy on the Uganda Question.

It is thus not impossible that the ultimate fall of the Baggara tyranny may be due to concurrent if not combined pressure from the south and from the north. In that case, the time may not be so far distant, when order will be restored throughout the whole of the Sudan, its childlike races relieved from the oppression under which they have suffered for centuries, and the slave trade finally extinguished in that part of Africa. But, attractive as such a vision is, the possibility of Egypt being assisted, directly or indirectly, in her advance upon the Sudan, by a corresponding movement from the south, is evidently not a thing to be counted upon. And even without such aid she ought ultimately to be able, in the manner already indicated, to recover so much of the Upper Nile Valley as is of absolute importance to her.

I have been looking far ahead. Let me repeat that, fair as I believe the prospects of Egypt in the direction of the Sudan to be, they might easily be spoiled by excessive haste. Time fights on her side. Every year her finances are growing better able to stand the strain of an important military expedition. Every year her army becomes better organized, more consolidated, more confident in itself. Every year the tyranny of the Khalifa becomes more intolerable, while he himself, whose strong personality alone makes the continuance of that tyranny possible, is one step nearer the grave, to which care and debauchery are rapidly hurrying him. Egypt can afford to wait, though, for the sake of humanity, we may hope that she will not have to wait very long.

But, of course, when I speak of Egypt being able to wait, of time fighting on her side, of her army growing stronger as the years go on, I mean the army as at present constituted, the army with British direction at its head, and with a certain number of British officers. The presence of the British officers has been the essence of the reorganization of the Egyptian army so far. Were that influence to disappear, I do not say the army would collapse (though I have my own opinions on the subject), but I do say that it would be absolutely impossible to predict anything with regard to it. You could no longer make any calculation as to the future, based upon the immediate past, because you would have struck out of the calculation precisely that factor which in the immediate past has been the most important.

I am not one of those who hold that everything that has been done in Egypt since 1882 is due to Englishmen. I am the first to recognise the very important part which has been played in the revival of the country by natives and other Europeans. I do not believe that the indefinite continuance of British control in its present form is essential to the ultimate welfare of Egypt. I see great improvement in the self-governing capacity of its inhabitants, and I look forward to still greater improvement in the same direction. But optimist and Egyptian as I am, I cannot conceal from myself or from my readers, that the command of the army is one of the last things that it will be safe to hand over entirely to native management. No doubt the quality of the native officers is much improved. As juniors they are often excellent, and even in the command of regiments some of them have proved a success. But can anyone say that, taken all round, they as yet possess that initiative and that sense of responsibility which would justify their being entrusted with the exclusive direction of affairs? Have they sufficient confidence in themselves, or would they, unsupported, inspire sufficient confidence in their men? I do not believe that any honest man, acquainted with the facts, could answer these questions with a confident affirmative.

It was a fatal flaw in the Wolff Convention, which in other respects had many good points, that it bargained for the cessation of British control over the Egyptian army within two years after the withdrawal of the British troops from the country. The only thing to have made the withdrawal of the British troops reasonably safe would have been to maintain for a long period the British direction of the native troops. If our dealing with the army has been perhaps the most conspicuous success in the whole of our labours for the reorganization of Egypt, it must be remembered that this is the field in which we have had the most absolutely free hand. Nobody thought of interfering with Sir Evelyn Wood or Sir Francis Grenfell. It is not probable that anyone will interfere with the new Sirdar, General Kitchener, who succeeded Sir Francis in April, 1892. But the more absolute British control has been, the more serious are likely to be the consequences of its withdrawal.

Do not let me be supposed to suggest that we must abandon the hope of ultimately training a sufficient number of natives competent to fill positions of command. Quite the contrary. In making soldiers we have had a splendid success. To crown the work, we ought to end by making officers. Nor can there be the smallest doubt that the British heads of the army recognise this duty and do their best to accomplish it. But it is another question whether they are quite bold enough in making the necessary experiments. If the native officers are still wanting in initiative and self-reliance, there seems nothing for it but to multiply their opportunities of practising these qualities. To do so would probably lead to some failures, and there certainly was a time when affairs were so critical that nothing whatever could be risked. But that is not quite the case to-day. The present, if any, is the moment for trying gradually to increase the number of native officers in responsible positions. When the army was first formed, there were twenty-seven British officers to six thousand men. To-day there are seventy-six British officers to twelve thousand five hundred men, and there are about forty British non-commissioned officers besides. The proportion, instead of diminishing, has increased. The heavy duties, suddenly thrown on the young army at a most critical moment, explain and justify that increase; but it certainly would seem that, in the interests of both British and Egyptians, it is not desirable to go much further in this direction.

I have referred already to the existence of a certain covert discontent among the native officers, on account of the slowness of promotion in the higher grades. And this is perfectly natural. The commanders of companies to-day include a great number of young men who have come into the army since 1882, having passed through the Military School. The whole period of their service has been under the English system. We have given them a thorough training, and, though we may know that many of them suffer from some want of character which unfits them for further advancement, it cannot be supposed that they can see with equanimity a number of young English subalterns passed over their heads, to occupy at once the positions of majors. Without taking at all an alarmist view of such grumbling—for, after all, what army in the world is not full of complaints about the slowness of promotion ?—it is evidently desirable to remove any reasonable grounds for it which may exist. From every point of view it would be a wise policy to increase as soon as possible the number of native officers advanced to the higher posts, always provided that British control at headquarters remains strong enough to ensure promotions being made rigidly by merit, as without this control they certainly would not be.

There is another reason, of more importance, perhaps, than the fear of native discontent, which should weigh against the multiplication of British officers in the army. Here, as elsewhere in the Egyptian service, what is essential to the success of British influence, is not the quantity of Englishmen, but their quality. There is no point in the whole wide sphere of our power where it is more important to select most carefully the Englishmen whom you employ. And, of course, if you are going in for picked men, you handicap yourself by demanding large numbers.

The Egyptian army has in the course of years necessarily lost many of those Englishmen who were in it from the beginning, who had taken part in the work of its creation, and who had gained an invaluable experience of the country and the people. Fortunately, there are some of that class remaining, such as the new

Sirdar himself, the Adjutant-General, Colonel Rundle, the Military Governor of the Frontier, Colonel Wodehouse, and several other excellent officers. But there are also a number of young and as yet inexperienced men, and, what is perhaps more serious, there is some danger of a considerable substitution of new for old officers at an early date. There is no reason to doubt that the former will in time be as much improved as their predecessors by the wonderful opportunities which the Egyptian service affords for the development of the best qualities of English soldiers. But it is not a good plan to introduce too many new hands at once, especially as it is quite impossible that they should possess for some time to come the same influence over the native officers as the old men whom they replace and whom the natives have been accustomed to obey and to look up to from the first.

Nothing, indeed, is more to be deprecated than a too frequent change of the British officers in the army. It is reported that the British War Office, impressed by the special efficacy of the Egytian service for turning boys into men, desires to pass a large number of young officers through that service as quickly as possible. This plan may be very good for the English army, but it is not at all good for the Egyptian. Egypt is a very peculiar country, which it takes some time to know. Arabic is a very difficult language, which even with a serious effort—not always, I fear, made by Englishmen—it takes several years to learn. Yet a knowledge of the peculiarities of the country and people, and a good command of the colloquial language, are most important elements in the utility of Englishmen, and above all of English officers in Egypt. The men who have acquired these qualities are much too valuable to be lightly dispensed with. Of course, no one expects English officers to stay in the Egyptian army all their lives. But neither is it desirable that their passage through it should be a very hurried one. Moreover, that is not at all the desire of the officers themselves. As a rule, they grow very interested in the country and the work, and the more interested they are, the greater is their value. They like to stay, and, where they have proved themselves efficient, they should be allowed to do so as long as possible. For the maintenance of the authority of British officers, not by virtue of their numbers, but of their character, capacity, and experience, will remain, for some time longer, essential to the well-being of the army, and to the safety and repose of Egypt.

CHAPTER VIII.

THE RACE AGAINST BANKRUPTCY.

FEW people realize the fascination of Finance. This is the more remarkable because, in a way, there is nothing which men love to talk about so much as money. How many thousands A has got, in what venture B made his fortune, who lost most heavily in that last panic on the Stock Exchange—such topics possess a perennial attraction in the club no less than in the market-place. But when it comes to be a question of the resources, not of an individual, but of a society, a municipality, or a state, the subject, except among experts, is generally voted dull. The human interest, somehow, seems to be wanting. In reality it is not wanting, only it does not lie on the surface. It needs to be extricated from the superincumbent mass of repellent details, from columns of figures about debts and sinking funds, exports and imports, rates and incidence of taxation, and, in the special case of Egypt, from the artificial and complicated restrictions under which the business of the Treasury has to be carried on.

And yet, if only they could find a skilful exponent, the financial vicissitudes of Egypt during the past twenty or thirty years would make a stirring tale. Some day, it is to be hoped, a man will be found bold enough, and with patience enough, to relate that tale with all its incidents, which are so dramatic, so humorous and so full of surprise. And if he does his work well, the book will read like a novel. It would be vain to hope that this element of romance will not disappear in the present necessarily brief and business-like résumé. But I can at least indicate where the treasure lies for him who has time and energy to work the mine.

The story naturally presents itself in the form of a trilogy: Prodigality, Ruin, Recuperation. And each successive stage of the threefold drama has been remarkable for its intensity. Never was there a wilder career of public extravagance than that of Egypt under Ismail Pasha. Rarely has the inevitable retribution been so sudden, so thorough, fraught with such widespread misery, resisted by such extraordinary shifts, or productive of such momentous consequences. And even more rarely, perhaps, has the recovery from utter collapse been so unexpected or so signal.

But there is another attraction about Egyptian Finance, deeper and more permanent than the sensational ups and downs which characterize its recent history. I mean the closeness of its relation to human life. The men who control the Exchequer in more highly developed countries are, of course, well aware that it is not with statistics, and balance-sheets, not with the mere paraphernalia of Finance that they are really dealing, but with the well-being, the comfort, the happiness, even the morality, of their fellow-citizens. This is the great fact underlying Finance, a fact more or less important according to the special circumstances of each community, yet of vast importance even for those nations, among whom, as in the United States, individual wealth is comparatively independent of the action of the State. But nowhere in the world is the bearing of public economy upon private welfare either more direct or more evident than in Egypt. In other countries it is possible to lose sight of it. In Egypt it is always before one's eyes. The man must be a fool indeed, who, sitting in the Finance Office at Cairo, in any position of command, is not constantly reflecting upon the condition and needs of the people. Can he afford to lighten taxation in such and such a province, where agriculture is staggering under an intolerable burden? Can he somehow squeeze out money sufficient to make a canal in one district, where irrigation is inadequate, or to drain another district, where irrigation is excessive? Will he be allowed to add to the 'administrative expenditure' the sum necessary to sanitate Cairo, or to fill up the stagnant pools, which breed fever in so many of the country towns and villages? What funds can be spared for the construction of railways, which shall bring the rich produce of remote corners of the country to a profitable market? Is it yet safe, from the financial point of view, to extend primary education, or to establish Courts of Summary Justice in every locality? In what order are all these clamorous and competing needs to be approached and grappled with?

Such problems are, no doubt, familiar to all who have had experience of public work in India. The attraction they possess must be felt, wherever a backward country is under the control of civilized administrators. But nowhere, it may safely be asserted, are questions of this sort more numerous, more urgent, or more absorbing, than in the Valley of the Nile. In Egypt the State is everything. Upon it, and its capacity to help them, depend the very food and health of the people. Prosperity—nay, decent existence—is impossible with a disordered Treasury.

The kind of work which I have been describing is different indeed from what in many quarters is still regarded as the great preoccupation of Egyptian financiers. How long, I wonder, shall we have to struggle against the hardy anachronism, that the interest of Egyptian Finance centres in the Debt, and that the financial authorities of the country are the mere bailiffs of the bond-holders? As a matter of fact, now that it has once been established that the resources of Egypt, under present management, can bear the interest of the Debt, at its present rate, the last people whom an Egyptian Finance Minister, nominal or virtual, need trouble his head about, are these very bond-holders. The creditors of Egypt, he is well aware, are safe enough. Except when an occasion presents itself to reduce the interest by the legitimate method of conversion, the Debt need no longer have a foremost place in his mind. It is a great unpleasant fact, but it is far from being a subject of constant solicitude. Even the Commissioners of the Caisse, who only exist to protect the creditors, and who from time to time, to justify their existence, get up a little fuss about some supposed danger to interests, which in their hearts they know to be perfectly secure—even the Commissioners of the Caisse, I say, are more occupied nowadays with projects for employing their Reserve Fund in developing the wealth of the country than with needless anxieties about the coupon. And in their new capacity, it is only fair to add, they have acquired a new usefulness, and have sometimes shown a wise and far-sighted liberality. There was a time, no doubt, when the Debt was everything, when the qualities most needed in the financial administration of Egypt were the gifts and experience of a banker. But at present the head of that administration does not need to be a banker. It is not essential that he should know much about the Stock Market. What he does need to be is a political economist. What it is essential that he should know about is the economic and social condition of the people.

And for a political economist I can imagine no experience more interesting or more instructive than that of practical contact with Egyptian affairs. The working of great economic laws, which is apt to be obscured by the complexities of an advanced civilization, may here, under simpler conditions and in a limited area, be clearly traced by any intelligent observer. Economic causes produce their theoretically correct results with a swiftness and an exactitude not easily visible in other lands. The removal of a burdensome tax, whether paid in money or in labour, is promptly justified by an increase in the productive and the purchasing power of the people. A growth of exports, resulting from the heightened fertility of the land, is followed with remarkable precision by a corresponding growth of imports. The very nature of the goods imported affords unmistakable evidence as to what class of the population has benefited by the increase of production. Or, to take an illustration of a different kind, the value of a particular outlay upon irrigation may be calculated within a very few years in terms of sugar or of cotton.

And this is true, not of economic doctrines only, but of the deeper laws, which connect economics with politics and with morality. Of these laws also the recent history of Egypt affords the most impressive illustration. Nowhere does the condition of the people respond more rapidly to good or to bad government. No country is easier to ruin by misrule. The tremendous financial smash which marked the closing years of the reign of Ismail Pasha was the result of a disregard, not only of every economic, but of every moral principle.

Ismail himself is as fine a type of the spendthrift as can well be found, whether in history or fiction. No equally reckless prodigal ever possessed equally unlimited control of equally vast resources. He came to the throne at a moment when there seemed no limit to the potential wealth of Egypt. The whole land was his to do what he liked with. All the world was ready to lend him money to develop it. Moreover, Ismail combined in himself every quality, good as well as bad, that goes to make the ideal squanderer. Luxurious, voluptuous, ambitious, fond of display, devoid of principle, he was, at the same time, full of the most magnificent schemes for the material improvement of the country. Over and above the millions wasted in entertainments, in largess, in sensuality, in the erection of numerous palaces—structurally as rotten as they are æsthetically abominable—he threw away yet other millions upon a vast scheme of agricultural development, started with inadequate knowledge at inordinate cost.

When with the close of the American War the fall in the price of cotton threatened to sweep away the foundations of Egypt's sudden but precarious prosperity, Ismail conceived the notion of recouping the loss by the production of sugar on an enormous scale. The idea was in itself a good one. Sugar has already turned out a very valuable crop in Egypt, and we are likely to hear more of it in the future. But undertaken, as Ismail undertook it, the new form of cultivation proved, at the outset, a gigantic failure. A whole countryside—part, by the way, of the vast estates which the Khedive confiscated from their rightful owners and cultivated by forced labour—was turned into a sugar plantation. Twelve large factories were started, and supplied with the most costly machinery, much of which was never used. The whole system was wasteful and unintelligent to a degree which is past belief. But the crimes and follies, colossal as the Pyramids or the Temple of Karnak, which belong to that epoch of financial madness, need not detain us here. It is their consequences, and the means by which Egypt is at length escaping from those consequences, with which we have to deal.

And the consequences were appalling. When Ismail came to the throne in 1863, the debt of Egypt was only a little over three millions. The annual revenue of the country was amply sufficient to meet all needful expenditure, yet by the end of 1876 the debt had risen to eighty-nine millions. It had been increased nearly thirtyfold in thirteen years. A country of six million inhabitants and only five million acres of cultivated land had added to its burdens at the rate of seven millions a year. And at the same time the taxation of the land had been increased by something like 50 per cent. There is nothing in the financial history of any country, from the remotest ages to the present time, to equal this carnival of extravagance and oppression.

No doubt it would be unfair to set it all down to the account of the Khedive himself. Ismail has long since fallen beyond all hope of recovery. Once an omnipotent despot, filling a conspicuous place in the eyes of mankind, he is now a despised suppliant, and indeed virtually a captive, at the Court of Constantinople. It is impossible to pity him, even in this depth of degradation. But let me not make him out worse than he was. If the personality of Ismail was an essential factor in the ruin of his country, it needed a whole series of unfortunate conditions to render that personality as pernicious as it actually became. It needed a nation of submissive slaves, not only bereft of any vestige of liberal institutions, but devoid of the slightest spark of the spirit of liberty. It needed a bureaucracy, which it would have been hard to equal for its combination of cowardice and corruption. It needed the whole gang of swindlers—mostly European—by whom Ismail was surrounded, and to whom, with his phenomenal incapacity to make a good bargain—strange characteristic in a man so radically dishonest—he fell an easy prey.

Too much importance is commonly attached, in accounting for the financial disasters of Egypt, to the amount of Ismail's borrowings on the Stock Markets of Europe. It is true that his methods of raising money in that quarter showed a progressive degeneration. His first loan—and it was one of moderate proportions—was brought out through a house of high credit and reputation, and its terms, though stiff, were very far from being exorbitant. As his demands increased, he had recourse to agents of a more speculative character. The sums actually received for every £100 of nominal capital rapidly diminished. Of the great £32,000,000 loan of 1873, for instance, only £20,700,000 reached the Egyptian Treasury. But these transactions, though extravagant, were not dishonest or hopelessly insane. The same cannot be said of the multitude of short loans which, renewed at ever-increasing rates, and swollen at each renewal by arrears of interest, resulted in the accumulation of an enormous Floating Debt, the total of which was treble or quadruple the amount of the original advances.

Nor was this the whole extent of the mischief. The money actually realized was often not Ismail's to spend, even upon his own extravagances. Not less than £3,350,000 had to be paid, under an award of the Emperor Napoleon III., to the Suez Canal Company, as an indemnity for modifications or breaches of the original concession. The total amount sunk by the Egyptian Government in the Canal is given in Mr. Cave's Report of March, 1876, as £16,075,000; yet Egypt has no longer any share whatever in the vast profits of that undertaking. Reference has already been made to the large sums required to meet preposterous claims brought against Ismail by foreign adventurers, to whom his speculativeness, his trickery, and his unbusiness-like character gave ample opportunities for extortion. And even when he could afford to spend some of his borrowings upon himself or upon the country, he always contrived to get the least possible value for his money. The contracts entered into by the 'Daira'* or the Government were monuments of wastefulness. The prices paid in hard cash for material obtained from Europe were on the scale of those at which a fashionable tailor supplies goods upon credit to young men of large prospects but no immediate income. Attempts have often been made to calculate what proportion of the debt contracted by Ismail was really spent for the good of the country. In view of the absolute chaos of the accounts previous to 1876, such calculations are wholly futile. One thing alone is certain: that the proportion was incredibly small. I doubt myself whether the portion of Ismail's loans devoted to works of permanent utility—always excluding the Suez Canal—was equal to 10 per cent. of the amount of debt which he contracted.

And all this time, be it remembered, while money was being raised in these enormous quantities by profligate borrowings at home and abroad, the people were subjected to the most cruel exactions. Not only was the rate of taxation increased, but no regard was paid to the nominal rate in the sums actually extorted. This is, after all, by far the worst feature in that era of frightful misgovernment. But bad as the system was, it had one saving merit. It was so bad that it wrought its own cure by making foreign intervention inevitable. That intervention, no doubt, perpetuated the Debt, but it also, in the long-run, put an end to the habitual plunder of the people by their own rulers. The condition of Egypt to-day, even with the burden of more than £100,000,000

* The 'Daira' was the Khedive's private estate, ultimately surrendered by him to one section of his creditors.

tied tightly on her back, is better than it would have been, had she been able to repudiate every penny of these millions, but had remained, at the same time, subject to the reign of official tyranny and extortion, which preceded the establishment of European control.

But it took a long time to place the Debt of Egypt upon an endurable footing, and meanwhile the country was destined to meet with many fresh disasters. The first general settlement of all its liabilities, which was effected on the proposals of Mr. Goschen and M. Joubert in November, 1876, was of very short duration. The arrangement, indeed, was a reasonable one upon the facts as stated to those gentlemen, but unfortunately the statement was wholly misleading. Whether or not the accounts were deliberately cooked, they certainly did not reveal the true position of things.

Indeed, that position remained a mystery until the Khedive in April, 1878, after a long struggle, consented to the appointment of a Commission, armed with full powers to examine, not only the revenue, but the whole administrative system. As soon as this Commission had finished its elaborate and searching inquiry, it became evident that a reduction of the interest on the Debt was inevitable if the work of government was not to come to an absolute standstill. That reduction was, after a series of desperate manœuvres on the part of the Khedive, ending only with his deposition, carried into effect by the Law of Liquidation of July, 1880. The effect of this law was to wipe out the Floating Debt, to consolidate the obligations of Egypt in a few great loans, and to fix the interest at a rate, which under normal conditions it was possible, though still very difficult, for the country to pay. But in the interval of nearly four years between the Goschen settlement and the Law of Liquidation, the liabilities of Egypt had been increased by something like ten millions, owing to the frantic expedients to which Ismail, in the death-agony of his power, had been forced to have recourse.

Ismail's financial policy was never more reckless than in the latter days of his reign. The short loans constantly prolonged on ruinous terms, the anticipation of revenue, the staving off of urgent creditors by the delivery of depreciated securities, all destined to be ultimately paid off at par (in one instance a debt of £72,000 was redeemed by the surrender of not less than £230,000 of Unified Stock), such and suchlike follies succeeded one another thick and fast during the disastrous years 1877, 1878, 1879. It was certainly high time that this insensate mismanagement should, by whatever means, be brought to an end.

Immediately after the passing of the Law of Liquidation the Debt of Egypt was composed as follows:

Privileged Debt	£22,629,800
Unified Debt	58,043,326
Daira Loan	9,512,804
Domains Loan	8,500,000
Total	£98,685,930

The rate of interest was 5 per cent. on the Privileged and the Domains Loans, and 4 per cent. upon the Unified and the Daira, but the Daira was entitled to a further 1 per cent. contingent upon certain circumstances which have, however, never arisen. Leaving out of account the interest on the Daira and Domains Loans—which would, it was hoped, be defrayed by the yield of the respective estates—the charge upon the revenues of Egypt, for the service of the Debt, amounted to £E3,410,000* per annum (£E1,157,000 for the Privileged, and £E2,253,000 for the Unified). Adding to these figures the tribute due to Turkey, the interest on the Suez Canal shares bought by England, the Mukabala (an annual payment to certain land-holders, whose

* It is one of the pleasures in the life of an Egyptian financier that, in addition to the other complexities of his business, he has to be constantly dealing with two different pounds—the pound sterling and the pound Egyptian, which latter is, roughly speaking, equal to £1 0s. 6d. The Egyptian pound is divided into 100 piastres, 97½ of which are the exact equivalent of the English pound. I shall always designate Egyptian pounds by the sign '£E,' leaving to '£' its usual significance as indicating the pound sterling. The amount of the capital of the Debt is always stated in pounds sterling.

taxes had been anticipated by Ismail), and a few minor charges, the total encumbrances of the country fell only just short of £E4,500,000, not reckoning the sums which might be necessary to make up the deficits of the Domains and the Daira. As the whole revenue of Egypt at that time amounted to little more than nine millions—in 1881, a very prosperous year, it was £E9,229,000—it will be seen that just about half the receipts were, under the most favourable circumstances, diverted to the discharge of the liabilities, which had been piled up during the preceding fifteen years.

The burden was enormous, but, heavy as it was, it had only been rendered bearable at all by heavy sacrifices on the part of the bond-holders. The 4 per cent. interest on the Unified Debt was vastly lower than any of the various rates at which the loans amalgamated into that debt had originally been borrowed, and was only two-thirds of the rate assigned to it in the settlement of Mr. Goschen and M. Joubert. In many quarters it is still the fashion to speak of the Egyptian Bond-holders as if it was they who were the bloodsuckers that ruined the country. But it is high time to abandon such pernicious nonsense. The ultimate holders of the bonds are the last people in the world who can be held responsible for the misfortunes of Egypt, while the real criminals are well out of reach of all the misdirected abuse which is constantly poured forth upon this subject.

The arrangement embodied in the Law of Liquidation, the work of able and conscientious men who had made themselves masters of the subject, was based on just and reasonable ideas, but it left no margin for contingencies. We can see now, looking back upon it, that it was a mistake to make at that time any immediate provision for a Sinking Fund. The intention was excellent, but Egypt was not yet in a position in which she could afford to begin reducing her liabilities. It would have been wiser to rest content, for the moment, with putting a stop to the continual increase of them, and to devote all the revenue that remained, after the payment of the interest, to the administrative needs of the country, which had been shockingly neglected during the preceding years of desperate embarrassment. It was good —indeed, it was essential—to check administrative waste; but the Law of Liquidation went further. It not only suppressed the extravagances, but it trenched upon the necessaries of government. By reducing too rapidly the expenditure on the public services, and especially on the army, it contributed in some degree to that revolutionary movement which was destined to upset the financial equilibrium of Egypt almost as soon as it had been re-established.

During the brief period of tranquillity and better government which intervened between the Law of Liquidation and the rise of Arabi, the Debt was reduced by something like a million. But the revolution and its consequences, more especially the great fire of Alexandria and the disastrous events in the Sudan, added to the burdens of the country an amount nearly ten times as great as that by which they had been diminished during this brief but delusive period of revival. As soon as order had been restored, the Finance Ministry, under the able guidance of Sir Auckland Colvin, and subsequently of Sir Edgar Vincent, made heroic efforts to grapple with an impossible situation. The most rigid economy was enforced from end to end of the administration, and great ingenuity was displayed in developing all possible sources of revenue by every means compatible with honesty and sound economic principle.

In this painful struggle the successive Financial Advisers derived invaluable assistance from Blum Pasha, at that time Under Secretary of State for Finance. Blum Pasha, who is of Jewish extraction and Austrian nationality, left Egypt in 1890 to fill an important place in the financial world of Vienna; but during the fourteen years of his presence at the Finance Ministry in Cairo, and especially during the period of great perplexity immediately succeeding the revolution, he rendered memorable services to the country. His industry, patience, and tact, coupled with a natural resourcefulness in matters of finance, which had been developed by his training and experience as a banker, were qualities admirably suited to the situation. It is one of the greatest advantages, which Egypt has in recent times derived from the direction of her policy by a civilized power, that the country has been able for the first time to make full use of men of this character. The Government of Ismail was not wanting in European experts, whether in finance or in other branches of administration, at the very time when it came so hopelessly to grief. But its wisest and most capable employés were without influence. Their counsels were disregarded and their capacity rendered useless. It is not enough to have well-qualified Europeans in the Egyptian service in order to keep things straight. It is necessary that there should be some power behind them to give effectiveness to their advice.

But, despite all the skill devoted to finance during the troublous years 1883 and 1884, it was perfectly evident to everybody that no amount of good management could pull Egypt through without some fresh external assistance. A new loan had become inevitable, if the question of the Alexandria Indemnities was to be settled, or the debts due to the rebellion and to the war in the Sudan cleared off. Without such a loan the Treasury would soon be absolutely empty, and the means of paying for the everyday work of government would not be forthcoming. And if it was necessary to raise a new loan, it was no less necessary to readjust the existing distribution of the revenue between the government and the bond-holders. During the year 1883, the revenues assigned to the Debt produced so large a surplus that, after full payment of the interest, it was found possible to redeem £800,000 of the capital. But in the very same year the revenues assigned to administration fell short of the expenditure by more than £E1,600,00c. It was clearly ruinous to pay off a funded debt, bearing only 4 or 5 per cent. interest, if while so doing the Government was obliged to borrow on short loans at much higher rates. In addition to the new loan, therefore, the circumstances imperatively demanded some change in the Law of Liquidation.

To be able to modify the Law of Liquidation, the Egyptian Government required the consent of the Great Powers. To raise a new loan, it required the consent, not only of the Great Powers, but of Turkey. It was in order to bring about an agreement between all these parties that the London Conference met in the summer of 1884. The discussions of that body resulted in nothing; but the minute examination of the resources of Egypt, which was made by the financial delegates attached to the Conference, was not wasted labour. There was an English proposal for the re-establishment of financial equilibrium, based on a report of great ability drawn up by Sir Evelyn Baring, Sir Reginald Welby, Sir Rivers Wilson, and Sir James Carmichael. There was a French counter-proposal, not less able, though animated by a less liberal spirit, the author of which was M. de Blignières. These proposals, together with those made by Lord Northbrook after his short visit to Egypt in the autumn of the same year, served as the basis of the negotiations, which took place between the Powers in the winter of 1884-85, and which ended in the conclusion of the London Convention in March, 1885.

That Convention is the organic law of Egyptian Finance to the present day. The system established by it, though not without faults, was a great improvement on the Law of Liquidation, and for the first time rendered the financial salvation of the country possible. Indeed, the wonder is how, in view of the indifference of most of the Powers to the welfare of Egypt, and the bitter annoyance of France at our presence in that country, the English Government ever succeeded in inducing all the parties concerned to agree to so reasonable an arrangement. It would probably never have done so, had it not been for the interest felt by the Powers, and especially by France, in the payment of the Alexandria Indemnities. Great Britain was in a perfectly inexpugnable position in refusing to settle those claims unless all other outstanding liabilities of the Egyptian Government were provided for at the same time. It is to the lever given to the British Government by the question of the Indemnities, and to the concession made to Germany and Russia in allowing each of them to appoint a Commissioner to the Caisse de la Dette (which henceforth consisted of six instead of four members), that the Egyptian Government owes the London Convention.

There are two great points to be noticed about that important agreement.* In the first place, it empowered Egypt to raise nine millions sterling by means of a loan guaranteed by all the Powers, and to make the annuity of £315,000, set aside for the service of this loan, a first charge upon the revenues assigned to the Debt. With the security afforded by the guarantee of the Powers, the new money was obtained on excellent terms. The nominal amount borrowed in order to obtain £9,000,000 of ready money was only £9,424,000, and as the interest did not exceed 3 per cent., the annuity of £315,000 not only sufficed to cover that interest, but left a substantial sum over for the reduction of the capital.

To obtain nine millions in cash for an annual payment of £315,000 was something quite unheard of in the history of Egyptian Finance. No fairy godmother ever produced a richer or more unexpected gift. The sum in question not only paid the Alexandria Indemnities, and wiped out the deficits of the years 1882-85, but provided a round million for new works of irrigation.

The history of that million is one of the most marvellous chapters even in the romantic history of Egyptian Finance. The old saw recommends 'a hair of the dog that bit you.' The million in question was, to all appearances, a remedy quite as illogical. That a country which had been ruined by excessive expenditure and reckless borrowing should borrow once more in the very moment of insolvency, and should do so, not merely to clear off existing liabilities, but actually to plunge into fresh expenditure, seemed contrary to every maxim

* See note to p. 56.

of financial prudence. There were not wanting critics of the highest repute, who were vehemently hostile to the proposed new outlay. And in principle they were entirely right. Not in one case out of a hundred would such a policy have been justifiable. But Egypt, the land of exceptions, supplied just that hundredth case. It was life and death to her to put the great central works, upon which the irrigation of the Delta depended, into proper working order. To do so required a capital expenditure which was beyond the means of the annual budget of the Public Works Ministry. This extra million just provided the necessary capital. It saved the irrigation system, and with it the finances of Egypt. It has brought in cent. per cent. Of all the extraordinary contrasts of which the history, and especially the financial history, of Egypt is so full, there is none more striking than that of the countless millions borrowed by Ismail and this single million for irrigation; the former raised with ease in the heyday of fortune, the latter only obtained after a hard struggle when Egypt's power of borrowing seemed almost extinct; the former squandered with so little benefit to the country, the latter of such incalculable value in the re-establishment of her prosperity.

Less easy to explain than the Guaranteed Loan, but not less necessary to understand, for anyone who wishes to grasp the problem of Egyptian finance in its present form, is the new principle which the London Convention introduced in the distribution of the revenues of Egypt between the Caisse and the Government—or, to put it in another way, between the service of the Debt and the expenses of administration. I do not now refer to the provisional relief afforded by allowing Egypt to make a small deduction from the interest on her Debt during the years 1885 and 1886.* That arrangement was a compromise between the views of England, who was favourable to a permanent reduction of the interest, and those of France, who, faithful to her traditional policy of championing the bond-holders, was opposed to any re-

* See p. 109.

duction whatever. But the Convention contained another readjustment between the creditors and the Government, which was of far greater and of permanent effect.

It was the fault of the Law of Liquidation that it made an ogre of the Funded Debt. In their natural but exaggerated desire to reduce the enormous liabilities of the country, the framers of that law had left an inadequate provision for the immediate needs of the Government. The Convention of London remedied this mistake in an ingenious manner. It did not take away any portion of the revenues assigned to the service of the Debt, so that the security of the bond-holders was in no way diminished. But recognising that the revenues, which had been reserved to pay the expenses of administration, were insufficient, it provided that, within clearly defined limits, the Government should have a claim upon the funds received by the Caisse, as soon as the interest on the Debt had been satisfied. A certain scale of administrative expenditure was 'authorized,' and the Caisse, after paying the coupon, was to make good to the Government any deficiency on this 'authorized' expenditure. Moreover, if, after making good that deficiency, the Caisse should still have a surplus, this surplus was to be divided equally between the Caisse and the Government, one half going to the reduction of the Debt, and the other half to any object which the Government might choose.

This sounds, and is, very complicated. But it can be explained by a concrete illustration. To simplify matters, I will not cite the Budget of any particular year, but will draw up, in round figures, an imaginary Budget, fairly representative of the actual situation in an average year, or, rather, in what was an average year before the recent great development of Egyptian prosperity. The total revenues of Egypt are, let us suppose, £E9,500,000, of which £E4,000,000 go to the Caisse, and £E,5,500,000 to the Government. But, whereas the Caisse, with receipts amounting to £E4,000,000, requires only £E3,500,000 to pay the interest on the Debt, the Government, with receipts of £E5,500,000, is, let us say, obliged to spend, for purposes of administration (including the payment of the tribute to Turkey and of the interest on the Suez Canal shares) £E5,850,000. The total expenses of the country are thus £E9,350,000, leaving a surplus of £E150,000. But the Government is in a deficit of £E350,000, while the Caisse is £E500,000 to the good.

How does the London Convention provide for this deficit of the Government? That all depends upon the question to what extent the £E5,850,000, which the Government has actually spent, come within the description of 'authorized' expenditure. The Convention of London accorded to the Government a fixed annual sum of £E5,237,000, plus one or two variable sums, depending upon the financial results of each particular year, and subsequent agreements between the Powers have further augmented the 'authorized' figure by allowing certain novel items to be added to it. In 1891, for instance, the total 'authorized' expenditure amounted to no less than £E6,071,000. Now, up to the limit of this 'authorized' expenditure the Government is entitled to draw upon the money remaining in the hands of the Caisse after payment of the interest. But whatever is beyond that limit, it must defray, if it can, out of its half-share of any surplus which the Caisse may still have after making good the deficit on the 'authorized' expenditure.

Let us apply these principles to our imaginary case. The actual expenditure of the Government, in that case, has exceeded the receipts by £E350,000, but we will suppose that the 'authorized' expenditure has exceeded them by no more than £E300,000. It is only £E300,000, therefore, that the Government can demand from the Caisse. When this sum has been transferred, the Government is still £E50,000 to the bad, and the Caisse has still £E200,000 in hand.

Now comes the last stage in these complicated proceedings. The £E200,000 still remaining to the Caisse have to be equally divided between it and the Government. With the £E100,000 which the Government obtains by that division it clears off the difference of £E50,000 still existing between its means and its outgoings, while the remaining £E50,000 are its own to do what it likes with. The £E100,000 retained by the Caisse go to the reduction of the Debt.

This is a typical Egyptian Budget for any year since 1885. In my imaginary illustration the Government is able, by one means or another, to cover all its expenditure. But it is easily conceivable, though the case has never arisen since the Convention of London, that the Budget of the State as a whole should show a surplus, and the Government, nevertheless, come out with a balance on the wrong side. To illustrate this possibility it is only necessary to suppose that in the above calculation, everything else remaining unchanged, no more than £E5,600,000 of the £E5,850,000 spent by the Government should fall within the category of 'authorized' expenditure. In that case the Government could not draw upon the Caisse for more than £E100,000. After this operation it would find itself in a deficit of £E250,000, while the Caisse surplus would be £E400,000. That surplus would, it is true, have to be divided equally between the Caisse and the Government; but the £E200,000 which the latter would derive from such a division would still leave it, at the end of the account, £E50,000 short, while the Caisse would be left with £E200,000 for the reduction of the Debt. Thus, it is even now possible, though far less likely than under the unmodified Law of Liquidation, that the Egyptian Government should be in a deficit while the country really had a surplus.

As I have said, the case just supposed has not arisen since 1885, nor would the consequences nowadays, if it did once in a way arise, be very serious. For by this time the Government has, out of the ultimate surpluses of preceding years, accumulated a sufficient Reserve Fund of its own—as distinguished from the Reserve Fund of the Caisse, which I shall explain presently—to meet any such occasional deficit. It is therefore, under normal conditions, in no kind of danger. But, on the other hand, it is exposed to one constant and grave inconvenience. There is an unavoidable, and I may add a wholesome, tendency on the part of the Administration to exceed its 'authorized' expenditure. What was 'authorized' in 1885 was the absolute minimum necessary to carry on the business of the State. That minimum has been augmented on several occasions by the consent of the Powers, but it has not been augmented in proportion to the growing needs of a progressive Government. Now that the resources of the country are so greatly on the increase, its rulers are naturally and rightly desirous to spend more money on many objects of public utility, which were necessarily starved in the moment of extreme embarrassment when the 'authorized' expenditure was fixed. In the figure of £E5,237,000 originally 'authorized,' only £E70,000 was allowed for Education, while the actual expenditure on Education last year was £E91,000, and was still not enough. The sum allowed for Justice was £E324,000, while the actual cost of Justice last year was £E364,000. This, again, is an item which ought to be still further increased if many useful reforms are to have a fair chance. It would be easy to multiply instances, but I have said enough to illustrate the general tendency. In the year 1891 the total expenditure of the Government exceeded the 'authorized' figure by not less than £E141,000, and it is inevitable that this excess should be still greater in the future if the administration is to be carried on in a liberal spirit, and in accordance with the growing needs and the increased resources of the country.

But for every pound by which the Government exceeds the 'authorized' expenditure, it has to raise two pounds in taxation. Let this fact be well grasped, for it is a central principle of Egyptian Finance. The reason will be at once apparent to any reader who has followed closely the preceding explanations, but as the point is both difficult and important, I will state that reason once more. It consists in the fact that, with the existing distribution of the resources of the State, the only fund out of which the Government can defray any 'unauthorized' expenditure is its half-share in the ultimate surplus of the Caisse—I mean that surplus which the Caisse still possesses after paying the interest on the Debt, and making good to the Government the difference between its receipts and its 'authorized' expenditure. It is evident, therefore, that for every extra £E100 required for administrative needs the country must pay £E200 in taxation, the other £100 going to the reduction of the Debt. Unless the system is changed, this necessity will, in the course of years, become a very burdensome business, and a serious check to the development of national prosperity.

I have said enough—perhaps the reader will think I have said too much—about this ingenious financial puzzle. If his patience has not been equal to grappling with it, he may console himself by the reflection that he is no worse off, in this respect, than the vast majority of Egyptian officials. I do not believe that, outside the Finance Ministry, there are ten men in Cairo who understand the financial system of the country. Let me illustrate this assertion by the sort of discussion which I have myself heard at least a dozen times. An enthusiastic administrator belonging to some other office —Public Works, let us suppose, or Education, or Justice, or the Sanitary Service—comes to the Finance Ministry, and makes out an eloquent case for an extra credit of, say, £5,000 for a new object of unquestionable public utility. His financial colleague, to whom the request is addressed, cuts a wry face.

'What,' says the applicant, 'you don't mean to say that what I propose is not worth £5,000, especially in these days, when things are looking brighter, and we are no longer so desperately hard up for money?'

'Yes, my dear sir, it may be worth £5,000, but I am not sure that it is worth £10,000.'

'But I do not ask for £10,000. I only want £5,000.'

'I know you only want £5,000; but the fact remains, that it will cost the country £10,000.'

And then the financial man plunges for the hundredth

time into a desperate effort to explain to his friend the effects of the London Convention: how the expenditure of the Government already exceeds the 'authorized' limit, how unauthorized expenditure can only be defrayed out of the Government's half-share of the ultimate surplus of the Caisse, and how, therefore, every fresh pound devoted to administration involves two pounds to be taken from the taxpayer. But it is all no use. The applicant goes away in disgust, with the firm conviction that the whole thing is an abominable juggle, invented by a parsimonious Treasury, which has no sympathy with the aspirations of reforming administrators. Yet all the time it is no juggle, but a simple statement of hard facts, which no one, perhaps, regrets more than the financial authorities themselves.

There is, as we have seen, only one way in which the Government can increase its expenditure without raising double the amount it actually requires. That way is to induce the Great Powers to add the new outlay to the sum already 'authorized.' But Egypt has had bitter experience of the difficulty of obtaining the consent of the Powers to any financial change. It is not worth while to enter into negotiations which may last six months, or, for the matter of that, six years, except for an object of really vital importance. There have, however, been some objects of sufficient magnitude to make an appeal to the Powers appear desirable, and the first and greatest of these was the abolition of the Corvée. If I enter at some length into that story, it is with a twofold object. For the abolition of the Corvée is at once the largest of recent reforms, and that which illustrates most clearly the international difficulties by which all reform is beset.

The estimates on which the Convention of London was based allowed a sum of £E450,000 for the reduction of the Land Tax. In other words, it was calculated that, with the relief afforded to it by the terms of the Convention, the Egyptian Government would be able to make both ends meet, even if it collected £E450,000 less than the £E5,118,000, which was the full legal amount of the tax. But the whole of this £E450,000 was not available for direct reductions. Experience showed that the actual receipts of the Land Tax fell short of the sum assessed by an average of at least £E200,000 a year. There thus only remained £E250,000 with which to diminish the assessment.

How was this sum to be applied? An all-round reduction of 5 per cent. would, in view of the great inequality of the burden in different parts of the country, be neither just nor politic. It would afford inadequate relief to the most heavily burdened cultivators, while it would be a needless gratuity to those whose taxation was already moderate. If, on the other hand, it was decided to reduce the tax in certain districts only, great difficulties would present themselves in the choice of such districts, and the rest of the country would be filled with jealousy and discontent. Under these circumstances it occurred to the authorities—and it was a brilliant idea—that instead of using the £E250,000 for a haphazard reduction of the tax taken in money, it would be better to devote that sum to reducing the much more oppressive and wasteful tax exacted in labour, which fell with tolerably equal weight upon all parts of Egypt.

It was estimated that the work of clearing the canals of silt, which was annually performed by the forced labour of the peasantry, could be done by contract for about £E400,000 a year. But the loss which the people suffered in being dragged away from their homes, often at the very season when their presence was most necessary in their own fields, would, if calculated in terms of money, amount to more than twice that sum. I am speaking now, be it observed, of the cost of the Corvée, even after the system had been cleared of abuses. What damage that system inflicted on the country in the old days of despotism, when unlimited numbers of the fellahin might be dragged away from their villages at any moment for any purpose—public or private, legitimate or illegitimate—upon which the Khedive chose to employ them, it is quite impossible to guess.

These abuses were summarily stopped with the British

Occupation. But even under the reformed system, by which forced labour was limited to necessary works of public usefulness—such as the clearing of the canals—the burden of the Corvée was a grievous one. It imposed upon the people sacrifices out of all proportion to the money which it saved to the State. It was, in fact, taxation of the worst and most wasteful kind, only justified by the want of money which made the employment of paid labour impossible. The proposal, therefore, to devote £E250,000 a year to reducing, by more than one half, the forced labour of the peasantry all over Egypt, instead of devoting that sum to an inconsiderable reduction of their burdens in the shape of Land Tax, was as sound economically as it was eminently humane and popular.

But the manner of settling accounts between the Caisse and the Government, as fixed by the Convention of London, placed a tremendous obstacle in the way of such an application of the money. To reduce taxation by £E250,000 was not a very serious matter for the Government. For, inasmuch as it had the right to call upon the Caisse to make good the difference between its receipts and its 'authorized' expenditure, a reduction of £E250,000 in these receipts simply involved an increase of that amount in the contribution made by the Caisse to the expenses of the Administration. No doubt there would be a corresponding decrease in the ultimate surplus of the Caisse, and the Government, which had a half-share in that surplus, would be the poorer by one moiety of the decrease, or £E125,000. But such a sacrifice was possible. What was not possible for the Government, in the then state of its finances, was to take upon itself an 'unauthorized' expenditure of £E250,000. For this course, as we have seen, would have cost the country £500,000, and that was more than it could afford, even for the best of objects.

There was no alternative, therefore, but to go to the Powers and ask them to add the £E250,000 in question to the 'authorized' expenditure. The case was clear. The benefit of the proposed measure to the great mass of the Egyptian people was indubitable. Nevertheless, it took three mortal years to get France to give anything more than a provisional sanction to the arrangement. French diplomacy was not above keeping Egypt in suspense about this vital matter, in order to bring pressure to bear upon her Government for the concession of some rather shabby demands about the pay and position of certain French officials.

This £E250,000 a year enabled the Public Works Ministry to reduce by more than 50 per cent. the number of men called out for the clearance of the canals. The boon thus bestowed upon the peasantry was enormous. Indeed, so great was its popularity, so apparent, from the outset, was its excellent economic effect, that no sooner had the Corvée been abolished in part, than everybody began to demand that it should be abolished altogether. Nubar Pasha had initiated the good work. His successor, Riaz, was burning with honourable emulation to complete it. To do so he required another £E150,000 a year. Riaz, however, did not shrink from the bold proposal to put a special tax upon all the land of Egypt in order to raise that sum. The idea was as courageous as it was equitable. For the new tax, being raised at an equal rate per acre, fell most heavily on the large land-holders, while the burden of the Corvée had, with great injustice, fallen almost entirely on the poor. Yet so strong was the general feeling in favour of the total abolition of the Corvée, that the National Assembly, whose assent was necessary to the imposition of the new tax, although composed almost entirely of landlords, passed the measure without a dissentient voice. This was in December, 1889.

The new tax, however, was never levied. The finances had by this time made such a wonderful recovery, and Egyptian Stock stood so high, that in the summer of 1890 it was found possible to convert the Privileged Debt, and to reduce the interest from 5 to 3½ per cent. with only a very slight increase of capital. It is true that the nominal amount of this debt rose from £22,296,000 to £29,400,000. But then the latter figure included a small loan of £2,330,000 raised in 1888 to relieve the Treasury of certain heavy annual payments to the Khedivial family, and now merged in the Privileged Debt. It included also a fresh sum of £E1,300,000, the greater part of which was devoted to irrigation works, not less profitable in their consequences than those executed by the million taken out of the Guaranteed Loan. The net result of these changes, together with the conversion of the Daira Loan—which was effected at the same time, and which took the form, not of a reduction of interest, but of a reduction of the capital by 15 per cent.—was to relieve the Egyptian Budget by no less a sum than £E314,000 a year.

Here, then, was money enough to pay for the abolition of the Corvée, without the collection of the new tax, to say nothing of a handsome balance which would still remain over for other useful expenditure. But it is one thing for Egypt to have money—quite a different thing for her to be allowed to use it. The question, how the saving effected by the Conversion of the Debt was to be applied, led to a renewal of the old French tactics in a still more oppressive and indefensible form. The Conversion itself, involving as it did a change in the Law of Liquidation, had only been rendered possible by the consent of the Great Powers. In the first instance, France had refused her consent, unless Great Britain would name a day for the evacuation of Egypt. When that position became untenable, she had, indeed, consented, but 'with proviso and exception.' The condition she made, or, rather, the principal condition—for there were several others equally vexatious, though less important—was, that the money annually saved by the Conversion should be retained by the Commissioners of the Caisse, and should only be spent for such purposes as the Powers might subsequently approve. At the time when these terms were accepted, the Egyptian Government was looking anxiously to this money as the means of paying the £E150,000 still required to complete the abolition of the Corvée. It never occurred to anyone that France would refuse to agree to its application for so beneficent a purpose. But that is just what France did. Under great pressure she allowed the sum saved during 1890, which was about £E110,000, to go towards the much-desired object, and the Egyptian Government was thus enabled, by putting its hand into its pocket for the extra £E40,000, to dispense with the special tax. But when, in the following year, Egypt appealed to the Great Powers to permit her to make the necessary £E150,000 a year a permanent charge upon the savings effected by the Conversion, France flatly refused, and she has steadfastly adhered to that refusal. It was only with great difficulty, and after fresh concessions had been extorted from the Egyptian Government, that France could be induced to allow the £E150,000 in question to be added, like the previous £E250,000, to the 'authorized' expenditure. No thanks are due to her if, owing to the progressive improvement of the country, even this niggardly concession has sufficed to enable the Government to get rid of the Corvée, while abolishing the fresh tax created for that purpose.

This is a thoroughly typical story. Egypt is the classic land of baksheesh. But there is no form of baksheesh more extraordinary—perhaps I might say more repulsive—than the blackmail which is so often levied upon the Egyptian Government by Foreign Powers, before granting their consent to any of the modifications which a change of circumstances frequently renders necessary in the financial system imposed upon Egypt by International Agreements. Every single Great Power must give its approval before that system can be modified in any particular. Perhaps it is only natural that, if one of these Powers wishes to get something out of the Egyptian Government, it should be tempted to use the occasion of being asked for such approval, in order to obtain what it desires. But France has been by far the greatest sinner in this respect—for France always has something which she wishes to get out of Egypt, and she has never shown the smallest scruple in her methods of obtaining it.

It is true that, with the revival of her finances, Egypt

is now less at the mercy of the Powers than she used to be. If she is not allowed to add a particular outlay, however useful, to her 'authorized' expenditure, she can in many cases find the money out of her own resources. This is one of the reasons why it was of such vast importance that the country should, at whatever sacrifice, not only make both ends meet, but accumulate a reserve which might give it, in the long-run, a certain latitude in matters of expenditure. The Egyptian Government can never afford to be without some savings of its own to fall back upon. It is a question not merely of financial stability, but of political independence.

I have spoken repeatedly of the financial revival of Egypt. It remains to consider what is the extent and what have been the causes of that revival. The true point of departure in any such review is 1886, the first year in which Egypt enjoyed the benefits conferred on her by the London Convention. That Convention gave Egypt a last chance. But it was a difficult chance, and few of the best judges believed at the time that, even with the concessions then made, the country could pull through and become permanently solvent. Certainly no one believed that in less than ten years Egypt would attain such a degree of financial prosperity as has actually fallen to her lot.

I will only give one proof, but it is a very striking one, of the degree in which the financial resuscitation of the country has exceeded even the most sanguine expectations. During the discussions of the experts attached to the London Conference in 1884, one of those present threw out the idea that Egypt might be allowed to redeem the Unified Debt at 80. None of the delegates were opposed to the proposal in principle, and certainly the holders of Unified, which then stood at 59, would have been only too delighted at the thought of ever being paid off at 80. Had the proposal to make the Stock redeemable at that figure been adopted, Egypt would in the long-run have saved £11,000,000. But the notion that Unified could by any possibility reach such a price appeared so fantastic to the financial experts that the proposal was simply dropped, not from any doubt as to its fairness, but from a total disbelief in its practicability. Yet, as I write, Unified Stock stands at 98, and seems likely to stay there.

Is this great increase of credit justified by the facts of the situation? The question can be best answered by a glance at a few figures. The total Revenue, taking the receipts of the Caisse and the Government together, has during the six years been as follows:

1886	£E9,574,000
1887	9,616,000
1888	9,661,000
1889	9,718,000
1890	10,236,000
1891	10,599,000

The increase has all along been steady. Latterly it has been enormous. From nine and a half to ten and a half millions in six years is not bad progress. But what makes that progress all the more promising is the fact, that the increase in the Revenue of the State has been concurrent with a decrease in the burdens of the people. Indeed, the decrease of burdens has been, to a great extent, the cause of the increase of Revenue.

It is true that some new taxes have been imposed since 1885. The duty on tobacco has been raised from 10 to 14, and again from 14 to 20 piastres per kilogramme—that is to say, to about one shilling and tenpence a pound, or rather less than one-half the English duty. The House Tax has been extended to foreigners. We may estimate the growth of receipts consequent upon these new charges at about £E500,000 in the former, and about £E70,000 in the latter case. But, on the other hand, there have been reductions of taxation exceeding, in all, £E600,000 a year, and the taxes which have been abolished or diminished were taxes of the most obnoxious kind. The tax on sheep and goats, which was very injurious to agriculture, the tax on all trades and crafts, which was collected in innumerable small sums from the poorest of the people, as well as a number of vexatious minor imposts, have totally disappeared. The price of salt, which is a Government monopoly, has been reduced by 40 per cent. In the least prosperous parts of Upper Egypt—the Province of Kena and the Frontier Province—the Land Tax has been reduced by 30 per cent. Not only, therefore, has the amount of taxation remitted exceeded the amount imposed, but the new taxes are fewer, simpler, fairer, and economically more sound than the old ones.

In addition to the relief afforded by this readjustment of taxation, the Government has freely abandoned arrears of Land Tax amounting to something like a million. But, of course, the greatest reduction of all in the burdens of the people has been the suppression of the Corvée. That measure has cost the Government £E400,000 a year, but it has saved the peasantry from losses which, reduced to terms of money, would represent a vastly heavier sum. No exact calculation is indeed possible, but it is certain that the people would gladly pay for the cleaning of the Canals twice over rather than see the Corvée back again.*

While the Revenue of the country has thus advanced by leaps and bounds, the Expenditure shows no corresponding expansion. It has varied very little from year to year, nearly always amounting to about nine and a half millions. In 1886 it was £E9,585,000. In 1891 it was £E9,525,000, against a Revenue of £E10,599,000, thus leaving the huge surplus of

* When I speak of the 'suppression of the Corvée,' I mean its suppression as a regular system of forced labour for the execution of Public Works. The inhabitants of all parts of the country are still liable to be called out in any sudden emergency, such as the Locust Plague of 1891. An annual levy of this sort is made for guarding and, in case of a breach, repairing the Nile banks during the season of the flood; and the number of men required for this purpose is very large. Nor is it easy to see how the peasantry can be relieved of the liability to personal service of this kind. But the obligation to guard the river-banks in flood-time—a duty in which every fellah feels a direct interest—neither is, nor is regarded as, a hardship at all comparable to the tremendous labour of clearing the canals, to say nothing of the hundred and one illegitimate objects for which the Corvée was at one time employed.

£E1,073,000. Yet, though the total expenditure shows no increase, the sums now devoted to objects of public utility are larger than they were six years ago. In addition to the £E400,000 paid for free labour in lieu of the Corvée, more money is spent on schools, railways, the Post Office, the administration of Justice. How has all this been possible without an increase in the total? It is because, while the useful items of expenditure have been developed, the wasteful items have been kept down. We have seen that a large saving has been effected in the interest on the Debt. There has been a great reduction likewise in the annual deficit of the Domains, while the Daira deficit has been converted into a surplus. There has been a diminution in the Pension List, and in the number of superfluous officials. The salaries of the Ministry of Finance alone have been brought down from £E104,000 to £E82,000. Yet no one can say that the work is not done with greater efficiency.

Lightened taxation and improved receipts, increased outlay on good objects, and decreased outlay on useless ones—these are the essential features of the change which has come over the aspect of Egyptian Finance, and they augur well for the future. But I have not yet finished my tale of promise. At the end of 1885 Egypt had not one stiver in reserve, whether in the hands of the Caisse or in those of the Government. At the end of 1891 the Caisse had a Reserve Fund of £E1,822,000, the Government had a Reserve Fund of £E665,000, and there was besides a third Reserve Fund of £E324,000, consisting of the economies effected by the Conversion of the Debt which France has insisted on locking up in the manner already described. Altogether, Egypt had in 1892 nearly three millions in hand against a rainy day.

Against all this it may be urged that since 1886 the Debt of Egypt has once more increased. And this is true, but the increase is rather apparent than real. We have seen that the Debt at the time of the Law of Liquidation amounted to 98 millions. After the re-adjustment of the finances, resulting from the Convention of London, it stood at 104 millions. On July 31, 1892, the figures were:

Guaranteed Loan	... ...	£8,991,000
Privileged ,,	... ...	29,400,000
Unified ,,	... ...	55,986,000
Daira ,,	... ...	7,236,000
Domains ,,	... ...	4,845,000
Total	... ...	£106,458,000

There is thus an increase of between two and three millions during the last six years. But this increase is not all due to fresh borrowing. About half of it merely represents the addition to capital necessitated by the Conversion, and is far more than counterbalanced by the great reduction in interest consequent upon that operation. The total amount of fresh borrowing is £1,465,000, and this has been entirely devoted to the redemption of pensions and to reproductive Public Works. To add less than a million and a half to your debt, while reducing your interest by more than three hundred thousand, and increasing your annual revenue by more than a million, is evidently neither rash nor unprofitable finance.

But it may be asked, Why borrow at all? Is there not an anomaly in borrowing on the one hand, while piling up a Reserve Fund on the other? The objection is specious; but in view of the peculiar circumstances of Egypt it is not well founded. It was a fatal flaw of the first reforms introduced into Egyptian Finance that they did not provide for a Reserve Fund. At that time the great specific was to keep down the Debt. But Egypt is a country the revenue of which is exceptionally liable to be affected by physical accidents. An abnormally high or an abnormally low Nile may, in any given year, completely upset the Budget, although the general position of the finances of the country is thoroughly sound. Under these circumstances, a Reserve Fund is of the first necessity. What is the use of paying off, say, a million of Debt one year, if you run the risk of finding yourself short of cash in the following year, and having to resort to a fresh loan, which, raised at a moment of temporary embarrassment, is certain to cost you dear?

If the Reserve Fund of the Government is important on account of the political situation of Egypt, the larger Reserve Fund of the Caisse is no less essential by reason of the singularity of her physical condition. It was, therefore, a wise policy which, four years ago, led the Caisse and the Government to propose, and the Powers to agree, that the process of reducing the Debt should be suspended until a Reserve Fund of two millions had been accumulated in the hands of the Caisse. As soon as that figure has been reached, the amortization is to be resumed. And there can be little doubt that that figure will be reached at the end of 1892. From 1893 onwards, there will be a large sum annually available for the diminution of the Debt, and that without the smallest danger to the financial stability of the country, which in case of accident will have a large Reserve to fall back upon.

So much for the extent of the financial revival. It will not be necessary to dwell at any great length upon its causes. Their operation has been slow, but sure. If the reader will glance back at the table on page 200, he will see that the great elasticity which now characterizes the Egyptian Revenue has only begun to show itself during the last two or three years. The sensational surpluses of 1890 and 1891—not fictitious surpluses, be it observed, but genuine results of really solid progress—have disarmed, though they have not silenced, criticism. It is impossible, in these days, not to pity the hack writers of the Opposition Press, who, for their poor pittance of French or Turkish baksheesh, have to strain their ingenuity to prove that white is black, and that the progressive increase in the resources of the State is a symptom of the ruin of the country.

But in the early years of the Occupation the critics of the Finance Ministry, and of its English counsellors, had a much easier task. Nor do I deny that, in that period of strain, recourse was often had to expedients which, while perfectly legitimate, were far from glorious, and which, had they stood alone, would neither have achieved nor deserved a permanent success. The economies then practised were often harsh, and sometimes petty. In several cases equilibrium was only attained by extraordinary shifts. There was one year, 1886, when the Budget would not have been balanced without a vigorous enforcement of the recruiting law, which was out of all proportion to the military needs of the country, but which produced large sums in ransoms paid to escape the burden of compulsory service. In 1887 a surplus was manufactured by the simple device of deferring the payment of the salaries for December till the beginning of January, and thus throwing the charge forward upon the Budget of the succeeding year.

It was these and similar ingenuities, which gave the enemies of Sir Edgar Vincent a handle for attacking him as a juggler, who had no real genius for grappling with the difficulties of finance, but only great skill in avoiding them. As a matter of fact, no charge could have been more unjust. During the six years of Vincent's administration, the seed was sown and was steadily ripening, which has since then yielded so bountiful a harvest. In many cases the reforms, which have borne the richest fruit, were due directly to his initiative. No doubt he was full of expedients, but expedients are only contemptible when they form the whole stock-in-trade of a financier. They are pardonable, and even laudable, when they are merely resorted to in order to gain time for radical economic reforms to produce their slow but certain effect. Sir Edgar Vincent left Egypt in the summer of 1889, too soon to see the complete vindication of his policy, which, ably and prudently continued by his successor, Sir Elwin Palmer, has since then produced such brilliant results. But he did not leave until he had assured himself that Egyptian Finance had definitely turned the corner, and that his zeal, his courage, and his fertility of resource had not been exercised in vain.

It was Vincent who reformed the monetary system, and substituted a simple and convenient currency for the chaos of coins of all metals and all countries, which used to cause so much confusion, and to constitute so great an impediment to trade. It was Vincent who was the first to see what could be made of the tobacco duty, and who, by negotiating the Commercial Treaty with Greece, enabled the Egyptian Government to develop that duty. But apart from these particular measures, of which he deserves the almost exclusive credit, Vincent will always be remembered as the most gifted and one of the most energetic of the little band of Englishmen who, under the presiding genius of Baring, rescued the finances by restoring the prosperity of Egypt. It is, however, not to one man, or to one measure, that this result is due. It is due to better government all round, to a careful husbanding of the income of the State, accompanied by a vigorous attention to the springs of national wealth, which had for some time been most shamefully neglected.

Two great factors have combined to bring about the financial recuperation of Egypt: the prevention of waste on the part of the administration, and the development of the productive powers of the country. As far as the prevention of waste is concerned, the first essential was a proper system of accounts. Accounts are the foundation of finance. You may have good accounts and a bad financial administration, but you cannot have good finance with bad accounts. There was nothing more fatal in the financial chaos of the days of Ismail than the manner in which the private property of the Khedive was jumbled up with the property of the State. This mischievous confusion was put an end to when Ismail's vast estates were surrendered to his creditors, and a regular Civil List substituted for the multifarious revenues which at one time flowed into the coffers of the Sovereign of Egypt. But the reformation of the Public Accounts, which began as far back as 1877, took a good ten years to complete. It is thanks to Sir Gerald Fitzgerald, who held the office of Director-General of Accounts from 1877 to 1885, and to Sir Elwin Palmer, who subsequently filled that office until he succeeded Sir Edgar Vincent as Financial Adviser, that Egypt owes a system of accounts, which can bear comparison with those of any other country in Europe. Irregular expenditure has been put a stop to. No official, however powerful, can nowadays spend money not accorded by the Budget, or, in case of emergency, by a Supplementary Credit, which has had to run the gauntlet of the Committee of Finance and the Council of Ministers.

Nor is the State the only gainer by the order thus introduced. The tax-payer has been benefited in an equal degree. The poorest peasant in the country is now annually furnished with a tax-paper—'wird,' as it is called—which shows him exactly what he has to pay to the Government, and at what seasons the instalments are due. The dates of these instalments, moreover, which vary in different provinces, have been arranged so as to correspond as nearly as possible with the seasons, when the cultivator realizes his produce, and is therefore in the best position to discharge his debt to the State. I have shown in a previous chapter* how terribly the fellah suffered in old days from the absence of any such provisions for his protection. It was not the amount of the sums due—heavy as these often were—which ruined the people. It was the exaction of sums not due, the constant uncertainty how much the tax-gatherer might demand and when he might demand it, the necessity of resorting to bribery as a protection against official extortion.

It is indeed difficult to realize to what extent the burdens of the poor were at one time aggravated by the tyranny and corruption of the official classes. That tyranny is now a thing of the past. I wish I could say with equal confidence that corruption also had been eradicated. Corruption, however, if not destroyed, has been greatly diminished. In old days the action of the Government itself directly fostered this vice in its servants. By maintaining a swarm of officials with wretched salaries, which were generally in arrears, it compelled men to choose between dishonesty and starvation. At present official salaries are paid with the same

* Pp. 81-83.

regularity as in England. Moreover, while the numbers of the bureaucracy have been considerably decreased, the pay of the lower ranks has been raised. And if the chief incentives to corruption have been thus removed, incessant war has been waged against it in every grade of the Civil Service. Innumerable examples have been made, and that not only in the case of subordinates. Among those punished for peculation, or for winking at peculation, have been officials of the highest rank, including several Governors of provinces and one powerful Minister. The effect of such salutary severity has made itself felt throughout the Administration. Corruption, even where it still exists, is no longer flaunted in the market-place, but hides its head in constant terror of detection. From being a fashion it has become a stigma. A whole new chapter has been added to the code of official morality.

But the work of financial reform has not been confined to reducing the burdens of the people. It has done more than that. It has increased their means of bearing the burdens that remain. The greatest vice of all in the old system of government was that, while the demands made upon the people were constantly increasing, their capacity to meet those demands was being steadily impaired. The Government took from them twice as much as it was entitled to take; it did not give them in return what it was bound to give. While the coffers of the State and the pockets of its servants were being filled by the plunder of the peasantry, the soil was deteriorating from the neglect of those great Public Works upon which its fertility depended.

Except in abnormal cases, the Egyptian cultivator can afford to pay his taxes, if he receives a proper supply of water for his crops. From time immemorial Egyptian law has recognised the intimate connection between land-tax and water-supply. The land which, in any given year, gets no water is for that year legally exempt from all taxation whatever. As soon as it gets water its liability is established. But it is evident that the mere fact of receiving some water, though it may set up the liability of the cultivator to pay, does not necessarily ensure his capacity to do so. In order to ensure that, he must get his water in proper quantities, and at the proper times. But this is just what, in thousands of instances, he could not get, as long as the Irrigation System remained in that state of unutterable neglect and confusion into which it had fallen in the period preceding the British Occupation. Of the long catalogue of beneficent measures, by which the tax-paying power of the Egyptian people has been increased, the greatest and most essential is the reform of the Irrigation System.

Of the details of that reform I shall have a word to say in the succeeding chapter, but its financial effects must be noted now. They have manifested themselves directly in the greater ease with which the Land Tax has lately been collected; but they have had a no less important effect in augmenting other items of the Revenue. The Land Tax accounts for fully one-half of the total receipts of the Egyptian Treasury. About three-fifths of the remaining half are derived from the Customs Duties, and from the Railways, which are the property of the Government. Now, the total amount of these three sources of income in the year 1886 was £E7,337,000. In 1890 it had increased to £E8,040,000, and in 1891 to £E8,366,000. To the extent of about one-third, this augmentation is due to the heavier taxation imposed upon tobacco. But the remainder is not the result of any increase of taxation. On the contrary, it has been attained in the face of a considerable decrease in the rate of the Land Tax in certain provinces. It is an effect of the growth which is taking place in the producing and consuming powers of the people, in consequence of the care now devoted to nourishing the sources of national wealth.

The Land Tax in 1886 brought in £E5,116,000. In 1891, even after the large reduction already referred to, it still brought in £E5,098,000. And both in 1890 and in 1891 it was collected with a facility such as had never been experienced in recent years. This is not surprising, when we consider that the cotton crop, which is by far the most important of all the products of Egypt, representing more than two-thirds of her exports and about one-third of her whole agricultural wealth, had risen from less than three million kantars* in 1886—which itself was a good year compared with its predecessors—to three and a quarter millions in 1889, to upwards of four millions in 1890, and to upwards of four and a half millions in 1891. The net result of the recent improvements in irrigation has thus been to increase the amount of the great staple of agriculture by something like 50 per cent. Not only, therefore, is the cultivator able to pay his taxes more easily, but he has more left for his own needs.

The increase in the amount of agricultural produce, coupled with the decrease of extortion, has worked a complete transformation in the condition of the fellah. It is impossible to take up any book or report about Egypt written twelve, ten, or even six years ago, which is not full of gloomy forebodings based upon the indebtedness of the peasantry. And no doubt that indebtedness is still very heavy in many quarters. But it is no longer, in the great majority of cases, overwhelming. It does not threaten Egypt with the dissolution of social order. No one talks, as the most conservative writers did ten years ago, of the necessity of a general liquidation of agricultural debts. The problem of enabling the peasant to borrow at lower rates than those which he still has to submit to is one of capital interest. But compared with the rates once prevalent, the interest at present paid is moderate. There is much yet to be done in lightening the burdens of the people in this respect. But no mere financial arrangements, however wise, can equal the relief already afforded, and still to be afforded, by the attention now given to their great primary need—the regular supply of water.

Unfortunately the effect of the agricultural development of recent years has been to a large extent counteracted by the prodigious fall in prices. During the ten

* The kantar is about 100 lb.

years 1880-1889 the cultivator could obtain, on the average, some 252 piastres a kantar for his cotton. But in 1890 cotton only averaged 228 piastres a kantar, and in 1891 the mean price had fallen as low as 188. And most of the other principal products of Egyptian agriculture have experienced a concurrent, though a less marked, decline in value. Had it not been for this unfortunate circumstance, the revival of the prosperity of the country and the growth of the revenue, great as they are, would have been even more signal. The efforts of the Government to improve the condition of the people have not succeeded through any external good luck. They have succeeded in the face of a run of bad luck, so far as prices are concerned, which it would be difficult to parallel. One shudders to think what would have been the burdens and the sufferings of the unfortunate Egyptian cultivator, if that fall of prices had come upon him in the old days, when his burdens were so much heavier and the produce of his land so much smaller than to-day.

The most striking evidence of reviving prosperity is furnished by the receipts of the Customs. The yield of the Customs Duties has risen sharply in the last three years. For some time previously it had shown, if anything, a tendency to decline. If there was an increase in any particular year, it was due, not to natural, but to artificial causes, such as the stimulus given to imports by the payment of the Alexandria Indemnities, and by the British Campaign in the Sudan. During the last few years, on the other hand, there have been no such exceptional reasons for inflation. The condition of trade has been perfectly normal. Yet the Customs Revenue (excluding the tobacco duty) has risen from £E585,000 in 1889 to £E651,000 in 1890, and to £E808,000 in 1891. Of the last figure something like £E60,000 to £E70,000 is, indeed, due, not to the increase of trade, but to a Convention with the Porte, by which Turkish goods have, for the first time, become subject to the ordinary import duty. But, even after making this deduction, the progressive increase of receipts is very marked, and, inasmuch as, apart from the tobacco, there has been no change in the uniform *ad valorem* duties levied upon all goods coming into or going out of the country, the growth of the Revenue is an accurate gauge of the growth of Trade.*

But the Trade Returns themselves are so significant that they deserve a rather closer examination. The exports amounted to £E11,953,000 in 1889, to £E11,876,000 in 1890, and to £E13,878,000 in 1891. The latter is the highest figure ever attained. The next highest is that of the year 1876, when the exports amounted to £E13,561,000. But this slight difference in the value is no indication whatever of the difference in the quantity of produce exported respectively in the two years. At the prices ruling in 1876, the exports of 1891 would have amounted, not to fourteen millions, but to nearly nineteen.

And this is not all. An increase of exports is not necessarily a sign of increased prosperity. Indeed, in a country like Egypt, it may at certain times be evidence of the exact reverse. The great question is, What proportion of the exports goes to pay the interest on the Debt and other external obligations, and what proportion represents the free exchange of surplus produce, for which the country gets value in return? The hopeful feature of the recent great increase of exports is the fact that it is concurrent with a reduction in the sums due by Egypt to the outside world. In the only two previous years, in which the exports exceeded £E13,000,000, namely 1876 and 1879, the tribute which Egypt had to pay to Europe was much greater than it is to-day. What she received in return for her exports was proportionately much less than what she receives at the present time. In the years 1879-81—the most favourable triennium which I can find in the fifteen years preceding 1892—the average annual exports of Egypt

* The Customs Duties are 1 per cent. *ad valorem* on all exports, and 8 per cent. *ad valorem* on all imports, excluding tobacco, which is subject to a uniform tax of 20 piastres per kilogramme, irrespective of its value.

were just over £E13,000,000. During the same period her average annual imports were just under £7,000,000. In 1890, on the other hand, with exports under £E12,000,000, her imports were just over £E8,000,000, and in 1891, with exports at £E13,878,000, her imports were £E9,201,000. Instead of benefiting by little more than half of what she sends to foreign countries, she now gets something in return for nearly two-thirds of what she sends.

Never before 1891 has the value of the imports been anything like £E9,201,000. And the best of it is, that this figure has been reached without any artificial inflation whatsoever. It is a genuine indication of the increased purchasing power of the country. There have been altogether eight years, prior to 1890, in which Egypt has imported more than £E7,000,000 of foreign goods. In one instance, 1885, she even imported upwards of £E8,000,000. But in almost every one of these instances, and above all in 1885, the imports were very far from being purchased out of the ordinary resources of the country. They were swollen by the introduction of goods bought with borrowed money, or by supplies intended for the British troops engaged in the Nile Campaign. But the deductions, which have to be made from the figures of the last two years on account of influences of this kind, are quite inconsiderable. The growth of imports, which set in with the closing months of 1889, and has gone on increasing ever since, is due to the greater power of the Egyptian people to buy, and to nothing else.

And what is it that they buy? The details of their purchases are even more encouraging than the growth of the total figure. Comparing 1891 with 1890, Egypt, owing to the increase in her wheat crop, imported £E151,000 worth less of foreign cereals and vegetables than she had taken in 1890. But she imported £307,000 more of cotton goods, £E280,000 more of metal goods, and £E77,000 more of wood intended for purposes of building. Now these are just the articles which are required by the body of the people. They represent the clothes of the peasantry, their domestic utensils, and the materials with which, whenever they can afford it, they try to substitute a better class of dwelling for the rude mud huts in which the majority of them live.

And, lastly, from whom do they buy? The answer to that question is of less relevance to the immediate subject; but it is so interesting to our own country, that a brief digression with regard to it may perhaps be excused. We in Great Britain are the chief customers of Egypt. We take three-fourths of her exports. But, on the other hand, we also supply a far greater quantity of the articles which Egypt derives from abroad than any other nation. British goods constitute nearly two-fifths of the total imports of Egypt. The increased purchasing power of the Egyptian people is therefore a matter of direct interest to British manufacturers and workmen. Since 1890 the exports of Great Britain have in general been on the decline; but not so our exports to Egypt. They have risen from £E2,536,000 in 1889 to £E2,999,000 in 1890, and to £E3,425,000 in 1891. It is true that other countries, such as France and Austria, which rank next in importance to Great Britain in the trade of Egypt—each supplying about one-tenth of what she buys—have benefited in an equal degree. The advantage which England derives from the revival of Egyptian prosperity is no exclusive advantage. She shares it with the rest of Europe. Indeed, in some respects other countries have, in proportion to their total trade, benefited more by that revival than Great Britain. In Egypt, as elsewhere, the greater enterprise shown by our Continental competitors in pushing their goods, and in adapting themselves to the wants of their customers, has told against us in the distribution of trade. But even if relatively somewhat diminished, the interest we have in the purchasing power of the Egyptian people remains incomparably greater than that of any other nation.

These facts are worth noting because of two opposite misconceptions which are widely prevalent with reference to the material interest of England in the Occupation of

Egypt. On the one hand, there is the foreign, and particularly the French, misconception, according to which Great Britain employs her position of virtual though unrecognised guardianship in a spirit of selfishness and exclusion, and in order to obtain special advantages for British trade and enterprise in the Nile Valley. As a matter of fact, no view could be more erroneous. So far from unduly favouring the commercial interests of their own countrymen, the British administrators in Egypt err, if anything, on the other side; so intense is their anxiety, that in the position of trust which they occupy they should be above the least suspicion of partiality. Neither directly nor indirectly has Great Britain drawn from her predominant position any profit at the expense of other nations. In the total trade of Egypt—taking exports and imports together—the share of England, which was 57 per cent. in the years immediately preceding the Occupation, was in 1891 only 54 per cent.

But although the action of England has been unselfish in this matter, she has not therefore been without her reward. The foreign misconception, just referred to, has its counterpart in the mistaken idea—which is confined to Great Britain—that though our work in Egypt may be a good thing for the Egyptians, and may be honourable and praiseworthy from the point of view of humanity, yet it is of no advantage to ourselves. Even if this were true, I do not know that it would be a condemnation of our work. But it is not true. The improvement of Egyptian administration leads directly to the revival of Egyptian trade, and in that increase England, which has more than half the trade of Egypt in her hands, possesses a direct interest of the most unmistakable kind. Our own country does thus, after all, obtain a recompense, and a recompense at once most substantial and most honourable, for any sacrifices she may make for Egypt. She gains, not at the expense of others, but along with others. If she is the greatest gainer, it is simply because she is the largest partner in the business. I will not discuss the question whether, in view of her predominant interest, she has not a strong moral claim to play the leading rôle in protecting the welfare of Egypt, and the commercial interests of all nations which have dealings with that country. I will not ask whether, if another Power, whose material interests in Egypt are not one-fifth of our own, wished, for whatever reason, to upset the Egyptian coach, we should be under any obligation to allow it. I simply state the facts. Political inferences must be left to others.

A word about the third great item of Egyptian Revenue—I mean the Railway Receipts. These were £E1,301,000 in 1889, £E1,408,000 in 1890, and £E1,631,000 in 1891. The figures of 1889 are higher than those of any previous year, except 1884 and 1885, when the receipts were swelled by the movement of troops and stores for the Nile Campaign. But if the receipts of 1889 were the best which the railways had ever had under normal conditions up to that date, those of 1891 exceeded them by 25 per cent. This great expansion, moreover, is not only due to the carriage of a larger quantity of goods going out or coming into the country. There has been a concurrent development of local traffic, and more particularly a great increase in the number of passengers. I do not refer to the first class, the growth of which is no doubt principally due to the annually increasing influx of tourists. The third-class traffic shows an even more remarkable development. In 1888 the third-class passengers were 3,300,000, in 1889 3,700,000, in 1890 4,000,000, and in 1891 4,800,000. Not only, therefore, do more goods pass to and fro, but more people travel, and especially more poor people. The lesson of these figures is clear, and it is reinforced by the immense augmentation which has taken place in the number of inland letters and telegrams. Just as foreign trade has extended, internal intercourse shows greater vitality. As evidence of the improved condition of the people, the statistics of the Railways, the Post Office, and the Telegraphs, are even more striking than those of the Customs.

We are now in a position to take stock of the present

condition and future prospects of Egyptian Finance. If the re-establishment of solvency is due to the growth of the Revenue, that growth itself is directly traceable to increased production. Herein consists the most hopeful feature of the situation. The revival of the last few years is no artificial one. It rests upon really solid foundations, and, striking as it has been, there is no reason why, with fairly good luck and sensible management, it should not continue, until it reaches proportions of which few men have at present any conception. The Valley of the Nile is a land of strange surprises. If anyone had suggested five years ago that the Egyptian accounts would in 1891 show a surplus of more than a million sterling, he would have been thought a lunatic. As I have no wish to be regarded in that character, I will not say to what extent the productiveness of Egypt may, in my opinion, be developed within the next ten or twenty years. Let me confine myself to the remark, which no one can gainsay, that that productiveness is still far from having reached its limit, and that, if proper measures are taken to encourage it, Egypt may in less than a generation attain a degree of prosperity as undreamt of now as her present position of solvency was undreamt of only as far back as 1885 and 1886.

It is all a question of water. If the water-supply were increased by means of a system of storage, the cultivable area might be enormously extended. Hundreds of thousands of acres might be restored to fertility, while other large tracts might be made to bear crops for the first time, or to bear two crops a year where they now produce only one. And, with the expansion of agriculture, trade would receive a further enormous impetus. Nor is there any reason why agriculture should remain the only Egyptian industry. Egypt will never be a great manufacturing country. But there is room for industrial enterprise in many directions, if European capital can but recover that confidence in Egypt which a number of egregious swindles and the protracted feeling of political insecurity have undermined.

Yet, however bright the prospect, the financial problem

is as difficult and as interesting as ever, though the difficulty and the interest are of a novel kind. The race against bankruptcy has been won; but taxation is still very heavy—especially the taxation of the land. And, on the other hand, the fresh expenditure necessary, if the Government is to do its duty in raising the standard of civilization and developing the latent wealth of the country, is very considerable. Nor is it easy to decide whether relief of taxation or fresh expenditure has the first claim upon the increased resources of the State.

This is a question on which the best authorities are divided. But there is one point about which it would be difficult to have two opinions, and that is the claim of the Egyptian Government to dispose, with greater freedom than it at present possesses, of its surplus revenue. The provisions of the Convention of London, already explained, which have the effect of obliging Egypt to pay twice over for new items of expenditure, are utterly indefensible under existing conditions. The effect which those provisions at present exercise is the very opposite of what their authors intended. It is one of the contradictions which meet you everywhere in dealing with Egyptian affairs, and especially with Egyptian Finance, that this arrangement, which was devised as a relief, has turned out a burden, and that it has so turned out in consequence of the unexpected prosperity of the country. It was not in the interest of the creditors that the Convention provided that one-half of the ultimate surplus of the Caisse should be devoted to the reduction of the Debt. It was in the interest of the Government. The framers of the Convention were convinced that Egypt was too poor to pay a fixed sum annually for amortization. It was as an escape from the necessity of imposing such a fixed payment that they hit upon the idea of giving the creditors a claim to one-half of a contingent surplus, which they probably regarded as highly problematical. But this half-surplus now bids fair to reach annually a far higher figure than anyone would have dreamt of fixing as the annual contribution to the reduction of the Debt.

As things stand to-day, it would be immensely to the advantage of Egypt to accept a heavy annual charge for amortization, on condition of being free to deal with the rest of her Revenue as she pleased. Nothing could be fairer than such a proposal. Let the Egyptian Government pay the interest on the Debt, plus such a sum as may be agreed upon—£E200,000, £E300,000, or even £E500,000—towards its reduction. But then let it be at liberty to dispose of the rest of its resources as it thinks fit, free from any hocus-pocus about 'authorized' or 'unauthorized' expenditure, and from any interference on the part of the Caisse and the Powers. If it fails to discharge these new obligations, then let the old arrangement revive. But as long as it fulfils them, let it have that liberty of action which all the world over is the privilege of solvency.

The reform just suggested is the most important and the most beneficent change which remains to be effected in the international arrangements relating to Egyptian Finance. It would be one of its many advantages that the Egyptian Government would thereby be put in a position to decide, on the merits of the case, between the competitive claims of a relief of taxation and a new form of useful expenditure. The present system creates a strong prejudice in favour of the former alternative. If the Government remits taxation to the extent of £E100,000, it loses £E100,000 and no more. But if it decides upon fresh expenditure to the same amount, the cost to the country is not £E100,000, but £E200,000. The absurdity of such a system is self-evident. Everybody would agree that, if by a reproductive expenditure of £E100,000 the country could obtain, say, £E150,000, such expenditure would be fully justified. But as things at present stand, the Government would be actually a loser by undertaking it.

Personally, if I may venture to express an opinion upon so thorny a point, I am disposed to think that anything which creates a prejudice against reproductive expenditure is a misfortune to Egypt. Reduce taxation by all means, and above all reduce the Land Tax. But remember that while £E300,000 a year, properly distributed, will suffice to relieve all the districts where the Land Tax is really crushing, by far the most effectual way of ultimately lightening that and every other burden of the people is to develop still further the productive powers of the country. I do not go so far as one high native authority, who once said to me: 'If you are going in for charlatanism, relieve the Land Tax. If your object is the prosperity of Egypt, create a Reservoir.' The remark is too epigrammatic to be entirely true. But there is more truth in it than falsehood.

For Egypt is a country which cries aloud for the application of capital to elicit its great latent wealth. The recent expenditure of the Government on Public Works has been reproductive to a degree surpassing the most audacious forecasts. But there is much more to be done in this direction. The time will soon be reached when the amount of water at present available in the summer months will have been made to render the greatest service of which it is capable. After that there can be no considerable stride forward until the supply is augmented. If the amount of summer water could be doubled, or even increased by 50 per cent., the effect on agriculture would be stupendous. The question of creating a vast Reservoir, to collect the river water in the months of abundance, in order to give it out again in the months of drought, is therefore the most interesting problem which now confronts, not only the Engineers, but the Financiers of Egypt. This question, however, can be better discussed after we have cast a glance at the Irrigation System.

CHAPTER IX.

THE STRUGGLE FOR WATER.

THE early Greek poet, who declared that 'water was the best of all things,' the early Greek philosopher, who saw in water the primal element of creation, must surely have drawn their thought, perhaps unconsciously, from Egyptian experience and sentiment. We know that Greece, in her beginnings, owed much to the influence of Egypt. May not the theory of Thales, and even the poetical hyperbole of Pindar, have been inspired by some contact, direct or indirect, with the land where a single great River is the lord and giver of life, the source and sustenance of all existence and all civilization? Egypt, as a geographical expression, is two things—the Desert and the Nile. As a habitable country, it is only one—the Nile. Every square foot of cultivable land has, at some time or other, been brought down by the river which now flows in its midst—at one season a shallow and sluggish stream, of which but little reaches the sea; at another, a sea itself, here spreading in a vast lake over the whole face of the country, there pouring along through numerous channels towards the ocean, and filling the remotest corners of the land with the rush and the sound of many waters.

The ordinary visitor to Egypt knows nothing of these things. He goes up the Nile, but, as far as the stream itself is concerned, he is almost invariably disappointed. Passing over the bridge at Cairo, he looks down upon the most remarkable river in the world, a river with which no other can compare in the strangeness of its character, the richness of its gifts, the immense rôle it has played in human history. But it makes no more impression on him than the Thames at London Bridge. The breadth of the stream is not remarkable—about a quarter of a mile—the volume of water is not great, the colour is dull, the pace of the current is, if anything, slow. Yet the Nile, as the tourist sees it, from December to March, is full and strong and stately compared to what it afterwards becomes.

In April, May, and June, and sometimes into the beginning of July, the water at Cairo falls and falls. The lowering of level would be even more marked if the Nile were not nowadays pounded up at the Barrage, some fourteen miles further down, in order to feed the Summer Canals, which keep the cultivation of the Delta alive. Meantime the two branches of the river below the Barrage are almost dry. There are many points at which, during the season of low water, a child might walk across. The fields, except where artificially nourished by the careful doling out of water from the Canals, are parched and seamed with fissures. The air is full of dust. The brilliant green of the crops, which so strikes the visitor during the winter, has given way to more sombre hues. The trees have shed their leaves. Nor is the animal world less oppressed by the lack of water. Man and beast alike languish. And all day long the fiery sun, undimmed by the lightest cloud, proceeds on his stately but pitiless march through a sky of deepest blue, as if determined to dry up what still remains of life-giving moisture, and to restore the tiny strip of cultivated Egypt to the vast surrounding Desert, in which, for hundreds of miles, it forms the only break.

Towards the end of the dry season the physical distress of the people becomes great and visible. And that physical distress is heightened by mental anxiety, as to how long this tyranny will continue. The level of the water is still sinking. Already some of the least valuable crops have had to be given up. The more valuable ones are threatened. High and low, rich and poor are united in one common solicitude: What is the news from Assuan?* Has the river risen? Is it not later than usual? Does it not look like a bad year? Will it ever rise sufficiently to save the cotton? One day a message of hope is flashed over Egypt. There is a rise of some inches at Assuan. The next day there is again a rise. From one end of the country to the other the countenances of men show signs of relief. But their joy is premature. The next day the river has gone down again. It was a false rise, the precursor, as so often happens, of the real flood. Such alternations of hope and disappointment frequently continue for a week or a fortnight before the true rise unmistakably begins.

At the commencement of the flood it takes ten or twelve days before a rise at Assuan makes itself felt at Cairo. When that time has elapsed, anyone watching on the river bank at the latter place may note how, from day to day, at first slowly, then with ever-increasing rapidity, the water creeps up the bank. After the first week or two, it is no longer only the level, but the whole demeanour of the river, which shows signs of the coming change. Gradually, surely, the current quickens, the water assumes a deeper colour. During the low season, a bather in the Nile may easily make headway against the current. In the first eight days of the descending flood he may still swim up stream, though with increasing difficulty. Another eight days, and all his efforts will only keep him stationary. Eight days more, and all swimming is impossible. By the middle of August the river has risen some twenty feet, and nears the summit of its banks. Its discharge has increased from thirty millions of cubic metres a day to six hundred

* Of course the earliest news of the state of the Nile comes, not from Assuan, but from the frontier at Halfa, as, before the loss of the Sudan, it came from Khartum. The engineers go by the reports from Halfa. But what the mass of the people, by immemorial habit, are accustomed to look to, is the height of the river at Assuan—the boundary of Egypt Proper. The meaning of so many 'pics' (cubits) of water at Assuan is understood by every peasant in Egypt.

millions.* Cross the bridge at night—in one of those balmy Egyptian nights which are unequalled for their purity and their brilliance—and listen to the great river, which six weeks before hardly made its presence felt—so low down was it, so sluggish, and so noiseless—but which now swirls and roars about the piers, as if it would sweep everything before it! There are few more striking manifestations of the might of Nature. And the impression is heightened by the fact that, for months past, not a drop of rain has fallen. No cloud has crossed the sky. There has been no sign of storm or thunder. It is to the tropical rains of countries fifteen hundred and two thousand miles off that this tumult of waters is due.

And now the basins of Upper Egypt are rapidly filling with water. By the middle of September, as you stand on one of the low desert hills and look over the country, it is all a huge lake, while in the Delta both branches of the Nile and the numberless artificial channels are flowing at full speed. The whole land is a land of rivers, as erstwhile it was a land of dust. Physical comfort is restored. The spirits of men have risen as the waters rose. Crops, cattle, human beings, all rejoice together in the abundance of the first necessary of life. The water, charged as it is with quantities of fine mud, is murky to look at, but it is refreshing to bathe in and wholesome to drink. Wherever you go on the banks of the Canals you see brown-skinned men and boys plunging with delight into the life-giving stream. Women are drawing from it, dogs are lapping it, the great patient buffaloes are standing up to their necks in it, pictures of content.

But soon a new anxiety, the opposite of that which lately possessed them, begins to cloud the gladness of men's hearts. The longed-for flood has come with a

* The average daily discharge of the Nile at Cairo in the flood months—which are, roughly speaking, August, September, and October—is upwards of six hundred million cubic metres. In the lowest years it has been as little as four hundred and fifty millions, in the highest it has sometimes exceeded one thousand millions.

vengeance. The question now is: Will it go, or, rather, will it go in time? In Upper Egypt the basin land has by this time been thoroughly saturated The moment will soon come when the water ought to be running off the fields if they are to be sown in season. But it cannot run off while the river is flowing brim full. Moreover, throughout the whole length of the country the embankments of the Nile are being nervously watched. Strong barriers as they are, the strain which two months of flood has put upon them is sure to find out some weak points. And as the river, especially in the Delta, is running high above the level of the adjoining land, the consequence of a breach might be to inundate a whole district, and to carry destruction to the homes and the harvests of thousands of the inhabitants.

As September wears on, people begin to look as anxiously for news of a fall of the Nile at Assuan, as in the middle of June they were looking for news of a rise. In this instance, too, the issue may long be a doubtful one. As the river often has a false rise, so it often has a false fall. And the vicissitudes of the fall, like those of the rise, become known with extraordinary rapidity throughout the country, and are followed with the same strained and universal interest. It is not till the fall has been steady and continuous for a number of days that the general concern is allayed, and the state of the river ceases, for the first time for six months, to be the predominant thought in the minds of the people of Egypt.

By the beginning of October, in an average year, the crisis is over, though the water-level at Cairo is often at its highest at that time, as the river begins to be swollen by the discharge from the basins of Upper Egypt. But in a year of very high Nile, like 1887, or in 1892, the tension may be greatly prolonged. Throughout the flood, and especially towards the close of it, when the danger is greatest, the embankments, for hundreds of miles, are watched day and night by an army of men called out for that purpose. Every eighty yards or so there is a post consisting of one or more sentinels, who never leave the bank, their only shelter —though shelter is scarcely needed—being a rude hut of durra stalks. At night each post hangs out its lantern, the long line of lights along the brimming river producing a picturesque and striking effect. But the sentinels alone would be of little use to cope with a disaster. At intervals of a few miles are stationed gangs of men supplied with the materials and tools necessary to repair a breach, and ready to rush off at a moment's notice to any point from which danger is signalled.

The least alarm is passed along with the speed of lightning from post to post, until it reaches the nearest gang. If the danger is more serious, reinforcements are hurried up, and the engineer of the district is at once summoned. The Inspectors of Irrigation are constantly on the *qui vive*. During high flood they spend most of their time on the river, reviewing their long line of fortifications and its innumerable garrison, stopping repeatedly at the most dangerous points to see that everything is in order, and that all provisions have been made in case of accident. And if for a few days they are able to return to headquarters at Cairo, where piles of papers are always awaiting them, they are momentarily liable to a summons to rush off to any part of their districts where a breach has occurred or is foreseen. Their steamers are in constant readiness, and they may have to start at any hour of the day or night. Sometimes they may have taken a journey of fifty or a hundred miles at full steam, only to find on arrival that the alarm was a false one. And perhaps they have hardly time to turn round before a fresh alarm is signalled, and off they dash again to a new and possibly distant point of attack. This state of things generally continues for about a month. In an exceptional year, like 1892, the battle may last much longer, and then it is certain that, however skilfully the flood is dealt with, some damage will ensue. Even if any serious accident is avoided, the infiltration from the river is always more or less injurious to the neighbouring lands, and in a year of prolonged flood the losses resulting from this cause are very considerable.

It is hard to imagine a more interesting life than that of an Irrigation Engineer in Egypt. But at the same time I can think of few lives more trying. He is for ever playing the most exciting of games, in which the stakes are the welfare, possibly the existence, of numbers of his fellow-creatures. Great indeed must be the satisfaction of success. There are not many people who can look back upon so much good—palpable, unquestionable, far-reaching—bestowed upon their kind as the men who can husband the Nile to the best advantage in the period of drought, and keep it innocuous in the period of flood. But there are few also whose success is threatened by more incessant and more various dangers. For nearly one quarter of the year is it only by minute and constant calculation, and by the most scientific management of an elaborate artificial system, that they can succeed in making the water last, in sending it at the right moment to the right place, in giving to each district its fair share, in saving all the cultivation that can be saved, and in taking care that they sacrifice—if sacrifice there must be—the less valuable in order to preserve the more valuable crops. For something like another quarter of the year they are harassed by an exactly opposite, but equally difficult, problem—how to get rid of the water with the least injury to the country and the channels, with the smallest deposit of silt in the canal beds, and, during that great struggle at the end, with the least risk of any great breakdown in their long line of artificial defensive works. And when the successive crises of low flood and high flood are over, how enormous is the labour which lies before them throughout the winter in clearage, in repairs, in putting right such parts of their system as they know to be still defective, in renewing and strengthening those works upon which the strain has been too great! For the embankments of the river, after the flood has gone, are somewhat like fortifications that have been exposed to a long siege, with this difference: that in a twelvemonth the siege will surely come again, and the interval must not be allowed to pass without preparing for the emergency.

To understand, even in outline, the Agriculture of Egypt, two great facts must be borne in mind. The first is that the country is watered, not by rain, but by the river. In Upper Egypt rain practically never falls. Even in Lower Egypt it is a negligible quantity. The second great fact is, that the river is not only the irrigator, but the fertilizer of the soil. The fine reddish-brown mud which the Blue Nile washes down from the volcanic plateaus of Abyssinia, mixed with organic matter from the swamp regions of the White Nile, does more than any manure can do for the annual renovation of the land.

For thousands of years the agriculture of Egypt depended entirely upon the unaided action of the river. The valley was intersected by dykes, running at right angles to the Nile, and forming with the embankments of the latter, and with the rising desert land which bounds the valley on either side, a series of basins so contrived as to regulate the course of the flood and to compel it to deposit the rich matter with which it was charged. These basins were in a series of chains, each chain being fed by a separate canal from the river, and having a separate escape, by which the water, after doing its work, was let out into the river again. In some, but not in all cases, communication was also provided from the bottom basin of one chain to the top basin of the chain immediately below it. By these means the water was retained upon the land—which was generally flooded for six or seven weeks—till it was covered with a thick coat of rich mud. On this mud, after the water had run off, the seed was cast, and the husbandman had nothing to do but to tend his crop, and in the fulness of time to harvest it. The harvest was in March and April, and after it was over the land lay fallow till the next flood.

Throughout the greater part of Upper Egypt* this

* By Upper Egypt I mean the whole country from the apex of the Delta to the southern frontier. It is sometimes divided into Middle and Upper Egypt, but the distinction is only confusing.

primeval system still exists. But in Lower Egypt, that is, the Delta, the last sixty years have seen the introduction of a new agriculture. The old method had great advantages. Cultivation cost little in labour and nothing in manure. The flood itself annually revived the soil and kept it perpetually in heart. But, on the other hand, there was only one crop—though a very rich one. For nearly half the year the land was idle, and the single harvest, which consisted principally of wheat, beans, and clover, though it amply sufficed to nourish the population, was of little value for exportation. In ancient days, no doubt, Egypt was one of the granaries of the civilized world, which was at that time practically confined to the shores of the Mediterranean. But the vaster civilization of to-day requires vaster granaries. Europe now draws its supplies from the great plains of North America, of Russia, and of India. The small contribution of the Nile Valley is of little importance. That barbarian of genius, Mehemet Ali, who made himself master of Egypt in the beginning of the present century, saw that, if the country was to play any rôle in the commercial life of mankind, it must look to other and more valuable crops.

The climate was singularly favourable to the cultivation of two of the most profitable of the earth's products—cotton and sugar. But sugar grows all the year round, and cotton grows just during the six months when, under the old system, the country—all but the strip of high land near the river*—was first waterless and then flooded. In order to grow these crops in large quantities, it was necessary to depart from the old methods and to substitute perennial irrigation for six weeks of flooding. Sugar and cotton must be watered, but they must not be drowned. It was well to deposit the fertilizing mud upon the fallow, but it would not do to deposit it upon growing crops. Hence a double change was necessary. Water had to be supplied all the year round, but it had to be supplied in limited

* The Nile Valley, being of deltaic formation, slopes away from the river to the foot of the desert hills.

quantities. So far as the land was devoted to growing the new crops, it must be constantly watered, but it must never be inundated.

It was in order to receive and distribute water in the shallow season, and not only during flood-time, that the 'Sefi'* or Summer Canals were dug. They are, of course, deeper than the old 'Nili' or Flood Canals, inasmuch as their business is to draw from the river when it is low, and not merely in the flood-time. In order to understand the irrigation of Egypt, this distinction between Summer and Flood Canals must always be borne in mind.

The changes introduced by Mehemet Ali have drawn a sharp line of division between the Irrigation System of Upper and of Lower Egypt. From the apex of the Delta to the southern boundary of Egypt Proper at Assuan—a distance by river of about six hundred miles—the agriculture of the Nile Valley is still the agriculture of the Pharaohs. There is, indeed, a single district, where one of the new Sefi Canals, the Ibrahimía, gives perennial irrigation to some two hundred and forty thousand acres comprising the greatest sugar plantations in Egypt, and, by means of one of its branches, the Bahr Yusef, to the oasis known as the Fayúm. Moreover, the lands immediately adjoining the river all along the valley, the islands, and certain patches in the centre of the basins, watered by wells, bear crops in summer as well as in winter. But, speaking broadly, Upper Egypt is a land of single-crop winter cultivation, annually soaked with Nile water, and renovated by Nile mud, just as it has been any time these six thousand years.

Irrigation under these conditions is comparatively a simple matter. It has puzzles of its own, as we shall see hereafter, and can be carried out very well or very badly. But it presents nothing like the tangle of difficulties which attend the modern system, prevalent throughout the Delta. The object of the latter system is to render the land more fertile, by allowing it to be

* From 'Sef,' pronounced like our English 'safe,' the Arabic word for summer.

cultivated in summer as well as in winter, in the season of low water and of flood, as well as when the flood is over. And the result has undoubtedly been an extraordinary development of the wealth of the country. The richest crops, the crops which give Egypt her position in the markets of the world, are grown on the lands of the Delta, or of the exceptional district of Upper Egypt just referred to, which are preserved from inundation, and fed with water in driblets all the year round, by means of the Sefi Canals.

But this enormous increase in the produce of the soil has not been without its drawbacks. You cannot take an extra crop out of the land, especially when it is an exhausting crop like sugar or cotton, without diminishing its natural fertility. And if the new system of cultivation takes more out of the land, it at the same time puts less into it. For since it is essential, wherever cotton and sugar are being grown, that the flood should not cover the country as it did formerly—as it does in the greater part of Upper Egypt to-day—but should be carried right away into the sea, the soil is deprived of the fertilizing and recuperative effect of the rich mud which the high Nile brings down in such abundant quantity. Twice as much is demanded of it as in the old days, and the revivifying substance, better than any manure, which in the old days was annually given to it, has been taken away. The inevitable consequence is a marked deterioration of the soil, which can only be remedied by a free use of artificial manure, or by giving the land, from time to time, a thorough soaking with flood water. The latter method amounts, in fact, to a partial and occasional return to the basin system.

This deterioration was aggravated by the unscientific manner in which summer cultivation was introduced, and especially by the neglect of the great essential of proper drainage. It was the want of drainage which completed the ruin of the Birríya, that broad belt of land which occupies the northern and lowest portion of the Delta, adjoining the great lakes. There are upwards of one million acres of this region, now swamp, or salt marsh, or otherwise uncultivable, which in ancient times were the garden of Egypt. Fortunately, a great portion of the Birríya may be reclaimed with comparative ease. The salted lands, especially, which form so large a part of it, can be rescued by thorough washing, and by the cultivation of rice, the restorative nature of which crop is well known to the Egyptian agriculturist. Rice cultivation, indeed, must be on a restricted scale, as long as the present dearth of water in summer continues. But there is always the possibility of washing the land in winter, when water is abundant. For all these purposes, however, drains are indispensable, and it is only in the last few years that a beginning has been made in supplying this want.

The truth is, that the system of perennial irrigation, conceived by Mehemet Ali, was too difficult and too complicated a business for the men who had to carry it out. Up to 1882 the condition of that portion of the country in which the new system had been established was steadily going from bad to worse. In ancient times Egypt must undoubtedly have possessed engineers of first-rate capacity. But in this, as in many other respects, her present inhabitants fall far behind the tradition of their ancestors. Mehemet Ali himself recognised this fact. He called in the assistance of highly-trained engineers from France to supply the lack of native capacity. But the Frenchmen, who, up to the time of the British Occupation, were supposed to represent the scientific element in the business of irrigation, are not to be blamed if, despite their counsels, that business was a failure. They failed where the English have succeeded, but the fault was not theirs. It was not due to any want of capacity on their part, but to the falseness of their position. They were advisers, and advisers merely. And what is the good of skilled advice, without authority to secure its adoption? Sitting at head-quarters at Cairo, they could not see what was being done by their agents in the provinces, done, often, against the better judgment of those agents themselves, in deference to powerful local influences, or to the commands of ignorant Mudirs. And if they had seen those mistakes, they would have had no power to prevent them.

The position of the English Engineers is different. They do not sit at head-quarters, but traverse the country from end to end. And they have a power behind them, which ensures their advice being followed. 'I must deprecate,' says one of the most eminent among them, 'any invidious comparison between the French and the Anglo-Indian Engineers. The comparison must be made really between the Arab Engineers *advised* by French Engineers and the Anglo-Indian Engineers *directing* the Arab Engineers.' That is the root of the whole matter. European skill—in this as in other respects—is necessary for the regeneration of Egypt. But European skill is useless without European authority. Wherever you turn, that cardinal fact stares you in the face.*

It was during the fifty years before such authority was established that the irrigation of the Delta was reduced to chaos. To make the land of Egypt cultivable all the year round, without ruining it, is under any conditions an intricate problem. It requires a network of main and subsidiary Canals, each member of which must be scientifically designed, in respect of capacity and level. These Canals must be supplied with regulating sluices, which have to be judiciously located and carefully worked. And the skill needed to bring the water to the land is not greater than that needed to take it off again. As I have said, irrigation is fatal without drainage. And the two systems, each very complicated, must be kept distinct, like the veins and arteries of the human body, if the most direful confusion is not to ensue. But the difficulties which beset perennial irrigation are, in Egypt, vastly augmented by the fact that, under existing circumstances, there is a considerable portion of the year during which water is very scarce. If you want science to make the Canals

* See pp. 185-187, and, indeed, see this volume *passim*.

properly, you want, not merely science, but good husbandry and equity to ensure the proper use of them during the painful period when only the most rigid economy and most impartial distribution of water can do justice to the needs of all. Egyptian Irrigation is a moral as well as a scientific problem.

But in the creation of the new irrigation works in the Delta, science and morality had alike been wanting. Private interest had ruled supreme in their construction. Technical skill had been conspicuous by its absence. As a consequence, every conceivable blunder and injustice had been committed. The Canals were faulty in slope, in capacity, and in alignment. Moreover, they were not adequately supplied with regulating sluices, and where such sluices existed, they were often found in the wrong places, and were constantly closed at the wrong times. The channels were accordingly choked with silt, for the removal of which enormous numbers of men were obliged to submit to weeks and months of forced labour, without, in many cases, being able to effect the desired result. Irrigation outlets were cut from the main Canals, regardless of all considerations of level and of the area which they were intended to supply. Hence reckless waste of water in one place, impossibility of obtaining water in another. Moreover, pumping engines had been erected on the Canal banks by permission of the Government—for no engine could be put up without such permission—regardless of the capacity of a particular Canal to feed the engine, and with consequent detriment to the other proprietors along its banks.

But perhaps the worst feature of all was the neglect of drainage, which was steadily ruining large tracts of country. Even where drains existed, they were frequently used also as irrigation channels, than which it is impossible to conceive a worse sin against every sound principle of agriculture. In some cases these channels would be flowing brim full for purposes of irrigation, just when they should have been empty to receive the drainage water. Elsewhere the salt-impregnated drainage water was actually pumped back upon the land.

I have only mentioned a few instances of the almost incredible tangle of mistakes, fatal to the fertility of the soil, and wasteful of the money of the Government and the labour of the people, with which the Anglo-Indian Engineers, who were summoned to Egypt in 1883 and 1884, found themselves compelled to grapple. To bring order out of such confusion was the work of years. That work is not completed even yet, though in the most important districts of Egypt the glaring faults of the old system have been remedied, and irrigation is now conducted on scientific principles. But at the outset the difficulty was tremendous. It was almost impossible to see one's way through such a network of error. And what made it all the worse was, that there had grown up, intimately intertwined with these blunders, a countless number of vested rights.

In order to rectify a mistake which might, perhaps, be injurious to a whole district, it was often necessary to interfere with some powerful private interest, and before private interests could be made to give way to public necessity, the struggle was long and fierce. It was fortunate that, even in the first year of their presence, the Anglo-Indian Engineers, though they possessed neither the experience of the country nor the command of money necessary to effect anything great, were able to make such a number of minor but striking improvements that the chorus of general approbation soon drowned individual complaints and protests.

The excellent results which from the very outset have attended the labours of the Anglo-Indian Engineers are greatly due to the skilful manner in which Sir Colin Scott Moncrieff organized his new service, and to his happy knack in choosing his subordinates. The innumerable errors of detail confronting him in the system, which he had undertaken to put right—errors, each one of which required the incessant attention of a skilled, energetic, and determined man to deal with it—pointed unmistakably to the necessity of dividing the work.

Sir Colin saw that he could accomplish little without some lieutenants of first-rate ability, and, having got the right men, he wisely accorded them great latitude in the management of their respective districts.

The country was divided into five Circles of Irrigation (three in the Delta and two in Upper Egypt), of which four were entrusted to the new-comers from India.* This plan of localizing the engineering talent, which it had been found desirable to import into the country, proved a complete success. It is not too much to say that, among the English Inspectors of Irrigation, there has not been one weak or second-rate man. Differing widely—even extraordinarily—in character and gifts, they have all displayed in a high degree sound technical knowledge, untiring industry, absolute contempt for hardship or misrepresentation, and the most perfect impartiality. Viewed as a whole, there can be no question that the Irrigation Department is, of all the branches of the Egyptian Service managed by British Chiefs, the one upon which, from first to last, it has been possible to look with the most unmixed pride.

With men of this calibre stationed in every quarter of the country, seeing with their own eyes, and entrusted with a wide discretion to act to the best of their judgment, the work of improvement marched as rapidly as the limited amount of money at the disposal of the Irrigation Service would permit. While a great deal was left to the initiative of the individual Inspectors, and the methods of each of them presented considerable diversity, there was still a general harmony of purpose running through their work. The same evils existed everywhere, and

* These Inspectors were Colonel Ross, Mr. Willcocks, Major Brown, and Mr. Foster. When Moncrieff became Under-Secretary of State, and Colonel Ross took his place as Inspector-General, the latter was replaced by Mr. Garstin. These six men, together with Colonel Western and Mr. Reid, who between them restored the Barrage, have been the saviours of Egyptian irrigation. Western and Reid left when their special work was finished. Moncrieff and Ross both retired in 1892, Moncrieff being replaced by Garstin, and Ross by Foster in Lower, and by Brown in Upper, Egypt.

they were dealt with on the same principles, though with varying degrees of boldness and ingenuity. The great problem everywhere was to better the machine without interrupting its action. 'Egypt,' wrote Sir Colin Moncrieff in his first report, 'was no *tabula rasa* on which to lay down the most perfect Canal System, but a country whose very life depended on a fully developed but very bad system. It has been necessary to introduce reforms without for a day stopping the existing machinery. When a canal has been closed, it has been necessary to have another canal to take its place.'

In spite of these difficulties, the work was vigorously pushed on all over the country. Old drainage channels, which had been allowed to become blocked, were cleared and prolonged. New drains were cut for the relief of salted and water-logged districts. Lines of Irrigation were disentangled from lines of Drainage. The direction and level of many Canals were rectified. New regulators were built, and the existing regulators were worked in a novel fashion. They were now for the first time closed in the season of low Nile, thus greatly diminishing the cost and labour necessary to raise the water on to the fields. On the other hand, the old habit of closing them during the flood was as far as possible discontinued, and the result was a great reduction of the silt deposit in the canal beds, that fertile source of expense to the State and oppression to the peasantry.

In no respect, indeed, were the new methods more productive of benefit to the people than in this important matter of preventing excessive deposits of silt. I have shown, in the preceding chapter, how the improvement in the finances of Egypt has enabled the Government to dispense with forced labour for the great annual task of removing these deposits. But long before the practice of clearing the Canals by means of the Corvée was abandoned, the amount of clearance necessary had been enormously reduced by the skill of the Engineers. In the case of a single Canal, the Ismailía, which connects the Nile with the Suez Canal, the changes introduced by Colonel Ross brought down the amount of silt deposit from 300,000 cubic metres in former years to 120,000 cubic metres in the year 1884. This represented a saving in the annual cost of dredging of no less than £9,000. The Nagar Canal in Menufía had, up to 1884, suffered from an annual deposit of between 500,000 and 300,000 cubic metres, which it required the Corvée of the whole province—20,000 men working on an average for 40 days—to remove. But by the expenditure of less than £2,000 Mr. Willcocks succeeded in reducing this deposit to only 30,000 cubic metres, thus economizing between seven and eight hundred thousand days of work, or, in terms of money, at least £15,000 a year.

Improvements of this kind were events in 1884. Since then every successive year has had its share of them, and people have come to regard them so much as a matter of course that nowadays it would be looked upon as a failure if any season passed in which the irrigation works were simply kept in order, and no new change for the better effected. As a matter of fact, every year since 1884 has seen some fresh district restored to fertility, and in some cases brought for the first time under cultivation, in consequence of the patient, intelligent, unwearying work which Egypt has learned to expect from the heads of the Irrigation Service, and never expects in vain.

But the achievements of the Irrigation Engineers have not been confined to a number of local improvements, however valuable. The summer irrigation of the Delta, as they found it, was not only faulty in all its details; its great central machinery had completely broken down. In order to make the system work satisfactorily, it is absolutely necessary to raise the level of the river during the low season. Only by this means can the supply of water, at a time when every gallon is worth money, be fully utilized, and its distribution properly controlled. To clear the great arterial Canals every year to such a depth as would enable them to take in the water required from the Nile at the low level of the spring and early summer was a work beyond the resources of the country in the way of labour, even under a powerful despot like Mehemet Ali, who could command the Corvée of the whole population. And when the Canals had been dug to this needless depth, they did not, after all, do their work with anything like the same efficiency as if they had been less deep, and had been filled by artificially holding up the water at their heads. In summer-time they ran at so low a level that it was a difficult and costly business to raise the water on to the land. During the flood and winter months they carried a most superfluous quantity of water at an inadequate slope, and the silt deposits were consequently enormous. Moreover, under this system it was impossible to divert the whole river into the Canals during the low season. The bulk of the precious summer water still flowed down the two natural branches of the Nile, and had to be lifted from them into the irrigation channels by mechanical means.

From the first introduction of summer cultivation it had been recognised that its complete success depended upon the power of damming up the river at the apex of the Delta. Given this power, the last drop of water could be used up, and the whole supply distributed fairly to the different parts of the country by the network of Canals. But without it the system was paralyzed at its central point. Napoleon, during his expedition to Egypt, was one of the first to see of what enormous value a dam across the two branches of the Nile, just below their bifurcation, would be to the agriculture of the Delta. As early as 1833, Mehemet Ali, appalled by the annually recurring difficulty of clearing the Canals to a depth which should enable them to receive the low summer supply of the river, began to lay the foundations of such a dam. But after a year or two the work was abandoned. It was not till 1842 that the French Engineer, Mougel Bey, succeeded in persuading the Viceroy to take up the idea again.

The design of Mougel Bey was a magnificent one, and the mighty dam, which owes its inception to his genius, is one of the greatest irrigation works in the world. This is the famous Barrage (or 'Barrages,' as it is at times more correctly but somewhat pedantically called), which is situated about fourteen miles downstream from Cairo, and spans the two branches of the Nile immediately below the point at which they divide. The work consists of two bridges, one across the Rosetta and one across the Damietta Branch of the river, each of sixty-one arches.* They are connected by a revetment wall, a thousand metres in length, which runs across the intervening peninsula, and in the middle of which is the head of the Menufía Canal, the main source of water-supply to that portion of the Delta lying between the two arms of the Nile. The arches of both bridges are constructed so as to leave a free passage for the water when high, but to be closable by means of iron gates, whenever it is thought necessary to raise the level of the river. With the gates completely closed, the Barrage thus constitutes a barrier pounding up all the water in the river, and enabling the main Canals to receive their full supply by free flow from the reservoir so created.

The Barrage took nearly twenty years to build. It cost £E1,800,000 in money, to say nothing of the unpaid labour of the peasantry who were employed upon it. But it was practically useless till Sir Colin Moncrieff came to Egypt. The arches of the bridge over the Damietta Branch had not even been supplied with gates. The bridge over the Rosetta Branch had indeed been used, but in a tentative and half-hearted fashion, which rendered it of little value. When it was first completely closed in 1863, a settlement took place, and the passage was almost immediately re-opened. In 1867 a further accident occurred, causing serious damage to ten of the arches, and after this the work was virtually despaired of. In 1883 it was officially declared valueless, except to regulate the flow of water in the two branches of the river. The most that had ever been got out of it was an additional head of water of about half a metre.

Such was the deplorable condition of this splendid

* The Damietta Branch Barrage originally had seventy-one arches, but ten of these have been suppressed.

and costly work at the time of Sir Colin Moncrieff's arrival. But this was not the whole of the mischief. The comprehensive scheme of irrigation of which the Barrage was the basis included the construction of three Main Canals, taking off from it and watering respectively the Eastern, the Central, and the Western provinces of the Delta.* Of these three Canals, only the middle one, the Rayah Menufía, was in working order. The Eastern Canal had been commenced but abandoned. The Western Canal, the Rayah Behera, had, indeed, been completed, but sand-drifts having choked up the portion nearest its head, it could take in little or no water direct from the river at low level. In order to supply the province of Behera, the Government had therefore entered into a thirty-three years' contract with an Irrigation Company to pump water out of the river into the Canal at two stations on the Rosetta Branch of the Nile. By this contract, the Government bound itself to pay a minimum of £E26,000 a year to the Company plus a varying sum depending upon the amount of water actually pumped. This outlay would have been entirely unnecessary if the Barrage had been in working order, and the Rayah Behera cleared of sand-drift. In 1891-1892 this pumping has been dispensed with, and the Government is now paying its £E26,000 a year for nothing.

But, wasteful and uningenious as the plan of pumping the river into the main Canals may appear, it was just about to receive a great extension. When Sir Colin Moncrieff came to Egypt, he found a scheme under the consideration of the Public Works Ministry, and on the point of being accepted, by which a system, similar to that already employed in Behera, was to be adopted for the whole of the Delta. Engines were to be erected at an initial cost of £E700,000 and kept going at an annual

* The Eastern provinces—those to the right of the Damietta branch of the Nile—are Dakahlía and Sharkía ; the Central provinces—those between the Damietta and the Rosetta branches—are Menufía and Gharbía ; the Western province—to the left of the Rosetta branch—is Behera.

cost of £E250,000, in order to supply all the principal Canals by lifting water into them out of the river. There is something very bizarre in the idea that the Egyptian Government was actually on the verge of trying to lift the whole river, or as much of it as could be thus intercepted, by means of pumping engines, when all the time the same object could have been accomplished far more easily and efficiently by holding up the water at the Barrage, if that work had only been put in order. There can, of course, be no comparison between the two methods. The former is costly, the latter cheap. The former only utilizes part of the water, most of which is running away while you are pumping at it. The latter enables you to utilize the whole of it. No one would have dreamt of adopting the former counsel of despair, if the possibility of proceeding by the latter and better method had not been abandoned, and abandoned without adequate trial.

It is the most extraordinary thing in the world that for the sixteen years preceding Sir Colin's arrival no serious effort had been made to repair the Barrage. There was plenty of talk about it. A great scheme was in existence, involving an outlay of £1,250,000. But nothing practical had been attempted. No doubt the idea of repairing anything is alien to the Arab mind. An Egyptian builds a house; but the last thing which ever occurs to him is to look after it when built. He is quite content to live in it, and watch it deteriorate year after year without anything being done to arrest the process, until it threatens to tumble done about his ears. Then he leaves that house and builds another. It is a pious act to build a mosque. But what Egyptian thinks of preserving the magnificent mosques already existing? Up to quite recent years the finest monuments of Arab art were being allowed to crumble to ruin without a finger being lifted to prevent it. And how much costly machinery has not been imported into Egypt during the last half-century, which has either been suffered to rust unused or been spoilt in the use with incredible rapidity for want of the most ordinary care? That 'a stitch in time saves nine' is the last proverb to be recognised in Egypt.

But even when full account has been taken of this unfortunate idiosyncrasy, the total neglect of the Barrage still appears inexplicable. Perhaps it was due to the fact that the undertaking, being indissolubly connected with the name of Mehemet Ali and his immediate successor Abbas, the following Viceroys, Said and Ismail, preferred spending all their money on new schemes of their own to devoting a comparatively small sum to the maintenance of this great work of earlier and better rulers. And by the time Tewfik came to the throne, the Barrage was almost forgotten, and there was, moreover, no longer any money to spend.

But, whatever may have been the cause, the fact remains that nobody had tried the experiment of restoring the Barrage. When Sir Colin Moncrieff started the notion of doing so, he was good-naturedly forgiven for his 'ignorance of the country, natural in a foreigner'—that favourite Egyptian excuse for escaping the trouble of improvements. But the new-comer was not to be daunted by such discouragement. The pumping contract was laid aside, and when the low-water season of 1884 came round, a first attempt was made to see how much water the Barrage could hold up if both the bridges were closed. The enterprise was entrusted to Mr. Willcocks, and it turned out a signal success. By a number of ingenious temporary measures he succeeded in holding up two and a quarter metres on the Rosetta, and about one metre on the Damietta Branch.* The effect produced was extraordinary. The discharge of the Rayah Menufía was doubled, and that of the Rayah Behera and of the three Sefi Canals, which draw from the river between Cairo and the Barrage, greatly increased. Water in abundance made its appearance as late as the middle of June in districts where it had not been seen for

* Of course the water surface level above the two dams is the same. The reason why the Barrage on the Rosetta side has to bear a greater head than that of the Damietta side is, that the bed of the river is lower in the former than in the latter branch.

years except during flood-time. And not only was the quantity increased, but, owing to the delivery being at a higher level, an immense saving was effected in the trouble and cost of lifting. The cotton crop for 1884 was nearly half a million kantars above the highest figure of previous years.

The experiment of 1884 was repeated in 1885 with even better results, so far as raising the level of the river was concerned. And, having succeeded for two successive years in patching up the Barrage, the Irrigation Engineers were able to make a very powerful appeal for a special grant to carry out its complete restoration. The sum required was quite beyond the resources of the annual Budget of their Department; but, fortunately, it was found possible to provide it out of 'the million for Public Works' included in the guaranteed Loan of 1885.* The necessary money thus secured, the work was pushed on with great energy. Two new experts were brought from India to take it in hand, Colonel Western as Director-General of Works, and Mr. Reid as Resident Engineer. Their task was a very heavy one. To ensure the stability of the Barrage against the pressure of a great body of water is a matter of remarkable difficulty. The gigantic weight of this structure rests on nothing but fine mud and sand. There is no solid foundation attainable. Moreover, all the time that the Barrage was being repaired it had to be used, too; for after the successful experiments of 1884 and 1885, there would have been a tremendous outcry if something had not been done every summer to keep up the level of the Nile. It was thus necessary to isolate those portions of the work which were under treatment while the remainder of it continued to hold up the river. Every year, as soon as the flood was over, one half of one of the bridges was enclosed by a coffer dam, out of which all the water was pumped, so that the floorings of the arches were left dry. An enormous number of labourers were employed, and the task of repairing the floor and strengthening and extending the great apron of masonry, which constitutes

* See p. 187.

the defence of the structure against the subversive action of the water, proceeded without a day's cessation, and for a great part of the time both night and day. Working thus under the highest pressure, and in the face of innumerable and unforeseen perils arising from the treacherous nature of the river-bed, the western half of the Rosetta Branch Barrage was finished in the winter and spring of 1886-87, and the eastern half in 1888-89. The eastern half of the Damietta Branch Barrage was similarly completed in 1887-88, and the western half in 1889-90. The arches of both bridges were supplied with iron gates in double leaves, moving in parallel grooves, and raised and lowered by overhead travelling winches. By the low-water season of 1891 the work was finished, and for two successive summers the Barrage has now held up the river to the full height required for the proper distribution of the whole available water-supply among the great arterial Canals. The maximum head of water which it has borne in the past and the present year has exceeded four metres—the amount contemplated in the original design.

The cost of the restoration of the Barrage was £E460,000, and at least £E30,000 a year will probably be required to keep it in order, as no reasonable expense must be spared for the defence of a construction which is at once so invaluable and exposed to so much danger. But for this expenditure the Barrage does, and does with incomparably greater efficiency, the work which in 1883 it was proposed to perform by pumping engines at an initial expenditure of £E700,000, and an annual expenditure of £E250,000.

The economy—to say nothing of better regulation—effected by the restoration of the Barrage, is not confined to the cost of pumping. It has also been the most potent, though by no means the only, factor in diminishing those enormous silt deposits which, as we have seen, are the bane of Egyptian Irrigation. Now that it is no longer necessary to dig the Canals to as great a depth as formerly, they do not take in so large a quantity of flood water, and it is the flood and not the summer water which causes deposit. Moreover, the beds of the Canals at their intakes being now at a higher level, their slope is increased. The water thus flows down them with greater velocity, and consequently a smaller amount of the matter carried in suspension sinks to the bottom.

The total effect of the new methods in reducing the cost of clearance is very remarkable. The labour required for this purpose, in the Delta alone, under the old system, was estimated in terms of money at £E530,000, and this is probably below the mark. Nowadays, with a greatly increased mileage of Canals, and with a large number of drains into the bargain, which formerly either did not exist or were not kept in order, the annual cost of clearance is only £E200,000.

From every point of view, indeed, the Barrage has been an immense success. Of course it has its critics, but they have the poorest case of any critics of my acquaintance. There was no conceivable change that could have been introduced into Egyptian Irrigation, not even the change from a bad system to a good one, which was not certain to injure somebody. No doubt there are some lands which, owing to their exceptional situation, are worse off now than they were in former times. But the handful of people who profited by the old chaos is absolutely insignificant compared to the numbers benefited by the new order. It is not by hunting up every solitary instance of the few individuals injured, by exaggerating it, reiterating it, making a grievance of it, that our critics can shake the credit of a work from which the agriculture of the Delta, as a whole, has derived such enormous advantage.

And, indeed, nobody seriously contends that the Barrage, so long as it holds out, is not a great boon to the country. What those foreign cavillers—for I do not think there is a single Egyptian who belittles the Barrage—what those foreigners, I say, to whom every good thing done by the English is a stumbling-block, seek to console themselves with, is the alleged instability of the structure. For my own part, I am prepared to maintain that, even if it were to give way next summer, it has already saved Egypt more money than has been spent upon it since 1884. But it is not going to give way. Every injury which it sustains, every accident—and there are often slight accidents—which reminds us of the treacherous character of the subsoil, sends a tremor of hopeful excitement through certain jealous breasts. But disappointment always follows. Oh, if it would only burst! It is to be feared that, if nothing serious happens to it, there are certain persons in Egypt who will themselves burst from baffled spite!

It is surely a strange thing that among those to whom the success of the Barrage is a source of chagrin there should be any Frenchmen. The conception of the work was French. The great design, which the British Engineers have, after all, done nothing but bring to completion, was due to a Frenchman. Sir Colin Moncrieff himself has always been foremost to give full credit to Mougel Bey. He found the poor old man in poverty and oblivion. He was incessant in sounding his praises. He left the Egyptian Government no rest till it had recognised by an adequate pension the services of the man who was the author of the Barrage. If Mougel Bey lived to see the great idea of his life realized, if in his extreme old age he was restored to honour and comfort, the chief thanks are due to our own countryman, who rescued the work and fame of his French predecessor from undisturbed neglect. There is nothing in such a story which should estrange two nations, each of whom has good reasons for looking upon the Barrage with pride.

If there is any charge which can be justly brought against the Barrage, it is that it does its work too well. The storing of the summer water and its diversion into the main Canals is now so complete that, during May and June, the two branches of the river are for a certain distance almost entirely dry. Of course the towns and villages along them are supplied with drinking as well as with irrigation water from one or other of the main Canals, or their branches, and supplied more easily and conveniently than they could be from the river at its lowest. Navigation, too, has been maintained and, indeed, improved. There are now two complete main lines of Canal-Navigation, by which boats can pass during the season of low water from above the Barrage to Alexandria on the one side, or Damietta on the other. Still, when all has been said, the drying up of the river-beds has serious disadvantages, if only from the sanitary point of view. The excuse for it is, that every available drop of water is needed for the crops, and, indeed, given to them. But as soon as the quantity of summer water can be increased, it would certainly be desirable to allow some of it to flow down the two river-branches to the sea.

I have said that the Barrage cost £E460,000. The remainder of 'the Irrigation Million' of 1885 was devoted to making the third or Eastern of the three Main Canals taking off from the Barrage*—begun, as we have seen, years ago, but never completed for any distance—to the improvements in Navigation just referred to, and to Drainage. There still, however, remained some works to be undertaken in the Delta—of more than local importance—both in the extension of Drainage and in improving the Rayah Behera, the great Western Canal. Moreover, Upper Egypt was beginning to push its claims for a share of the extraordinary expenditure on Public Works. Relying on the phenomenal results of the Million Expenditure, the Irrigation Department accordingly appealed for a second special grant for the above-named purposes. The sum asked for was £E1,250,000. The sum actually obtained—as part of the operation for the conversion of the Privileged Debt in 1890—was £E910,000. The bulk of this money has gone to Upper Egypt, though considerable amounts have also been devoted to the Rayah Behera and its branches, and to the extension of Main Drains.

So far as the Delta is concerned, it may be said that the Irrigation System, in its main outlines, has now

* It was called 'Rayah Tewfikía,' in honour of the late Khedive, who opened it in the spring of 1890.

been put on a proper footing. Many minor improvements remain to be effected, and year by year some of them will be taken in hand. But there already exists a complete network of main and subsidiary Canals, having the Barrage as its starting-point, and designed on scientific principles. The System of Drainage is not yet equally complete, for here, as we have seen, the previous neglect had been most conspicuous. But even in this respect enormous progress has been made, and whatever else is urgently required will, in all probability, be carried out during the next few years by means of the ordinary Public Works Budget. Even then the limit of useful expenditure in the way of Drainage will not have been reached. But it must be remembered that, before reclamation on a large scale can become profitable, the summer supply of water will have to be increased.

Such are the main features of the work, which has revolutionized—I can say nothing less—the agricultural condition of the Delta, and saved its inhabitants from the widespread bankruptcy and possible famine which were staring them in the face in the early eighties. Totally different in character, though scarcely less important in their results, have been the operations carried on in Upper Egypt—that is to say, in the long narrow valley—where basin irrigation with inundation in flood-time are the rule, and perennial cultivation the exception. Upper Egypt, indeed, has seen no single enterprise so large or so striking as the restoration of the Barrage. The special expenditure on irrigation in this part of the country has taken the form of a great number of constructions, most of them individually small, but constituting in their totality a comprehensive and elaborate scheme known by the name of the 'Sharáki' Works.

'Sharáki' is the term which is applied in Egypt to those lands which have, in any given year, to be relieved of all taxation on account of their receiving no water whatever. In Upper Egypt the amount of 'Sharáki' used to be very considerable. It averaged at least forty-five thousand acres a year, while in exceptionally bad years it reached many times that amount. In 1888, when there was a very low Nile, the loss to the Government, in taxes abandoned on account of 'Sharáki,' was nearly £E300,000. Evidently it was worth while to face even a very large expenditure in order to avoid the recurrence of such disasters, to say nothing of the habitual loss of about £E50,000 from 'Sharáki' in average seasons.

But the £E600,000 or thereabouts, which was granted for the prevention of 'Sharáki,' has not been utilized for that purpose alone. The opportunity has been taken to remodel generally the Canals of Upper Egypt in such a manner as to make them far more satisfactory in every respect. It is true that the basin system had never fallen into anything like the same disorder as that which we found existing in the Delta. It was the ancient system of the country and, thanks to the experience of centuries, was never wholly mismanaged. But, while not vicious in principle, it was very primitive in many of its details. The number of masonry works was inadequate, so that in order to pass water from one basin into another, or from the tail-end of a chain of basins into the river, recourse was frequently had to the primeval method of breaching the bank. Moreover, the several chains of basins were not so connected as to give each other the maximum amount of assistance in the distribution of the flood. When, owing to the inadequate filling of the principal Canal of any one chain of basins, the higher basins belonging to that chain were insufficiently flooded, there were often no means of supplying the deficiency from the main Canal of the chain immediately above.

It would be obviously impossible to enter here into the details of the scheme by which Colonel Ross, who designed the whole of the 'Sharáki' Works, has solved the chief problems of Basin Irrigation, ingenious as many of these details are, and interesting even to non-technical people. But it is worth while to note that he had constantly to keep in view two distinct objects, not always easily combined. The first was to make sure that every basin—and he was dealing with a hundred and twenty of them, varying in size from five hundred to thirty-five thousand acres—should, even in a year of low Nile, be adequately flooded. The other was to give to every part of each basin, as far as possible, not merely water, but water of the 'red' or fertilizing quality. Whether the water he receives is 'red' or 'white' makes a vital difference to the agriculturist of Upper Egypt. The 'red' water (I think *we* should call it brown) is that which has not yet deposited its precious mud, the annual regenerator of the soil. The 'white' water is that which has already parted with its mud. Land inundated by 'red' water every year, for a sufficient time, never deteriorates. Land inundated only by 'white' water rapidly becomes exhausted. In traversing the fields of Upper Egypt, any observant traveller must be struck by the remarkable contrast often exhibited in the quality of the crops on adjoining lands, where all the natural conditions appear at first sight to be identical. On inquiry, it almost always turns out that, where the crops are poor, it is due to some defect in the irrigation works, or perhaps to some insuperable disadvantage of situation, which has prevented these particular fields from being inundated with 'red' water.

Were it not for this necessity of flooding the land with water of a certain quality, Basin Irrigation would be comparatively easy. As it is, the filling of the basins is a most complicated business. Very varied means have to be adopted, and a great multiplicity of feeders devised, especially in large basins, in order to distribute the precious mud equally over the land. The number of individual works, such as canal extensions or widenings, syphons, regulators, culverts, etc., on which the 'Sharáki' grant has been expended, amounts to several hundreds. It required the great scientific attainments, the memory, the minute knowledge of the country, and the mastery of detail, which distinguish Colonel Ross, to bring this complicated enterprise to a satisfactory conclusion.

As to the good results of the expenditure, local testimony leaves no room for doubt. Some of the most neglected districts in the provinces of Kena and Girga now confess to receiving good 'red' water with as much regularity as their neighbours. The efficacy of the work in increasing the area of flooded land in a year of very low Nile has yet to be tested by a season like the summer of 1888. But we have already some evidence on the point. In 1891 the Nile flood, though not a bad one, was considerably below the average. I have it from a competent authority that there were fifty thousand more acres under water in Upper Egypt in 1891 than could possibly have been inundated without the new works. I cannot vouch for the accuracy of the statement, but from all that I know on the subject—and it is one about which I had to make a good many inquiries on the spot—the estimate appears a moderate one. Now, the yield of average basin land in Upper Egypt is at least £E4 an acre. The amount saved to the country in a single year—and that not by any means of the worst—would thus be £E200,000. In this, as in other instances, what is so striking about Egyptian Public Works is the largeness and the rapidity of the return when capital is wisely expended.

This is, I feel, a very imperfect and superficial account of a big subject. But it will have served its purpose if it has given some idea of the great variety of difficulties by which the problem of artificially supplying water to a whole country is beset, and of the industry, ingenuity, and, on the whole, remarkable economy with which that problem has been dealt with by the small body of able and devoted men who have been gathered under the command of Sir Colin Scott Moncrieff. The longer I remained in Egypt, and the more I saw of the country, the more clear it became to me that the work of these men had been the basis of all the material improvement of the past ten years. We at the Finance Office have, so to speak, registered that improvement in our easier budgets and growing surpluses; but it is the engineers who have created it. Any share which the financiers have had in the matter consists in the fact that, by the repression of wasteful expenditure, they have rendered possible the beneficent outlay of which the engineers have been the directors. If the old waste had gone on, the sums which could have been allotted to Public Works would not long have sufficed even for maintenance. If the credit of Egypt had not been restored, the fresh capital which was necessary to put the Irrigation System straight could never have been obtained. And the experience of the past in this respect is the best guide for the future. As long as the Irrigation of Egypt is in the hands of men like its late or its present chief and their principal assistants, the best thing that the Finance Ministry can do is to place as much money as it can safely afford at their disposal, confident that whatever is thus spent will bring in a splendid return.

There is one respect in which the British Irrigation Officers are more fortunate than most of their countrymen engaged in the service of the Khedive. Their work is not only successful, but it is appreciated. Whatever may be the feeling of the Egyptians about the British Occupation, however great may be the prejudice existing in some quarters against the presence of British officials, there is no doubt that the chiefs of the Irrigation Service have overcome all the odium naturally attaching to them as foreigners and Christians, and enjoy an almost universal popularity throughout the length and breadth of the land. And not only popularity, but extraordinary and even touching confidence. This they themselves probably regard as the highest reward of their ceaseless and unselfish labours. In remote country districts, where the name of England is scarcely ever heard, and where the ignorant country-folk are hardly aware of the difference between one European people and another, the Inspector of the Circle is not only a personality known to all the world, but is trusted and sought after in the most various troubles and disputes. Wherever he goes he is liable to be appealed to, not only about matters belonging to his special department, but about every other conceivable question in which the inhabitants are interested. It is often difficult for him to explain that some of the subjects brought before him—questions of land-ownership, for instance—are absolutely no business of his, and that the petitions addressed to him should be submitted to some quite different authority. The people recognise in him the great benefactor of their district, and, with a child-like simplicity, they turn to him for help and counsel, even in concerns the least related to his actual functions.

I remember once discussing the question of our position in Egypt with a native statesman, honest but narrow-minded, who avowed himself bitterly opposed to our presence and to our policy. I could not help asking him how he thought the country would get on without the British Engineers. He promptly answered, 'You do not suppose that if Great Britain were to retire from Egypt we should let the engineers go. I myself should be the first to do everything I could to retain them.' Whether the engineers, deprived of the power which the predominance of English influence gives them, would be of anything like the same utility as they are to-day; whether, indeed, their efforts might not be rendered wholly useless, is a question I will not discuss here. I merely mention the incident as a proof of the way in which, even among the most anti-English natives, the work of these officers is appreciated.

Only one case in point to conclude with. It is a story which I think I have seen in print before, but it is so remarkable that it will, perhaps, bear repetition. In the bad year 1888, when, as has been stated, the Nile flood was an exceptionally poor one, there was a large area in the province of Girga which was threatened, like many others in Upper Egypt, with a total failure of the inundation. The Canal which ordinarily flooded this particular district was running at a level at which the water could not possibly spread over the fields, and many thousands of acres seemed doomed to absolute barrenness. A cry of despair arose from the whole neighbourhood, What was to be done? One of the English Inspectors of Irrigation, who happened to be on the spot, promptly determined to throw a temporary dam across the Canal. The idea was a bold one. The time was short. The Canal was large, and, though lower than usual, it was still carrying a great body of water at a considerable velocity. Of course no preparations had been made for a work the necessity of which had never been contemplated; but the Inspector was not to be daunted by the apparent hopelessness of the undertaking. Labour, at any rate, was forthcoming in any quantity, for the people, who saw starvation staring them in the face, needed no compulsion to join gladly in any enterprise which offered them even the remotest chance of relief. So the Inspector hastily got together the best material within reach. He brought his bed on to the Canal bank, and did not leave the scene of operations, night or day, till the work was finished. And the plan succeeded. To the surprise of all, the dam was, somehow or other, made strong enough to resist the current. The water was raised to the required level, and the land was effectually flooded.

The joy and the gratitude of the people knew no bounds. It was decided to offer thanksgivings in the Mosque of the chief town of the district, and the event was considered of such general importance that the Minister of Public Works himself made a special point of attending the ceremony. But the enthusiastic population were not content with the presence of the high native dignitary. They insisted that his English subordinate also should be there. They were not willing to give thanks for their deliverance without having amongst them the man who had wrought it. Everyone knows how deep a prejudice exists in Mohammedan countries against the presence of a Christian in a Mosque. In the great tourist-visited cities of Egypt this feeling is wearing off, but in the country districts it is as strong as ever. In those districts it is an unheard-of thing that a Christian should be present at a religious ceremony—more than unheard of that he should be present at the instance of the Mohammedan worshippers themselves. But in this case the universal feeling of thankfulness and admiration was too strong for the most deeply-rooted fanaticism. For the first time, doubtless, in the history of that neighbourhood, an Englishman and a Christian was allowed, and even compelled, by the natives, to take part in a solemn function of their usually exclusive and intolerant faith.

The work of the Irrigation Engineers has during the last ten years been tested by trials as severe as any to which it is ever likely to be exposed. The season of 1888, as we have seen, was one of very low flood. The seasons of 1887 and 1892 have been marked by two of the highest floods on record. In the ten years preceding the Occupation, there had also been very high Niles in 1874 and 1878, and a very low Nile in 1877. But while the high Niles of 1874 and 1878 burst the embankments right and left—that of 1878 more especially breaching the left bank of the Damietta branch, and sweeping over the crops and villages for thirty or forty miles—the high Niles of 1887 and 1892 were directed safely into the sea with but inconsiderable loss. And while the low Nile of 1877 cost the Government £E1,100,000 in 'Sharáki,' and was followed by a regular famine, the low Nile of 1888 cost the Government less than £E300,000, and did not lead to anything that could be called a famine, although there certainly was scarcity and great hardship in certain districts. But this, as we have seen, was before the execution of the special works destined to secure the inundation of the basins even in years of inadequate flood. Alike in high and in low Niles, Egypt, if we may judge from the experience of the immediate past, is now safe-guarded, not of course against some damage, but against anything like a general catastrophe.

The result of ten years' work in the Irrigation Department may be summed up in the statement that the very most is now made of the existing resources of the country in the way of water, while the dangers incident to a high flood are reduced to a minimum. There remains the great problem whether the water available for irrigation may not be largely increased by the creation of one or more Reservoirs, which shall retain part of the superfluous discharge of the flood or winter seasons, in order to increase the supply during the succeeding summer.

The creation of a Reservoir is indeed the burning question of Egyptian Irrigation at the present day. Into the comparative merits of the various proposed sites and projects I do not propose to enter. The Egyptian Government is, I believe, resolved to submit these competing schemes, as soon as they are in an adequate state of preparation, to a Commission of experts, and it would be folly for any unscientific writer to attempt to forestall the decision of such a body. But it may be interesting to point out the extent of the benefit which Egypt might derive from the execution of any such scheme, and to consider how the means of executing it might be obtained.

The cultivated area of Egypt is about five million acres, of which two million eight hundred thousand are in Lower, and two million two hundred thousand in Upper, Egypt. With an augmented supply of water, cultivation in both parts of the country might be greatly increased, but in two different ways. In Lower Egypt the increase would take the form of additional land, either reclaimed or brought under cultivation for the first time. In Upper Egypt it would take the form, not of an extension of the cultivated area, but of the introduction of summer culture in districts which at present only bear crops in the winter and spring.

What is the extreme limit of possible extension in either case? The total amount of land which could possibly be cultivated in Lower Egypt may be estimated at four million eight hundred thousand acres—that is to say, two million more than now, of which about two-thirds would be land reclaimed, and the rest land cultivated for the first time. But no reasonable person imagines that either the enterprise, the money, or the labour for so great an extension as this could be forthcoming in the next fifty years, even if the water were found. The most which any sane advocate of the Reservoir scheme, however enthusiastic, contemplates as within immediate prospect is an addition of six hundred thousand acres to the cultivated area of the Delta. But even this amount would add very greatly to the wealth of the country. Ordinary Delta land, even at the present low prices, will bear crops worth at least £5 an acre. So here is a certain promise of £E3,000,000 a year, if the necessary water can be obtained in summer.

In Upper Egypt the problem is different. All the cultivable land is already under crops in the winter time. What the Reservoir men urge is, that, given the extra water, it would be highly advantageous to assimilate the culture of Upper to that of Lower Egypt by introducing in the former a system of perennial irrigation. It is, indeed, problematic whether the proposed conversion of all the basins into Sefi—or Summer Cultivation tracts—would not be accompanied by great disadvantages. The object is of much more doubtful practicability than that of reclaiming the six hundred thousand acres in Lower Egypt. If successfully realized, however, it would, as its advocates maintain, add £E4,000,000 to the annual value of the produce of Upper Egypt.

But, in order to carry out both the above schemes, the amount of storage water required would be enormous. Of the six hundred thousand new acres in Lower Egypt, four hundred thousand might be expected to be under cultivation every summer, and at the outset, at any rate, they would be growing a large proportion of rice. Under these conditions they would require forty cubic metres of water per day per acre, or a total of sixteen million a day. Upper Egypt, if converted into Sefi, would require about twenty-six million cubic metres of summer water a day more than it gets at present. Total: forty-two million cubic metres per day, for the whole country, and that for near one hundred days, on the average, every year. The amount of storage water required would thus amount to somewhere about four thousand million cubic metres per annum.

I know that every one of these figures, though they are the result of careful study, is disputable. What is more, I know that there is no man in existence, not even the highest technical authority, who could set up a calculation on this subject which would not be open to much question. But allowing the widest margin for error and for difference of opinion, the above account gives a fair general impression of what is involved in the Reservoir scheme in its most ambitious developments. For my own part, strong advocate as I am of the principle of a Reservoir, I am perfectly convinced that all this will not be done at once. Egypt may be well content if by the end of this century she finds herself in possession of a Reservoir, discharging annually as much as one-half of the grand total stated above, and adding, say, five hundred thousand acres a year—four hundred thousand in Lower and one hundred thousand in Upper Egypt—to the average amount under summer crops.

Such an increase would be small compared with the gigantic schemes which haunt some people's imagination. But even this modest plan would add three or four millions a year to the produce of the country. And if, as Sir Colin Moncrieff has estimated in his last word on this subject, the necessary Reservoir, together with all subsidiary works, could be obtained for £E2,600,000, it would be about the best investment of money on a large scale that can possibly be conceived. The case for a Reservoir, in some form or other, is more than made out. Assume that Sir Colin Moncrieff under-estimates, and that it would cost, not £E2,600,000 but £E3,000,000. Assume, to be unquestionably on the safe side, that it would cost as much as £E5,000,000. It would certainly even then bring the country a net profit ten times as great as the expense of its creation within the lifetime of one generation.

But, of course, you must first settle the tremendous controversy—where the Reservoir is to be. Shall it be Assuan, Kalabsha, Wadi Halfa, or some other point in the Upper Nile Valley; or shall we follow Mr. Cope Whitehouse's* advice and adopt as a site his beloved

* It is very difficult to deal with Mr. Whitehouse. He is an enthusiast, not to say a fanatic, for the Wadi Rayan scheme. He

Wadi Rayan, the great depression in the Libyan desert to the south-west of the Fayúm? No one who cares about Egypt can fail to look forward with the deepest interest to the answer which the contemplated Commission may give to that momentous question.

And when the site is decided on, how is the money to be got? If Egypt had a free hand in financial matters there cannot be the shadow of a doubt that for so remunerative a scheme, endorsed by the judgment of a powerful Commission of experts, she would not have the smallest difficulty in raising money at a moderate rate of interest. But Egypt, we know, cannot borrow without the consent of Turkey, and even with that consent she could scarcely charge her Budget with the annuity necessary for the new loan—an annuity which might amount to as much as £E200,000 or £E300,000 —without the consent of the Powers to add that sum to her 'authorized' expenditure. There are no doubt the economies resulting from the Conversion of the Debt, which amount to upwards of £E300,000 a year, and which could not be better employed than in defraying the annual charge for the new loan. But here, again, nothing can be done without the consent of the Powers. In one shape or another that consent is requisite if Egypt is to raise the money on her own account.

I do not like to anticipate difficulties with the Powers in this matter when once the magnitude of the end in

---

is utterly incapable—it is not his fault, but his misfortune—of judging fairly anything or anybody that seems to stand in the way of the realization of his pet project. Everything he says or writes about irrigation in Egypt must, therefore, be received with the greatest caution. Still, it is impossible not to feel admiration for a man who devotes his whole life and his remarkable abilities to the advocacy of a great work of public utility, however deplorable may be his controversial methods. The Reservoir which Mr. Whitehouse recommends may not be the best possible Reservoir, but there are some strong *primâ-facie* arguments in its favour. No Commission which may be appointed to examine into this subject should, and I feel confident that no Commission will, dismiss the Wadi Rayan plan without the most careful consideration view and the practical certainty of success are generally realized. But the experience of past years forbids us to look forward very confidently to the unanimity of all nations concerned. That depends upon the temper of France, and the good temper of France in Egyptian matters is evidently not to be counted upon.

Supposing that the worst comes to the worst—supposing that, after the usual interminable discussion, the Powers, or one of them, cannot be induced to allow Egypt to devote some portion of her resources to the best of all conceivable purposes, is it therefore necessary that the scheme should fail? Surely that would not reflect great credit upon the powerful and wealthy State which at present stands towards Egypt in a position of semi-guardianship. The relations between Great Britain and Egypt have not so far been rendered any smoother by excessive generosity on our part in matters of money. The British Treasury, in its natural and very proper jealousy for the interest of the British taxpayer, has insisted upon Egypt paying the last penny which can possibly be regarded as due from her for any services rendered by Great Britain, from the extra cost of the Army of Occupation, which is entirely borne by the Egyptian Treasury, down to the small sum necessary for burying the British soldiers who fell at Tel-el-Kebir. Such financial severity is all very well for the Treasury, but looked at from the broader standpoint of national policy, a more liberal attitude might not only be politically sound, but in the long-run financially remunerative.

Indirectly, Great Britain has made a great deal of money at the expense of Egypt. Sixteen years ago we bought for £4,000,000 Egypt's interest in the Suez Canal, which, had she only clung to it, would soon have become so fertile a source of income to her. What we bought for £4,000,000 will in another year or two be worth something nearer £20,000,000. Would it really be a very enormous sacrifice, or a very extraordinary act of generosity on the part of Great Britain, if we were to devote say one-fourth of the clear profit that we have made out of this fortunate transaction to the benefit of the country at whose expense we have made it, especially when that country is one the interests of which are so intimately bound up, economically and politically, with our own? And would the fitness of such an act of liberality be in any way diminished if the object to which the money was to be applied were the increase of the agricultural wealth, and thereby of the exports and imports of Egypt, in whose external trade we are interested to the extent of more than 50 per cent.?

I hope that the necessity for considering such a proposal may never arise. I hope that Egypt may be allowed to pay for her Reservoir, as she very well can pay for it, out of her own resources. And even if the question did arise, I have not much confidence that any British statesman would be found bold enough to propose to his countrymen to make even this comparatively small sacrifice, however just and politic it might appear. The spirit which might dictate great strokes of statesmanship in the conduct of our foreign affairs seems to be, if not extinct, at least in abeyance. The suggestion just made is likely to be a shot in the air, but it may be a good suggestion, all the same. Personally, I can think of no act which would commend itself more promptly to the equitable judgment of mankind, or which would do more to render Great Britain beloved in Egypt. Any improvement in his water-supply is a thing which goes straight home to the heart of every Egyptian. It is the one sort of benefit which you can confer upon him of which the value is not only indisputable, but universally recognised. The most successful, the most creditable, the most unquestionably useful, of all the services rendered by our country to Egypt have been connected with this vital problem of water. But the work done, great as it is, remains incomplete without the Reservoir. I trust that we may live to see this crown put upon it under British direction, and, if need be, not only under British direction, but through British generosity.

CHAPTER X.

EXPERIMENTS IN JUSTICE.

It was till quite recently a common saying in Egypt, heard as often from the lips of Englishmen as from those of any of their critics, that the progress made since 1882 in the sphere of Justice was nothing much to boast of. This sounds, at first, like the severest possible condemnation of our whole proceedings. To secure justice is the great end of Government. Its radical injustice was the fundamental vice of the old system of Egyptian administration. 'Justice! justice! justice!' were the words in which Sir E. Malet summed up the needs of Egypt when taking leave of the country. How can it be said that the work of the past years has been a solid or an enduring success, if in respect of Justice it leaves so much to be desired?

In truth, such a criticism is only a play upon words. If by 'justice' is meant the spirit of equality and fair dealing in the relations of man and man or in the action of the Government towards its subjects, then it can truly be said that the promotion of justice has been the central principle inspiring our work during these ten years in every department of the State, the essence of all the improvement which has been achieved. It is justice, in this sense of the word, which has raised the Army by securing to the soldiers fair treatment, proper pay, food, clothing, and leave, and by establishing for the officers promotion by merit. It is justice which has lightened the financial burdens of the people by fixing the amount of the taxes, and introducing regularity into their collection. It is justice which has inspired the irrigation officers in distributing water and adjusting the supply to the legitimate needs, and not to the wealth of the recipients. If the methods of the Administration have been radically changed in all its branches and in all its ranks, it is because the idea of equal treatment of men of different classes, of a fair apportionment of public burdens, and a fair distribution of benefits and rewards, has entered into the spirit of the Executive.

But if we use the word 'justice' in its narrower sense, to designate simply what appertains to the Courts of Law—their codes, their procedure, and their personnel—then it must be admitted that, in this special sphere, progress has not been so marked as in many other directions. And the reason is simple. Justice in this sense of the word is a branch of government from which British influence has been largely excluded. Our effective interference in it only dates from 1889, and is still limited in extent. There is not one judicial system in Egypt, but four. There is the old Koranic system, worked by the Mehkemehs or Courts of the Religious Law, which are now mainly confined to dealing with the personal status of Mohammedans. There is the system of the Mixed Courts, which deals with civil actions between foreigners of different nationalities, or between foreigners and natives, and in a small degree with the criminal offences of foreigners. There is the system or no system of the Consular Courts, which deals with the great body of foreign crime. Finally, there is the system of the new Native Courts, which deals with civil actions between natives, or crimes committed by them. Of all these, it is only the Native Courts which the English have taken in hand, and that not till within the last few years. The Religious Courts, full of abuses though they be, are yet hallowed ground upon which it has been thought unwise to suffer the foot of the Christian foreigner to intrude. The system of the Mixed Tribunals is exceedingly difficult to modify, inasmuch as each modification requires the unanimous consent of the fourteen Powers who established them. Such consent could only be obtained after years of discussion, and in the absence of any crying evils in these Tribunals—with so many other things more urgently demanding reform—it has not been worth while to seek it, except for some minor changes. The Consular Courts, again, gross as are the scandals which frequently occur in them, can only be touched, either by extending the criminal jurisdiction of the Mixed Tribunals, or by improving the new Native Courts to such a degree that foreigners can fairly be asked to submit to them. And the time is not yet ripe for so radical a proposal.

There remain, then, only the Native Courts. These, no doubt, are the most important of all from the point of view of the general welfare, both because they affect the greatest number of people, and because it is through their development that the best way out of the existing tangle of jurisdictions can be found. But with these Courts, as has been already explained, it was, for a long time, Great Britain's policy not to meddle,* except by very ineffectual Platonic advice. There are tons of wisdom on the subject in the reports of Sir Benson Maxwell and Sir Raymond West. But in the absence of any pressure upon the native authorities to induce them to listen to such wisdom, these reports simply served to increase the size of Blue Books. It was not till after the fall of Nubar Pasha that the British Government first showed a serious interest in the condition of the Native Courts. It was only with the appointment of Mr. Scott, in the spring of 1890, that practical steps began to be taken to improve them.

I do not say that the preceding six years—for the Native Courts were first established in the beginning of 1884—had been entirely wasted. The mere recognition of the necessity of reformed tribunals, administering a civilized system of law, according to prescribed rules, was in itself a great step in advance. Nor were the new Courts conceived in any illiberal, though certainly in a too theoretical, spirit. Their Codes and Procedure

* See p. 93.

were, with some unimportant alterations, copied from those of the Mixed Tribunals, which in their turn had been borrowed from the French Codes and French Procedure. That was not a bad basis; but a serious error was made in taking too little account of the points in which the French system, as the experience of the Mixed Tribunals had already shown, was unsuitable to the special circumstances of Egypt. The majority of cases which come before the Native Courts are small matters of a simple character. Cheapness and expedition are, under these conditions, the first essentials of a good administration of justice. But the methods actually adopted were in many respects too elaborate for the understanding, and too costly for the means of the people.

It is the besetting sin of Orientals, when attempting to copy European institutions, that they do so without a sufficient regard to the difference of conditions. In Egypt, as in other Eastern countries, there are, roughly speakly, two attitudes of mind towards the civilization of the West—the religious and conservative attitude, to which the whole thing is anathema; and the progressive and free-thinking attitude, which is prepared to bolt Western ideas whole, but has not the power to digest them. Where the latter attitude prevails, the consequence is the importation of some European system, without any adequate recognition of the modifications which are required to make it suitable to its new home. This was the original flaw in the constitution of the Native Courts. Their founders sought to establish a system of ideal perfection, alike beyond the requirements and the capacities of Egypt. In order to ensure in the long-run a flawless decision, it may be desirable to have cases tried by a posse of judges, and to multiply appeals. But for practical purposes, especially in a backward country, something much more rough and ready—always provided it be incorruptible—is greatly to be preferred.

And there was a special reason why, at that time, it would have been better to restrict, as far as possible, the number of the judicial body. The finances were at a low ebb, and if there were to be many judges, it followed that, as a rule, they must be badly paid, and proportionately open to temptation. Moreover, the available material was scanty. There were far too few competent men in the country to man eight Tribunals of First Instance, with about a dozen judges each, to say nothing of nearly twice that number in the Court of Appeal.*

Of the first occupants of the Native Bench only about one out of four had had a regular legal training, and even of these a considerable portion were lawyers in name rather than in fact. They were, for the most part, armed with degrees from the Law Schools of Paris or of Aix. But the latter University enjoys a rather dubious popularity among Egyptian students on account of the facility with which it is supposed to grant diplomas to foreigners—*diplômes d'exportation*, as they have been sarcastically called. A European education is, at the best of times, not without its dangers for Orientals. Unless a man has real capacity and character, he may lose more by it on the moral side than he gains on the intellectual. There were not a few among the young judges whose smattering of French jurisprudence was a very poor compensation for the estrangement from the faith, the habits, and in some cases even from the language, of their native country, which they had undergone in acquiring it.

Under these circumstances an increase in the number

* The Decree of June 14, 1883, provided for the creation of five Courts of First Instance in Lower Egypt: at Cairo, Alexandria, Benha, Mansura, and Tanta; and three in Upper Egypt: Beni-Suef, Siut, and Kena. There were to be two Courts of Appeal, one at Cairo for Lower Egypt, and one at Siut for Upper. The three Courts of First Instance in Upper Egypt were, however, not established till 1889, while the Court of Appeal at Siut has been dropped. The minimum number of judges was fixed at five for a Court of First Instance (besides as many as four assistant judges) and eight for a Court of Appeal. As a matter of fact, this minimum was, from the very first, largely exceeded, the earliest Courts of First Instance consisting of ten, eight, and seven judges, while the Court of Appeal started with no less than fourteen. But of these four were Europeans.

of judges was far from implying an increase in judicial strength. Nor, if the choice had been ever so large, could there have been at that time any certainty that the right man would be selected. In the years 1883 and 1884 it was too soon to expect that appointments should be made by merit, especially in a branch of the public service which we took a certain pride in leaving entirely to native management. Jobbery and nepotism are difficult habits to eradicate in any country. They still flourish among the most progressive nations, although war may have been waged against them for generations. But in Egypt, up to quite recent years, it never occurred to anybody that there was anything wrong in appointment by favour. No doubt there might be a feeling against the nomination of bad characters to public positions, though that feeling was not always strong enough to prevent such nominations. But as long as a man was a decent sort of person, why on earth should you not appoint him to any vacant post, if you liked him and wished him well? The idea of special qualification as a necessary condition of the efficient discharge of special duties is one of very recent growth. When the Native Courts were first constituted, it was still in its earliest infancy. The judgeships were simply regarded as so many opportunities for giving worthy people whom it was desired to benefit a modest income.

With a novel and elaborate Law, and with a weak Bench to administer it, the new Native Courts, though a great improvement on what had gone before, could hardly be expected to prove from the beginning a conspicuous success. But their efficiency was still further impaired on the criminal side—and the criminal side was the most important—by the mess in which the system of criminal prosecution then was, and, to some extent, it must be admitted, still is.

The organization of the Police has been one of the weakest points in the reconstruction of government in Egypt. No doubt the problem was a very puzzling one. A perfect Police system is one of the latest developments of civilization. It is no easy matter to unite vigour and promptitude in the maintenance of order and the repression of crime with a jealous respect for the rights of individuals. A strong and energetic Police force, free from any tendency to high-handedness and from the spirit of bullying, is a blessing which few, even among European nations, can boast. But in the East it is particularly difficult to attain this ideal of combined energy and self-control in persons holding positions of public authority. Restrict the autocratic power of an Oriental official, and you run a great danger of rendering him impotent. If he is not allowed to keep the peace and to punish crime in his own heavy-handed and arbitrary fashion, he is apt to become bewildered, and to give up the game of maintaining order altogether. It takes a long time to teach him how to make the law respected by others, while keeping within the strict bounds of legality himself. In Egypt it has been found an easier business to put a stop to the abuse of the power of the Police, and to protect private individuals from violence and injustice on the part of the authorities, than to maintain a strenuous administration of the law under the new and milder régime. The abolition of the kurbash was the earliest and one of the greatest of all our reforms. But it must be confessed that, especially at the outset, its disappearance was attended by considerable drawbacks.

No doubt the double object which reformers had in view, when dealing with the Police and the local authorities, might have been more rapidly achieved, if a clear course of action had been decided upon from the first and firmly adhered to, and if its execution had been entrusted to a single man possessing the rare combination of qualities necessary for the work, and armed with something like dictatorial powers. As a matter of fact, neither of these desirable conditions has existed. So far from there having been one policy steadfastly maintained, there have been a succession of different policies. The organization of the Police has been the battle-field of conflicting principles. Everything about them, down to their uniforms, has been changed, and changed and changed again. And if the direction given to reform has been uncertain, the heaven-born administrator, clothed with ample authority, has never yet made his appearance on this particular field.

The Egyptian Police, indeed, have had no luck. Their first English Chief, General Valentine Baker, was not fitted by disposition, or intended by those who invited him to Egypt, to be a police-officer. He was brought from Constantinople to Cairo in the first months of the British Occupation, not to command the Police, but to command the Army. When insuperable difficulties presented themselves to his being allowed to fill the latter post, the office of Inspector-General of Police was offered to him as a kind of compensation; but it was not one for which he had any real aptitude. A brave soldier and a brilliant leader of troops in face of an enemy, he never reconciled himself to his new rôle, although he strove conscientiously to do his duty in an uncongenial sphere of work. There was always at the back of his mind the belief and the hope that he would some day be called upon to serve Egypt in the field. His whole management of the Police was influenced, from the first, by the conviction that they would sooner or later be wanted as a military reserve, when the Army had proved inadequate to save the country from invasion.

And the original organization of the Police lent itself to such a conception. As first constituted, they were divided into two separate bodies, the larger of which was a semi-military Gendarmerie, while only the smaller and less important was a genuine police force. And it was upon the Gendarmerie, and upon their development into soldiers, that the best part of General Baker's attention was always concentrated. The disaster which befell him at El Teb in February, 1884, so far from diverting him from his fixed idea, only made him keener than ever to achieve some great military success, which should wipe out the memory of that unfortunate engagement. Throughout the whole of his period of command, which only ended with his death at the close of 1887, General Baker never ceased to devote his best energies and a disproportionate amount of the funds at his disposal to the improvement of the Gendarmerie, and the Police proper suffered in consequence.

Matters were not improved by the brief interlude during which the control of the Police, while nominally remaining in the hands of General Baker, really passed to a man of very different character and quite opposite views—I mean Mr. Clifford Lloyd. The period of Mr. Lloyd's activity in Egypt almost exactly coincides with the absence of General Baker on his unlucky expedition to the Eastern Sudan, and during that period Mr. Lloyd was virtually Head of the Police. He entirely changed the organization, getting rid for the time being of the Gendarmerie (which, however, General Baker subsequently re-established in a new form) and seeking to substitute a small and well-paid volunteer force for the conscripts of whom the Police originally consisted. The attempt to obtain volunteers was a complete failure. A certain number of Turks, who were all that Mr. Lloyd succeeded in enlisting, turned out useless and unruly, and were disbanded soon after his departure. But if he failed to change the composition of the Force, he succeeded in introducing new principles into the administration, and in stirring up a controversy, which has raged more or less fiercely ever since, and which even now is not absolutely settled.

Into the details of that controversy it is quite impossible to enter here, but I may just indicate the main issue. The question was, putting it broadly, whether the Police were to remain, as of old, under the orders of the provincial authorities—the Mudirs and Mamurs—or whether they were to be an independent body under the orders of their own officers and ultimately of the English Inspector-General. Mr. Lloyd had a great and not wholly unjustified distrust of the Mudirs. He knew that the old system, by which they were left free to deal with crime according to their lights, and to use the Police just as they thought fit, had led to great abuses.

Not only had it placed in their hands a powerful instrument of oppression, often employed for purposes of private greed or spite, but it caused the Police to be diverted, to a great extent, from their proper work, and turned into ushers and footmen. This tendency is an excellent illustration of the difficulty which an Oriental finds in distinguishing between subordination and servitude. If people are under his orders for any purpose, he cannot understand that they should not be at his bidding for all purposes—even to blacking his boots. Such treatment necessarily degraded the Police, and made the introduction of any general system of discipline for the whole body impossible. Mr. Lloyd was perfectly right in setting his face against it, but he unfortunately fell into the opposite error of making the Police too independent of the Mudirs and Mamurs.

For in the internal administration of the country everything depends upon these officials. The entire government of a district centres in the Mamur, and that of a province in the Mudir. If their authority is undermined, the whole machine falls out of gear. No doubt it is highly desirable—in fact, it is essential—that the exercise of their power should be rigidly controlled from headquarters, and that they should not be allowed to use it in an arbitrary manner, or to abuse it for their private ends. Indeed, the whole problem is, how to exercise this control, which is indispensable, without destroying the prestige of the provincial officials, which is equally indispensable. But to take the Police—the arm of the Executive, of which the Mudirs are the head—entirely away from the Mudirs does destroy that prestige. And it is quite certain that this was the effect, though doubtless it was not the intention, of the well-meant but ill-digested changes introduced by Mr. Lloyd. In his position as Under-Secretary of State for the Interior—the Ministry to which Police and Mudirs are alike subject—he had, it may be thought, a unique opportunity of putting the relations between the two parties upon a proper footing. But the shortness of his stay, if no other reason, prevented him from bringing about a workable arrangement. He had time enough to disturb many things; he had not time enough to erect a new and better system in the place of the bad one which he upset.

The fight over the control of the Police has never been so acute as during the period of Mr. Lloyd's administration; but it has gone on with more or less liveliness and with varying results ever since. In his day the Mudirs were almost deprived of all power over the Constabulary. With the reaction which followed his disappearance, they almost recovered their old absolute control. General Baker, when he returned to work after Mr. Lloyd had gone, was far too much occupied with the Gendarmerie (which, as I have said, he partially recreated) to interfere with the ideas of Police organization which found favour with the native authorities, and especially with Nubar Pasha. But when, after General Baker's death, the Gendarmerie were again abolished (the bulk of them being transferred to the army, where they now form the 11th Sudanese battalion), the English officers of the Police once more turned their attention to the organization of the Constabulary proper, and forthwith the old controversy about the position of the Mudirs was revived.

It is only in quite recent times that, through the efforts of General Kitchener, who was in temporary command of the Police from the spring of 1890 to that of 1891, and through those of his successor, Colonel Settle (Inspector-General in 1892), a tolerable understanding has been arrived at. The Police of each province, as matters are now arranged, are under the authority of the Mudir; but, on the other hand, his orders must be given to them through their own local officers. He has no power of interference with the discipline and organization of the force, nor can he make use of it except for the legitimate purposes of maintaining order and repressing crime. If he has cause of complaint against the conduct of the Police, his remedy lies in an appeal to the Ministry of the Interior, which, through the Inspector-General at headquarters, deals with the case. This is as it should be; but, of course, the success of the system depends on a spirit of give-and-take on both sides, and on friendly relations between the Mudirs and the chiefs of the Police. Fortunately, these relations have of late days been greatly improved. The officers of Police have now a better appreciation of the respect which is due to the position of the Mudirs; while the latter, on their part, have begun to recognise that a properly disciplined and independent police force, so far from impairing their authority, is calculated to strengthen their hands in the execution of the law.

The conflict which I have attempted to describe was necessarily unfavourable to a prompt dealing with crime. But the difficulty was complicated by the presence of a third authority, distinct from the Mudirs and the Police, to whom the system of native jurisprudence, copied as it is from that of France, has entrusted the investigation and prosecution of criminal offences. This was the Procureur-Général, a number of whose representatives are attached to each Tribunal. The latter are described collectively by the name of the 'Parquet,' their head being called 'Chef du Parquet,' and his assistants 'Substituts du Procureur-Général.' For the purpose of bringing criminals to justice, the Police are under the orders of the Parquet; but, unfortunately, it must be admitted that, especially at the first introduction of the new system, the Parquet worked very badly, alike with the Mudirs and the Police. The Mudirs were jealous of this fresh interference with their old powers, while the local Police officers disliked taking instructions from men outside their own body, whom they regarded as upstarts.

And the character and bearing of the Parquet were often little calculated to dispel these prejudices. It has been the practice of the Ministry of Justice to put the best young lawyers into these positions before promoting them to the Bench. The members of the Parquet are, for the most part, capable men; but not only are they, in many cases, too young to have much experience, but they are, by their previous training, little fitted for the rough and primitive life of the provinces. Town-bred, often educated in Europe, and with European ideas and manners, they feel themselves superior to those about them, not excepting the Mudirs, in intelligence and culture, while they are apt to be lacking in that intimate acquaintance with the ideas and habits of the people which is so important for the detection of crime. Hence arrogance and impracticability on the one side, distrust and apathy on the other, and as the result of all a want of co-operation among the agents of the law, which is greatly to the advantage of the malefactor.

This want of co-operation is aggravated by the fact that the Parquet send all their reports of current investigations direct to the Ministry of Justice, where the Procureur-Général is too busy to examine them, while the superior officers of the Police, who are located at the Ministry of the Interior, have no opportunity of seeing them. The latter are thus unable to detect the omissions and imperfections in the evidence for the prosecution, and to get such errors rectified in time. The consequence is, that cases frequently come before the Courts supported by inadequate evidence, and that the Judges, annoyed by what they consider the slovenliness of the Executive, acquit the criminals, and throw the blame for the failure of justice upon the Police.

There are many people who think that the institution of the Parquet was altogether a mistake, that the control of the Police in the detection of crime should have been left to the Mudirs, and that it would be better to restore it to them. But apart from the strong objections to a fresh change of system, it may be doubted whether the Mudirs are, even nowadays, properly qualified to conduct a criminal investigation. The members of the Parquet, whatever their faults, do know what evidence means. But the average Mudir, as the proceedings of the famous Commissions of Brigandage clearly showed, is still possessed with the old notion that the great thing is to get out of the prisoner, by hook or by crook, a confession of guilt. That confession once obtained, he is inclined to trouble himself very little about confirmatory evidence. Yet before a properly trained body of judges, one good piece of independent circumstantial evidence is worth any number of confessions. And this is especially the case in Egypt, where guilt is so readily avowed, and as readily denied again, when it comes to the actual trial, on the always specious ground that the confession has been extorted by illegal means.

In this, as in so many other matters, it is probably the wisest course not to change your machinery, but to improve it. And as a matter of fact, there is already a marked tendency towards greater harmony between the various authorities concerned in the prosecution of crime. Youth and inexperience, which were the chief faults of the Parquet, are being remedied by the lapse of time, while the practical spirit, by which the Ministry of Justice is now animated, tends to minimize causes of friction between the agents of that office and those of the Ministry of the Interior. It has been suggested that this friction might be still further reduced, and the prompt punishment of crime greatly facilitated, if the Police were entrusted, under the orders of the Mudirs, with the entire responsibility for the prosecution of minor offences, and if a greater latitude were given them in the investigation of more serious ones. With regard to the latter, they would still remain under the general direction of the Parquet, who in such cases would continue to conduct the prosecution. These proposals seem reasonable, and it is probably on such lines that the Judicial Adviser will seek still further to promote the important object of ensuring cordial co-operation between Parquet, Mudirs, and Police.

Another matter of first-rate moment in the interest of public security, and one which has been long neglected, is the reorganization of the Ghaffirs, or village watchmen. The Ghaffirs are the old indigenous police force of the country, and an indigenous institution is always to be preferred to imported foreign systems, if only it can be kept free from gross abuses. But in the present instance the abuses have been very great. The numbers of the Ghaffirs are enormous. There were, till 1891, when General Kitchener began to introduce a saner system, some two or three hundred thousand of them throughout Egypt, and they were selected in the most capricious fashion. Now, it is manifestly absurd that, among a quiet people like the Egyptians, one man in every seven should be set to watch the other six. And, of course, the watching has been most perfunctorily performed. The Ghaffirs, being unpaid and undisciplined, have had every inducement to neglect their duty, while some of the bolder spirits have not unfrequently paid themselves by doing a little robbery on their own account. Evidently what is wanted is greatly to reduce their numbers, to make the able-bodied men of a village do the work by turns—not compelling anyone to serve for too long a period—and to give them one or two competent officers, who should be properly paid. But the most necessary thing of all is to make the principal Sheikh of each locality (the headman or Omdeh, as he is called) feel himself responsible for the efficiency of the Ghaffirs.

The Omdeh, who is always appointed by the Government, is indeed a most important figure in Egyptian village life. Like other ancient institutions, his influence has suffered a certain eclipse with the advent of the Reign of Law. In the old days the Omdeh was nothing less than an autocrat. He could command any man's services, and no doubt he used his authority very much to his own advantage. But, on the other hand, it was he whom the Government held responsible if anything went wrong. The new system, while curtailing his arbitrary powers, has at the same time weakened his interest in, and his sense of responsibility for, the good order of his village. In a country where the monarchical principle is so deeply rooted as it is in Egypt, this is undoubtedly a misfortune. The Government cannot do without the Omdehs, and, that being so, it should seek to compensate them in a legitimate way for the loss of their old irregular privileges. Direct payment is out of the question, but there are other benefits—such as the free occupation of Government land, where it exists—which might be bestowed upon the Omdehs, in order to encourage them in the discharge of the multifarious duties which they are called upon to perform. But, whatever the means adopted, it is necessary to improve the position of these village headmen. And it is equally necessary to exercise greater care than has generally been taken of late years in their selection. This, again, is one of the points to which proper attention has only quite recently been directed.

It is on the improvement of the Ghaffir system, and on the zeal and goodwill of the Omdehs, that the Government must mainly rely for the suppression of the peculiar form of crime which is described in Egypt by the name of 'brigandage.' This term, as I have already explained, is somewhat of a misnomer. Regular professional brigandage is comparatively rare. What is commonly so called is simply the more or less organized raiding of the bad characters of a village upon outlying houses or hamlets, or, in some cases, upon other villages. There have been instances in which neighbouring villages have thus mutually raided each other. The motive of these outrages is sometimes want, and sometimes spite. In certain instances they have even been got up by the village Sheikhs themselves. But, whatever its origin, the evil, easily dealt with at the outset, may, if encouraged by the absence of repression, grow to formidable proportions. A small but vigilant body of watchmen would, however, in most cases, be well competent to cope with it; while on the rare occasions where they were not so competent they might at least track the gangs, and thus enable the regular Police, whose assistance would have to be called for in such emergencies, to find and arrest the criminals.

We have seen that it was the prevalence of brigandage which broke down the new Native Courts at the very commencement of their career. In 1884 and the following years, first the investigation, and then the actual trial, of crimes of this description was taken out of the hands of the regular Tribunals, and entrusted to special Commissions, having the character and powers of a

Court-Martial. These Commissions were originally created for a few months only, but their mandate was renewed by successive decrees, and for nearly five years they dealt with the great mass of criminal offences alike in Upper and in Lower Egypt. Every such Commission did no doubt contain a judicial element, but it was always presided over by a Mudir, and he was practically its guiding spirit. And as if to mark still further the arbitrary character of the Commissions, they were placed under the control, not of the Ministry of Justice, but of the Ministry of the Interior (the only administration, by the way, from which at that time European influence was effectively excluded). In other words, the fundamental principle of separating the judicial from the executive power was absolutely adandoned in practice, almost as soon as it had been proclaimed by the establishment of the new Courts of Justice. With respect to crimes of violence committed in the provinces, the Criminal Code, with all its elaborate provisions for the protection of the accused, was for the time being a dead letter.

These Special Commissions may, perhaps, have had a certain effect in diminishing crime, but they themselves were guilty of every sort of enormity in the process. When the nature of their proceedings was revealed by the inquiries of M. Legrelle and other judicial experts, it was discovered that torture had been freely used for obtaining evidence, that many persons had been imprisoned for years without trial, and that many others had been condemned to severe punishment on the flimsiest evidence. In one case, nineteen people, all innocent, were condemned on the confession of a single man, who, as it subsequently turned out, had been coerced into making a false charge against himself and his associates. The history of the Commissions of Brigandage shows how strangely civilization and barbarism may still exist cheek by jowl in the Land of the Pharaohs. Side by side with the new Native Courts, with their model Codes, elaborate Procedure, and Judges who mimicked, even when they did not possess, the character of civilized

European magistrates, there was another set of tribunals, far more powerful and important, which dealt with crime in a manner worthy of the Dark Ages.

The continuance of such a state of things was possible just so long as Great Britain could cling to her attitude of non-interference in the internal administration of Egypt, but no longer. In a previous chapter I have shown how the revival of British interest in the question of native justice resulted in the suppression of the Special Commissions, and how that step, by making the improvement of the Courts more imperative than ever, led directly to the appointment of Mr. Scott.*

It is not too much to say that the two and a half years which have elapsed since Mr. Scott's arrival have done more to raise the character of the Native Courts, and to make them equal to their work, than would have been achieved in a century, or in any number of centuries, under the old system of management. The credit of the progress which has been made is, indeed, not due entirely to Mr. Scott. It is due, above all, to the impression, which his appointment created, that Great Britain was in earnest about the business. For years past there had been plenty of people in Egypt, natives as well as Europeans, who were fully alive to the nature of the existing evils, and could indicate, more or less convincingly, the measures necessary to remove them. But the spirit of reform, though not absent, was, in this as in other matters, impotent without vigorous external aid. The forces of obstruction—an obstruction due to prejudice and ignorance quite as much as to any baser motives—are too strong to be overcome by Platonic arguments. It was not till the British Consul-General threw the weight of his powerful personality into the scale of judicial reform that the needful changes, which competent critics had long been suggesting, were actually initiated.

But Mr. Scott is certainly entitled to very special credit for the moderate and judicious spirit, greatly aided by his previous experience of the country, with which

* See pp. 131, 132.

he set about his delicate task. By a series of important changes of detail he has modified the judicial system which he found existing, and rendered it vastly more suitable to the conditions of the country. But he has never attempted to revolutionize it. No doubt, if he had had the work to do *de novo*, he would have preferred something more like the Indian system, which experience has proved to be so well suited to the wants of a backward country, where most of the litigants are poor, and most of the cases simple. He recognised, however, that the Egyptian Codes and Procedure, such as he found them, were the only ones which the native judicial body knew how to work, or to which the people were accustomed. He therefore wisely decided, not radically to alter the actual administration of justice, but simply to improve it in the points where it was most imperfect.

The chief faults were the slowness and costliness of legal proceedings and the absence of any means of bringing ready redress for small injuries within reach of the majority of the people. To remedy these defects, the Judicial Adviser has reduced the number of judges requisite for the hearing of the great number of cases, whether civil or criminal, and has extended the system of summary justice. Formerly, five was the usual complement of every bench, alike in the Courts of First Instance and in the Court of Appeal. Now, it is reduced to three, five judges being only occasionally required in the Court of Appeal in criminal trials of the most serious kind. Formerly there was only one judge attached to each Tribunal for the administration of summary justice, and his powers were of the most limited kind. Now, there are more than twenty judges so employed throughout the country, and instead of being fixed at the seats of the Courts of First Instance, they go on circuit in their respective districts, so that small actions and offences can be dealt with on the spot. Moreover, these judges have power to try all misdemeanours, and to hear all suits involving a sum of not more than £100, including suits about land, which, in a purely agricultural country like Egypt, are of course the most common.

An appeal lies from these single judges to a three-judge Court at the respective Tribunals of First Instance; but the decision of the latter Courts on all misdemeanours and suits under £100 is final. The time and energy of the Court of Appeal are thus saved for the examination of those graver cases—such as felonies and civil actions involving large sums of money—which a Summary Court is not competent to try, and which must therefore be brought, from the outset, before one of the Tribunals of First Instance. The general effect of these changes is to expedite the action of the law, to economize the time of judges and the money of suitors, and to reserve the full strength of the Highest Courts for questions of real moment.

But the extension of summary justice, and the reduction of the number of judges sitting in each Court, necessarily throws a great responsibility upon the individual judge. Incompetence is more dangerous than it used to be under the old system. Hence the changes of procedure introduced by Mr. Scott involved what was in any case most desirable, namely, the careful elimination of the less trustworthy elements of the old Bench, and the substitution of a number of new and better-qualified men. In this respect great progress has undoubtedly been made during the last year and a half. Between one-third and one-fourth of the old judges have been pensioned off, and great care has been taken to appoint in their place not only men of character, but men of adequate legal training. The present is the first year since the establishment of the Native Courts in which no man has been made a judge or a member of the Parquet who was not either a doctor or licentiate in law of some European University, or invested with the corresponding degree by the School of Law at Cairo. Moreover, fresh life has been infused into the latter institution; and under its new and excellent French head, M. Testoud, it is now turning out men who, as far as can be judged, are fully equal, if not superior, to their colleagues who have been educated in Europe.

But to bring the Native Bench up to the standard of

knowledge and character requisite for the proper discharge of its high duties is necessarily a work of time. For the present a great deal of supervision is essential, in order to keep the individual judges up to the mark. It is with this object that a Commission has been established, consisting of Mr. Scott, the Procureur-Général—M. Legrelle, and one of the Legal Advisers of the Government—M. Moriondo. With the aid of three native inspectors this Commission examines the records of a certain number of all the cases decided by the Summary Courts and Courts of First Instance. It does not usurp the functions of a Court of Appeal. It does not reverse decisions. But it calls the attention of individual judges to any flagrant errors which they may have committed, and at the same time it issues general circulars, containing explanations and instructions on important points of law or practice, on which, from an examination of the cases, it appears that the judges in general have a special tendency to go wrong. About sixty such circulars have been issued during the past year, and they constitute a body of practical jurisprudence, which is of great value for the education of the Native Bench. This method of supervision, which is analogous to the inspecting powers possessed by the High Courts in India, was at its first introduction violently criticised in many quarters, on no better grounds that I could ever discover than that it was a novelty. But now everybody is reconciled to it, and with reason. For it has proved a great success, not only in ensuring uniformity of action on the part of the Courts, but in promoting the zeal and efficiency of the judicial staff.

The increased capacity and reputation of the Native Tribunals is one of the most hopeful features in the progress of the country. The material of which they are composed is not bad, and it is steadily improving. The ablest and most ambitious of the educated natives, including a large proportion of Mohammedans, take readily to the law as a career. There is no want of capacity among them, nor, with proper selection, is it difficult to find men of principle. What they still for the most part lack is the spirit of independence and the willingness to take responsibility. The great object is to teach them respect for the dignity of their position. And this can only be done by keeping them up to their work on the one hand, and by defending them, on the other, against arbitrary interference, when they do that work conscientiously and well. From this point of view the presence of some Europeans on the Native Bench is of great utility. There are not many of them, but they have an invaluable effect on the morale of their colleagues, and it would be a great mistake to reduce their number.

The European element in the Native Courts is of further and special importance with a view to the future. If Egypt is ever to be an independent country, owing her stability to the soundness of her own institutions, and not to external support, it is impossible to contemplate the continued co-existence of four several judicial systems within her borders. Amalgamation is indispensable, but the only basis of amalgamation, compatible with independence, consists in extending the jurisdiction of the Native Tribunals. As late as 1884, the most that native reformers aspired to was to get rid of the Consular Courts by giving the Mixed Tribunals authority to deal with all criminal offences committed by foreigners. If that idea is now abandoned, it is not because the Consular Courts are any more tolerable, but because it no longer seems out of the question to look forward to an even greater and more comprehensive reform—I mean the extension of the powers of the Native Courts to include all civil and criminal cases, whether affecting foreigners or natives. But if this ideal is ultimately to be attained, it can only be by including a strong foreign element in the staff of the Native Courts. Without such a safeguard the Powers would never surrender the privilege now enjoyed by their subjects of being tried by their own judges. Hence the appointment of a certain number of Europeans to the Native Bench is by no means a mere temporary expedient, but a first step in the direction of the great object of unity of jurisdiction. The future of the Native Courts may thus be to approximate, as regards their composition, to the present Mixed Tribunals, but with this difference, that instead of being, like those Tribunals, virtually Foreign Courts, with a minority of native members who are nothing but ciphers, they will be genuinely Egyptian Courts, with a majority of native members, but strengthened by the presence of a few picked Europeans.

The development of the system of native justice, in such a manner as to absorb the powers both of the Consular Courts and of the Mixed Tribunals, is doubtless a bold idea. At present the possibility of realizing it may seem very remote. But there are two circumstances which militate in favour of such a solution. In the first place the mandate of the Mixed Tribunals is only a temporary one. It has to be renewed from time to time, and opportunities for revising it are thus constantly recurring. And in the next place it must always be remembered that the Native Courts already administer a European system of law. If their personnel can be so improved as to justify the assertion, that not merely the law they administer, but the spirit by which they are animated, is up to the standard of European ideas of justice, the only valid reason for maintaining separate European jurisdictions will have ceased to exist.

Complete amalgamation, I admit, is still a long way off. But even now the way could be prepared for it by the establishment of a Supreme Court of Revision, or Final Appeal, to which the most important cases decided by the two existing Courts of Appeal—the International and the Native—might equally be submitted. The existence of such a common Supreme Court would have an excellent effect on both systems. It would be good for the International Courts, for their present tendency is rather to degenerate than to improve, owing precisely to the want of any effective control or criticism of their decisions, in a country where there is neither an enlightened public opinion, nor an influential Press, nor a formidable Bar. And it would be good for the Native

Courts, because it would not only enhance their dignity by putting them on a level with the Mixed Tribunals, but excite the emulation of their members, to prove themselves equal to their foreign rivals before the neutral Court of Revision, by which the judgments of both parties would be examined and compared.

A word remains to be said about the reform of the Mehkemehs, or native Religious Courts, whose authority is now almost confined to the registration of land, and to matters affecting the personal status of Mohammedans, questions of marriage and inheritance being the most important. As this is a subject into which religious feeling enters, it evidently requires to be treated with special tact. But it is a mistake to suppose that even pious Moslems would be opposed to every effort to raise the character of these Courts, which are at present by-words for corruption. And this object might be achieved by greater care in the selection of the Kadis —as the judges of the Mehkemehs are called—by giving them somewhat better pay, and by insisting that in future they should possess some knowledge of the general principles of law. At the same time the Mehkemehs should be compelled to adopt a regular system of procedure—that most important guarantee for the proper administration of justice. Such changes might easily be effected without upsetting the religious basis of the Kadi's jurisdiction or wounding Mussulman susceptibilities. And if the staff of the Mehkemehs once consisted of properly trained lawyers, working in accordance with fixed rules, their jurisdiction might with great advantage be somewhat extended. The Kadis are a very numerous body, located in all the smaller towns as well as in the provincial capitals. As Juges de Paix, with powers to deal with all trifling cases, they might serve to relieve the pressure on the judges of the ordinary Tribunals, and might thus be worked into the general system of the Native Courts, without any infringement of their special authority in regard to questions depending on the Religious Law.

The measures which I have indicated, are, of course,

suggestions merely. I have no pretensions to be a legal expert. But a man does not need to be a legal expert to realize the direction which the reform of the Egyptian system of justice ought to take, and which as a matter of fact it is taking. The key of the situation must be sought in the Native Courts. If they go on improving as they have improved during 1890, 1891, a way is open out of the present chaos of jurisdictions. And this improvement, be it remembered, is the direct result of English interference. The history of the Native Courts contains a lesson which it would be worth while for the opponents of British influence to lay to heart. When Mr. Scott was first appointed Judicial Adviser, there was a tremendous hullabaloo. Riaz Pasha, acting for the nonce as the champion of the native party of obstruction, resisted the appointment tooth and nail. The French Consul-General was instructed to protest against it to the Khedive as an intolerable extension of British power. Right and left arose vehement complaints about the grasping policy of England and her supposed intention to swallow up the Egyption Administration, piece by piece. Yet, as a matter of fact, Mr. Scott's appointment has resulted in one of the greatest strides yet made by Egypt in the direction of ultimate self-government.

It is always the same story. If any man desires to help Egypt forward on the road of independence, the worst and most short-sighted thing he can possibly do is to resist the introduction of English control into any department of the Government. It would be a different thing if Egypt were an out-of-the-way country, with a homogeneous population, from which European ideas could be successfully excluded, and which could effectually 'stew in its own juice.' As a matter of fact, Egypt lies close beside one of the greatest highways of mankind. She has one of the most mixed populations in the world. She is already full of resident Europeans, and European visitors flock over the land in increasing numbers every year. Under these conditions Egypt must needs learn to govern herself according to European ideas, or she will cease to exist as a separate country at all. There is no necessity for such a consummation. Distributed among the various races, who jostle one another on her soil, there exist the qualities necessary to the maintenance of a civilized government, if only the people can be taught and encouraged to use them. At the present day there are already several departments of the State which work admirably under native guidance. But they are just the very departments which at some time or other have been radically reconstructed by Englishmen. The System of Justice is, I firmly believe, destined to afford the latest and most striking illustration of this general law.

CHAPTER XI.

ODDS AND ENDS OF REFORM.

In the preceding pages I have been obliged to dwell at considerable length upon those central reforms the success of which gives its chief interest to the work of England in Egypt. I could not hope to retain the attention of my readers if I were to describe, with anything like equal detail, a number of improvements which have been effected in other branches of the Public Service, but which, however valuable in themselves, are not of the same vital importance to the country as the changes introduced into the Army, into Finance, into Justice, or into Irrigation.

Nor is it necessary for my purpose that I should do so. I am not writing a Blue Book. I have no wish to give a catalogue of reforms. What I have sought to do is to illustrate the general tendency of our work and the spirit which has animated it, and these have been in all departments essentially the same. Everywhere the struggle has been against corruption, against formalism, against unjust preference shown to the wealthy and powerful, against backstairs influence of every kind. Everywhere it has been necessary to weed out the worst of an excessive number of mechanical officials, and to inspire the remainder with energy, self-respect, intelligent method, and to create a disposition to deal promptly and practically with difficulties, instead of simply covering them up and hiding them away under tons of paper. It has been necessary to demonstrate that honest and efficient work, and not lip-service, not the arts of the flatterer and the parasite, is the road to promotion.

Of course I do not say that even now the right man is always promoted. In Egypt, as in every country in the world, showy, but superficial, qualities may often usurp the place which of right belongs to solid merit. But where such mistakes have been made of late days, they have at least been honestly made. There is, on the whole, no more creditable feature of British administration than the manner in which the British Heads of Departments have sought to encourage and advance their best men, irrespective of personal predilection, and without any thought of political proselytism. Over and over again it has been represented to them—and I speak from personal knowledge—that such and such an official should not be promoted because he was 'hostile to English influence,' or a 'French sympathizer,' or a 'fanatical Mussulman,' or what not. Over and over again these objections have been put aside. Our countrymen in the service of the Khedive have steadily acted on the principle that their only business was to make that service as efficient as possible. I have often heard them criticised by outsiders for not trying to make it more of an English Service. As an Englishman I am proud to know that these suggestions have not been listened to, and that the object of the British officials has been, not to Anglicize the Egyptian bureaucracy in political opinion, but only to Anglicize it in spirit, to infuse into its ranks that uprightness and devotion to duty which is the legitimate boast of the Civil Service of Great Britain.

Let me repeat again, that there is nothing wonderful in all this. The qualities which we may have contributed to the Egyptian Administration are not novel or extraordinary qualities. They are the commonplaces of civilization. But it needs only a little experience of the East to realize how vast an improvement may be effected in the condition of a country by the introduction of nothing more than the ordinary methods and principles of civilized government. We have it on the authority of the classical poets, that it is as far from Tartarus to this commonplace Earth as it is from the Earth to the abodes of the Gods. It is the road from Tartarus to Earth along which Egypt has been travelling, and it is no small achievement to have covered the distance in a few years.

As this has been the nature of our influence, it is evident that it could never be out of place. And, as a matter of fact, I know of no Department in the State which has been touched by that influence without being benefited by it. The improvement may have been greater, or it may have been less; but there has been improvement everywhere. If, in certain directions, progress has fallen far short of what we might wish, the shortcomings have been due to those unfavourable conditions to which I have already alluded. They have been due to the impotence of the Egyptian Government to make laws of general application without the consent of Europe. They have been due, in an even greater degree, to the unwillingness which Great Britain at one time showed to interfere with any evils that were not absolutely flagrant, and to the lack of means which rendered it impossible to undertake reforms requiring a large outlay unless, like the improvements in Irrigation, they were of so urgent a character that they could not possibly be neglected.

These latter obstacles—the lack of will and the lack of means—have been less potent of late years than in the period immediately succeeding our first unfortunate attempts to deal with the internal administration of Egypt. What happened with regard to Justice has been repeated, more or less, in several other branches of the Public Service. We undertook a good deal at first which we afterwards abandoned, or grew callous about. When we found ourselves in hot water all round, and money was scarce, we determined to confine ourselves to one or two great Departments, and to let the rest take their chance. Step by step we have been forced to recognise that the policy of letting things take their chance does not answer, and to resume the responsibility which we had thought it possible to shake off. But we have resumed it under better auspices, strengthened by successes achieved in other directions, and by the greater ease of the financial situation.

When in the autumn of 1883 Mr. Clifford Lloyd was sent out to put everything right at once, he found that two of the greatest existing scandals were the state of the prisons and the grossly insanitary condition of the towns and villages. He accordingly created two new Departments, one of Prisons and one of Public Health—both being branches of the Ministry of the Interior—and put an Englishman at the head of each. With regard to the prisons, the work then initiated has suffered no serious interruption. It has, like so many other things, been starved for want of money, but in spite of the meagreness of its budget, the Prisons Department can show a good record of useful work. This is just one of those instances to which the simile of Tartarus emphatically applies. The management of the prisons, as revealed by the reports of Major Chermside in 1883, was inconceivably bad. It was at once so barbarous and so senseless that the introduction of civilized control could not possibly fail to effect an enormous change for the better. The provincial prisons at the present day, though still very defective in point of construction, are clean, decent, and properly managed—the greatest contrast to the hells they were in former times. The great convict prisons of Tura and Giza are in every way model establishments. Nowadays it is sometimes argued that the prisons are too comfortable, and positively afford an inducement to very poor people to commit crime. But in Egypt, as elsewhere, I believe this argument to be nonsense.

Very different was the fate of the second of Mr. Lloyd's creations—the Department of Public Health. This is one of the spheres in which the work of reform was most grievously prejudiced by Mr. Lloyd's failure, and by our consequent policy of retreat and concentration upon one or two central positions. In the beginning of

1885 Dr. Sandwith, the able and go-ahead man who had been placed at the head of the Public Health Office by Mr. Lloyd, was got rid of by a rather ignoble intrigue, due to the excessive zeal which he had shown in the dismissal of corrupt subordinates. His place was, it is true, filled by another Englishman, but English interest in the matter died away, and till quite recently this Department remained one of the least satisfactory in the Government Service. No particular blame attaches to anybody. There was simply a total inadequacy of means to ends. In Egypt the whole business of providing for the health of the population is thrown on the shoulders of the Government. In Cairo and Alexandria there are European hospitals and some good European doctors in private practice. But with these exceptions, there are no hospitals, no dispensaries, no doctors, no nurses, no sanitary institutions or appliances of any kind which are not supplied by the Government; and to supply all these things for six million people with only £E90,000 a year is manifestly impossible. Considering the inadequacy of the available resources, a good deal was done even in the six slack years which followed the resignation of Dr. Sandwith. The Government hospitals in the large provincial towns were put into proper order, and that at Cairo was brought to a high standard of excellence, thanks largely to the ability and energy of Dr. Milton.

But that is about all that can be said. No doubt a regular system of sanitary inspection was established throughout the country, and in the Official Journal almost every week you might read, on the authority of the Mudir, that 'public health in the province of —— was perfect.' But that was official optimism. As a matter of fact, but for the work done by the hospitals and their medical attendants, Public Health throughout Egypt is to this day about as imperfect as the fine constitutions of the people and one of the best climates in the world will permit. The habits of the Egyptians, if not wholly unclean—for they are fond of washing—are in other respects radically insanitary. The towns and villages are filthy. The Canals, which are the only sources of water-supply to the bulk of the population, are subjeet to every kind of pollution. In the neighbourhood of many populous places, there are 'birkas,' or stagnant ponds, which exhale miasma even when they are not—as they very often are—used for drinking. In the principal cities there is a certain amount of sweeping and carting away of refuse, but there is absolutely no drainage. People who have known Egypt for many years assure me that, bad as all this is, it is enormously better than what used to be, and the decrease of certain characteristic diseases, such as ophthalmia—which is still, however, very common—is quoted in proof of the assertion. It is, of course, quite possible to believe, though difficult to imagine, that there was an Egypt even more insanitary than the Egypt of to-day. But that does not alter the fact that the scope for improvement in sanitary matters at the present time is large enough to give employment for many years to the most ambitious and energetic reformer.

It is, I hope, to be regarded as the first sign of a more vigorous policy in this matter, that a man who assuredly lacks neither energy nor ambition has recently been placed at the head of the Sanitary Department. Rogers Pasha, who now occupies that position, had previously done most distinguished work as Principal Medical Officer to the Egyptian Army. It is certain that under a chief so clever, vigorous, and restless, the Public Health Office will enter upon a new career of activity. Rogers Pasha has already aroused the Sanitary Inspectors in a very effective fashion, and he may be trusted to worry the financial authorities into giving him at least some portion of the funds necessary to effect the most obvious improvements. This is one of the branches of the Administration in which the rate of progress is likely to be greatly accelerated in the next few years.

The revival of interest in sanitary matters is further proved by the preparations at present being made for the thorough drainage of Cairo. This is a tremendous undertaking, estimated to cost at least £500,000. Its necessity has long been recognised, but it has been put off from year to year, owing to want of money—not so much absolute want of money, as want of power to apply money that actually existed to the desired object, owing to the usual and ten-times-explained necessity of obtaining the consent of the Powers, or, more properly, the consent of France—for none of the others made any difficulty. France was finally appeased last year by the appointment of an International Commission to examine the various competing schemes. This Commission, composed of an Englishman, a Frenchman, and a German, sat last winter, and ended by proposing a scheme of its own, for which preliminary surveys are at present being made. So in two or three years we may hope to see Cairo drained, in which case that city, or at any rate the European quarter of it, will very likely be one of the healthiest places of residence in the world. And the example thus set will, in all likelihood, be gradually followed in other towns. At Alexandria the Municipal Council is already engaged upon the study of drainage schemes. The whole question of sanitation, in fact, is one which now, for the first time, is receiving serious attention.

No doubt there are certain special difficulties in the way. The body of the people know nothing about the laws of health, and care less. Moreover, the Mosques are probably the principal offenders against those laws, and to prevent the Mosques from becoming centres of infection, or from draining into the Canals, and thus poisoning the drinking water, is a matter which will require delicate handling. Any interference with the Mosques might easily excite a fanatical opposition, which would stand seriously in the way of all sanitary reform. But here, as elsewhere, there are good native influences as well as bad, if only they can be developed, and rendered effective. Among educated Egyptians there is a growing sense of the importance of enforcing sanitary regulations. I have known even orthodox Mohammedans who were prepared to advocate very severe measures to remedy the filthiness of the Mosques, and who declared—quite rightly, no doubt—that such measures were dictated by the very spirit of their religion, which has always laid so much stress on cleanliness. It is a hopeful symptom that there exist a certain number of pious men who are disposed to invoke the reforming tendency of the Founder of their Faith against the abuses of its later practice.

Nor is it with regard to sanitary matters only that there exists an inevitable antagonism between those who wish to adapt the teaching of the Prophet to the knowledge and aspirations of a progressive age and the obscurantist majority of the self-constituted religious guides of the people. The field of education presents another battle-ground for these two conflicting principles. Every student knows how high in the teaching of Mohammed is the rank assigned to Knowledge. In the theory of Mohammedanism, Piety and Learning go hand-in-hand. And so they did in practice during those early centuries, when the Religion of the Prophet displayed its greatest expansiveness and vitality. Nor was the term 'Learning' in those days, though always associated with Theology, interpreted in any illiberal sense. During some of the darkest ages of human history the lamp of science was, to a great extent, kept alive by Arab votaries.

The famous Mosque of El-Azhar at Cairo was a University and a centre of Eastern culture for some hundred years before the oldest European Universities were founded. And to the present day it still enjoys incomparably the greatest prestige of any seat of learning in the Moslem world. But so far as real knowledge and education goes, El-Azhar is, if not a dead, at least a dormant, institution. The old Arab erudition, related alike in substance and in method to that of Europe during the Middle Ages, has met with the fate which would have befallen European culture, had it not been breathed upon and revived, in the Renascence, by the spirit of Ancient Greece. The only thing which really flourishes at the El-Azhar nowadays is the study of the Arabic language. Besides this, there is nothing but a decrepit Theology and a still more decrepit Jurisprudence, both based entirely on the Koran and the commentaries of the old Arab doctors, both products of the scholastic method in its last stage of degeneracy.

Yet the influence of this petrified University rests like a blight upon the religious and intellectual life of the country. The Ulema, or, literally, 'men of learning,' whose Alma Mater and headquarters El-Azhar is, are at once the Priests and the Professors of Egypt. It is true that, in the strict sense of the term, the Mohammedan religion admits no priests—no intermediary between God and man. But it is peculiarly fertile in religious teachers who, though possessing no ordination and dispensing no sacraments, still exercise as despotic a sway as ever regular priesthood did over the minds of the people.

Just as the Ulema do not owe their religious influence to ordination, so their claim to intellectual distinction is not established by examinations and degrees. He is the religious teacher, he is the man of learning, who can get himself accepted as such by the general opinion of his fellow-students. This would not be a bad principle of selection if the ideals, either of Religion or of Knowledge, permeating the whole body, were sound ones. But while those ideals are narrow and perverted, the result simply is to set up as teachers—and teachers to whom an ignorant population looks up with superstitious reverence—the men most remarkable for the vehemence of their bigotry and for the profundity of their immersion in antiquated formulæ and barren traditions.

The system of education which has its root in the El-Azhar has innumerable branches in the Mosque schools, of which there are several thousands throughout the country. Egypt is rich in 'Wakfs,' or religious foundations, destined for the most part to the maintenance of the Mosques and of the schools attached to them. But the teaching of these schools is smitten with the sterility of the El-Azhar, which, directly or indirectly, has moulded all the teachers. The children learn a little reading, less writing, and the repetition of the Koran from masters who are ignorant of the very rudiments of the art of instruction. To get by heart a certain quantity of the Sacred Volume is the main object of the whole course. Now this is not only not education. It is not even paving the way for it, except in so far as there must always be some advantage in learning the letters of the alphabet. But to sit on the ground swinging your body backwards and forwards, and continually repeating, in a monotonous chant, a quantity of matter which you are taught to regard with religious reverence, but never taught to understand,* is, if anything, an anti-educational process. If the object of true education be intellectual gymnastics, if it be to exercise and render supple the joints of the mind, then this system is its very opposite, for it tends to stiffen them. It is not calculated to enlighten, but to obfuscate. Under these circumstances we cannot be surprised that no more advanced education has grown spontaneously out of the system followed in the Mosque schools. They have gone on for centuries without developing anything higher. As far as unaided native education is concerned, Egypt has got to the end of her tether.

So much is this the case that, when public instruction is spoken of in Egypt nowadays, no one thinks of the Mosque schools, or even of the El-Azhar. Knowledge, as it is understood in the present age, is disseminated, not by these institutions, but either by the numerous European schools existing in Egypt, or by the Government schools, in which there are European masters or native masters trained in European methods. It is now nearly eighty years since Mehemet Ali—who could not write his own name—recognised that, if there was to be any real education in his country, it must be brought from Europe. Curious and contradictory were the efforts made by him and his successors to endow Egypt with the learning of the West, the nature of which they

* The language of the Koran is, of course, as unintelligible to the ordinary Arab schoolboy of to-day as the language of Chaucer would be to English school-children in the first standard.

did not themselves understand, though they appreciated its effects. At one time the desired object was to be accomplished by bringing European teachers, especially Frenchmen, to Egypt; at another time by sending young Egyptians to be instructed in Europe, and especially in France. At one time the young Egyptians so sent were made to live together in a sort of *pensionnat* of their own, in order that they might the better preserve their national faith and traditions. At another time they were dispersed and made to live in foreign households, in order that they might become the more thoroughly Europeanized. In one way or another some six hundred Egyptian scholars have been maintained in Europe at the cost of the State during the present century. And meantime, in Egypt itself, schools destined to spread European education were being founded and suppressed and founded again. Scholars were being pressed into them by force, as in our own country we used to press men for the Navy, and when they got there they were being paid to stay.

For it was not till the reign of Ismail Pasha that any considerable number of Egyptians, even among the upper classes, learned to realize the value of European education. By this time the religious prejudice against it had begun to wear off. Moreover, incessant contact with Europeans, who were now pouring into the country in large numbers, could not but impress the natives with the disadvantage at which they themselves stood, in the practical business of life, by reason of their lack of instruction. But when they did begin to grasp this fact, it was not the Government schools to which they first turned. The richer men sent their sons to Europe. Others made use of the numerous European schools which had by this time become established in Egypt. In 1875 the number of scholars in these European schools was 8,961, of whom about two thousand were Egyptians. By 1887 it had increased to 22,764, of whom 15,132 were Egyptians.

Of the natives visiting the European schools, only a small number belong to the Mohammedan majority of the people of Egypt. And the reason is simple. The European schools are, for the most part, distinctively Christian institutions, and many of them have been founded with the direct object of proselytism. The most important of them are French Catholic foundations, but since 1860 the American Mission has also started some large and important schools in the interest of the Protestant faith. The Italian and Greek schools, which are generally secular, aim almost exclusively at the education of the children of their respective nationalities, which are very numerously represented in Egypt. Great Britain, it must be admitted, has done very little for Egypt in the way of voluntary schools.

I have said that, of the native scholars who attend the European schools, only a minority belong to the dominant faith. The majority are either the children of Syrian Christians established in Egypt, and therefore mostly members of the Roman Catholic Church, or else Copts — the Copts being especially numerous in the schools of the American Mission. Except for the Government schools, therefore, the Mohammedan population are at a disadvantage in respect of educational opportunities, and they are well aware of it. But despite this fact, the reputation of the Government schools was, till recently, so bad that Mohammedans of the better class, even when they felt the value of European education, hesitated to send their children to those institutions.

This bad reputation is now, however, fast passing away. Since 1887 a striking change has come over the character of the Government schools and the estimation in which they are held. This is not due to any great increase in their pecuniary resources. Indeed, the Convention of London largely reduced the budget of the Ministry of Public Instruction, and though since 1888 that budget has once more been on the increase, it does not even now stand at the same figure as it did in 1884. But if the amount of money has not increased, it is infinitely better employed. The public schools of the Egyptian Government are now, for the first time in their history, organized, and conducted in accordance with approved educational principles, and the result has been most gratifying. I am far from wishing to attribute the credit of this change solely to British influence, although it has been coincident with the employment of Mr. Douglas Dunlop, the first of our countrymen who has held any position of influence in the Egyptian Ministry of Public Instruction. But it certainly is due in great part to the increase in the number of European teachers, French as well as English, and to the improvement in their quality. There are now fifteen English and twenty-four French masters in the Primary and Secondary Schools, besides thirty-four Egyptians who teach in English and fifty-six who teach in French.

There were three main evils in the old system of training in the Government Schools, against which war had to be waged. The first was the practice of cramming the memory instead of developing the powers of thought. This, it may be said, is an evil not peculiar to Egypt. But in Egypt it has certainly been carried to extraordinary lengths. It is clearly derived from the traditions of Mohammedan religious education as practised at the El-Azhar, and in the Mosque schools. A kind of instruction which consists in learning a set of texts or a set of formulæ, and the ideal of which is to stereotype knowledge, naturally relies almost exclusively upon the memory. Reflection and observation are held of little account.

The second great vice of the old methods was intimately connected with this glorification of mere memory. It consisted in multiplying the number of subjects taught, and in sacrificing quality to quantity. This, again, is a common mistake of a lower civilization trying to adopt the results of a higher, without understanding them. The first attitude of the Oriental towards Western culture is to condemn it root and branch. The second is to appropriate it unintelligently, to grasp at a number of sciences, but miss the spirit of science. It was upon these principles that the old curriculum of the Government schools was framed. Any quantity of subjects were taught, but none was learnt. The present method is diametrically opposite. Instead of dabbling in several European languages, the pupils are taught either English or French, but they are taught the one language well. The importance of learning some European tongue is evident. It is not so much for the sake of the language itself, as for that which it contains. Arabic is a noble language, but its literature does not contain the great body of modern knowledge. The very terminology of physical science is wanting. Thus, the young Egyptian, in learning English or French, is not only making a useful practical acquisition. He is not only undergoing the invaluable training of translating his thoughts into a new form. He is obtaining the means of studying history, geography, and science, as they cannot at present be studied in Arabic. To teach the pupil one European language, but to teach it thoroughly, and to teach other subjects through it, is the principle at present adopted with most encouraging success in the Government schools.

The third great vice of the old system was the want of attention to discipline, to deportment, and to physique. The boys were slovenly, unruly, and untrained in bodily exercises. In all these respects the improvement in late years has been extremely marked. Drill is now regularly taught in the principal Cairo schools, and a class of native boys are being trained as drill instructors. English games have been encouraged, and the scholars take to them kindly. Quick and imitative as they are, their progress in manliness of bearing and *esprit de corps* is very remarkable.

If the spirit of reform has been slow in reaching the educational system, there is no branch in which of recent years it has borne richer fruit. The Government has often been criticised for spending so little upon education, although at any time during the last ten years it has spent twice as much upon it as the Government of Great Britain did only sixty years ago. But two things should be borne in mind in this connection. People must live before they can be taught. Famine is worse than ignorance. What the Egyptian Government had to fight for, in the early years of the occupation, was the very existence of the people. Essential as education is, the provision of education is not such a primary duty of Government as the defence of person and property, the maintenance of justice, or, in a country like Egypt, where human life depends upon Public Works, the careful preservation of those works upon which life depends. And, in the next place, it would have been no use simply to augment the budget of the Education Department, so long as the schools were being conducted on unintelligent methods. It was not for want of money that education made so little progress under the earlier Viceroys. They spent freely upon it, but they did not know how to make their expenditure effective. The time has now come when the Government may feel sure that whatever additional resources it can devote to Education will not be thrown away. But it is only in quite recent years that such confidence has been possible.

And even now a great crowd of scholars is not the thing to aim at, but rather the thorough training of a limited number. The Government is still far from being in a position to offer a decent education to the majority of the inhabitants. It has not got a sufficient number of properly trained masters even for the 6,800 scholars of its existing Primary and Secondary Schools.* Egypt has yet to create a native professional class. She has yet to educate the men who are destined to fill the Government Service. When these urgent needs have been supplied, it will be time enough to think of general public instruction. Fortunately, the country possesses, in the present Under-Secretary of State for Education, Yakub Artin Pasha (an able and highly cultivated Armenian), a man who thoroughly understands the wants of the country, and who knows that the efficiency of a few schools whose scholars will, in

* There were in 1892 forty-two Government schools in Egypt—six Primary of the Lower Grade, thirty-four Primary of the Higher Grade, and two Secondary, both of the latter being in Cairo.

their turn, spread the light of knowledge, is vastly more important than the multiplication of schools of an inferior description.

From this point of view, great importance attaches to the maintenance of a high standard in the Colleges for professional instruction, which are the apex of the Government system of education, and in so raising the level of the subordinate schools that they may be able to supply these Colleges with pupils capable of profiting by a higher curriculum. It was a fatal defect in the old methods, that boys were allowed to pass from the Primary to the Secondary Schools, and from the Secondary Schools to the Colleges, without having proved, at each successive stage, their capacity to benefit by superior instruction. It was no use improving the teaching staff of the Secondary Schools and Colleges, as long as the boys and young men entering them were not sufficiently well grounded to understand what they were being taught. This state of things no longer exists. Recent years have seen the introduction of a well-conceived and properly conducted system of primary and secondary examination. In order to enter a secondary school, a boy must now have his Primary Education Certificate, and in order to enter a College he must have his Secondary Education Certificate. The bad material is thus weeded out, and the energy of the professors and of the higher class of masters is no longer wasted upon pupils of whom they can make nothing.

The Colleges to which I have just referred are eight in number. There are the Schools of Law, of Medicine, of Engineering and of Agriculture. Besides these, there are three Training Colleges for native teachers of Arabic, English and French, and a Technical School—École des Arts et Métiers—at Bulak. The College of Agriculture, and the Training Colleges for native teachers of English and French, are new. The rest have existed for some time, but, with the exception of the Technical School, they were till recently in a very effete condition. But now fresh life has been infused into them all. I have already spoken of what M. Testoud has done for the School of Law. Improvements have also been introduced into the School of Medicine, which now has an English Vice-Principal. There is, however, still much to be done in bringing the School of Medicine up to the mark.

Special interest attaches to the Training College for native teachers of Arabic. This institution may become an important point of connection between the traditional Mohammedan education and the Europeanized system of the Government schools. The teachers of Arabic, and of the subjects taught in Arabic in the State Schools, are still for the most part ex-students of the El-Azhar. Their mental standpoint is the medieval one which clings to that University. The object of the College in question is to imbue them to some extent with the elements and the spirit of modern knowledge, and to teach them the art of teaching.

Time alone can show whether the movement, of which this College is the outcome, is destined to have a great development—whether the old educational foundation, which has so memorable a past, and even at the present day enjoys so great a reputation throughout the Mohammedan world, will gradually undergo a change that will bring it into harmony with modern ideas, or whether it is destined to remain in the old ruts, a perpetual drag upon the educational progress of Egypt. The result is evidently of the greatest importance to the future of the country. There are some critics who maintain that Mohammedanism and progress are irreconcilable; and if the tenets of the scholastic pietists of the El-Azhar are to be literally insisted on, so no doubt they are. But I do not know that the attitude of the Ulema towards Science at the present day is more apparently hopeless than that which various Christian Churches have adopted towards Science in the past. Yet that opposition has, in most cases, died completely away. What has happened in the West may happen in the East. *Avec le ciel il y a des accommodements*. There are not wanting those among the more live-minded of the Ulema who realize that, if they are to retain their old position in Egyptian society, they must march with the times.

An interesting illustration of this attitude was given not very long ago at the distribution of prizes in a Government School. One of the Government Inspectors, who happens at the same time to be a distinguished member of the El-Azhar University, was present on the occasion, and felt inspired to try and reconcile his educational with his religious convictions. Perhaps he thought that his presence at an institution which, to many of his compeers, would seem tainted with heresy required some explanation. So he made a speech, in the course of which he defended European instruction on the ground that, since the learning of the West was originally derived from Mohammedan sources, Mohammedans need not be too scrupulous in accepting the return to them of some of their own wares. On the whole, this is not a bad way out of the difficulty. But it must always be borne in mind that, in view of the present attitude of at least a majority of the Mohammedan religious teachers towards European education, the extension of the latter involves an uphill fight. No doubt, if the Government pushes on along its present lines, and insists on giving a thorough modern education to its pupils, while carefully avoiding any needless offence to religious prejudices, the new ideas will in the long-run prevail. The religious party will end by falling in with them. But without steady support at the outset from the protecting arm of the State, and without the presence of a strong and dominant European element in the Schools and Colleges, progress would soon be arrested, and Education would relapse into the old grooves.

At the same time, the new system is steadily gaining in popularity, as may be seen from the great increase in the demand for Government instruction on the part of Mohammedans. I have stated that in old days the Government schools could only be filled by force or by bribery. As late as 1882, not more than 30 per cent. of the total number of pupils paid for their instruction, and the income from fees did not exceed £2,300. In 1891 the percentage of paying pupils was seventy-one, and the amount of school fees exceeded £20,000.

There is one point about the development of the Government schools which, from the political side, should be of peculiar interest to Englishmen. Our object, as I understand, is to develop the capacity of self-government in Egypt. It was a great step in that direction when we set up the principle of appointment by merit, and not by favour, throughout the Government Service. But it would be misleading to pretend that that principle is rigidly adhered to at the present day. In theory no man can enter the service except after passing an examination. In practice, this preliminary is often dispensed with, and that for two reasons. The examining body, which is composed of representatives of the various Ministries, is not up to its work; and even if it were, there are not, at present, a sufficient number of natives who could satisfy the requirements of a high-class examination. The development of the Schools, if the present satisfactory state of things is maintained, will open a way out of both these difficulties. It will increase the number of competent candidates, while the Primary and Secondary Certificates already referred to will supply a better test of efficiency than the existing haphazard examinations for admission to the several offices. If the rule could be laid down, that no man should be admitted to the lower grade of the Civil Service without a Primary Certificate, and no man to the higher grade without a Secondary Certificate, a notable improvement would soon be seen in the personnel of the Government.

A very important step in this direction was taken in 1892 on the suggestion of Mr. Gorst. A decree was passed, providing that in future no vacancy should be filled among the higher class of Assistants (Muawens) in the Governing Staff of the provinces except by men who had passed the secondary examination. It is from these Assistants that the Mamurs and Mudirs are in future, as a general rule, to be chosen. The reform in question, therefore, when it has been at work for some years, will for the first time ensure a respectable standard of education, and the knowledge of at least one European language, among the chief provincial authorities. In view of the enormous power and influence exercised by these men in a bureaucratic country like Egypt, it is impossible to overestimate the importance of such a step.

For my own part, I attach much more importance in the immediate future of Egypt to the improvement of the character and intelligence of the official class than I do to any development of the Representative Institutions with which we endowed the country in 1883. As a true-born Briton, I, of course, take off my hat to everything that calls itself Franchise, Parliament, Representation of the People, the Voice of the Majority, and all the rest of it. But as an observer of the actual condition of Egyptian Society, I cannot shut my eyes to the fact that Popular Government, as we understand it, is, for a longer time than anyone can foresee at present, out of the question. The people neither comprehend it nor desire it. They would come to singular grief if they had it; and nobody except a few silly theorists thinks of giving it to them.

Do not let me be supposed to depreciate either the Legislative Council or the General Assembly. As far as they go, they are most useful institutions—especially the former. The Government does well to give them every encouragement, and jealously to respect their rights. There is no saying that a day may not come when their share in controlling the national destinies will be far greater than it is at present. But, for the moment, their strength is fully taxed in discharging the somewhat narrow, but certainly not too narrow, functions bestowed upon them by the Organic Decree of May 1, 1883, which was inspired by Lord Dufferin.

The Legislative Council meets once a month. It is composed of thirty members, of whom fourteen, including the President, are nominated by the Government. Its duty is to examine the Budget, and all proposed laws which affect the administration of the country. The Government, however, is not bound to accept the amendments which the Legislative Council passes, though it is bound, if it rejects them, to state the reasons for such rejection in writing. Moreover, the Council cannot initiate legislation. Its powers are thus very restricted, and at one time there was rather a tendency on the part of the Government, not indeed to disregard its legal rights, but to treat its opinions as of no consequence. But this tendency is a thing of the past. The Government, which has the right of delegating any functionary to be present at the Legislative Council, now takes considerable pains to explain to that body the *raison d'être* of the measures submitted to it. There is, at the same time, an increasing desire on the part of the Council of Ministers, who, in conjunction with the Khedive, are the ultimate legislative authority, to accept, as far as possible, the amendments introduced into draft decrees by the Legislative Council. And there can be no doubt that, in a good many instances, the decrees in question have been rendered both more popular and more practical by such amendments.

At the same time, it is a wise disposition of the Organic Decree which permits the Government, if it judges necessary, to disregard the suggestions of the Legislative Council. It was my duty on one occasion to explain and defend a proposed decree before that assembly. The subject was one which excited considerable interest among its members, and there was a good deal of discussion. Of the dignity and good humour with which the discussion was conducted it would be impossible to speak too highly. Moreover, most of the amendments proposed and carried were not only sensible in themselves, but supported by valid arguments temperately urged. There were, however, one or two others which, if adopted, would have wrecked the whole scheme, and which, as a matter of fact, the Council of Ministers subsequently put aside. I do not think the authors of these proposals had the least intention of defeating the object of the law they were discussing, but they were incapable of grasping the bearing of the particular amendments, in which they were individually interested, upon the measure as a whole. As critics of laws prepared by men of greater administrative experience, the members of the Council render valuable service. But as legislators with absolute power they would certainly produce some very grotesque and self-contradictory enactments.

A remarkable instance of the way in which the Legislative Council, despite its general good sense and moderation, may on occasion go utterly wrong is afforded by its treatment of a decree for the more drastic punishment of brigands, which was submitted to it in the spring of 1890. The draft of the Bill, as presented by the Government, simply enacted that, where an act of brigandage resulted in murder, the leaders and organizers of the band should be liable to capital punishment. A high religious authority, who was a member of the Council, proposed to amend the measure in accordance with the Religious Law, and his colleagues followed him like a flock of sheep.

Now, what was the nature of the amendment? In the first place, it converted the original draft, which, whatever might be thought of its provisions, was brief, simple, and intelligible, into a long-winded disquisition on brigandage in general, full of verbiage, irrelevance, and ambiguity. But the substance of the amended decree was even more appalling than its form. For it provided, among other things, that any brigand who was arrested before he had committed theft or homicide should, after being submitted to the bastinado, be imprisoned until he repented or died: that any brigand who had succeeded in committing a theft, but without murder, should have his right hand and his left foot cut off: that any brigand who had committed murder should be punishable, at the choice of the authorities, either (1) by amputation of the right hand and left foot, followed by execution, or (2) by amputation, followed by crucifixion, or (3) by amputation, followed by execution and crucifixion, or (4) by simple execution, or (5) by simple crucifixion. The Bill then went on to lay down in detail the method of crucifixion, enacting that the criminal should have his legs as well as his arms stretched out on cross bars, and that a spear should be thrust into his left breast, and twisted round in it until he died. But by way, presumably, of mitigation for these barbarities, it went on to provide that the punishments aforesaid should not apply if, after murder followed by theft, the brigands returned the objects stolen, or if one of the gang were a dumb man or a near relation of one of the victims. It is not to be supposed that this farrago of nonsense, which was of course rejected by the Government *en bloc*, would ever have commended itself to the Legislative Council, if it had not been brought forward in the name of the Sacred Law. But the fact that such barbarous bosh should have been accepted at all is a proof of the necessity of keeping the final decision in legislative matters in the hands of men more uniformly amenable to the influences of civilization.

So much for the Legislative Council. The General Assembly is simply the Council over again, with the addition of the six Ministers and of forty-six members popularly elected. This Assembly has no legislative functions, though it is entitled to pass resolutions on any subject of public interest—resolutions which the Government is free to take as much or as little notice of as it pleases. It has, however, one most important power of a negative kind, inasmuch as no new taxes can be imposed without its consent. This is a provision which might evidently some day or other enable the Assembly to play a very considerable part in Egyptian politics. But since 1883 the Government has been in the fortunate position of not requiring to impose new taxes upon its native subjects, except the tax necessary to facilitate the abolition of the Corvée, which, for reasons already explained,* the Assembly made no difficulty about accepting. That body, therefore, has not been summoned oftener than four times since its creation (the Organic Decree providing that it must meet at least once every two years), and its discussions have generally been brief and colourless. As far as

* See p. 195.

can be judged, its characteristics do not differ materially from those of the Legislative Council, though as the proportion of Government nominees, who form the best element of both bodies, is smaller in the Assembly than in the Council, the decisions of the former would be more likely to prove fantastic and unworkable than those of the latter.

The time, in fact, has not yet come for applying the principle of Representative Government, in any great degree, to the national affairs of Egypt. It would be sounder policy to begin by introducing it into the management of local business, and even then tentatively and with caution. The only local representative institution having administrative powers, which at present exists, is the Municipality of Alexandria. That city, by virtue of its large European population, has probably more of the elements requisite for the success of local self-government than any other town in Egypt. On the other hand, the mixture of Europeans and natives on this body gives rise to certain special difficulties.

It is impossible to say that during the three years of its existence the achievements of the Alexandria Municipality have been of a very brilliant character. It hobbles along, though of late days, especially since it has been provided by the Government with an able President in the person of Shakur Bey, it is becoming more business-like and less polemical. In any case, it has a certain educational value, and the Government has no cause to regret the experiment of creating it—an experiment which, according to the latest reports, seems likely to be repeated in certain other large towns. If the new Municipalities are wisely constituted, and if too much is not expected of them at first, they will, no doubt, especially with the spread of education, do useful work and constitute a desirable check upon the all powerful bureaucracy. But let me say once more that it is to the improvement in the character of the latter body, and to its judicious control by the European authorities at headquarters, that we must, for a long time to come, mainly look for the maintenance and development of reforms.

CHAPTER XII

ENGLISH AND EGYPTIANS.

So far we have been considering the course of the reforms which have marked the recent history of Egypt —reforms simple in their essence, but difficult of introduction; destined at the outset to encounter many vicissitudes, but justified in the long-run by their brilliant results. It remains to cast a glance at the probable future of this good work, and the forces favourable or unfavourable to it, at the prospects and the conditions of its continuance.

One thing, indeed, seems clear. Whatever may be the troubles yet in store for Egypt, the ultimate issue is not doubtful. Egypt will never be allowed permanently to relapse into the barbarism of the Mameluke period, or into the semi-barbarism of Mehemet Ali, and even of Ismail. No crucifixion of brigands, no cutting off of right hands and left feet, no other medieval barbarism or absurdity, will long be tolerated in this small and central country of unique interest and attraction, which is becoming more and more the common meeting-ground of civilized mankind.

No; it is not the ultimate result which is doubtful, but the manner in which it will be attained. Is the progress of the last few years to be steadily consolidated? Is the education of the Egyptian people, in the conception and habits of justice and good government, to continue smoothly and unchecked, until justice and good government become a matter of course? Or are we to see that progress and that education interrupted, and, as a consequence of such interruption, fresh impoverishment, fresh discontent, fresh anarchy, ending in the final subjection of the country to some great European Power? As a potentially independent State, Egypt is having a last chance. Is she capable of profiting by it? Will she be allowed to do so?

It is to the examination of these questions that I propose to devote the brief remainder of this book. But first of all, who are they, these Egyptians? What is the character of the masses to be guided, and of the classes who should be their guides? The bulk of the people are a primitive peasantry.* They are healthy, industrious after their own fashion, extraordinarily conservative in their habits and traditions, prone to obedience, devoid of initiative, good-humoured and pacific. In the scale of intelligence they certainly stand high, considering the centuries of darkness and oppression through which they have passed. But they lack the strenuousness and the progressive spirit which would characterize any equally intelligent race tilling a less bounteous soil and breathing a more bracing atmosphere.

Such a race will not of itself develop great men or new ideas, or take a leading part in the progress of mankind. But under proper guidance it is capable of enjoying much simple content. A vast deal of nonsense has been talked about the misery of the fellahin. They have been subject to a crushing tyranny in the past, but it has not knocked the natural cheerfulness out of them. And now that the tyranny is over, it may be doubted whether their lot contrasts unfavourably with that of the mass of the people in many more advanced countries. Poor they certainly are, but, except in a few districts where water is scarce or the

* According to the census of 1882, which is fairly accurate, the population of Egypt numbered 6,715,000 natives and 91,000 foreigners. Of the former no fewer than 4,200,2co, or 62 per cent., belonged to the agricultural class. It is probable that there has been a considerable increase of population since 1882.

land ruined by overcropping, they are not poverty-stricken. For what, after all, is the great hardship of poverty—provided always you have enough to eat—when you can spend your whole life in sunshine and fresh air, when the lightest clothing will supply sufficient warmth, the rudest cabin sufficient shelter, when you have no hard winter to provide against, no coals to buy, no shivering children to shield from frost or tempest? If the means of the Egyptian peasant are scant, his wants also are few, and his position, always supposing that he can be protected from injustice on the part of the Government, is a fairly independent one.

A large proportion of the fellahin are small proprietors living on the produce of their fields. A great number more, though they gain their livelihood chiefly by working for larger land-holders, have yet some little property of their own. The absolutely landless class is in a minority, and even these are nowadays in a much better position to earn a decent subsistence than they were ten years ago. The introduction of paid labour, in lieu of the Corvée, and the large expenditure on new public works, causes annually the distribution of a very considerable sum in wages among the poorest of the peasantry. No doubt the land tax is heavy, in a few districts crushingly heavy, and it is most inequitably distributed, some of the very best lands paying less than some of the worst. But looked at as rent, twenty-five or thirty shillings an acre—and these are the commonest rates—can hardly be called an excessive burden for land which bears rich crops with comparatively little delay.

Under present conditions the lot of the peasant is far from wretched. Indeed, to all appearances, the poor of the country are much better off than the poor of the towns, which are densely crowded. How they live, all these thousands of small tradesmen and artificers, seems at first sight a mystery. Yet even here there are few signs of extreme want. Disease and deformity abound, especially repulsive forms of blindness, but the physical infirmities of the people are due to the neglect of sanitary laws, and not to hunger. Though the death-rate of

Cairo, of Alexandria, and of the larger provincial towns is high,* there are probably fewer deaths from starvation, or from illness due to inadequate nourishment, than in the great cities of many civilized countries. There is no Poor Law, but a good deal of charity, and the common people are generous to one another.

Alike in town and in country, the poorer classes are of the same manageable temperament—cheerful, sociable, and easily contented. They are never tired of talking, and their delight in what they call a 'fantasía,' that is to say, any sort of show or entertainment, however simple and commonplace—in music, recitation, a masquerade, a marriage festivity, above all in fireworks—is exhilarating to witness. They are not only light-hearted, but light-natured. Unchanging in their habits and ideas, they are changeable enough in their moods. An Egyptian quarrel is like summer lightning. It blazes up in a minute, and then, if you watched the men engaged in it, you would certainly think it an affair of the most alarming character, so loud are their voices, so violent their gesticulations, so threatening their attitudes; but in nine cases out of ten it ends without a fight. Essentially the people are very far from pugnacious, despite their superficial excitability. Yet accidental circumstances may render this excitement dangerous. If an Egyptian happens to have a deadly weapon, he may, in the heat of the moment, make use of it in a quarrel, which otherwise would not even have led to blows. I remember several cases of homicide, due to the hasty use of fire-arms, where the provocation was absurdly slight. Weapons of any kind, however, are seldom carried in Egypt. The peasantry, as a rule, have neither the means nor the desire to acquire them, and their importation is subject to severe restrictions.

To govern such a race is, under ordinary circumstances, a simple task. As long as they are not grossly abused, as long as the great duty of government in the matter of water is not too scandalously neglected, there is no fear of widespread public discontent. It is the

* Between forty and fifty per thousand.

strongest proof of the intensity of the old misgovernment that a revolution like that of Arabi should have been possible among a population so easy-going and so submissive. A repetition of that movement under present political conditions is more than improbable. There is no large amount of smouldering disaffection which might, if opportunity offered, break out into destructive flame. But, on the other hand, there is always some danger of the people being carried away by a spasm of excitement—especially religious excitement. The Egyptian, if easily governed, is also easily led. He is not by nature in the least fanatical. But he has been brought up in fanatical traditions, and he is greatly under the influence of religious teachers, who are fanatics by profession. Every now and then an incident happens which shows how easy it is to get up a religious émeute against some section of the Christian population. But with vigilance and firmness on the part of the Government, such disturbances can very easily be put down. Under the existing régime they present no serious danger, and even their occurrence becomes increasingly rare. The bulk of the people are only too glad of an excuse for not obeying the instigation of bigots with whom, despite all their superstitious reverence, they have at heart little sympathy, though they might not, if left to themselves, have character enough to resist such incitement.

I have often been asked whether British influence is popular with the mass of the Egyptian people. It would be absurd to reply to that question in the affirmative; but to answer it with a simple negative would be no less misleading. There is unquestionably a certain prejudice against Englishmen, as there is against all Christians, though that prejudice is easily overcome in individual cases where the people have learned to recognise the stranger as a benefactor. But on the broad political issue they are much too backward to have any opinion one way or the other. The ordinary peasant has probably only the vaguest notions as to how the government is really carried on. That he is satisfied with the results, that he is well aware of being treated much better than formerly, cannot be doubted. But he is not in a position to reason about the causes of the change.

The docile and pacific disposition of the race, their ignorance, and their lack of independence, increase enormously the responsibility resting on their governors. There is nothing in the character of the people to check the abuse of power, nothing to guide its exercise. And at the same time the wise exercise of power is probably of greater importance to the whole community than in any other country in the world. Bad government must everywhere be injurious to public welfare. In Egypt it is simply destructive of it. I am afraid of wearying the reader with a repetition of this idea, but the truth is so fundamental that I trust I may be pardoned for my insistence.

And if the burden of responsibility that weighs upon the rulers of Egypt is exceptionally heavy, the stumbling-blocks in their path are also exceptionally numerous. While the native population is childlike and dependent, the foreign residents, and especially the Greeks—who are the most numerous, and may be found in every corner of the country—are obstreperous and exacting. The Capitulations remove them, to a great extent, from the control of the authorities, and their consuls are disposed to push foreign privilege to its extremest limits. Moreover, the constant assertion of such privilege gives rise to an infinite number of embarrassing questions. If the men charged with the conduct of Egyptian affairs require to be firm and upright, they have no less constant occasion for the exercise of tact, patience, and diplomatic skill. Great indeed are the demands which the peculiar circumstances of Egypt make upon those who are called upon to guide her destinies.

What does the country possess to-day, in the shape of administrative capacity, equal to rising to the height of these demands? Where are the Egyptians who can govern Egypt? To answer that question, it is necessary to pass in brief review the various classes and races which compose the higher ranks of native society.

Egypt possesses, strictly speaking, no aristocracy. There are, indeed, a few families of hereditary wealth, a very few of hereditary influence, though that influence generally rests on religious rather than social distinction. But such hereditary influence carries with it no legal privilege and no title of honour. The rank of Bey or Pasha is entirely personal. It belongs only to those upon whom it is directly bestowed by the Khedive. Moreover, Mussulman feeling is, in some respects, very democratic. The Egyptian bows—indeed, he bows very low—before the fact of wealth or power, but he cares very little about the tradition of it. The great man of to-day is no less great because he has risen from nothing. The poor man is no more honoured because he has a distinguished ancestry.

What represents the nearest approach to our idea of an aristocracy is the small clique of great Turkish families which contribute a large proportion of the men upon whom the rank of Bey or Pasha is bestowed. A few of these families have been established in the country for generations, but the majority are immigrants of the present century. They are, like the Turkish upper class in general, of the most varied origin—Kurds, Circassians, Turks from Algiers and Tunis, Turks from the Isles, Turks from Constantinople, etc. Some of them are really not Turks at all, but Christians, or even Jews, from different portions of the Levant, who have adopted the religion and fallen in with the habits of the dominant race. But, whatever their history, they nowadays form a coterie who have a tendency to hold their heads higher than their neighbours, and who are easily distinguishable by their common use of the Turkish language in social intercourse. Of course they are all perfectly familiar with Arabic, both in its literary and in its colloquial form. But, among themselves, they prefer to speak Turkish, and, indeed, the use of Turkish as the tongue of polite conversation is rather a mark of bon-ton in the upper grades of Egyptian society.

Politically, the Turks of Egypt have no particular affection for the Porte. The last thing in the world which they desire is to see Egypt become an ordinary province of the Turkish Empire. On the other hand, they are not in sympathy with the Arab population, which they claim to govern, but in their hearts despise. Their Egyptian patriotism is, in most cases, limited to the conviction that it is their natural right to fill the best places and to live upon the fat of the land. But their capacity is not altogether equal to their ambition. Speaking broadly, they have all the ordinary faults, with something less than the average merits, which distinguish the ruling caste in Turkey itself. What the upper-class Turk generally possesses is courage, dignity, good manners, the habit and air of command. What he generally lacks is energy, industry, public spirit, a sense of duty. He is quick to catch up the externals of civilization, but he is apt to miss its essentials. Where to the common qualities of his class he adds the uncommon quality of moral rectitude, he may, despite all his shortcomings, make an excellent ruler. But such cases are rare. Self-indulgence and corruption have eaten the heart out of the Turkish oligarchy. It is the curse of the whole vast region which still lies under the blight of Ottoman dominion, that the men who have the power of governing are devoid of the morality which is essential to governing well.

The failings of the Turkish grandees—arrogance of race alone excepted—attach, more or less, to the whole Pasha class of Egypt. When I speak of the Pasha class, I mean not only those having the actual title of Pasha, but the men of wealth, and especially of landed wealth, generally, to whom the highest places in the Government Service most frequently fall. Of course there are many honourable exceptions. And, of course, also, the vices just noted are the natural consequences of a bad system. For centuries the idea of power has been dissociated from that of the performance of duty. Power was a thing to be aimed at for the benefit of yourself and your friends, not a trust to be discharged for the benefit of those below you. As it came to you without having earned it, so it might be taken from you without having abused it. You must make hay while the sun shone.

It is the unfitness of the Pasha class to fulfil the functions naturally appertaining to them which constitutes one of the chief obstacles to the realization of the ideal of a self-governed Egypt. Nor is there much sign of a desire on their part to overcome their besetting sins. As a body, the Pashas are in the sulks. They are angry at being no longer able to do as they please. They are annoyed at having to work for the first places in the State, instead of stepping into them as a matter of course. If they would only accept the new order of things, their future would not be jeopardized. Governing capacity, readiness to assume command and to take responsibility, are qualities scarce among Egyptians. The men who have got them will always be sure of a career. But they must recognise that, under a civilized system, power means something more than the opportunity of serving personal interests and gratifying personal caprice, and that, in order to rule successfully in modern Egypt, as in any progressive community, it is necessary to 'scorn delights and live laborious days.'

The Egyptian upper classes are not wholly blind to the advantages and requirements of civilization. They learn French. They send their sons to Europe. They like to demonstrate at least a superficial familiarity with European fashions, habits, and ideas. The commonplaces of political progress are on their lips. But the assimilation is often only skin-deep. In their hearts, in most cases, there is still a hope that the irksome restraints of that progress—as applied to themselves—may yet be swept away, together with the obnoxious tutelage which has imposed them. Some of the younger men have, no doubt, read the signs of the times, and are fitting themselves for high posts, not only by the same studies, but by the same industry and application which are found necessary in European countries by ambitious men of the upper classes. But the old generation must die out before this practice can become general. At present the older Pashas vegetate in their palaces and country houses, while the majority of the younger men devote themselves to a life of pleasure. Thus, when a native gentleman is wanted for a position of responsibility and command, it is very difficult to find him.

How stands the case with that class of native society which fills the interspace between the small body of dissatisfied aristocrats at the top, and the vast mass of toiling peasants at the bottom ? In rural Egypt there is nothing between the two except the Sheikhs or village elders. The Sheikhs are land-owners of very various magnitude. Some of them only possess a few acres. Others have large properties, and are rich men. But as a class they have many distinctive characteristics, and are sharply separated from the Pashas. They live, not in isolated country seats, but in the big houses of the villages and small towns. They do not spend the winter in Cairo. They do not learn European languages or adopt European habits and ideas. They do not wear clothes of a modern cut, but retain the rich colours, the flowing robes, and the full turbans, in which painters of Eastern scenery find such delight. Indeed, so far as externals go, they are vastly superior to the class above them. Compare a stately village Sheikh, picturesque in dress and dignified in demeanour, with the poor imitation of a European gentleman which is all that the Pasha usually succeeds in appearing, and how can you hesitate to think the former the better man ?

And as a matter of fact, the grave and impressive bearing of the Sheikh is not wholly superficial. Within the limited sphere of their immediate surroundings, these men have the capacity of governing. They need to be kept under control, otherwise they are almost certain to abuse their power ; but they do know how to deal with the mass of their rustic fellow-countrymen. In questions of agriculture and irrigation, in all the simple problems of village administration, they are useful, and, indeed, indispensable, agents of government. But for the exercise of any wider authority they are at present useless. It is only necessary to see one of these grave and reverend seniors moulded like wax by a little Mudiría official in a shabby frock-coat and a greasy tarbúsh !*

The impotence of the Sheikh in such circumstances is due not only to his awe of the official uniform. It is due to the fact that the man he is dealing with has some sort of education, however limited, whereas the Sheikh has none. And the worst of it is, that if the Sheikh, conscious of this deficiency in himself, determines to give his son a regular schooling, the latter ceases to be a Sheikh, and becomes like the official. He loses his familiarity with country life, and his touch with the common people. He can no longer reconcile himself to sitting on a rug on the floor, and tearing away at a roast sheep with his fingers. He wants to live in Cairo, to receive so much a month from the Government, and to add to the files of his particular Ministry.

Yet for all this, there is stuff in the Sheikh class. They have many faults—selfishness, avarice, narrow-mindedness. They have the common Oriental combination of servility to those above, and arrogance to those beneath them. But they have physique, shrewdness, energy, and they are not without principles of a kind. If education is apt to upset instead of improving them, that is a sufficiently familiar effect of education in its first contact with semi-barbarians. Perhaps it is as much the fault of the education as of its victims. Doubtless the more thorough and more manly spirit, which is now being breathed into the Government Schools, will be less ill-suited than the former system of training to the sons of the country Sheikhs, and the latter may be expected to enter these schools in larger numbers in the future.

It remains to notice the bulk of the official class—the great body of Government servants below the Ministers, Governors of Provinces, and other high functionaries who are generally either natives of the Pasha type or Europeans. This official class is very numerous in

* The tarbúsh is what we commonly call a fez, and is the invariable head-dress of an Egyptian official, whatever his rank.

Egypt. It takes the place which is occupied by the middle class in most European countries, for the independent native middle class is very small. Professional men are as yet scarce in Egypt. The few who exist are generally looking out for employment in the Public Service. A place under Government is still the highest ideal of the fairly educated Egyptian.

I use the term 'Egyptian' here in a comprehensive sense. The bureaucracy contains men of the most various races. The Copts,* or native Christians, form about one-tenth of the population of the country. They are to be found in every rank and in every calling, though the proportion of Copts is larger in Upper Egypt than in Lower, in towns than in the country, in trade and in handicrafts than in agriculture. But in the Government Service they are especially numerous, and more particularly in everything that has to do with accounts. Besides the Copts, moreover, there are a large number of Syrians and Jews. The Syrians, who are mostly Christians of the Catholic faith, are particularly disliked, but they are also particularly useful. Their

* The Copts, as most of my readers are doubtless aware, are the direct descendants of the old inhabitants of the country, prior to the Arab conquest. They are easily distinguishable from the rest of the Egyptians, not only by their appearance and their names, but by their religion—a primitive form of Christianity, most closely allied to the Greek faith, though not identical with it—and to some extent by their habits and character. They are still somewhat looked down upon by their Mohammedan fellow-countrymen, a contempt which they repay by generally getting the better of them in business transactions. In Upper Egypt, especially, a large portion of the land is now in the hands of the Copts. They are credited with being shrewder, but less honest and less cleanly, than the Mohammedans. There is some truth in these allegations, but also a good deal of exaggeration. Speaking generally, the Copts have, no doubt, some of the vices of a subject race, as well as its suppleness and adaptability, for until recent years their position was decidedly one of social inferiority. With equal treatment, some of these characteristics, as well as the sharpness of distinction between them and the native Mohammedans—who are originally the same race, crossed with Arab blood—are tending to disappear. The Copts are, as a general rule, better educated than the majority of Egyptians.

superior education, and especially their great knowledge of languages—for many of them speak and write French perfectly, while there are some who have a good knowledge of English—makes them invaluable as translators and draughtsmen. There are also throughout the Civil Service—leaving the Europeans for the moment out of account—a certain number of Armenians and members of other Eastern nationalities. It is only the posts involving command over the common people, such as the governorships of provinces or districts, of which Mohammedans have, for good reasons, a practical monopoly.

Taking this motley mass as a whole, it is usual, I think, to exaggerate its demerits. There is a good deal of rubbish which could easily be dispensed with, for, even after the clearances of late years, there are still far too many officials in Egypt. But it would be inhuman and short-sighted, considering the great want of outside employment for men of this kind, to reduce the number too fast. The Government Service, in its lower ranks, is a system of outdoor relief for needy men of clerkly training, which in a country without a Poor Law cannot be hastily abolished. But apart from this lumber which, if retained at all, is only retained for reasons of charity, there is a good deal of capacity among the Egyptian officials. And this remark applies not only to the higher ranks, 'the clerks of the Upper Division,' as we should call them in England, among whom are many men of fair education, good manners, and trustworthy character, but even to the mass—externally most unattractive—of the lower ranks. The crowd of small officials are known individually by the title of 'Effendi,' which is appended to every Government servant who is neither a Bey nor a Pasha, and which is about as dubious, regarded as a title of honour, as the English 'Mr.' when it is a written prefix, or 'Gentleman' when it is a written affix. Anybody who knows the social life of modern Egypt is well acquainted with the Effendi class. Their familiar characteristics, the obsequious manner, the slouching gait, the short-sightedness which is often so extreme as to amount almost to blindness, the worn official frock-coat buttoned up to the chin,* the general air of dinginess and servility —all these are calculated to make the most unfavourable impression upon the typical Briton.

And the effect which this unpromising exterior naturally produces is heightened by the traditional reputation for shiftiness and corruptibility attaching—and in many cases most unjustly attaching—to the Effendis as a body. For my own part, I have found—and I believe it is the experience of most of my countrymen who have had many of these men under them—that, if treated properly, they are far more capable and trustworthy than anybody would think possible at first sight. The fact is that the rank and file of the Civil Service, like the rank and file of the Army, used to be ruined by ill-usage. They were ordered about like slaves, ordered often to do what they knew themselves to be wrong, yet they durst not for their lives breathe an objection to the commands of their superiors. They were liable to dismissal on frivolous pretexts, not only for breaches of duty, but for the inopportune performance of it. And as they were almost always penniless, except for their official salaries, and generally had large families, they dreaded dismissal like a sentence of death. Discipline under these circumstances was no doubt perfect, but it was discipline of a wrong sort. It degraded the subordinate, and made a tyrant of the chief. The members of each class of the official hierarchy revenged themselves for the maltreatment they received by maltreating, in their turn, the class beneath them. And they all maltreated the common people.

Here, as elsewhere, a change of system was the first condition of a change of character. Treat the Effendi like a man; let him understand that you expect from him obedience, but not servility, that a reasonable objection properly urged will not be resented, and that, if he does his duty, his rights are secure—and you will be able to get plenty of good work out of him. No doubt

* To button your coat up to the neck is a sign of respect. It is sometimes amusing to see the haste with which this operation is performed on the approach of an official superior.

there are many black sheep—the hopeless legacy of a bad past. No doubt the general standard of education is low, though we may now look forward to a rapid improvement in this respect. But the prospect is by no means desperate. At bottom the Egyptian is intelligent and adaptable. He is by nature no more inclined to be dishonest than other people. Of course, if you put a premium on dishonesty, as the old system did, you will get it, as you would anywhere else. But an exactly opposite policy will produce—and, indeed, is producing—an opposite result.

At the same time, the average of capacity in the Civil Service would be lower than it is if it were not for the presence of a number of men who are sometimes denied the title of Egyptians. I refer particularly to the Syrians, Armenians, Jews, and other foreigners of Oriental extraction. These men are the objects of much jealousy on the part of their Mohammedan and Coptic colleagues, and there is a false kind of Egyptian patriotism which aims at excluding them from the Public Service. Yet Egypt, of all countries, is the least able to dispense with intelligence and capacity, wherever she can find them. If the principle of 'Egypt for the Egyptians' is ever to work, it can only be by giving a broad interpretation to the word 'Egyptian.' That term must include, not only Mohammedans and Copts, but all persons, whatever their race, and whatever their faith, who are permanently established in the country, who have their property and their families there, and who have definitely thrown in their lot with that of Egypt. Of course, if these people of foreign origin are admitted to the full rights of Egyptian citizenship, they ought by the same token to accept its obligations. It is a legitimate complaint, on the part of the ordinary natives, that their Syrian and other alien rivals, even when born and permanently resident in Egypt, are generally not amenable to Egyptian Law, but have become the protected subjects of various foreign Powers. Nothing was more natural than that these aliens should seek such protection in the past, when the native laws afforded them no defence against arbitrary ill-usage. But as long as the present régime continues, they do not need the shield of a spurious nationality. If they claim to be regarded as Egyptians, they claim no more than their right. But in that case they should give up masquerading as Frenchmen, or Austrians, or Italians, or Spaniards.

In speaking of the Egyptian bureaucracy as a whole, I must be taken to include these semi-foreign elements. I do not for the moment refer to the men of genuine foreign nationality whose connection with the service of the Khedive is necessarily a temporary one. Now, of the Egyptian bureaucracy, as just defined, it may be asserted that it is not lacking in capacity, in habits of business, in industry, or in discipline. What it does lack is backbone. That the majority of Egyptian officials enormously prefer civilized methods of government, that they would rather live under a reign of legality, principle, and probity, than serve as agents of the old system of tyranny, muddle, and corruption, there can be no doubt whatever. But, left to themselves, they do not possess the strength of character, the independence, or the *esprit de corps*, to resist the gradual return of the former evils. To render them efficient defenders even of a system with which they sympathize, they would require an amount of moral courage and cohesion which are still very far to seek. It is easier for the younger men, who have never been trained in habits of suppleness and servility, to develop the virtues of firmness and self-reliance. But it will take a long time before these qualities permeate the whole body.

Such are, from the political point of view, the chief component elements of Egyptian society. There is a vast passive populace. There is a middle class—mostly official—which is intelligent, docile, and sympathetic towards reforms, but timid and disunited. There is an upper class, devoid of the best traditions of a genuine aristocracy, with little sense of *noblesse oblige*—just a certain number of rich and powerful families who still hanker after the monopoly of office and of privilege which formerly belonged to them. This class is not without the desire to rule, or a certain instinct for ruling. But it is singularly deficient in the industry, the education, and the principle which, under the new conditions, are requisite before men can rule to any purpose. The great body of this class are, therefore, unserviceable for the work of government. And while they are unserviceable to-day, with European influence in the saddle, they might become dangerous to-morrow if that influence were withdrawn. Last of all, there are the Ulema, who, as I explained in the preceding chapter, claim to be the depositaries of religion and learning. But their religion is a bitter fanaticism, and their learning a string of barren scholastic dogmas. The majority of them are hostile to reform, because it comes from Christians, and they might almost certainly be counted on to throw their weight into the scale of reaction.

Where in all these bodies do we find the elements of a native party, having at once the will and the capacity to hold the field which has been won for civilization? In time, no doubt, the middle class will become more numerous and more courageous, and may furnish an adequate body of supporters to the cause of progress. In time the younger men of the upper class may realize, as the best of them realize already, that the days of privilege are over, and that they had better buckle to and fit themselves for that position of leadership in the new society which is theirs whenever they care to take it. In time, perhaps, even the keen edge of fanaticism may be blunted, and the religious party may find a way to reconcile their obstructive doctrines with the imperious necessities of the age. But all this requires time—time—time. The reforms of recent years have been momentous, and they have struck root; but the roots need to grow down deeper into the soil. At present there is no one acquainted with Egypt who would not tremble for these reforms, if it were not for the small body of Europeans in high positions, whose power is out of all proportion to their numbers.

The question, indeed, is not one of numbers at all.

There could be no greater error than to try and crowd the Egyptian Service with Europeans. Europeans in the lower ranks are a mistake, and many Europeans in any rank are a superfluity. It is not quantity but quality which is required, not many men, but picked men, and picked men with something at their backs. I have already exposed the fallacy of thinking that the mere presence of Europeans, however capable, is sufficient to keep Egypt straight. Their presence is, indeed, essential, but it would not be effective without the conviction that they will, in case of need, have the support of a Great Power which has made the cause of progress in Egypt its own. It is the shadow of the world-wide Empire behind them upon which their influence, and with it the whole fabric of reformed government, ultimately rests. Great Britain looms large in the Egyptian mind. '*L'Angleterre et toutes ses colonies*,' as a native ojurnalist—a hostile journalist, by the way—once said to me, with irritable emphasis on the '*colonies*,' is evidently not a thing to be trifled with. Of course, Superior Persons are aware that this is all nonsense, that a wide-spread Empire is a source of weakness and not of strength, and that there is no such thing as Prestige. But such Superior Persons have not generally lived much abroad. If they knew the East, they would recognise that Prestige is no delusion. If they knew—more particularly—Egypt, they would be forced to admit that it may be one of the most potent of the factors that 'make for righteousness.'

There is, however, a misunderstanding which I am most anxious to guard against when extolling the influence of my country. To say that British influence is the foundation of the work of reform is not to pretend that the whole structure has been raised by British hands. Far from it. Among those who have taken a foremost part in the regeneration of Egypt have been many Europeans, who are not only not English, but in some cases not even friendly to England, though their power for good has been enhanced by England's action. And there have also been many natives. This is the most hopeful element of the situation. It is not only, or principally, upon what Englishmen do for Egypt that the case for England rests. It is upon what England is helping the Egyptians to do for themselves.

And the great body of native reformers are perfectly aware of this. They are conscious of their own weakness. They want to do right. They thoroughly understand the essential principles of good government, and desire to see them applied to their own country. They are willing to face prejudice and opposition in that behalf, but not without support. 'Il nous faut un appui' is the simple but sufficient formula in which I have heard their point of view summed up. How often have I not had to listen to complaints against England for not interfering more! How often has it been pointed out to me that the battle would be definitely won if only it were certain that we never meant to go away! But perhaps enough has been said to show what is the true nature of British influence. It is not exercised to impose an uncongenial foreign system upon a reluctant people. It is a force making for the triumph of the simplest ideas of honesty, humanity, and justice, to the value of which Egyptians are just as much alive as anybody else. It is a weight, and a decisive weight, cast into the right scale, in the struggle of the better elements of Egyptian society against the worse.

When I say that we have the reforming party in Egypt with us, the remark is subject to two reservations. In the first place, it must not be supposed that all those who are at heart on our side would be willing everywhere and at all times to say so. They gladly work with us, but they like to be able to pretend that they do so under compulsion. And, after all, this is very natural. Our ultimate intentions have always been doubtful. The natives in question, to whatever branch of the Public Service they belong, are quite clever enough to know that, if we stay, they will never be made to suffer for any mere expressions of opinion, so long as they have performed their duty faithfully. But if we were to go, and the expected era of reaction were to follow our departure, then the fact of having expressed anti-English opinions might be pleaded in mitigation of their faithful performance of duty in the past. So, on the whole, it is just as well to keep in touch with the Mammon of unrighteousness. Therefore they do England's work, while professing a desire that England should go, and they profess that desire, while offering up secret prayers that she never may.

On the other hand, there certainly are some, and those among the most able and vigorous of the party of progress, who are sincere in their desire to see the back of the British troops and of British Officials. It is not that they do not sympathize with the work which has been done during the last ten years. But they are convinced that they could have done it by themselves, or at least that they are now quite able to continue it by themselves. There is something, to my mind, very humorous, as well as pathetic, in this self-confidence. Most of the men who feel it are Egyptians only in that wider sense for which I have argued above, but the acceptance of which it has, on certain recent occasions, required the whole influence of Great Britain to hammer into the heads of the Egyptian proper. These persons have all along been on the side of European civilization and European reforms. But what were they able to make of things in the old days, when the foreign influence which they now think so superfluous was not predominant? Where were they in 1882? They were, for the most part, safe out of the country. It is difficult not to smile when men of this stamp, whom the bulk of the natives have to be coerced into regarding as their fellow-citizens, and some of whom hardly know Arabic, put themselves forward as the champions of 'Egypt for the Egyptians.'

There are among the highest grades of Egyptian society, side by side with the Turkish and Arab Pashas, equal to any of them in rank and wealth, and superior to almost all of them in education and intelligence, a certain number of Christians—principally of Armenian origin—who have played a large and honourable rôle in

Egyptian public life. I need only recall, as an instance, the name of Nubar Pasha, the greatest of them all. It is in the minds of some of these men that the idea that Egypt could get on very nicely left to herself—provided always that they had the management of her—has most firmly established itself. One might have thought that the failure of Nubar to avert the ruin of his country would have been a sufficient warning. Which of them can hope to succeed where Nubar, with all his high ideals and pre-eminent capacity, was unsuccessful? The fact is that these Christian Pashas, eminent by their ability, but few in number, and without hold on the body of the people, are only accepted on sufferance by the Mohammedan majority of their class. The latter will be quite prepared to use them, as the Porte uses men of the same race and qualities, but only so long as they are prepared to govern in accordance, not with their own enlightened notions, but with the spirit and the views of the Pashas as a body. In reality, these men, if they only knew it, have more interest than anybody else in the maintenance of the controlling influence of some European Power. With that force behind them, they will be able to render valuable services to a country which stands greatly in need of capacity such as theirs. Without it, they might easily become the mere tools of the Party of Reaction.

So far, it seems, the case is pretty clear. If there was nothing involved in the Egyptian question but the maintenance and the development of the reforms of recent years; if we had nothing to think of but the training of the Egyptian people in self-government on civilized lines; if there was nobody concerned but Egyptians and English—the desirability of going on as we are going, of giving a hopeful experiment sufficient time to render possible its permanent success, would not, I conceive, be open to any sort of question. Unfortunately, the problem of the future of Egypt is not so simple as that. It is complicated by the international element in Egyptian politics, and especially by the attitude of France.

CHAPTER XIII.

THE DIFFICULTY WITH FRANCE.

THE reader, who has followed me thus far, will not need to be reminded that almost all European nations have interests in the Nile Valley, and that these interests are entrenched in a manner which has no parallel elsewhere. We have seen that many acts of government cannot be performed in Egypt without the concurrence of the European Powers. It is not too much to say that the work of England in that country, however excellent, could not go on if the Powers in general were opposed to it.

Fortunately, European sentiment is rather with us than against us. And it is increasingly with us. Its direction has varied very much during the past ten years, but, as far as the foreign residents in Egypt are concerned, there is no difficulty in explaining these successive changes of feeling. The foreign residents were enthusiastic at our coming. Very soon the disappointment, which resulted from our first tentative and half-hearted dealing with Egyptian affairs, turned many of them against us. But the revival which has taken place in recent years, and the discovery that, though slowly and by indirect methods, Great Britain is nevertheless moulding the laws and administration of the country into closer conformity with civilized principles, has now brought most of the better elements to our side. With the exception of the French, and a small minority who are completely under French influence, the respectable portion of European society is favourable to the present system. While critical of our methods, they recognise the good results of our work, and would be dismayed at our withdrawal. When, nowadays, you find Europeans who are opposed to British influence, the motives for their opposition are generally the reverse of reputable. Those who prefer troubled waters, because they are the best to fish in, naturally disapprove of the effects of our Occupation.

The better feeling of the resident Europeans has reacted upon the political attitude of their respective nations. I do not say that this is the only cause which has influenced the Egyptian policy of the majority of the Powers in our favour. But into the other causes I cannot enter. To do so would take me altogether outside the scope of this book into general questions of foreign policy—into the relations of Great Britain with the Triple Alliance, and other controversial topics. After all, the only thing which concerns us here is the effect of these influences on the situation in Egypt itself. At one time, Italy was our only friend among the Great Powers in Egyptian matters, while the others—I do not now speak of France, who has always been uniformly hostile—were coldly indifferent to our difficulties, and sometimes not indisposed to increase them. Of late years, on the contrary, we have experienced general cordiality, and a good deal of quiet but effective help, not only from the Italian, but from the German and Austrian representatives. The minor Powers, also, as a rule, are not otherwise than friendly. Russia, on the other hand, always inclines to back France, not so much, I think, from any annoyance at England's position in Egypt, or at the use which England makes of it, as from general political considerations. But Russia's opposition—for it cannot be called hostility—is of a somewhat perfunctory description. Her individual interest in Egypt is too small, and her sense of the indecency of obstructing necessary reforms is too great, to permit of any very active interference with our work on the part of Russian diplomatists.

There is one respect in which the fact that Great Britain now has the majority of the Great Powers on her side is of special importance to the Egyptian Government. We have seen how constant are the questions arising between the Government and the Commissioners of the Public Debt. It is true that, with the recovery of the finances, the time has gone by when a hostile policy on the part of the Commissioners was able to put the Government into a position of embarrassment. But a friendly attitude on their part is still, and always must be, of great importance to the smooth working of the administrative machine. And under present circumstances the friendliness of the Caisse is generally to be counted on. Four out of the six Commissioners—that is to say, the German, the Austrian, and the Italian, as well as the Englishman—are always predisposed to side with the Government in any reasonable proposal. And the two others are kept in wholesome check by the knowledge that they are in a minority, even if they should be—and I do not say that they often are—inclined to raise troublesome questions. Disagreements with the Government may still occur. A system which sets up two concurrent authorities in one of the most important branches of administration, and which creates an *imperium in imperio* like that of the Caisse, must always give rise to a certain amount of friction. But, at any rate, there is no longer an inclination to create difficulties. The Government has less cause than it once had to regard the Caisse as a financial ogre, barring the way to reforms. On the contrary, it now very frequently finds that body prepared to give cordial support to a policy of reproductive expenditure.

Space will not permit me to dwell on the hundred little ways in which the gradual conversion of European sentiment to the side of England facilitates the task of the Egyptian Government. But I feel bound to put the question, whether the fact that English policy now commands the sympathy both of the resident Europeans and of the Powers is not the best answer to the charge, so often flung in our faces, that we have broken faith with Europe. I should be the first to admit the formal discrepancy between the repeated statements of British Ministers and the policy which, as a matter of fact, Great Britain has been compelled to pursue. But I deny that this is any proof of bad faith. We misunderstood the situation at the outset. When we first went to Egypt we believed—and it was natural that we should believe—that the duty before us was a comparatively simple one. We thought that all we had to do was to put down a military rebellion. Only actual experience of the internal condition of Egypt could teach us that the rebellion was the least part of the matter, and that the real difficulty lay in the utter rottenness of the whole fabric of government.

Our conception of the task before us was mistaken. Hence our original declarations have proved impossible of fulfilment. But if you go below the mere letter of those declarations, and consider their spirit, the essence of them all was a profession of disinterestedness. To that profession we have been true. And the best proof of the fundamental honesty of our action is the fact that the unprejudiced body of civilized opinion endorses it. Would it have done so if Great Britain had used the position of vantage which she has acquired in Egypt for her own individual and exclusive benefit? But Great Britain has done nothing of the kind. No nation is able to say that any legitimate right or privilege which it once possessed in Egypt has been infringed by any action of ours. Such rights and privileges remain absolutely untouched, even where it would be just and reasonable that they should be modified. And, on the other hand, what European people, having any interests in Egypt, has not benefited by the fact that that country has been preserved from disorder and restored to prosperity? That this is the true view of the character of British policy is shown by the willing acquiescence, if not the outspoken approval, of the majority of civilized nations.

There are, no doubt, two Powers who raise a protest—Turkey and France. And there are excellent reasons in each case why they should do so. With regard to Turkey, I shall have something to say later on. The grievance of France is of a particularly acute and obtrusive character, and it is aggravated by her belief, or pretension, that in giving voice to her own individual dissatisfaction she is speaking on behalf of the civilized world.

As it happens, the civilized world does not agree with her. It would not at all gratify the civilized world if Egypt slipped back into chaos. That world, as a whole, has no wish to hold England to the letter of her engagements while she remains true to their spirit. It has no desire to see the Egyptian Question reopened. It would much prefer that England, having the largest interest in the matter, should look after the maintenance and development of civilized government in the Nile Valley, always provided that she does not use her position there to the detriment of others.

We may, then, dismiss the absurd contention that France, in perpetually worrying us about Egypt, represents anybody but herself. But, of course, she is perfectly entitled, on her own account, to bring up against us the awkward declarations which we made *urbi et orbi*. Neither is it unnatural that France should feel sore at the fact that England now holds, among all European nations, the first position in Egypt. That position once was hers. It is true that it is not our fault if France, after dragging us into the Egyptian embroglio in 1882, shirked at the last moment, and left us to settle the whole business alone. It is not our fault if, by her foolish action at Constantinople in 1887, she prevented our withdrawal from Egypt, when we had already come to a complete understanding with Turkey as to the conditions of such withdrawal. As a matter of fact, France is far more responsible than we are ourselves, whether for our first going to Egypt or for our still being there. In strict logic she is the last of all the Powers that has any right to complain of our occupation. All this is incontestable. But it is no use hurling strict logic at the head of wounded susceptibilities. France is hurt. She is unreasonably hurt. No man is bound to give in to his neighbour because the latter is unreasonably hurt. But no man is any the worse for trying to understand the cause of his neighbour's ill-humour, even though it be ill-founded.

And it is in the comprehension of what irks the French in this matter that Englishmen often appear somewhat deficient. I have frequently seen it stated, on the British side of the controversy, that France made a piratical expedition to Egypt at the end of the last century, and that, solely on the strength of that aggressive and unsuccessful enterprise, she has asserted her right to a predominant influence in the country ever since. But the claim of France to a special interest in Egypt rests on something more solid and more creditable than the invasion of Napoleon. It was France who supported Egypt in her struggle for independence from Turkey when all the other Powers were against her, and when by their opposition they prevented that independence from becoming complete. It was to France that Mehemet Ali turned for aid in his attempt to civilize Egypt, as he understood the meaning of civilization. For something like half a century French lawyers, French engineers, French men of learning, were engaged in doing their best—often under most discouraging circumstances—to endow Egypt with the fruits of European culture. Except in the field of Egyptology, in which France has achieved such splendid triumphs, their efforts were not crowned with immediate success. But much good seed was sown, which has since come to ripeness. And in any case Frenchmen may claim to have been the pioneers of European influence. Whatever Egypt borrowed from Europe, whether in the material or the intellectual sphere, came to her first through French channels. Her upper classes, if educated at all, were educated by Frenchmen, and in French ideas. French even became an official language—side by side with Arabic. To this day the Englishmen in the Egyptian service write official letters to one another in halting French.

Last, but not least, the Suez Canal is French. It was carried out by a Frenchman, in spite of English opposition and the indifference of the rest of the world, and its administration has always remained exclusively in French hands. The officials of the Company in Egypt are nearly all Frenchmen. The banks of the Canal, and the town of Ismailia, though nominally Egyptian territory, are virtually a French colony. Of course, it may be said that, if the Canal itself is French, the trade which passes through it, and to which it owes its success, is, to the extent of no less than four-fifths, English. But this does not detract from the merit of its creators. It may be said also—and the observation is more pertinent to the present theme—that the Canal, while a blessing to mankind, has been of doubtful advantage to Egypt. But this does not alter the fact that we have in the Canal a gigantic French enterprise, a radiating sphere of French influence located on Egyptian soil, and that its existence adds a large item to the long list of claims which France may set up to a peculiar interest in Egypt.

This is the French side of the case. I have done my best not to understate it. But there is another side. The tremendous clamour which French writers keep up on this question sometimes leads us to forget that other nations also are entitled to special consideration in Egypt. The trade of Austria with that country is nearly equal to the trade of France. The number of Greeks and Italians resident in Egypt is greater than that of Frenchmen. Moreover, Austria and Italy have both in various ways contributed largely to the work of civilization. And if their influence in this respect has been less extensive than that of France, it has also been far less tainted with evil elements.

For when the services of France to Egypt are considered, it is needful, though it is disagreeable, to call to mind also her disservices. The part she has taken in the development of Egypt has been large, but it has been far from disinterested. The Suez Canal swallowed up millions of Egyptian money, and involved the sacrifice of thousands of Egyptian lives.* In the days prior to the establishment of the Mixed Tribunals—which France resisted with all her might—French adventurers exploited Egypt in the most merciless fashion, and they frequently enjoyed the support of French diplomacy in their nefarious game. No Great Power has clung with such tenacity as France to all the advantages, however indefensible and galling, bestowed on its subjects by the Capitulations. She has shown no consideration for the weakness of Egypt. She has never hesitated to use her immense superiority of power to push the interests of French traders, French contractors, and French financiers. In the years immediately preceding the Arabist Revolution, when England and France were acting in concert in Egyptian affairs, it was France who was for getting the last pound of flesh out of the Egyptian debtor. It was England who was in favour of showing some consideration for the people of Egypt, and not of treating the question purely as one of pounds, shillings, and pence.

It is sometimes assumed that the unfriendly attitude of France towards the Government of Egypt is due to the fact that she regards that Government as the mere tool of England. Even if this were true, the system of punishing Egypt to spite England might seem an ignoble one. But it is not altogether true. The disposition of France to bully Egypt does not date from 1882. Ask any of the older Egyptian statesmen, who had to do with the foreign relations of his country in pre-Occupation days, what is his experience and opinion of French policy—and watch his face! Cordial detestation of French diplomacy, bitter resentment of the manner in which France took every possible advantage of the dependent position of Egypt—these are, perhaps, the only sentiments which men like Nubar and Riaz have in common. The predominance of the French language

* The forced labour of the peasantry in digging the Canal, which was promised in the original concession, was found to involve such intolerable hardships that Ismail Pasha was obliged to put a stop to it, compensating the Company by a very heavy indemnity.

and of French culture ought to give France a position of immense influence in Egypt. But her political action has been so short-sighted in its selfishness that it has gone far to weaken the hold which she would otherwise have had on all educated Egyptians.

And if French policy towards Egypt was bad before the Occupation, since the Occupation it has been simply detestable. I do not wish to dwell on this nauseating theme. When an individual allows jealousy to become master of him, good feeling, and even intelligent self-interest, go to the wall. And it is the same with nations. It seems useless to demonstrate to the French that, in opposing every reform in Egypt simply because British influence is predominant there, they are cutting their own throats. France, after all, is very nearly as much interested in the good government of Egypt as we are. She has nothing to gain by the perpetuation of old abuses. Yet that has not prevented her from obstructing the abolition of the Corvée and the just taxation of foreigners. It has not prevented her from locking up money which the Egyptian Government sorely needs for public improvements. It has not prevented her from opposing reductions in the number and the salary of superfluous officials,* from withholding her consent to a reasonable Press Law, or from throwing obstacles in the way of the Government when seeking, with the aid of the Mixed Courts, to make Police regulations for purposes of such undoubted necessity as the control of the drink traffic or the sale of poisons. It has not even prevented her from making herself ridiculous by maintaining a separate Post Office in Egypt,

* The attitude of France on the question of the French officials is the most extraordinary thing in the world. If an English or other foreign official is no longer wanted, his services are dispensed with. But attempt to dispense with the services of a French official, and you have a diplomatic representation at once. Moreover, France practically insists that any office once filled by a Frenchman should always be so filled. And so anxious are we to avoid fresh causes of friction that the Egyptian Government, under English pressure, has repeatedly yielded to this monstrous pretension.

although all the other Powers have abandoned that antiquated privilege, which, in view of the admirable management of the native Post Office under Saba Pasha, is now purely vexatious.

But I have no wish to go through a catalogue of the offences, varying from grave injuries to mere petty annoyances, of which France has been guilty towards the Government of Egypt. I would rather, if possible, find an excuse for them, and there is one excuse which, I think, may reasonably be urged. The majority of Frenchmen, and even of responsible French politicians, are, I believe, entirely ignorant of what is really going on in Egypt, of the manner in which, and the objects for which, British influence is exercised. They needs must be so, if they take their notions from the newspapers which appear in Egypt in the French language, and which are among the most libellous prints published anywhere in the world. According to these newspapers, the power of England is used without regard for the feelings and the welfare of the people, and with the sole object of furthering her own commercial interests and paving the way to annexation.

Such a version of our acts and aims is not only wide of the truth: it is the exact opposite of the truth. And the men who write this balderdash are perfectly aware of its inaccuracy. They do not intend any great harm. They only want to turn out spicy articles, and they know that the Europeans on the spot, including the Frenchmen, will not take their tirades too seriously. But such tirades do great mischief nevertheless. For these articles are solemnly reproduced by French newspapers, and are read and believed in France itself by sensible people, who have not the least idea that the sallies in question have just about as much substance as had those of M. Rochefort in the *Intransigeant*, of which they are, in fact, inferior imitations. Thus, the good relations between two great countries may be materially impaired by the half-humorous extravagances of a handful of witty, needy, and dare-devil penny-a-liners.

The unscrupulous polemics of the French newspapers in Egypt would be of less importance, if they were controlled by a solid body of local French opinion. But the majority of the French colony in Egypt are, to put it mildly, not of a good type. France is honourably, most honourably, represented in that country by the higher French officials in the Government Service. It would be difficult to speak too strongly of the loyalty with which—in a position that is evidently one of great delicacy—these officials continue to render able and ungrudging service to their adopted country. As a general rule, they work most harmoniously with their British colleagues. Personally, I have every reason to remember with pleasure and gratitude the generous help which I have received from Frenchmen who were, like myself, in the service of the Khedive, and who were as keenly desirous as any of their English fellow-workers to sink political jealousies in the common object of promoting the welfare of Egypt.

But the bulk of the French and quasi-French residents are, unfortunately, not animated by similar sentiments. They give no heed to the counsels of moderation which proceed from their fellow-countrymen of the official class. They are carried away by personal interest and narrow racial antipathy, and, unfortunately, they often drag after them the Government of France. It has happened before now that the French Minister in Egypt—recognising the true state of affairs, the real nature of England's policy, and the little interest that France had in opposing it—has sought to counteract the evil influence of local French opinion, and to preserve his Government from being misled by it. In such cases the Minister has found to his cost that the hot-headed leaders of local opinion were too strong for him; that they had means of making their influence felt at home behind his back; and that he was being discredited with his Government as a coward and a weakling for taking a reasonable view of Egyptian affairs.

The fractiousness of the French colony and the ill-natured action of the French Foreign Office, which is largely due to that fractiousness, have sorely hampered the work of reform in Egypt. But they have not been able to arrest it. As the position of the Egyptian Government grows stronger, and especially as the financial situation becomes more assured, the retarding and weakening effect of French hostility is steadily on the decrease. France can do a great deal to make our position in Egypt uncomfortable, but she cannot, after all, defeat the main objects of our policy by any action on the spot. It is from another point of view that her persistent ill-humour presents so serious an aspect. The danger which threatens the welfare of Egypt must be sought, not in Egypt itself, but in England. As long as Great Britain chooses to stick to the task upon which she is engaged, France cannot upset the Egyptian coach. But the question is, whether Great Britain will think it worth while to stick to that task at the cost, or supposed cost, of the continual irritation of France. If there is one thing which Englishmen desire more than another in respect of foreign policy, it is to live on good terms with their nearest neighbours. And undoubtedly the position we at present occupy in Egypt makes it difficult—I do not say it makes it impossible—to live on good terms with the French.

It is sometimes rather hastily assumed that, if this stumbling-block were removed, there would be nothing to mar the harmony between the two countries. Considering the great number of points at which the interests of France and Great Britain clash, this view appears, perhaps, rather too optimistic. At the same time, it cannot be doubted that the Egyptian Question ranks high amongst the causes of difference. And it is not unnatural that many people should be inclined to doubt whether it is worth while to aggravate any strain which may exist in the relations of Great Britain and France, even for so important and honourable an object as that of securing the welfare of Egypt.

It is not for me to discuss whether we should be justified in abandoning our work in Egypt, in its present unfinished state, because France is angry at our doing that work at all. That, again, is a question involving wider political considerations than any into which this book—confined as it is to the position of affairs in Egypt itself—professes to enter. But, from the purely Egyptian point of view, there are some remarks which remain to be offered on the subject. The suggestion has been made that the retirement of England from Egypt might be facilitated if France would engage never under any circumstance to occupy the position from which England had retired. It is stated that France would be ready to enter into such an engagement. I will not consider how this arrangement might affect England and France; but as far as Egypt is concerned, it would certainly make matters not better, but worse. For the problem, from the point of view of Egyptian welfare, is simply this: How can the work of reform be maintained and consolidated? How can the country be kept steadily advancing along the road of European civilization, on which it is now fairly launched, and prevented from slipping back into chaos? If all that has been said in the preceding pages is not wasted ink, if every competent and disinterested European observer is not mistaken, there is no guarantee that Egypt may not thus slip back, except the maintenance, for a considerable time longer, of the controlling influence of some civilized Power. A compact, by which the two Powers best qualified to exercise such influence should agree with one another not to exercise it, would simply be the greatest conceivable encouragement to all the reactionary forces in Egypt to try and undo the good that has been accomplished.

Even as it is, no year passes without some intrigue, more or less formidable, directed against European influence. Now it is one British official, and now it is another, who is singled out for depreciation, and secretly calumniated to the Khedive. But it is not at individuals that such blows are really aimed. They are aimed at the odious restraints of civilization, of which the European officials are the upholders. As long as Great Britain occupies her present position in Egypt, such machinations are bound to end in failure. If France occupied that position, she would be equally influential, and perhaps equally disinterested. But a self-denying ordinance never to interfere, mutually accepted by France and England, while it would be fine fun for the reactionaries, might prove the death-knell of Progress.

Assuming that France were willing to take the pledge just mentioned, does it follow that she would be able to keep it? Circumstances might easily arise in which she could not—nay, in which she ought not to—abide by such an engagement. Nobody, of course, can say how soon—if the influence of England were to be withdrawn from Egypt—things would begin to go wrong. It is hardly likely that they would go wrong all at once. But can any man, knowing the social and political condition of the country, maintain with confidence that, if Egypt were left to herself to-morrow, favouritism and corruption would not once more raise their heads, that justice would not once more be venal, that the administration would not gradually fall back into disorder, and that, as a consequence of such disorder, financial equilibrium would not again be jeopardized? And then should we not have the old story: the embarrassments of the Treasury causing the impoverishment of the people—such impoverishment leading to discontent and agitation—that agitation directed not only against the Government, but, under the inspiration of mischief-making fanatics, against all the progressive elements of society—another Arabi—another Revolution? And if, in prospect of a fresh cataclysm threatening every European interest, after all diplomatic means had been exhausted, France were to declare that she could stand it no longer, if she were to take the line which we took in 1882, what moral right should we have to say her nay? Could we fight to restrain her from interfering?

It is impossible to say whether we should or we should not; but it is certain that nothing could produce a more dangerous tension in the relations of France and Great Britain than a situation such as that just described, and for that situation we should then have nobody but ourselves to blame. Nor could we expect the smallest sympathy from any side if we sought to hamper France in taking whatever steps she might, under such circumstances, think necessary to prevent a repetition of the disasters of 1882. As long as we accept the responsibility for decent government and for the protection of civilized society in Egypt, we can fairly, and with general approval, resist any attempts on the part of France to interfere with us in our work. But if we grow weary of that duty, and abandon it, we shall not be justified in trying to prevent France, in case of necessity, from assuming a position deliberately relinquished by ourselves.

CHAPTER XIV.

THE FUTURE OUTLOOK.

THE anxiety felt by many Englishmen to conciliate France by the abandonment of Egypt has led to a variety of suggestions for averting the possible evil consequences of such abandonment. Perhaps the commonest of these is the proposal that Egypt should be neutralized. There is always something seductive about the term 'neutralization.' 'Hands off all round,' 'a fair field and no favour,' and other specious phrases of that kind, are extremely soothing to the British mind when bothered by awkward questions of foreign policy. But, unfortunately, neutralization misses, in the case of Egypt, the whole point of the difficulty which it is intended to meet. It is open to all the objections just urged to mutual pledges of non-intervention on the part of France and Great Britain. The problem is, to ensure the internal good government of Egypt, both for the sake of its own people and for the sake of the general tranquillity—for a disturbed Egypt is a danger to the peace of the world. But how could neutralization accomplish these objects?

It was a capital plan to neutralize the Suez Canal. The Company can take excellent care of the internal arrangements of the Canal, and the only danger to it lay in interference from outside. Nothing could be better than to neutralize countries which, while they offer a temptation to the greed of their neighbours, are, if left alone, perfectly able to take care of themselves. 'Hands off all round' in such cases by all means. Hands off

Belgium all round. Hands off Switzerland all round. But it is impossible to conceive anything more dissimilar to the internal condition of Belgium or Switzerland than that of Egypt.

It is worth while to consider how Egypt would look to-day if this fine-sounding principle had been adopted some years ago. Would neutralization have suppressed the kurbash or reduced the Corvée? Would it have repaired the Barrage? Would it have created an Egyptian Army, or improved the native administration of justice? And would it, if introduced now, afford the slightest guarantee that all the ground gained might not again be lost? It is difficult to believe that Europe would seriously adopt so impotent a policy. For it simply means this—that from unwillingness to allow any one of their number to do the work, in which all are interested, the Powers should determine that that work must be left undone.

Conscious, perhaps, of the futility of their panacea in its naked form, some of the advocates of neutralization have saddled that proposal with a rider, which makes it appreciably worse. If it is true, they argue, that the principle of 'hands off all round' does not provide for internal order, then why not entrust the maintenance of such order to its natural guardian—the Suzerain Power? In other words, Egypt, while guaranteed against interference on the part of Europe, is to be left to the protection—shall I say at the mercy of?—the Turk!

I admit that, from a purely selfish point of view, this idea may possess certain attractions for Great Britain. Next to the disturbance of our relations with France, the irritation of Turkey is the most serious disadvantage resulting to Great Britain from her position in Egypt. Some people might even regard the irritation of Turkey as the graver evil of the two. It is true that our presence in Egypt does Turkey no practical harm. Her virtual authority in that country had dwindled to nothingness long before 1882, while her nominal suzerainty has been most carefully respected by Great Britain. Moreover, the heavy tribute which Egypt pays to the Porte, and which is the only material advantage that Turkey now derives from her suzerainty, has been rendered more secure by the re-establishment of Egyptian solvency. But the Sultan has been taught to think that the influence of Great Britain, and especially the presence of British troops in the Nile Valley, is an injury to his prestige throughout the Mussulman world. The injury is very slight, perhaps altogether non-existent. But the idea is rooted in the Sultan's mind, and it is sure to be sedulously cultivated. France, to use a common expression, is always pulling the tail of Turkey with regard to Egypt, and trying to work upon her pride to cause us trouble in that region.

It is probable that the difficulty with Turkey will be easier to get over than the difficulty with France. Turkish politicians must be well aware that, though they might possibly gain something by an upset of the existing order of things, they would also run the risk of losing, not something merely, but everything. As long as England continues to control the destinies of Egypt, the nominal authority of Turkey over that country, and the very substantial tribute she receives from it, are perfectly secure. But if England were to go, and if, as a consequence of her going, there were to be a fresh Egyptian crisis, it is more than any man can say that the Egypt which might ultimately emerge from such a crisis would retain any connection whatever with the Porte. It might be found to have gone the way of Algiers and of Tunis. Moreover, the natural development of England's policy may afford more than one opportunity of gratifying Turkey in a manner harmless to Egyptian interests. Whenever, for instance, the time arrives at which our troops can be withdrawn, their withdrawal would probably take the form of a concession to the Porte—a concession which would go far to soothe its offended dignity.

Of course, I do not pretend that, from the point of view of gratifying the Porte, such a step would have anything like the same effect as the proposal, not only to withdraw ourselves, but to invite Turkey to replace us. But, unfortunately, this idea of neutralization with Turkey as policeman is, in view of our duty to Egypt, quite inadmissible. What form is Turkey's responsibility for order in a neutralized Egypt to take? It must either be that of a permanent garrison, or of a right to send troops in case order were disturbed. There are capital objections to both alternatives. A disturbance of order in Egypt is not likely to arise except as the final outcome of renewed misgovernment, and misgovernment prolonged over a considerable time. But why wait to deal with the evil in its final stage, when it is so easy—by maintaining the present system—to check its beginnings? It would be a poor satisfaction for Europe, looking on at the gradual reversal of the work of reform and progress in Egypt, to know that, when the ball had finally rolled to the bottom of the hill, Turkey would be entitled—if by any miracle she were ready—to suppress an actual outbreak. And when the outbreak had been suppressed, where would Egypt be? She would be where she was in 1882, with all the work of reconstruction to do over again. And who could be trusted to do it? Turkey?

But then there is the other alternative—a permanent Turkish garrison. I will not allude to a hundred minor difficulties, easy to imagine, which the presence of such a garrison would cause. They are all thrown into the shade by one great dilemma. Would the Turkish troops be there as policemen merely, or would their commander—or whoever the Turkish representative might be—have a voice also in the internal administration of the country? In the former case, their presence would leave unaffected the real problem, which is, how to keep the Government moving along the present reformed lines. In the latter case, we have a *reductio ad absurdum*. The idea of entrusting Turkey with the maintenance of reforms, the chief aim of which has been to differentiate Egyptian from Turkish administration, is like substituting the wolf for the sheep-dog as the guardian of the flock.

But our choice of nostrums is not yet exhausted. If

'neutralization' will not do, why not 'inter-nationalization'? The word has an equally soothing sound, and it has the charm of being three syllables longer. But what does it mean? It means at one moment the same as neutralization, at another moment the exact opposite—not 'hands off all round,' but 'hands on all round.' According to this principle, the safety and good government of Egypt would, I presume, be entrusted to an International Commission, like the Caisse de la Dette. And that Commission would be supported by a Mixed Military Force, recruited from the scum of all nations and commanded by a polyglot staff of officers.

In the boundless mercy of Providence, let us hope that Egypt may at least be saved from this settlement of the difficulty. Here we have the worst of the whole list of proposed solutions. On that point all Egyptians would be unanimous. Much as some of them may dislike any foreign control, there is not one who would not agree that—whether such control be desirable or simply inevitable—it is far better that it should be exercised by one Power than by half a dozen or a dozen. Some might prefer France, and some England, and some, perhaps, another nation, but they would all prefer a single master.*

And they are perfectly right. The political constitution of Egypt suffers from an excess of Internationalism already. Is not the veto of the Powers on the legislative authority of the Egyptian Government Internationalism? Are not the mischievous restrictions on her financial freedom Internationalism? And was not Egypt in an ideal state of Internationalism at the time when the

* I have received a letter since I left Cairo from an Egyptian Pasha, one of the most cultivated and popular of his class, who, although a personal friend of mine, is certainly not a particular friend of England. He has been educated in France. His ideas and sympathies are entirely French. Yet, speaking about the work of Great Britain, he says, 'In one respect Egypt owes you English all her gratitude. You have saved my country from the curse of internationalism.'

representatives of all the Powers were vainly vying with one another to restrain Ismail Pasha in his wild career along the road to ruin? A notable object-lesson that!

It was a great step in advance when the political chaos of those days gave way to the Dual Control. But if the Dual Control was comparatively good, the Single Control has been better. Anomalous as the present situation is, it has been justified by the results. The position of England may, indeed, be delicate. The necessity for any foreign interference in Egypt may be regrettable. So long, however, as that necessity exists, the disadvantages of interference are reduced to a minimum when it is exercised by a single great Power. And, on the other hand, these disadvantages are at a maximum under the system of Internationalism—everybody meddling, nobody responsible.

But if it be admitted that, to guide Egypt in the direction of civilized independence, and to protect the various foreign interests which are bound up with her peace and prosperity, it is desirable that she should remain for a time under the guardianship of some one great Power, then there are obvious reasons why England should remain her guardian. The position that we occupy in Egypt may be said to be the result of accident. But it has more than accidental justification. Alike by the nature of our interests, by the nature of our power, and by certain special qualities in our national character, we seem marked out for the discharge of this particular duty. Our interests in Egypt are absolutely identical with those of the Egyptian people. We are their principal customers, and they also are very important customers of Great Britain. With the deficiency of outlets which threatens our vast foreign trade, the great and growing market of Egypt is evidently not a thing which we can afford to despise. And if Egyptian prosperity is a British interest, so is Egyptian independence. We have no desire to possess ourselves of Egypt, but we have every reason to prevent any rival Power from so possessing itself. And there is no sure, no creditable manner of providing permanently against such a contingency, except to build up a system of government so stable as to leave no excuse for future foreign intervention.

And while we have the strongest interest in such a result, we have also the greatest power to accomplish it. There is no nation in the world which is in a position to deal with any trouble that might arise in Egypt as easily as England. From a military point of view England is comparatively weak, but not the greatest military Power could have crumpled up Arabi as promptly as we did. It is not necessary to have a large army in order to keep the peace in the Nile Valley. A small army is sufficient, provided it can be on the spot quickly. Egypt is in the hands of the nation which commands the sea.

So much for the material advantages which England has in dealing with this problem. But she has also a moral advantage of a singular kind. I refer to the great number of her sons who have special aptitude and special experience in the work of governing or directing more backward nations. India has furnished many of the men who have done the best work in Egypt; and they have done it despite the fact that the conditions of their service in the two countries have been very different. In India they were masters, with a free hand and a more or less ample purse; in Egypt, while really responsible for the conduct of government, they are under the orders of native chiefs whose prejudices they must humour, and whose dignity they must be careful not to offend. They are hampered by a thousand restrictions, and by a painful lack of the sinews of war. They have been set to make bricks without straw. Yet here, again, they have been helped by one of the most marked characteristics of their race—the practical instinct which enables men of British birth—when it is a question of business—to fit into the most incongruous situations, and to make the best of limited opportunities, without troubling their heads about theoretical imperfections of system.

In the art of government, the Englishman seems to be as handy and adaptable as he is clumsy and angular in society. There are other nations with equal and perhaps greater gifts for the creation of an ideally perfect administration, if they have *tabula rasa* whereon to construct it. But I doubt whether any of them could have made anything at all of a system so imperfect, so incongruous, and so irritating, as that which we found in Egypt, and which we have not been permitted radically to alter. The logical Frenchman would have been maddened by its absurdities. The authoritative temper of the German would have revolted at its restrictions. They would have insisted on governing in their own way, or they would have despaired of governing at all. It needed that incarnation of compromise, the average Briton, to accept the system with all its faults, and to set to work quietly, in his sensible, plodding way, to do the best he could under untoward circumstances.

The qualities of the race have triumphed. But our success might have been less complete, perhaps that success might never have been attained at all, had it not been for one remarkable piece of good fortune. The stars were indeed gracious when, at the beginning of our greatest troubles, it occurred to the British Government to entrust the conduct of its policy to the hands of Sir Evelyn Baring. It would be difficult to over-estimate what the work of England in Egypt owes to the sagacity, fortitude, and patience of the British Minister. His mental and moral equipment—very remarkable in any case—was peculiarly suited to the very peculiar circumstances in which he found himself placed. Perhaps the most striking feature about him has been a singular combination of strength and forbearance. And he needed both these qualities in an exceptional degree. On one side of him were the English officials, zealous about their work, fretting at the obstruction which met them at every turn, and constantly appealing to him for assistance to overcome it. On the other side were the native authorities, new to our methods, hating to be driven, and keen to resent the appearance of English diplomatic pressure. The former were often induced to grumble at him for interfering too little. The latter were no less prone to complain of his interfering too much.

What a task was his, to steer an even keel between meddlesomeness and inactivity! Yet how seldom has he failed to hit the right mean. Slowly, but surely, he has carried all his main points. And he has carried them without needlessly over-riding native authority, or pushing his own personality into the foreground. He has realized that the essence of our policy is to help the Egyptians to work out, as far as possible, their own salvation. And not only has he realized this himself, but he has taught others to realize it. By a wise reserve, he has led his countrymen in Egypt to rely upon patience, upon persuasion, upon personal influence, rather than upon rougher methods, to guide their native colleagues in the path of improved administration. Yet on the rare occasions when his intervention was absolutely necessary he has intervened with an emphasis which has broken down all resistance. Criticise him as you will—and he has made mistakes like other statesmen—the record of his nine years of arduous labour is one of which all Englishmen may well feel proud. The contrast between Egypt to-day and Egypt as he found it, the enhanced reputation of England in matters Egyptian, are the measure of the signal services he has rendered alike to his own country and to the country where he has laid the foundations of a lasting fame.

But achievements of this magnitude involve a penalty Master the Difficult, and you will surely be asked to perform the Impossible. There is no pleasing certain people about Egypt. When we first plunged into that apparently hopeless thicket, they cried out about our failure. Now that we are emerging from the wood, they cry out on the very score of our success. 'If you really have done as well as you say, why haven't you finished? Surely the Egyptians must be capable by this time of looking after themselves.' This argument is head-splitting in its stupidity. One blushes to have to explain that the ingrained evils of some fifteen centuries cannot be eradicated in a decade. Material progress surely has been fast enough to satisfy the most impatient. But the wit of man has not as yet discovered the means to accelerate a moral revolution. And it is the moral revolution which is the essence of the business. To questions as to the date when our work will be finished and our controlling hand withdrawn, it is simply impossible to give a definite answer. No man can say when, no man can say whether, the attempt to educate the Egyptians in the habits of civilized government is destined to be crowned with success. What I do say is, that the past of the experiment is full of encouragement for its future; and that if the problem is capable of solution at all, it is along the lines of our present policy—the policy of Baring—that the solution is to be reached. And this, it appears to me, is more material than the amount of time required to reach it. It is interesting to know when you will arrive at the end of your journey: but it is more important to know that you are on the right road.

The truth is, that the idea of a definite date for the conclusion of our work in Egypt is wholly misleading. The withdrawal of Great Britain, if it is not to end in disaster, can only be a gradual process. An intangible influence, made up of many elements, like that of England in Egypt, cannot be withdrawn, any more than it can be created, at a certain hour or by a single act. Throughout this book I have been careful to speak of British Influence, not of the British Occupation. The two things are intimately connected, but they are not synonymous. No doubt our influence, as the predominant factor in Egyptian politics, would never have existed without the military conquest. No doubt the presence of the troops is even now an important element in its maintenance. It would be difficult to deprecate too strongly their immediate retirement, especially with so young a sovereign so lately raised to the throne. Nor can that retirement at any time be contemplated without uneasiness. But it does not follow that if, for whatever reasons, it should be thought desirable to withdraw the troops at some future date, our influence would necessarily suffer. No doubt it would, if they were withdrawn in deference to menaces—if anyone could say that we had been pushed out. But if they were withdrawn at our own time, and on our own conditions, it is not certain that the moral impression which they create, and in which their principal utility consists, might not be maintained by other means. The Wolff Convention sought to find a substitute for the effect produced by the Army of Occupation in a permanent right of re-entry on the part of Great Britain, in case order in Egypt were threatened by external or internal danger.* Such a right of re-entry, recognised not only by Turkey, but by the other Powers, and depending for its exercise upon our own judgment with regard to its necessity, might be very effective, though it would certainly never be quite so effective as the Army of Occupation, in giving weight to our advice.

But if the British troops were to be withdrawn, it would be more than ever necessary that the position of the British officers in the Egyptian Army should be maintained. And not only the position of the British officers, but that of a limited number of high British officials in the Civil Service. No doubt, in time, even these safeguards might gradually be dispensed with ; but that is looking forward to a more distant period than it is of any use trying to speculate about just at present. The circumstances must decide. As native governing capacity develops, as natives come forward who are fit for responsible posts now held by Englishmen, these posts should be resigned to them. Perhaps some British element in the Government would always be necessary. Perhaps the British Minister would always need to exercise some control on the most important questions of policy ; but that control might in the end be very light, and almost imperceptible. And to it also the automatic principle would apply. As the advice of the British Minister ceased to be necessary, he would cease to give it.

* See pp. 122, 123.

Such would be the natural, the wholesome, development of British policy in Egypt. Foreign jealousy may interfere with the programme. Native impatience may upset it. In that case, the game of Egyptian independence is up. The material progress of recent years might still be maintained, but as a political experiment our work would have been a failure. For my own part, I do not despair of a happier termination. And, in any case, I do not see how we can do otherwise than go on as we are going, and hope for the best. The difficulties already overcome should surely encourage us to face with a good heart the difficulties that we may yet have to encounter. They cannot possibly be more serious than those of the past.

I am speaking from the Egyptian point of view. Of course, Egypt is only one, and by no means the chief, of the responsibilities of Great Britain. There may be reasons of high policy in favour of our retiring from that country. If so, by all means let them be fully weighed. But the case for abandonment is certainly not advanced by simply quoting, for the fiftieth time, the declarations of our intention to withdraw, and refusing to recognise the facts which have prevented us from carrying out that intention. If it can be proved—and I maintain it is proved—that we have been true to the spirit of our declarations, and that the literal fulfilment of them would be fraught with ruin to the Egyptian people, and with mischief to Great Britain and to Europe, then we are undoubtedly justified in persevering in the course on which we are engaged.

No doubt the case would be different if the European Powers were agreed to declare that Egypt no longer needed the guiding hand of Great Britain, and were prepared to prove their confidence in Egypt's capacity for self-government by abolishing the Capitulations and the other international fetters upon Egyptian freedom. For clearly it is impossible to say at one moment that Egypt is competent to take rank among autonomous States, and to say at the next moment that she is not competent to punish a foreign pickpocket. But it will be time to consider the consequences of such an attitude on the part of the Powers when the majority of them show a disposition to adopt it.

And, lastly, let us hope that there may be no more attempts to confuse the issue by antiquated tirades about the bond-holders. Financial swindling may have helped to produce the state of things which made our intervention necessary. And it has certainly been one result—an honourable result, I venture to think—of our intervention that, while the burdens of the people have been greatly lightened, the rights of the Egyptian bond-holders are now absolutely secure. But the interest of the bond-holders—though, like every other legitimate interest, it has been benefited by England's action—has never been the inspiring motive of our policy, least of all of our policy during recent years. Nothing could be more false than any suggestion to that effect. The inspiring, the predominant, motive of that policy is the welfare of the Egyptian people. We have done much to promote their welfare, but there is something yet to do. The desire to complete that work is surely a worthy one. It is an effort in which, if we would be true to ourselves, we are bound to persist as long as we have the power.

Of course, it may be contended that, though financially the enterprise costs us nothing, Great Britain has not the strength to carry through the regeneration of Egypt consistently with the fulfilment of other and prior duties. To such arguments, if they can be established, all reasonable people would be prepared to listen, including, I hope, the present writer, who has now said his last word on this thorny subject, and whose constant aim has been to state the Egyptian Question temperately—recognising to the full all the difficulties of our position, honestly admitting all its weaknesses. But in the absence of such arguments—and they are not yet forthcoming—the case for Perseverance holds the field.

APPENDIX I.

(*Originally printed as a Preface to the Fifth Edition.*)

EGYPT IN 1894.

'ENGLAND IN EGYPT' was first published in December, 1892, and has run through four editions in its original form. In the present (fifth) edition nothing has been altered, except the type and the size of the pages. The whole work has been reprinted without omission or modification of any kind. But the important political events which have occurred in Egypt during the last fifteen months seem to call for some supplementary observations.

I venture to hope that these events have been rendered more intelligible to some portion of the British public by the outline of the Egyptian problem contained in the present work. The main object of my book was to give the English reader, who might not happen to be acquainted with Egypt at first hand, a clue to the complexities of the unique political situation existing in that country, to enable him to understand, not only the work which Great Britain is doing on the banks of the Nile, but also the strange conditions under which it has to be accomplished. And this clue to the Egyptian labyrinth—this Guide-Book to Political Egypt—may still be of service in the years to come. Great and unexpected as have been the events which have taken place since this book first appeared, they have not altered the fundamental conditions of the problem, as expounded in the following pages. Indeed, I am presumptuous enough to think that what has happened is calculated to illustrate and confirm the general correctness of the picture which I drew two years ago, and which I now again submit to the world without any fear that its accuracy will be impugned by the events of the future any more than it has been by those of the immediate past.

But while there is nothing to retract, there are, no doubt, some things to add, in order to bring the book up to date. As far as the material condition of Egypt is concerned, its most recent history is one of continued and even accelerated progress. Two more annual balance-sheets have to be added to those enumerated in Chapter VIII., and they show the following results:

	Revenue.	Expenditure.	Surplus.
1892 ...	£E10,363,000	£E9,595,000	£E768,000
1893 ...	£E10,321,000	£E9,601,000	£E720,000

The various Reserve Funds have now reached a total of £E3,554,000. And these surpluses, and this accumulation of resources against a rainy day, have been brought about in spite of fresh and important reductions of the Land Tax,* of a further diminution of railway rates, and of other minor concessions to the taxpayer. At the same time the amount of the State Debt has been reduced by more than a million, and a sum exceeding £30,000 has been knocked off the annual interest by the conversion of the Domains Loan from a 5 per cent. to a 4¼ per cent. security. The Domains Loan is of comparatively small amount, but another conversion of far greater moment—that of the Unified Debt, amounting to £56,000,000—is now in contemplation, and there is little doubt that, if the Bourses of Europe can be induced to allow it, the interest of this huge stock might easily be reduced from 4 per cent. to 3½ per cent. But whether this change is effected or

* During the last five years the Land Tax has been reduced by £E427,000 a year, or more than eight per cent.

not, the reduction in the interest of the Debt is already considerable, while the reduction of the burden of the Debt, relatively to the resources of the country, is enormous. In 1880 no less than 66 per cent. of the revenue of Egypt was absorbed by the charge for Debt and Tribute. In 1893 Debt and Tribute took less than 45 per cent. of the revenue. That fact alone ought to dispose for ever of the clap-trap we still occasionally hear about our administration being solely in the interest of the bond-holders. Under British administration the amount of Egypt's income which is available for Egypt's own purposes has risen from one-third to more than one-half. And this process is still going on. Year by year an increasing proportion of the revenue is spent for the benefit of the country. Yet the bond-holders have not suffered. On the contrary, the value of their investments has been doubled. It is one of the most remarkable financial phenomena of recent times that the 4 per cent. Unified Debt—the largest and, in point of security, the lowest of the Egyptian loans—should to-day be quoted at 103½! When we first occupied the country, it was but little over 50. There was a time, not so long before that event, when it was quoted at 27!

With regard to Finance, then, the revival described in Chapter VIII. has been well maintained; the anticipations there expressed have been more than realized. And the best of it is that this steady upward movement is due to no temporary or accidental causes. Financial expedients have nothing to do with it. What has brought Egypt from ruin to solvency, from solvency to financial ease, is the cumulative effect of a number of years of sober, orderly, and equitable administration. Accounts properly kept, taxes fairly collected, waste of all sorts sternly repressed, relief given where it was most sorely needed, the public works (on which the life of the country depends) properly cared for—these are the simple secrets of Egypt's present prosperity.

Chief of all these factors in the development of public welfare is the zealous and ingenious attention devoted to public works, or, in other words, to irrigation. No one who may do me the honour to read Chapter IX. will desire that I should explain further why this matter is one of supreme moment. Suffice it to say that since that chapter was written additional progress has been made, both in protecting the land from the alternate dangers of drought and flood and in extending the system of drainage. The work of Sir Colin Scott Moncrieff and Colonel Ross has been steadily carried on by Mr. Garstin and his lieutenants. Above all, the scheme for the creation of a gigantic Reservoir, intended to retain the surplus water of the winter months for use in the months of drought, has made rapid strides towards realization. The report of the Public Works Department on the various possible sites for the Reservoir, their comparative advantages and disadvantages, the probable cost of each of them, and the increase of cultivable land, of produce, and of revenue to be hoped for from each, has recently been published. It is a splendid piece of work. Only the stupendous industry of Mr. Willcocks, who has been exclusively engaged upon this subject for several years, could have rendered possible the completion within a comparatively short period of so exhaustive a summary of all the aspects of this difficult problem. Mr. Willcocks's report is accompanied by a very full and judicious memorandum from the pen of Mr. Garstin, and by a number of valuable appendices. Moreover, the whole book is illustrated by a series of elaborate plans of the different proposed sites, and of the hydrographical features of the Nile Valley from Wadi Halfa to the sea.

With these materials before them, the International Commission appointed by the Egyptian Government to consider the vexed question where the Reservoir should be placed must have found their task greatly lightened. The report of the Commissioners, Sir Benjamin Baker, M. Boulé, and M. Torricelli, has now been presented, and its contents will probably be made known to the public before these pages are in print. It would therefore be idle to attempt to anticipate its conclusions.

But even if this report puts an end to discussion about the site of the Reservoir, there still remains the question how money can be raised for its construction. Were Egypt financially free, the answer would present no difficulty. But in view of the complicated international fetters which restrict the action of the Egyptian Government in the application of its surplus revenue, he would be a bold man who should predict that obstacles will not be raised which may retard the execution of the scheme for some considerable time. Enough has been said in Chapter IV. about the difficulty of carrying out any reform in Egypt which requires the consent of the Powers. The drainage of Cairo, agreed to in principle more than two years ago, is still delayed, owing to their slowness to sanction the necessary Decrees. For the same reason the chief provincial towns, except Alexandria, are still without municipal government. It can hardly be hoped that the far greater question of the Reservoir, which, with its subsidiary works, may require some four or five millions, will be settled without infinite haggling. In the long run, no doubt, the matter is certain to be arranged. But meanwhile, unless England is prepared to cut the Gordian knot, precious years will be wasted.

The spectacle of Egypt, with her Treasury full of money, yet not allowed to use that money for an object which, on a moderate calculation, should add 20 per cent. to the wealth of the country, is as distressing as it is ludicrous. Every year that passes illustrates more forcibly the injustice of maintaining, in these days of insured solvency, the restrictions imposed upon the financial freedom of the Egyptian Government at a time of bankruptcy—restrictions justifiable then, but wholly unjustifiable now. No one would object to the continuance of the arrangement by which certain revenues are paid in the first instance to the Caisse de la Dette. But as long as these revenues suffice to cover the interest on the Debt and to provide any Sinking Fund which the Powers may deem adequate, the balance ought simply to be handed over to the Egyptian Government to deal with as it pleases, and the antiquated distinction of

'Authorized' and 'Unauthorized' Expenditure* should be swept away. No reform is more necessary than this, if the country is to derive the greatest possible benefit from the improved condition of its finances which has been attained by such severe privations.

Besides Finance and Public Works, the only branches of the administration which call for special mention here are the departments of Justice, Education and Public Health. And in all of these some further advance may be noted since 1892, though that advance is more marked in the first-mentioned department than in the others. Educational progress has no doubt been retarded by the revival of fanatical prejudice consequent upon the recent political troubles; and both Education and Sanitation suffer sorely from a lack of funds, for which the antiquated financial system already referred to is largely responsible. But in respect of the administration of Justice the reforms introduced by Mr. (now Sir John) Scott have already borne good fruit. The increase of Single Judge Circuit Courts for purposes of summary jurisdiction, by which twenty-five thousand small actions were disposed of last year, has justified the expectations of its author. The number of appeals from the Courts of Summary Justice is small, and the result of these appeals seems to indicate that the single judges are, as a rule, fully able to cope with the class of cases submitted to them. Thus the peasantry are benefited by having their small disputes cheaply and quickly settled, while the higher Courts are relieved from a mass of unimportant work, and enabled to devote their undivided energies to cases of greater moment. Meanwhile, the composition of these higher Courts is being improved, and the School of Law in Cairo, on which the country must mainly rely for a supply of competent native judges in the future, is steadily growing in efficiency and popularity. There is nothing more essential to the preservation of the whole fabric of administrative reforms than the existence of a body of educated and independent

* See pp. 188-193.

native judges. It is upon the attainment of this object that Sir John Scott, who takes for his motto *tant valent les juges, tant valent les lois,* has wisely concentrated his energies.

Thus the good work of our countrymen in Egypt, directed, in the words of Lord Granville's despatch of January, 1883,* to the establishment of 'an order of things possessing the elements of stability and progress,' has gone on uninterrupted since this book was written—uninterrupted, but not unretarded. On the contrary, that work has never before met with more persistent obstruction from those who have most to gain by its success. At no previous period have the relations between the British and the native elements in the Egyptian Administration been more strained than during the whole of the year 1893 and the first month or two of 1894. In this respect we have temporarily gone back to the 'years of gloom'; and it is only the great advance of Egypt in material prosperity, and the improved position of Great Britain in international politics, which have enabled the Foreign Office and Lord Cromer to grapple successfully with the difficulties of the situation. Had Egypt in 1893 been like Egypt in 1883, a country practically insolvent, with its administration in hopeless disorder, and had England's authority in Egypt still been an object of jealousy and suspicion to almost all the Powers, instead of having conciliated the opinion of impartial mankind by its success, the recent crisis would certainly have ended in local disorder, and might have ended in European war. It is no disparagement to the dexterity and spirit with which England's Egyptian policy has been conducted during the past eighteen months to say that, but for the work of the preceding ten years, that policy, however able, could not possibly have met with the measure of success which it has actually achieved.

For the latest difficuly which has confronted us, in dealing with this intricate problem, is certainly the

* See p. 27.

most formidable that we have yet had to encounter. I refer to the undisguised hostility of the young Khedive. At the time when 'England and Egypt' was written, Abbas Pasha had not yet shown his hand, although during the latter months of 1892 there were many indications of coming trouble. But within a month of the publication of this book—in January, 1893—the Khedive startled the world by suddenly dismissing Mustafa Fehmi, who had committed no offence but that of working harmoniously with the Anglo-Egyptian officials, and by appointing Fahkri Pasha Prime Minister in his place. As all the world knows, the instant protest of the British Government obliged the Khedive to cancel the appointment of Fahkri, and a compromise was effected by the succession of Riaz Pasha to the premiership, with the consent of Great Britain. But the mischief was done. Mustafa Fehmi was accompanied in his retirement by two of his colleagues, the Ministers of Finance and Justice, who, like himself, had always worked peaceably with the British, and their places were taken by Butros Pasha and Mazlum Pasha, who, though hitherto sufficiently neutral in their attitude, were at least free from any suspicion of avowed sympathy with British policy.

Thus a striking object-lesson was given to the whole Egyptian bureaucracy of the danger of cordial cooperation with the British officials. They saw Ministers unceremoniously dismissed for no other reason than that they were friendly to the English; they saw others raised to power because they were ready to obstruct England's work. All the constant causes of friction between British and Egyptian administrators were thus aggravated to the highest degree. I have said enough in Chapter III. about these causes of friction. It is there shown how the complete success of the strange experiment in government which we are making in Egypt can only be assured with the aid of the Khedive. Of that aid we were now deprived. Moreover, Riaz Pasha, though appointed with the concurrence of Great Britain, threw himself, from the first moment of his return to power, into a policy of stubborn opposition to British influence. The spirit manifested at headquarters spread like wildfire through every rank of the Administration. If an Order had been published in the *Official Journal* enjoining all the Egyptian authorities to obstruct their British colleagues whenever they could safely do so, it would scarcely have been more effective in causing such obstruction than was the example set by the Khedive and his new advisers.

Nor was the anti-British movement confined to the official world. The spectacle of the Khedive at open variance with the British naturally gave fresh encouragement to all those elements of Egyptian society which are permanently hostile to us, and incited them to unprecedented activity. I hardly know whether it is necessary to recall what these elements are. There are the fanatics, to whom even intercourse with foreigners is more or less repugnant, and foreign predominance intolerable. There are the old-fashioned Pashas and their following, who, from self-interest or mere Conservatism, long for the return of autocratic native government. There are a certain number of young men, ambitious, clever, sympathizing with modern ideas, who believe themselves capable of governing the country on progressive principles without external aid. Finally, there are the turbulent elements of the population, partly Egyptians, partly low-class foreigners and Levantines, who are always in favour of change, and who find the orderly and honest administration of to-day less congenial than the system which preceded it. No one of these parties is very formidable by itself, and their positive aims are quite inconsistent with one another. But in the negative policy of Anglophobia they were all able to unite; and, encouraged from above, they made an influential coalition. The greater portion of the Press, whether native or European, is inspired by one or other of these factions; and though the Press is still an inconsiderable power in Egypt, its vehement tirades, however childish and mendacious, were not without effect in creating the appearance of a genuine national movement. Moreover, the bulk of the people, who at heart are far from dissatisfied with the *status quo*, found it prudent to give a demonstrative, though hollow, support to the policy of their rulers. It did not occur to them to doubt that the Khedive and his Ministers, before placing themselves in open opposition to the English, had made sure that they were strong enough to carry such a policy to a successful issue, and this being so, they naturally desired to be on the safe side.

Herein lies the simple explanation of the 'unpopularity' of the English in Egypt, of which we have lately heard so much. To Englishmen at home the demonstrations made against us have been a matter of surprise. 'How is it,' they not unnaturally ask, 'that, if we have done so much good to the country, we are not more popular there?' Yet the answer is easy. As strangers of an alien faith, possibly of unsympathetic manners, we shall never be popular in the sense of being personally beloved. But neither are we unpopular—at least with the great mass of the people—in the sense that they desire to be rid of us. Free to choose without fear of the consequences, they would undoubtedly prefer the present state of things to the arbitrary system that preceded our advent. But with the Khedive and the native magnates conspicuously hostile to us, they shrewdly reason thus: 'If we do not take sides against the English, we shall be prejudiced while they remain, and punished when they go. If we do take sides against them, we shall curry favour with our native rulers in the present, and we are perfectly safe whatever may be the result in the future; for, should the English remain, they will not hurt us, and should they go, we shall be able to make capital out of the fact that we belonged to the patriotic opposition while they were here.'

Under these circumstances, it is not a matter of wonder to anyone who knows the Egyptian character that during the recent troubles we seemed to have few friends. It is true there was not much open defiance, but those who had always opposed us were more stubborn, and those who had hitherto sided with us were less cordial than before. Almost every Englishman engaged in the work of administration found the dead weight he had to lift appreciably heavier. His native subordinates yielded him a less cheerful obedience; his native colleagues, of equal or superior rank, gave him no help. Outside the official circle, men who had formerly been friendly now showed a disposition to shun us. In some cases they frankly explained that they were afraid to appear on good terms with the English. It has been alleged that the manner of the common people towards Englishmen, and more or less towards all foreigners, became visibly discourteous and almost menacing. This aspect of the case was perhaps somewhat exaggerated; but there is no doubt that many cool-headed observers began to grow uneasy as to the possibility of popular disturbances, which no one had dreamt of for some time.

It would serve no good purpose to recall the various unpleasant incidents, mostly insignificant in themselves, to which the attempt to annoy and obstruct the British officials gave rise. The covert opposition of the native element naturally made itself most felt in those departments of government in which our position has always been weakest; but to a greater or less extent the baneful influence was perceptible everywhere. The art of creating difficulties is well understood by the Egyptian bureaucracy, and it is no easy matter to grapple with a ubiquitous obstruction which is often ingenious and almost always polite.

The situation was a radically false one; but it is impossible to say how long it might have continued without the occurrence of any open rupture had not the impetuosity of the Khedive led him to adopt a method of attack which made the vigorous interference of the English Government once more inevitable. It is inconsistent with our general policy and peculiarly repugnant to Lord Cromer's temper and instincts to meddle with the every-day business of Egyptian administration, or to intervene, for any slight reason, between the English and the native servants of the Khedive. But when Abbas Pasha began to tamper with the discipline of the Army, the matter was too serious to be overlooked. The existing Egyptian Army has been created by British officers, and for ten years the supreme authority of the Sirdar in all purely military questions has remained undisputed. But with the promotion of Maher Pasha to the post of Under-Secretary of State for War, in the autumn of 1893, difficulties, unknown since the earliest days of the Occupation, began to arise in the administration of the War Office. With some trouble a truce was concluded which left the Sirdar's authority nominally unimpaired; but the attempt to undermine the position of Englishmen in the Egyptian Army did not stop there. On his now famous visit to the frontier in January, 1894, the Khedive lost no opportunity of publicly slighting the British officers who accompanied or received him; and his dislike to them was finally exhibited in so extreme a form that General Kitchener felt bound to resign the position of Sirdar. His resignation was, indeed, at the Khedive's request speedily withdrawn; but the manifest intention of Abbas Pasha to discredit the British officers, and to destroy their hold upon the troops, had brought about a situation not only absurd, but intolerably dangerous. Unless something could be done to rehabilitate the highest officers of the Egyptian Army in the eyes of their subordinates and the country-discipline would be at an end, and the internal tranquillity of Egypt, as well as the security of her frontiers, gravely imperilled.

These considerations led the British Government to take prompt and decided action. Under instructions from home, Lord Cromer demanded that the Khedive should issue a General Order, expressing his approval of the discipline and efficiency of the Army, and his satisfaction with the officers whose authority he had done so much to shake. In the painful position in which he was thus placed, the Khedive found himself without supporters. The Ministry of Riaz Pasha, which had up to this point encouraged him in his campaign against the English, was disconcerted by the rashness of his latest act, and counselled submission. The French Minister, and the other foreign elements usually most hostile to Great Britain, were dismayed at the possible consequences of an overthrow of discipline in the Army. Perhaps Abbas Pasha himself was taken aback by the evidence of the universal alarm which his recent conduct had inspired. Be that as it may, he retreated with the best grace he could, and issued the Order which had practically been dictated to him. In the first instance it was published only in French; but the British Government was not satisfied, and its publication in Arabic had to follow. Moreover, Lord Cromer was instructed to demand that Maher Pasha should be removed from his post at the War Office. Here again the Khedive was at first inclined to resist. He would remove Maher Pasha when another suitable post could be found for him. But this compromise was not accepted, and within a few days Maher Pasha was sent elsewhere, and another officer, Zohrab Pasha, whose loyalty to his English colleagues was beyond question, was promoted to his place.

Thus the result of the young Khedive's ill-judged crusade was to compel the reluctant British Government to inflict upon him a severer humiliation than has ever befallen the ruler of Egypt since the days of Arabi, and to demonstrate its own power with greater emphasis than on any previous occasion. The effect of that demonstration was precisely what any man who knows the character of the people would have predicted. For the moment, the 'Nationalist' opposition was completely disbanded, and Great Britain had once more a native party on her side. Moreover, the confidence of the Khedive in the anti-British Ministry, which had failed to support him at the critical moment, was destroyed. It is probable that he never got on really well with Riaz Pasha, and now that their joint endeavours had ended in such conspicuous failure, each no doubt threw the blame upon the other. Hence, Egypt has during the beginning of 1894 been once more in the throes of a ministerial crisis. The crisis was finally terminated by the announcement that after six years of retirement Nubar Pasha had returned to power. What may be the effects of this change it would be foolish to attempt to predict. Nubar Pasha is unquestionably the most capable of living Egyptian statesmen. His great ability, his enlightened mind, his sympathy with our principal objects, if not with ourselves, will cause all well-wishers of Egypt to long for his success. He, if any man, should be able to extricate the Khedive from the false position in which he has placed himself, and to re-establish good relations between him and the British Government; but if Nubar is to do this, Abbas Pasha must help him. Should the Khedive remain irreconcilable, no genius on earth could make the present system of Egyptian administration a workable one.

The immediate future is thus very uncertain. But the essential conditions of the problem remain unaltered. They only stand out more clearly in the light of recent events. There are two possibilities before Egypt. One is the frank acceptance by the Khedive and his native advisers of the helping hand which Great Britain still holds out to them, and their co-operation with us in that work of constructive reform which is honestly intended to make Egypt capable of ultimate autonomy. The other is their persistence in the recent policy of hostility and obstruction—a policy which renders the success of our work under present conditions impossible, and must therefore end in some radical change. That change would not necessarily take the form of the establishment of British dominion. Such might be the outcome, but there are other solutions at least equally probable. They are all, however, alike inconsistent with the ideal of Egyptian independence. The one thing which the attempt to shake off the guiding hand of Great Britain cannot result in, is a complete escape of Egypt from foreign control.

If any doubt previously existed as to the incompetence of the new 'Nationalist' party to grapple with the exceedingly delicate problems which the government of the country presents, the mad proceedings of 1893—1894 must surely have dissipated it. Even assuming that the Khedive and his 'Nationalist' sympathizers were right, and that Great Britain ought now to leave Egypt to her own devices, could any sane body of men have believed that that object was to be attained by the means actually adopted? Was it conceivable that, after all that had passed, the English would allow themselves to be ignominiously hustled out of the country, or that their withdrawal would be quickened by a deliberate attempt to wreck the work they have been doing, and the preservation of which is the only object of their continued presence? Such an idea convicts the men possessed by it of political imbecility. No reasonable critic will be inclined to take a very severe view of the Khedive's own action, disastrous as its effects have hitherto been. He was suddenly called to the throne at a very early age. He had had no opportunity of acquainting himself with the nature or the limits of the great power placed in his hands, and he was surrounded from the first by advisers who helped him to misinterpret the situation. But the same excuse cannot be made for the want of sense or of character which led the men, who ought to have instructed and restrained him, to become his ready tools in a course of action which, whether right or wrong, was certain to end in failure. It is not to feather-brained politicians of this type that the fortunes of any country, least of all of Egypt, can safely be entrusted.

The future must show whether Abbas Pasha, who is undoubtedly a man of courage, is also a man capable of profiting by experience. If so, the policy which Great Britain has all along pursued—of seeking to effect the regeneration of Egypt through the agency of her native rulers—may yet be crowned with success. I have never attempted to ignore the difficulties of that policy. I do not deny that during the last year and a half those difficulties have appeared greater than ever before. But this solution of the problem, if we can only arrive at it, is, after all that has happened, so much the best, that we ought, I think, to be very slow to despair of its achievement.

The chief obstacle to the attainment of our end is the fact that our intentions are generally misunderstood. Even in England there seem to be few people who have made up their minds what object we are, or ought to be, pursuing with regard to Egypt. The question is often asked why, if we do not intend to keep the country, we should be at such pains to improve it. What call have we to play the rôle of philanthropists? I have tried in the course of this book to supply an answer to such questionings. Let me briefly repeat that answer.

On the one hand, our commercial interests in Egypt are so great and growing that her prosperity, which would be immediately wrecked by misgovernment, is a matter of concern to us.* Secondly and chiefly, the geographical position of Egypt compels attention to her political condition. We have nothing to gain by owning the country ourselves, but we should have a great deal to fear from its falling into the possession of another Power. And the best means to provide against this—short of annexation—is to secure such tolerable conditions of life and administration in the Nile Valley as will prevent the recurrence of anarchy, necessitating foreign intervention.† Therefore our efforts to endow Egypt with a decent native government are not philanthropy, they are business. But they are business of a perfectly straightforward and honourable kind, and possessing the characteristic of all good business—namely, that both the parties concerned are benefited.

This, I believe, is a perfectly fair statement of the case. But it is a common impression in Egypt, sedu-

* See pp. 214, 215.

† See, for a fuller development of this idea, pp. 345-348.

lously fostered by our foreign rivals, that England's real desire is to convert her present informal protectorate by gradual stages into complete dominion. True, such a theory is wholly inconsistent with the tendency of all our actions. For why, if we simply desired to appropriate the country, should we spend our strength in painful and always misconstrued efforts to improve the native Army, the native Courts, the native Civil Service; to select the best men and to train them in the habits of civilized government; to discourage jobbery, and to stamp out corruption? It would be far easier to make no attempt to raise the character of the native administration. The worse it became, the better would be our excuse for staying on indefinitely. But the true interpretation of our reforming zeal is too simple for the suspicious minds of many native politicians. Believing that our every move conceals some insidious scheme for getting more power into English hands, they are easily tempted to intrigue against us, and thereby to protract our work and make our gradual withdrawal difficult, if not impossible. This is the latest of Egyptian paradoxes, that those who are most keenly desirous to see us go away are always doing the very things which are calculated to postpone our going till the Greek Kalends.

No doubt this misconception of the aim of British policy, steadily dinned into his ears from the first moment of his accession, has had much to do with the hostile attitude of the Khedive. If Nubar Pasha can succeed in removing that misconception, he will have rendered the greatest of all services to his master and to his country. It is only necessary that the Khedive should have faith in the honesty of British intentions, and should assist our work instead of thwarting it, in order that the progress of the country, political as well as material, may once again go on apace. We should then hear little more of 'Nationalist' agitation, or of the unpopularity of the British. For the 'Nationalist' movement of the past year, unlike that of Arabi's time, was no spontaneous uprising of the people against intolerable oppression. It was a factitious movement encouraged from above, and without such encouragement it would at once cease to be serious. If the signal for conciliation were given from headquarters, the steady, though often intangible, opposition which we have had to encounter of recent days would rapidly disappear, and the native officials, instead of wasting their energies in trying to circumvent their British colleagues, would be set free to co-operate with us in promoting the welfare of their country. As long as the Khedive is against us, these officials, even when at heart favourable to our work, are in a position of extreme difficulty. Loyalty to the English is represented as disloyalty to their master. There is no doubt about the sincere desire of the best of them that antagonism between the Khedive and the British should cease. And cease it evidently must if the present political constitution of Egypt is to endure.

A. M.

LONDON,
April 14, 1894.

APPENDIX II.

SPECIAL justification may be pleaded at the present time for another and final supplement to 'England in Egypt.' The year 1898 will be a landmark in the story of the British occupation. The foundation-stones of the great Assuan Reservoir have been laid, which will change the face of the country, and constitute one of the noblest monuments of civil rule in the world. A first blow has been struck at the international top-hamper of modern Egypt by an arrangement for securing the extinction of the Daira Sanieh debt in 1905. The increased facilities for credit afforded by the establishment of the National Bank with a right of note issue will meet the needs of commercial expansion, and help to lower the rate of interest in the provinces. With the capture of Omdurman, and the hoisting of the British and Egyptian flags over Khartum, the Sudan has once more been reunited to Egypt, but under totally novel conditions. Any further record of Anglo-Egyptian administration must include the organization and government of this vast Hinterland. Finally, there are symptoms of change in the essential conditions under which the regeneration of Egypt has hitherto proceeded, pointing to possible modifications in the very machinery of government, and even in the political status of the country.

A brief survey of the material progress of Egypt since 1894 will show that the rate of improvement has been more than maintained. Indeed, a richer harvest is reaped each year from the good seed sown in the form of security and honest administration.

The annual balance-sheets are eloquent; ordinary and extraordinary receipts are included:

	Revenue.	Expenditure.	Surplus.
1894	£E10,444,650	£E 9,995,641	£E 449,009
1895	£E10,698,023	£E 9,637,900	£E1,060,123
1896	£E11,015,702	£E10,540,502	£E 475,200
1897	£E11,442,937	£E10,752,776	£E 690,161
1898 (Approximate.)	£E11,624,000	£E10,248,000*	£E1,376,000

It must be noted that the growth of expenditure is principally due to a temporary cause: the reconquest of the Sudan, and the construction of railways—a valuable asset—beyond Wadi Halfa. In 1896-98 the expenditure side of the account was swollen by an aggregate sum of £E1,700,000* under these heads.

But Egypt still continues shackled by the international restrictions which prevent her making free use of the money she earns. It seems almost incredible, but it is the fact, that a Government, which is a model of severe economy, is prevented from easing taxation and increasing the country's resources by the self-same ingenious restrictions which were devised to keep a Government, notorious for its improvidence and recklessness, from extravagance, and from breaking faith with its creditors. Year after year there is swept away into international strong-boxes a large proportion of each annual surplus which, even after making every possible provision for debt and sinking fund, might be available for remission of taxation, for schools, prisons, hospitals, reformatories, and many other crying necessities. The Egyptian people ought really to be the most prosperous and lightly taxed in the world, and, in spite of the crushing load of debt with which Ismail saddled the land, the fellaheen might be fast advancing towards that ideal condition. They are advancing, it

* This figure excludes the £800,000 granted by the British Government. See p. 399.

is true; burthens are being lightened, and debt is being paid off or bought up. But the Law of Liquidation is a cruel drag on progress, and the sinking fund is made unnecessarily costly.

What could have been more natural than to suppose that, when the enhanced credit of Egypt allowed her to convert part of her debt, the Government which had built up this credit, and fortified the position of the bond-holders, would be allowed to use the difference between the old and new rate of interest to alleviate taxation?

But no! Every proposal to deal with the Economies Fund has been steadily resisted.

This fund, which can now be regarded as the Egyptian Sinking Fund, amounted, on December 31, 1898, to over £E3,100,000, bearing an annual and increasing interest of over £E110,000. It is invested in Egyptian bonds, and Egypt is therefore becoming *pro tanto* the holder of her own debt. But to buy up your debts at a premium of 8 per cent., instead of paying them off at par, a premium continually forced up by further obligatory purchases on your own part, is extravagant finance. It is an extravagance forced on Egypt by international conventions, for which, in the present case, the word 'France' might be read.

The General Reserve Fund stands in a very different position, and no serious complaint can be made of its administration, though unnecessarily large sums are passed into it every year. The amounts actually paid in up to December 31, 1898, aggregated over £E4,300,000. Thanks to the large and sensible policy of the Commissioners of the Caisse, this important fund has become a reserve on which Egypt is allowed to draw for public works. The Commissioners have made large grants and advances for such enterprises. Carrying still further the principle, that they are justified in devoting this fund to the improvement of the estate mortgaged for the bond-holders, they devoted in 1898 a sum of £E216,000 a year for ten years to the relief of the land-tax, and are contributing to the moral as well as the material progress of Egypt by voting money for schools and prisons. The various grants and advances made from the General Reserve Fund during the single year 1898 amounted to £E722,000, and large grants for canals and for the better equipment of the railways have already been announced for 1899. There is every prospect that the Commissioners, who are themselves sincerely interested in the welfare of the country, will persist in their enlightened policy. They have behind them the natural but not equally disinterested support of the bond-holders. If the free, *i.e.*, unpledged, part of the General Reserve Fund exceeded £E2,000,000, the excess would be by law devoted to drawing bonds at par which are now marketable at a premium.

Last of the three Reserve Funds, which are such distracting elements in Egyptian finance, comes the Special Reserve Fund, *i.e.*, the free balance of which the Egyptian Government can dispose as it pleases after allowance made for all adjustments. This fund on December 31, 1897, showed a *deficit* balance of £E570,847, a situation due to military operations and railway construction in the Sudan. But, thanks to the remission by Her Majesty's Government of the advance of £800,000 made to Egypt on current account in connection with the reconquest of the Sudan, and in spite of the extraordinary expenditure entailed by the Omdurman campaign and the prolongation of the Sudan Railway, the deficit of the Special Reserve Fund had at the end of 1898 been reduced to less than £E200,000. It is obvious that in normal circumstances this deficit will be converted into a surplus in the course of another twelvemonth.

For the most vivid illustration, however, of the advance of Egypt under British auspices, it is best to turn to the pages of the recent census. According to the enumeration of 1882, the population was then 6,813,919. The population returned in 1897 was 9,734,405, an increase of 43 per cent. Taxation has been reduced, while population has been growing and burthens have been lessened. Between 1881 and 1897 taxes to the annual amount of £E916,600 were reduced, while indirect taxes became immensely more productive, owing to better collection. The tobacco duty, which yielded £E97,000 in 1881, brought £E1,044,000 into the Exchequer in 1897.* The burthen of taxation per head of the population was in 1881 £1 2s. 2d., and that of debt £14 8s. 9d. In 1897 the corresponding figures were 17s. 9d. and £10 0s. 2d. In 1898 the taxation has been further reduced, as has been explained, by £E216,000; and 1899 opens with a still further remission of small taxes, pressing especially upon the poorer classes, to the extent of £E22,000 a year. With these remissions the last tax falling exclusively upon natives has disappeared.

It is a truism in Egypt that prosperity and water go hand in hand, and it is impossible to give too much credit to the zeal and skilfulness of the Irrigation Department for the growth of this well-being among the people. Happily, it has been found possible, in great measure through the assistance of the Caisse, to devote continually larger annual sums to public works. In 1897 the Caisse de la Dette granted £E250,000 for drainage works in the Delta, where the supply of water had outstripped the means of carrying it off after it had done its 'duty.'

For the same purposes a grant of £E154,000 was accorded in 1898, and a most important grant of £E530,000 was also made in the same year for strengthening the Barrage by the construction of two down-stream weirs in either branch of the Nile, which will reduce the pressure of the head of water on the existing structure. Most useful as these works will be, they are, however, dwarfed by the great project for the Assuan Reservoir.

The vital necessity of this project is so generally understood as scarcely to need explanation. The Barrage is now rendering the maximum amount of service it can render. On all sides comes up the cry for more water; from Lower Egypt for reclamation of land on the edge of the cultivated area, from Upper

* See p. 200

Egypt, at present dependent upon the flood, for a perennial water-supply to render the extension of sugar cultivation possible. But without the projected reservoir no more water can be stored, and the Public Works Department has to harden its heart and refuse to supply water to more distant lands, or to allow more water to be drawn from the upper river for new plantations, through fear of inability to supply sufficient in a year of low Nile to lands already cultivated. Not only, therefore, has the Barrage reached its maximum of utility, but the country may be said for the present to have reached its maximum of prosperity. Progress must be arrested unless more water can be given. The reservoir, however, will meet all these demands. The volume of water in Lower Egypt will be increased, and a very large 'flood-crop' area in Upper Egypt will be endowed with perennial water.

The project has at last been actually taken in hand! But the difficulties it encountered, and the manner in which these difficulties were overcome, afford a glaring proof of the absurd injustice which prevents modern Egypt having the free disposal of her own resources. Unjust! because precious years are wasted, and a costlier sacrifice than is really necessary has generally to be made. Absurd! because the ingenuity of those responsible for the conduct of affairs in Egypt manages in the long-run to get round the international restrictions in some always adroit and more or less plausible manner.

To begin with, the project had to be submitted to an International Commission as an indispensable condition for attempting to obtain funds from the international strong-boxes—funds which were not afterwards forthcoming. An International Commission on a technical question is no trifling matter, especially when its consideration is complicated by politics, but eventually, in 1894, a favourable report was obtained from the majority of the Commissioners.

The archæological world next rose in arm, but its opposition was disarmed by lowering the highest of the proposed dam, so as to avoid flooding the Philæ temples. Then arose the capital difficulty. How was the project to be financed? How was a country to find the money which could have raised a loan for so remunerative an undertaking on excellent terms, but was forbidden to raise a loan, or could have found the money in her overflowing coffers, but was prohibited access to them except under impossible conditions? The idea that the General Reserve Fund might contribute led to some months of careful negotiation, but had to be abandoned. The international control of a vast engineering work would be about as sensible as the international control of military operations. It was abundantly clear that the supervision and direction of the work must rest with Sir William Garstin and his able lieutenants of the Public Works Department, assisted by the advice of Sir Benjamin Baker, advice which has at all times been most generously and most willingly given to the Egyptian Government.

Ingenuity triumphed as usual in the end. An arrangement was concluded in February, 1898, whereby Messrs. Aird and Co. have contracted to finish the Assuan Dam and supplementary works for a sum of £2,000,000, and engaged to receive payment in sixty half-yearly payments of £78,613, to run from the completion of the works in 1903. The Egyptian Government is therefore relieved from the difficulty of paying for the works till a return is received from them—until, in other words, they pay for themselves. Meanwhile, Egypt will have to husband her resources to provide an additional £E1,180,000 for the subsidiary canals and drains which ought, if possible, to be completed during the same quinquennial period as Messrs. Aird's contracts. There can be no doubt of the value of the investment that Egypt will be making. A low estimate, which does not take into account the indirect profit to Government from increased railway and customs receipts, places the direct gain in increased land-tax at £E380,000 a year, while the value of reclaimed Government lands will be augmented by £E1,000,000. The annual addition to the wealth of the country, apart from the profit to the Exchequer, is computed at £E2,600,000, a moderate estimate. It is assuredly a matter of congratulation that this beneficent scheme will be due to British engineers, and that British capital will find the necessary means.

But the benefits of the reservoir are not entirely prospective. It is owing to the signature of the contract with Messrs. Aird that the price of land has shot up in Egypt, and that there has been a veritable rush of foreign capital towards the country. The Egyptian Government, which but a few years since found it difficult to entice capitalists to look at schemes equally beneficial to the country and to the investing public, has lately had its doors besieged by would-be concessionaires.

Another great feature of the last four years, in which the Public Works Ministry has played a large part, has been the initiation of light railways, which are carried out by private enterprise with a moderate Government guarantee. At the same time, the construction of agricultural roads, which have greatly assisted the making of the railways, has been steadily prosecuted. Over 1,700 kilometres of these roads are now open. The light railways should have a marked effect in cheapening the cost of bringing agricultural produce to the market, and thereby in counteracting any further fall in the price of Egypt's staple crops, a danger to which an agricultural country chiefly dependent on one crop must always be exposed. Already a line constructed by Belgian capital is open from Mansurah to Mataria, penetrating a secluded district, and giving an outlet to the fishing industry of Lake Menzaleh.

The provinces of Behera and Gharbia have been assigned to an English company—the Egyptian Delta Light Railways Company — which has made a good beginning. Eastwards the interesting province of Sharkia, which is destined to benefit very largely by the reservoirs, has been portioned out to a syndicate of local capitalists, and the Fayúm has been undertaken by a purely native group (an interesting experiment in association) who have wisely retained European advice and technical assistance. In short, every district where a light railway can exist will soon be equipped, and when the total lines now sanctioned are completed, Egypt will have 763 kilometres of agricultural railways. The State railways have also been extended, and the southern prolongation to Assuan has been completed, so that, except for the distance between Assuan and Wadi Halfa, where the Nile provides a free and excellent waterway, there is now, thanks to this prolongation and to the Sudan lines, uninterrupted railway communication between Alexandria and the Atbara, which will shortly be continued to Khartum. The number of passengers carried on the State lines has risen from 9,827,813 in 1894 to 10,742,546 in 1897. Over 720,000 of this increased number have been third-class passengers, a conclusive proof of the prosperity of the fellahin.

The chief administrative reform of the last four years has been that of the Ministry of the Interior. Lord Cromer is surrounded by a band of men all honestly eager to improve their particular departments. His policy among these conflicting appeals may be summed up as 'Ohne Hast, ohne Rast.' Energy has been successively concentrated on one reform after another in order of urgency, for the danger of dissipating force over a number of simultaneous reforms in Egypt is very real, as, however excellent the measures may be in themselves, it is only possible to steer one big project at a time through the maze of Egyptian obstacles into a safe haven. After Finance, the Army, Public Works, and Justice had been dealt with, the Interior had the next claim. Its reorganization is typical of the adaptation of indigenous institutions to modern uses and requirements. The Mudir in Egypt is the executive agent of the Government in the provinces. He is a blend of the French préfet and of the Indian collector, and it is to him that the people instinctively look. It was no easy problem to bring into line this functionary, who had often wielded despotic power in his district, without destroying his authority and shaking both the administrative and social fabric. The first step towards intervention was the proper control of the prisons and hospitals in the provinces, but this caused scarcely any difficulty, as the Mudir had little desire to interfere in such technical matters. They did not concern his prestige, and the English Inspectors were readily given a free hand. But the question of public security and of the police, the outward and visible sign of the Mudir's authority and prestige, was a very different affair. The police were under the orders of the Mudir, and to make the force efficient it was found necessary at an early stage of the occupation to reorganize it through English Inspectors stationed in the provinces, and directed by an English Inspector-General at headquarters. Naturally the Inspectors insisted on seeing that the new instrument was put to its proper use, but their ideas of its proper use did not always coincide with those of the Mudir, sometimes a survival of an earlier epoch, while their presence and activity impaired his authority. Hence arose friction, divided responsibility, and administrative confusion. The populace was puzzled, and with Mudir and Inspectors pulling different ways the prevention and detection of crime was not facilitated, and, indeed, the two sets of authorities were in some danger of actually working against each other. Now, the theory of Anglo-Egyptian administration, to quote Lord Cromer, is that of 'English heads and Egyptian hands.' It was decided to remove the English hands and rely upon the directing brain. Mr. J. L. Gorst,* at that time Under-Secretary of State for Finance, was transferred to the Interior in October, 1894. He was appointed as Adviser to the Minister of the Interior, and, while possessing no executive functions, was given the right to be kept fully informed with regard to all

* Mr. J. L. Gorst succeeded Sir Elwin Palmer as Financial Adviser in September, 1898, his post at the Interior being filled by Captain Machell. Mr. C. E. Dawkins, Under-Secretary of State for Finance, also resigned in 1898, to be succeeded by Mr. Mitchell Innes.

the affairs of the Ministry. At the same time, instead of Inspectors stationed in the provinces, Inspectors at headquarters, who were not to reside in, but to visit the provinces, were appointed. They were to be the eyes and ears of the Adviser, and it was his duty in turn to secure proper attention to their reports at the Ministry. The new system has borne good results upon the whole. But it must always largely depend for its success, and for the credit it may bring the English name in the provinces, upon the tact and reputation of the Inspectors, and upon the general tone and character imparted to their work by the Adviser.

A further measure more closely concerned the life of the fellahin. Here again it was determined to vitalize an indigenous institution. From time immemorial the Egyptian village has found its spokesmen in the Sheikhs and Omdehs (*lit.*, 'props,' or head Sheikhs), under whom the people spontaneously range themselves. These spokesmen were held responsible by the Government for order in their villages, and exercised an indefinite and fluctuating authority. This institution has been regulated. The duties and responsibilities of the Omdehs, upon whom limited judicial powers have been conferred, have been increased and defined, and in return they have been given greater dignity and accorded a certain exemption from taxation. To turn from an Egyptian village to an English county may seem at first sight a vain excursion of the mind, but the Omdehs, constituting as they do the middle class of land-owners, are to some extent parallel with the unpaid magistracy in England.

Other useful reforms have proceeded in the departments grouped under the Interior. Reformatories have been established, and under Coles Pasha useful prison labour is being enforced, and prisoners are taught handicrafts. Dr. Warnock has taken in hand the one lunatic asylum the country boasts, and in a very short space of time has substituted modern and humane methods for an almost mediæval treatment of the insane. Continuous progress has been made by the very energetic officers of the Sanitary Department under Sir John Rogers in improving sanitation, and the untiring zeal, energy and devotion, with which the Sanitary Department controlled and stamped out the cholera epidemic in 1896, have added a bright page to the story of the British Occupation.

Much has also been done in Education during the last four years. The number of pupils in the Government schools has increased, the proportion of non-paying pupils has decreased, and the overloaded Gallo-Byzantine programmes of instruction have been cut down and improved.

These changes correspond with an increased demand for education. Schools supported by native subscriptions have been opened for boys and girls alike, and their managers have engaged European teachers and solicited Government inspection. Even more remarkable is the fact that the El Azhar University—that conservative home of Islam's scholastic theology—has applied for teachers trained by Government to teach secular subjects within its walls. But the step forward which may prove the most momentous is the attempt to establish a system of primary instruction in the vernacular.

Education in Egypt resembles an inverted pyramid. High-class schools were created by the fiat of Mehemet Ali in order to turn out Government employés. The Ministry of Public Instruction has confined its attention to these higher schools ever since; the basis on which they should rest has been neglected. While the Government in 1897 spent more than £E93,000,* drawn from the pockets of the general mass of the taxpayers, on educating some 11,000 pupils, mostly of the well-to-do classes, and mainly for the careers of civil employés or lawyers, over 180,000 children found shelter in the village or mosque schools entirely supported by the voluntary efforts of the people. In these indigenous schools, which are not unlike the old dame schools of England, instruction is given—in theory, at least—in

* Excluding school fees.

the Koran, and in reading, writing, and simple arithmetic. In practice, owing to the ignorance of the teachers, instruction is usually confined to learning the Koran by rote. As a result of this neglect of primary education, over 91 per cent. of the population are unable to read or write. In 1898 the Government, clinging to its policy of vitalizing indigenous institutions, determined to try and improve the standard of secular education in these native schools. Grants in aid were offered to such Kuttabs as would submit themselves to Government inspection, and attain a certain minimum standard in reading, writing, and arithmetic. It was at first feared that the Kuttabs would not respond owing to an unfounded dread that the scheme involved interference with their religious teaching. Largely owing to the influence of Riaz Pasha, a warm advocate of improving these schools, and himself above all suspicion with his co-religionists, this apprehension was dispelled, and several hundred schools applied for the grant.

Turning from the Schools to the Courts, we may note that continuous effort has been directed, under Sir John Scott,* towards making justice more expeditious and accessible by increasing the number of summary Native Courts, and by facilitating the delegation of limited judicial powers to the Omdehs. At the same time, the Native Court of Appeal has been strengthened, and valuable changes have been introduced into the old Oriental law of evidence in trials for murder. Moreover, the Parquet—that institution so foreign to English ideas—has been taught that its duty is to prosecute, and not to judge, and has been brought into better co-operation with other departments. To complete this work it was found necessary, in 1897, to appoint an Englishman as Procureur-Général in the person of Corbet Bey.

Of late, however, public attention has been diverted from the Native Courts to the more sensational proceedings in the Mixed Tribunals. European interest

* Sir John Scott retired in October, 1898, to be succeeded as Judicial Adviser by Mr. Malcolm McIlwraith.

was excited in the suit brought by the minority of the members of the Caisse against the majority of that body and the Egyptian Government for the restitution of a sum of £E500,000, advanced for the expenses of the Dongola Expedition. The affair is still fresh in men's memories, and need not be more than shortly summarized.

When the Dongola Expedition was decided upon, the Government applied to the Caisse for a grant of £E500,000 from the General Reserve Fund, which, according to the decree constituting it, may be devoted, *inter alia*, to 'extraordinary expenditure incurred with the previous consent of the Commissioners of the Caisse.' The majority of the Commissioners acceded, and the money was given. But the French and Russian members applied to the Mixed Tribunals to order the refund of the half million. They were successful, and the money was repaid.

It is impossible for any impartial person to deny that the decision of the Court was open to the gravest criticism, and that its proceedings appeared animated throughout by partisan considerations. The Mixed Tribunals were never intended to have jurisdiction over the Egyptian Government in its acts of sovereignty, and their earlier decisions were inspired and guided by this obvious principle. But though the finding of the Court did not actually controvert this general proposition, yet it is difficult not to connect its decision with the pronounced tendency of the Mixed Tribunals in recent years to depart from the principle that formerly guided them and to seek to review the administrative acts of the Government. The second point involved was whether the extraordinary expenditure contemplated by the decree did or did not include grants for military operations. Here the question was rather one of fact than of law, the solution of which depended upon the intentions of the parties to the decree. Now the language of that document is certainly wide enough to cover the application of the fund to military operations. Such an application is not expressly excluded, and therefore, in all reason, the onus of proof that military expenditure lay outside the scope of the decree should have rested on the parties making that allegation. Surely it was in no wise incumbent on the Egyptian Government to show affirmatively that the decree applied to something which its actual words were certainly wide enough to cover. The Court, however, decided otherwise.

The juridical consequences of the judgment are less important than its political effect. This will be considered later on. But the heat and excitement generated by this debate naturally focussed attention upon the encroachments of the Mixed Tribunals. They are terminating a quinquennial period of their existence,* and the Commission which was appointed to discuss possible modifications in their procedure has brought this tendency to encroachment into strong relief. It has been shown that the Courts are constantly reviewing the administrative acts of the Government. At the same time they persistently seek to enlarge their jurisdiction by hunting for 'mixed interests' in every transaction, even where it is beyond the power of the most elastic legal fiction to establish a 'mixed personality.' As a result of the recent discussion, the Mixed Tribunals have been induced to define and limit their jurisdiction to some extent regarding 'mixed interests.' But they have refused to make any concession affecting the general position they have assumed towards the Egyptian Government.

The Mixed Courts have rendered valuable services to Egypt, but there are limits to an *imperium in imperio*, and it would be idle to ignore that by their recent action the Courts have involved themselves in considerable discredit. No one would willingly contemplate their extinction if this meant a resurrection of the chaos of conflicting Courts and jurisdictions which preceded their establishment. But the fact that Egypt has now refused

* The Mixed Courts have hitherto been renewed every five years by agreement between Egypt and the Powers represented in the Courts for a further period of five years.

assent to the continuation of the Mixed Courts for more than one year shows that the necessity for strictly defining their jurisdiction is urgent, and that some way may have to be found out of present difficulties, even if it is attended with temporary inconveniences. Foreign Powers might be willing to place their subjects, upon certain conditions, under the civil jurisdiction of the reformed Native Courts, which are being steadily strengthened, and it is certain that if two or three considerable Powers took this step the subjects of those who held aloof would find themselves at a commercial disadvantage.

But the question of the Mixed Courts, important as it is, and many other important questions have been thrown into the shade by the reconquest of the Sudan, which will make the years 1896-1898 ever memorable in Egyptian annals. Even in the earliest days, when the wise decision was taken to abandon those provinces, it was manifest that some day, when she had recuperated her strength and collected her resources, Egypt was bound to rid herself of the constant menace of invasion, and to re-assert her control over her vast Hinterland and the river that gives her life. Nevertheless, although the reconquest of the Sudan was felt to be getting nearer, and some anxiety had been aroused by the rumours of French movements in the direction of the Upper Nile, it was universally anticipated at the beginning of 1896 that the days of waiting were not yet over. Events were precipitated by the difficulties in which Italy found herself in Erythræa. Hard beset by the Abyssinians, the Italians were also threatened by a renewal of Dervish activity at Kassala. Accordingly they applied to the British Government in March, 1896, to make a demonstration beyond Wadi Halfa in order to relieve the Dervish pressure on Kassala. The demonstration originally proposed was quite insignificant: it was immediately transformed into a project for the re-occupation of Dongola, which in turn inevitably involved the reconquest of Khartum.

Necessarily very little warning or time for preparation

could be given to the authorities in Cairo. Happily, owing to the careful husbanding of her resources, to the assistance given in men and money by England, to the wonderful pitch of efficiency to which the Egyptian army had been brought by its English officers, and, above all, to the extraordinary energy and organizing genius of Sir Herbert (now Lord) Kitchener, and to the powerful and unswerving support given him by Lord Cromer, Egypt proved equal to the task. The British and Egyptian flags have been hoisted together over Khartum, and Great Britain has notified that foreign intervention will not be allowed in the Valley of the Nile while she remains in charge of the destinies of Egypt. The reconquest of the Sudan has been the triumph of hard work, perseverance, and economy, exercised through long years of patient waiting. Never, perhaps, has hard work so amply deserved success; assuredly, success so unequivocal and brilliant has never crowned hard work!

The opening campaign of 1896 was enough to strain the endurance of any army and the resources of any organization. Cholera, parching heat, alternations of blinding sand-storms and torrential rains, with unusual floods, beset the troops in the long, arduous task of dragging the railway up after them through the chaos of black rock and barren sand which hems in the Second Cataract for over a hundred miles. The grit and cheerfulness of the Egyptian troops were beyond all praise, and when the Dervishes, on June 7, stood their ground in the position they had themselves selected at Ferket, they were, in spite of several desperate charges, completely overwhelmed. They attempted to renew the contest at Hafir and at Dongola town, but the steady advance of the Egyptian force and the fire of the gunboats proved irresistible. By the end of September the entire province of Dongola was rid of its Dervish garrison, and Egyptian authority was established as far south as Merawi, at the foot of the Fourth Cataract. This closed the campaign of 1896.

The troops were not disturbed during the winter, but

the position in Dongola was obviously too extended and exposed. The conquest of the Sudan has been as much a victory over distances as over Dervishes. It was clear that the direct road into the Sudan was the desert route from Wadi Halfa across the great bend of the Nile to some point above the Fourth Cataract. The railway was therefore boldly launched into the desert; but the projected terminus, Abu Hamed, where it was to strike the river again, was held by a Dervish force, and as the rails advanced it became necessary to turn out the enemy's garrison. This arduous task, involving a forced march of 132 miles along the Fourth Cataract and over very difficult ground, was entrusted to Major-General (now Sir Archibald) Hunter. On August 7, 1897, Abu Hamed was attacked and taken, with the loss of 100 in killed and wounded. The effect of this blow was even greater than had been expected. The Dervishes hastily evacuated Berber, the second most important place on the Nile north of Khartum. The opportunity was too good to be lost. By a tremendous effort troops were pushed up along the river from Dongola, and Berber was permanently occupied. The railway was at the same time hurried forward, if possible with redoubled energy, and by the end of the year 1897 troops could be carried straight from Wadi Halfa to the neighbourhood of Berber.

Hitherto the Egyptian army had proved equal to the task. But with the near approach to the Dervish capital, and in view of the numerical superiority of the enemy, it was found prudent to call up English troops early in 1898.

In the spring of that year a large Dervish force, under the Emir Mahmud and Osman Digna, the notorious raider of the Eastern Sudan, advanced towards Berber, and entrenched itself in a *zariba* on the Atbara River, the first tributary that is met with in ascending the Nile from the sea, at a distance of some 1,500 miles from Alexandria. After a few days of anxious reconnaissance, the Sirdar determined to attack. His Anglo-Egyptian force numbered about 12,000 men, and Mahmud's army about 16,000. The enemy's position was well shaken by artillery fire, and then the British, Sudanese, and Egyptians raced each other into the *zariba*. There was a sharp but short tussle. The Dervishes lost over 3,000, and the attacking force nearly 500 in killed and wounded. The victory of April 7 seriously broke the Dervish power and prestige, but the Baggara clan, reviving its fanaticism, determined to make a last desperate stand under the walls of Omdurman. As the Nile rose, the Anglo-Egyptian army, now raised by various reinforcements to about 22,000 men, moved steadily and slowly up the river till, well within sight of the Mahdi's tomb that dominated the Dervish capital, the final struggle took place on September 2, 1898. The Dervishes displayed all their old intrepidity, but less than their customary skill in taking advantage of the ground. Discipline and weapons of precision triumphed over fanaticism, numbers, and desperate bravery. The Khalifa's army was virtually annihilated. Out of a total of perhaps 40,000 the Dervishes lost nearly one half in killed and wounded in a few hours, and on that same evening the Sirdar was freeing the few remaining Christian and Egyptian captives in Omdurman. Colonel Parsons, operating from Kassala, which had been restored to Egypt by the Italians in December, 1897, immediately took in hand the task of clearing the Eastern Sudan of its Dervish garrison. This campaign was remarkable for the fact that a newly-raised fellahin regiment, though completely outnumbered, and for the first time in action, inflicted a severe defeat on a far larger Dervish force. Towards the close of December the remnants of the scattered Dervishes were caught by Colonel Lewis in an attempt to retire westwards across the Nile and defeated after a sharp action, and organized resistance in the Eastern districts came to an end.

If the hard work, admirable management and forethought of the two and a half years' campaigning resulted in a brilliant military success, no less brilliant, and even more astonishing, has been the financial success.

Not only has the Dervish power been shattered, but the Sudan itself, with its interminable thirsty deserts and long stretches of stony cataracts, has been tamed. This more arduous conquest has been directed by English brains, but it may be doubted whether it could have been accomplished without the ever-patient endurance and unwearying labour of the fellahin battalions who laid the railway and hauled the gunboats through the cataracts. The financial triumph is largely due to their qualities. The usual result of a campaign is to leave a heavy debt. But Egypt has not been untrue to her character as the 'Land of Paradox,' and the Sudan campaign has bequeathed valuable and productive assets. They cannot be better enumerated than in Lord Kitchener's own words, spoken at the Mansion House on November 4, 1898.

'You may take it,' he explained to his audience, 'that during the two and a half years' campaign extra military credits to the amount of two and a half millions have been expended. In this sum I have included the recent grant for the extension of the railway from Atbara to Khartum, the work on which is already in hand. Well, against this large expenditure we have some assets to show; we have, or shall have, 760 miles of railways, properly equipped with engines, rolling stock, and a track with bridges in good order. . . . Well, for this running concern I do not think that £3,000 a mile will be considered too high a value. This represents two and a quarter millions out of the money granted, and for the other quarter of a million we have 2,000 miles of telegraph line, six new gunboats, besides barges, sailing-craft, and—the Sudan.'

It remains to cast a glance at the modifications which the events of the last four years, and especially the recovery of the Sudan, are likely to introduce into the external relations of Egypt and into her internal organization. When the Mixed Courts, set in motion by France and Russia, obliged the Egyptian Government to refund the half-million granted by the Caisse, the response was an immediate advance to Egypt of £800,000 by the British Government in account current to defray the expenses of the war. The promptness of this response—not a moment was lost —took political opponents aback, and it was obvious that this assistance gave Great Britain a special lien upon the Sudan, and, through the Sudan, necessarily affected our position towards Egypt herself.

The subsequent remission of the £800,000, and the employment of a considerable British force in the Sudan, has made the situation still clearer. It is true that there is no avowed and outward change in the position of the British Government towards Egypt. After the victory of Omdurman, and the retirement of the French Government from a false and untenable position at Fashoda, there was a confident expectation throughout Egypt that a Protectorate would be proclaimed, and the proclamation would have been accepted joyfully by all classes and communities in Egypt except the French colony. But Lord Salisbury, while maintaining that Lord Kitchener's victory has profoundly modified the situation, and while adopting a very different tone about Egypt to that which he formerly employed, has repudiated the idea of a Protectorate. There are some denials which are not far removed from affirmations, and Lord Salisbury's language, and the reception with which it met, have been generally interpreted to mean that the assumption of the Protectorate is only deferred. At any rate, even if the system of the veiled Protectorate is to continue, it must be allowed that the veil has become one of exceeding transparency.

How far, it must finally be asked, will the internal organization of Egypt and the machinery of Government be necessarily modified by events which are having so far-reaching an influence upon her external relations? The regeneration of Egypt through her native rulers has been our deliberate and consistent policy. In theory we still govern through the Khedive, we make use of the prestige of the dynasty, and the Khedive, in whose name all the acts of Government run, enjoys the full credit of them. Such a system can only work if both parties to it—the Khedive and the English—co-operate loyally. It may be objected that it was hazardous to suppose that an Oriental ruler could be found capable of appreciating and lending himself to such a system. Tewfik Pasha probably had by nature what may be termed—for an Oriental—constitutional inclinations. He had witnessed his father's downfall, had been through the fire of the Arabi rebellion, and had been restored by British bayonets. In spite of an occasional swerve, Tewfik played his part well, and readily identified himself in later years with every measure of improvement. He reaped his reward in increasing popularity and prestige, both amongst his own people and amongst the European community, as well as in a continuous relaxation of the beneficial but sometimes irksome English control.

It was hoped that Abbas Hilmi, after the unfortunate escapades into which evil counsels precipitated him at the beginning of his reign, would profit by experience and seek to follow in his father's footsteps. That hope has still to be fulfilled. The Khedive has not yet brought himself to definitely abandon a policy of obstruction in order to co-operate frankly and cordially with us in the work of constructive reform. The severe lessons of the army or frontier incident of January, 1894, and the restrictions placed upon his power of appointing Ministers, made a deep impression on the country, but they have not modified in essentials the Ruler's disposition. Unhappily, the arbitrary personal power wielded by his grandfather Ismail continues to be the young Khedive's ideal. His father's memory is out of fashion at the palace. Apologists may point to outward conformity with a constitutional régime, and to the apparently good terms on which the Khedive is with his principal English advisers. But one ugly fact remains, which cannot be explained away. It is in the native press that the Khedive's true attitude is reflected, and it is by his relations with these organs that his real disposition must be tested. Unfortunately, it is notorious that the violent section of this press is subsidized, and at times directly inspired, by the Palace. There is no necessity to go into the more delicate question of the actual relations of certain virulent journalists with the Khedive, or into that of his imprudent encouragement of absurd emissaries in Europe. It may broadly be affirmed, and no sane person conversant with Egyptian society would deny the proposition, that the hostility of the native press exists because it is agreeable to the Khedive, or because the Khedive allows it to be thought that it is agreeable to him. A word from Abbas Hilmi would change the tone of these papers, and confine their utterances within the limits of reasonable criticism. Will the Khedive speak that word? Or will he continue to allow himself to be identified with a propaganda that can lead to no good end? The remnant of the old Nationalist party, the only group that possesses a semblance of coherence or vitality in Egypt, urges him forward. But this party has its own axe to grind—devotion to the dynasty is not exactly a plank in its platform—and it has no hesitation in encouraging a young Ruler to venture further, perhaps, than he realizes, down a dangerous path.

The continuous and malignant misrepresentation of the measures of the Government, in which the Palace organs indulge, is seasoned, no doubt very much to the taste of these extremists, with constant appeals to fanaticism and with laudation of the present Sultan. At the same time, the native Ministers and officials who co-operate with us towards their country's welfare are incessantly held up to obloquy as false to the dynasty and to their religion. There is no present likelihood that Mohammedan fanaticism, though so constantly and mischievously stimulated, will issue in any serious outbreak. But ill-feeling on the part of the natives against the Europeans is undoubtedly promoted; and although the present Ministers have gauged the situation, and are not likely to relax in their patriotic labours, the perpetual attacks to which they are subjected are undoubtedly annoying, and to some extent weaken their authority, and put them out of touch with their co-religionists.

The Ministers have rendered, and are rendering, valuable services. When his increasing years and enfeebled health obliged Nubar Pasha to retire from public life in 1895, his place as President of the Council and Minister of the Interior was taken by Mustafa Pasha Fehmi, himself succeeded at the Ministry of War by Abani Pasha. Not only does the new President co-operate thoroughly with the occupying Power, but he has succeeded in imparting to his Cabinet a character of solidarity hitherto unknown in Egypt. A very short retrospect of Egyptian history will show what an immense step in advance is implied in the existence of a united Egyptian Ministry, pledged to a policy of conservative reform, furthering that policy with genuine conviction, and working in complete and cordial harmony with their English advisers. 'Immensum spatiis confecimus æquor.' We have attained a consummation that was devoutly to be wished, and for a long time seemed unattainable. It is not to be supposed that we shall allow the labours of the Ministers to be thwarted, or their prestige to be undermined. Any change that the present state of affairs, if it continues, may involve will rather be in an opposite direction.

C. E. D.

January, 1899.

APPENDIX III.

EGYPT IN 1904.

In the history of modern Egypt the year 1904 will be as memorable a date as that of the British occupation itself. In that year was signed the agreement between Great Britain and France which, in addition to its far-reaching consequences as regards the two countries primarily concerned, is destined to produce changes, equally far-reaching, in the Valley of the Nile. One of the minor results of that agreement has been to transfer some of Lord Milner's most eloquent and instructive chapters from the domain of actuality to that of history. No one will rejoice more than Lord Milner himself that all the complicated financial machinery prescribed by the London Convention, with its 'authorized' and 'unauthorized' expenditure, its reserve funds, its accumulating conversion economies, so lucidly explained in Chapter VIII., has now been swept away and become one of the curiosities of the past, and that 'the difficulty with France,' which formed the subject of Chapter XIII., has finally disappeared without leaving a trace of ill-feeling in either country.

By the terms of the Anglo-French agreement, France has recognised the permanency of the British occupation, and has given us a free hand in Egypt. With the cessation of French obstruction has also ceased all danger of international complications as regards other Powers. The attitude of France towards our occupation of the Nile Valley was based on a variety of considerations—historical, political, and financial, none of which apply in the case of the other European Powers. With the turn of the diplomatic wheel, the latter may have, from time to time, thought it their interest to aid and abet French hostility in Egyptian affairs, but they only came in as accessories after the fact, not as principals, and there is no fear that in future they will ever take the initiative in embarking on any such profitless enterprise. Henceforward—and this is a point of the first importance—we can pursue our task in Egypt without the feeling that the situation is a weak spot in our diplomatic armour. Above all, our occupation is no longer a bone of contention and an obstacle to the maintenance of friendly relations between ourselves and our neighbours across the Channel. From the point of view of Great Britain, it may be said that the Anglo-French arrangement has swept away all the political and diplomatic objections to the great undertaking to which we are committed in Egypt.

The change effected in the local conditions under which the country itself is administered is no less complete. All the cumbersome arrangements for the security of the bond-holders prescribed by the Law of Liquidation and the London Convention have been abolished. The whole complicated mass of Egyptian financial legislation has been swept away and replaced by a new Khedivial decree, which will henceforth be the sole law regulating the relations between the Egyptian Government and their creditors. The provisions of this decree were negotiated between England and France, and were subsequently approved by the four other Powers, whose consent was necessary—viz., Italy, Austria, Germany and Russia.

The broad principle underlying the new law is that suggested by Lord Milner in Appendix I. of this work ten years ago, where he says (p. 366), 'no one would object to the continuance of the arrangement by which certain revenues are paid in the first instance to the Caisse de la Dette. But as long as these revenues suffice to cover the interest on the debt and to provide any sinking fund which the Powers may deem adequate, the balance ought simply to be handed over to the Egyptian Government to deal with as it pleases, and the antiquated distinction of "authorized" and "unauthorized" expenditure should be swept away.' These words prophetically describe what is now an accomplished fact.

Under the new arrangement the Caisse de la Dette remains, but it is shorn of all its powers of interference in the financial administration of the country, and has reverted to its original functions of being a mere receiver of certain revenues specially assigned to the service of the debt. Those revenues have also been changed, and their amount brought into conformity with the annual charges which the Caisse has to meet. The Egyptian Government resume full liberty to deal as they please with their Customs revenue, and the receipts from the State railways and telegraphs and from the Port of Alexandria, and in their place pledge the land-tax in all the provinces of Egypt, with the exception of Keneh, the taxes of which were already contingently assigned to the Domains loan. The land-tax has been selected, firstly, because, being the most stable branch of the revenue, it provides the best security for the bond-holders; and, secondly, because it is the tax which the Government are least likely to wish to diminish. It is provided in the new decree that its assessment may not be reduced below four millions without the consent of the Powers. The annual charge on account of the debt, including the expenses of the Caisse de la Dette, fixed at £E35,000, amounts at the present moment to about £E3,600,000. The assigned land-taxes produce over £E4,200,000, so that there is an ample margin to insure the punctual payment of the Egyptian creditors. It is, however, undesirable to permit further accumulations in the hands of the Caisse, and it has therefore been provided that, as soon as the amount of land-tax in any one year paid into the Caisse reaches the sum required for the debt charge, during the remainder of that year the tax will be paid by the collecting authority directly into the Ministry of Finance. Further, as the receipts from land-tax come in principally during the autumn months, and will not, therefore, be sufficient to pay the interest, during the first half of each year, the Caisse has been provided with a working balance of £E500,000, which will be carried over from year to year. Lastly, the Caisse holds a sum of £E1,800,000, equal to a half-year's coupon, as a reserve fund, to which recourse may be had in the very improbable event of the Egyptian Government making default. The latter sum is invested in Egyptian stocks, and the interest thereon goes towards the payment of the annual debt charge, thereby preventing further accumulation. The Caisse retains its right, both individually and collectively, to bring an action against the Government in the event of any infringement of the stipulations of the new law. And that is the whole story, so far as the Caisse is concerned. It will been seen that its functions are no longer very arduous or very responsible.

On the other hand, the Egyptian Treasury has at last entered into possession of its own. The old reserve fund, with its liabilities and assets, the economies fund, and certain minor special accounts which had grown up under the former state of affairs, have all been transferred from the Caisse to the Ministry of Finance. At the end of 1903 these funds made up a sum of about £E7,800,000. Deducting the amount of £E2,300,000, which is retained by the Caisse, it will be seen that the Egyptian Government obtained possession of a lump sum of five and a half millions. The suppression of the Mixed Board which presided over the administration of the railways, telegraphs, and Port of Alexandria, has given the Government a free hand to deal with a department which, more than any other, stands in need of reform, and the efficiency of which concerns very nearly the material prosperity of the country. In the event of the sums placed at the disposal of the Government proving insufficient for the heavy capital expenditure required for the development of the resources both of Egypt and the

Soudan, the assent of the Caisse de la Dette will no longer be necessary before a further loan can be issued.

Without unduly extending this brief account, it would be impossible to enumerate all the many financial trammels which have now been swept away, but one point of considerable importance deserves special mention. Since the time when Egyptian bonds entered the category of gilt-edged securities, and the conversion of the Unified Debt on favourable terms came within the range of practical politics, Egypt's right to carry out that conversion has been seriously contested, not only by the bond-holders, but also by some of the foreign Governments in the countries where the debt is held. The question is a legal one, and the arguments on both sides are too technical to be reproduced here. It may, however, be said that the mere shadow of illegality would have been sufficient to prevent the conversion being carried through on anything like reasonable terms. The right of the Egyptian Government to convert all their debts has now been accepted by the Powers interested on the condition that the Guaranteed and Privileged Debts will not be paid off before July 15, 1910, and the Unified before July 15, 1912. The postponement of the proposed conversion for a few years is a small price to pay for the removal of all extraneous difficulties whenever the propitious moment for so extensive an operation arrives.

Such being the conditions under which Egypt begins a new epoch in her history, it may be of interest to give a brief account of her progress during the six years that have elapsed since Mr. (now Sir Clinton) Dawkins brought the story up to the year 1898. In the domain of finance the marvellous prosperity chronicled in the preceding pages has continued without a check, in spite of low Niles and epidemics of every description—misfortunes any one of which would, in former times, have sufficed to cause grave embarrassment to the Treasury. In this connection figures are more eloquent than words, and the following statement of the Egyptian revenue, including both ordinary and extraordinary receipts from 1899-1903, speaks for itself:

	Ordinary.	Extraordinary.	Total.
	£E	£E	£E
1899 ...	11,200,000	390,000	11,590,000
1900 ...	11,447,000	346,000	11,793,000
1901 ...	11,944,000	403,000	12,347,000
1902 ...	11,933,000	450,000	12,383,000
1903 ...	12,248,000	826,000	13,074,000

In order to fully appreciate the growth of revenue indicated by the above figures, it should be borne in mind that, during these five years, reductions of taxation were effected corresponding to an annual loss of £E358,000. During the first twenty years of the occupation, fiscal reform—or, in plain English, the abolition of unsound and burdensome taxes—held the first place in the financial policy adopted. That era may be said to have closed in 1903. The taxes that remain are established on sound and equitable principles, and press but lightly on the taxpayer, the taxation at the present time representing only 16s. per head of the population, as compared with 17s. 9d. in 1897, and £1 2s. 2d. in 1881. Any further growth of revenue will be most profitably utilized in providing the means for useful expenditure, rather than in lessening the already easily-met demands on the pockets of the people.

The ordinary and extraordinary expenditure incurred during these years is seen from the following table:

	Ordinary.	Extraordinary.	Total.
	£E	£E	£E
1899 ...	9,929,000	1,246,000	11,175,000
1900 ...	9,895,000	701,000	10,596,000
1901 ...	9,923,000	2,145,000	12,068,000
1902 ...	10,040,000	2,616,000	12,656,000
1903 ...	10,262,000	2,230,000	12,492,000

It will be observed that between 1899 and 1903 the ordinary expenditure increased by £E333,000, but practically the whole of this increase was due to the growth of the expenses of revenue-earning administrations, such as the railways, telegraphs, and post-office—an increase balanced by the corresponding growth in their receipts.

The extraordinary expenditure incurred during this period amounted to about nine millions, of which six and a half millions were devoted to objects of a directly remunerative character, such as irrigation and drainage projects, capital expenditure on railways, etc., and two and a half millions to sanitation, public buildings, and other works, which, though not technically productive, were necessary for the well-being of the community.

The most important financial reform taken in hand by the Government during the period under review was the reassessment of the land tax. The land tax as a whole is not heavy, but its assessment, which was made before the British occupation, is described by Lord Milner as most inequitable, and has long been condemned by all competent authorities. A law was passed in 1899 under which the burden will be distributed over the land in proportion to the fertility of the soil. The actual work of reassessment, holding by holding, has been energetically taken in hand; considerably more than half the cultivated area has now been finished, and a few more years will see this most important operation brought to a successful conclusion.

The indebtedness of the fellaheen has formed the text of many an Egyptian sermon. From time immemorial the village usurer has played a prominent part in Egyptian rural life, and once in the usurer's grasp, the poorer cultivator found it almost impossible ever to liberate himself. With a view to remedying this state of affairs, a series of experiments, at which not a few wiseacres shook their heads in disapproval, were conducted under Government auspices, culminating in the foundation of the Agricultural Bank. This institution lends money in small sums to the fellaheen at a reasonable rate of interest, the capital being repaid by instalments spread over a term of years. The interest and the annual amount for repayment of the loan together do not generally amount to what would formerly have been paid to the usurer merely as interest, and at the end of the period the cultivator has the advantage of finding that his debt has disappeared, instead of owing as much as, or perhaps more than, the original sum borrowed. The loans made by the bank are for very small amounts, and though the institution is a private enterprise, the payments due to it throughout the country are collected by Government agency. Moreover, the Government guarantees a return of 3 per cent. per annum on the capital employed. These advantages have been accorded to the bank in order that the fellaheen may be able to borrow on the most favourable terms possible. The dangers of measures of this description, especially in Oriental countries, are obvious enough. The only answer to be made is that, in practice, the experiment has been a complete success, and that it is enabling the peasantry, for the first time in their history, to shake off the yoke of the money-lender.

The most conspicuous event in recent Egyptian history has been the completion of the great Assouan dam, begun in 1898. Four years later, on December 10, 1902, in the presence of the Khedive and his Ministers, and a distinguished gathering representing all those of whatever nationality interested in the welfare of Egypt, the final stone completing the dam was laid by H.R.H. the Duchess of Connaught. The reservoir was actually used for the first time in 1903, and it will perhaps convey a clearer idea of its effect upon Egyptian agriculture—which is entirely an affair of irrigation—if, instead of giving the number of millions of cubic metres of water which it stores up, the simple fact be stated that, during the month of June, the most critical period for the irrigation of the summer crops, the available supply of water in the Nile was thereby doubled.

The total cost of this splendid monument of sagacious administration was under £E3,500,000, which sum includes the Assiout Barrage and certain minor works. Amongst the latter may be mentioned the consolidation of the foundations of the Temple of Philæ; and it is worthy of note that, when these foundations were examined as a consequence of the construction of the Assouan dam, it was found that many portions of the temple would have fallen before long without the measures which have now been executed. In spite, therefore, of the archæological protests to which the reservoir scheme originally gave rise, it would appear that the interests of Egyptology have gained, rather than suffered, by its execution.

The construction of the reservoir was not allowed to interfere with the normal progress of other public works. During these years about three millions were spent on irrigation and drainage, and 1,500 kilometres of new canals, 1,200 kilometres of new drains, and 700 kilometres of new agricultural roads were constructed. A fine building for the keeping of those priceless treasures of antiquity in which Egypt is so rich has been erected in Cairo, and the whole of these marvellous collections were transferred from the old museum at Gizeh within the space of eight months without the loss or destruction of a single object—a feat of which M. Maspero and his able assistants may well be proud.

The branches of government with which we have so far dealt show a continuous and steady progress that is almost monotonous. This is by no means the case with the two intimately connected and almost overlapping departments of Justice and the Interior. Of recent years these departments have had to bear the brunt of the attacks of hostile critics, and the police and parquet question is a hardy annual which even Lord Cromer has so far been unable to exterminate. Nor need this be matter for surprise. The application of a civilized judicial system to a people who had been accustomed to regard the law as one of the worst methods of administrative oppression was bound to be a long and difficult process. The abolition of the principle of vicarious punishment, and the introduction of the Western idea that a man is innocent until he can be proved guilty, have tended to weaken the authority of those responsible for the maintenance of public security during the transition period that must elapse until the people become accustomed to the new order. All change in the daily life and habits of thought of a people is slow and painful, especially when, as in the present instance, they are the product of centuries of mis-government. The problem was rendered more difficult by the fact that a judicial system, full of unnecessary complications and formalities, and altogether unsuited to the needs of an Oriental population, had already taken root in the country before our arrival. Since that time those responsible for the administration of the law have been struggling with varying success to produce good results under a system that cannot be described as satisfactory. Even so, however, many improvements have been effected. The work of decentralizing justice, of bringing it home to the doors of the people and reducing its cost, has made considerable progress. Something has been done to minimize the law's delay and to reduce the excessive period that intervened between the commission of crime and its punishment. The police are growing less corrupt and more efficient, and their officers show a distinct improvement. It cannot, however, be said that the departments of Justice or the Interior have as yet settled down into a normal and steady rate of progress, and doubts are still expressed as to whether their organization is being built on sure foundations.

While, however, our comparative want of success in this branch of administration may be attributed, in some measure, to defects of system, the real cause lies deeper, and is to be found in the inherent deficiencies of a population that has been oppressed for centuries. For this the only true and permanent remedy is to elevate the moral standard of the masses by means of a statesmanlike educational policy. This end the Ministry of Public Instruction endeavours to promote by the diffusion of an elementary form of education, consisting of the Arabic equivalent of the three 'R's,' throughout the whole country. The private village schools, known as kuttabs, have been improved and encouraged by means of a system of grants-in-aid to those schools that are willing to submit to official inspection and can show a certain standard of efficiency. During the past six years the Government have been gradually extending the area of their operations. In 1898 the number of pupils under Government inspection in the village schools was 7,500. In 1903 the number had increased to 76,000—representing the pupils of some 2,600 schools. There are altogether 10,000 of these schools in the country, and it will require the expenditure of much time and money before they can become even moderately efficient. There is, however, no other means of raising the general educational level of the mass of the population. The two other main features of the educational policy which has been adopted in Egypt consist in the encouragement of technical education for the artisan class, and the provision of a limited amount of higher instruction with a view to training young Egyptians for the Civil Service. In order to promote the first-named object, the Government have recently founded in Cairo an institution which is not so much a school, with its natural tendency to drift into book-work and theory to the detriment of practical application, as a model workshop where Egyptian boys of the artisan class are trained in good methods in the same way as they have hitherto been trained in inferior methods—namely, by the system of apprenticeship. The experiment has been very successful, and similar institutions are being created in other towns.

The Civil Service, both of Egypt and the Soudan, is composed, as far as possible, of local subjects, and the number of European officials is limited to what is absolutely necessary for the good administration of the country. For all places that can be efficiently filled by Egyptians no European need apply. Under these circumstances the choice of the few Englishmen that are employed in the Egyptian service becomes doubly important. Failures among our countrymen are not only formidable obstacles in the course of progress, but lower the prestige of the whole body of their compatriots in Egypt. It is impossible to overestimate the desirability of getting hold of a good stamp of man, suitable to the somewhat exceptional requirements of the case. Until recently the Service was recruited in a somewhat haphazard way by personal selection by the heads of departments. A new system has now been introduced, and in future the candidates will be, as far as possible, chosen from those who have completed a University course and passed out in honours. The final selection will be made after consultation with the University authorities, and after personally interviewing the applicants, by some of the high Egyptian and Soudanese officials. The accepted candidates will be given a year in which to pass an examination in Arabic, and they will then receive appointments as vacancies occur. Facilities for giving the necessary instruction in Arabic have now been created both at Oxford and Cambridge.

The story of the reconquest of the Soudan has already been told in these pages. It remains to give some account of the first steps by which this vast and remote country is being slowly brought from the abomination of desolation, which existed under the Dervish rule, into the peaceful and orderly conditions of a civilized community.

The Soudan problem differs, in many important respects, from that which has been so successfully solved in Egypt. It is both easier and more difficult—easier, because it is free from those artificial trammels, due to internationalism, which have hampered the progress of Egypt; more difficult, because the material obstacles to be overcome are far greater. The political status of the Soudan is defined by the Convention of January 19, 1899, between Great Britain and Egypt, which instrument declares the general principles under which the administration shall be carried on. It was framed for the express purpose of relieving the Soudan from all the cumbersome international institutions that the wisdom of Europe had imposed upon Egypt. The British and Egyptian flags float side by side at Khartoum and elsewhere throughout the Soudan, as a sign that the land, which was reconquered by the joint efforts of the two countries, is administered under their joint control, without any interference from outside. Again, since the destruction of the Khalifa and his followers in November, 1899, we have not had to reckon with either the open or the disguised hostility of any large section of the Soudan population, unlike the situation with which we had to cope at the outset of the occupation, when not only many of the Egyptians, but nearly all the foreign colonies, were on the side of the opposition. On the other hand, the natural conditions with which the task was surrounded were far more unfavourable than was the case with Egypt. Even the vestiges of a former civilization had been obliterated, and the edifice of government had practically to be built up from the very foundation. This remote country, with an area of 950,000 square miles, is inhabited by a population that is now roughly estimated at two millions. The people themselves are not an industrious race, in which respect they are the reverse of the Egyptians. Their wants are few and simple; they have no desire to improve their position; and they consider that the best use to be made of their freedom is to labour as little as possible. Lastly, the country seems devoid of that remarkable recuperative power which has been so considerable a help in the regeneration of Egypt herself.

The main lines of the administrative system which is applied to the Soudan are laid down in the Convention which has already been mentioned; but inasmuch as Egypt is responsible for the equilibrium of the Soudan budget, and has to make good any deficiency out of her own treasury, the ultimate financial control must necessarily be exercised from Cairo. In this, as in other branches of administration, the principle adopted has been to avoid over-centralization, and to reduce to a minimum the danger of unnecessary interference in matters of local detail. The Government so established is not, as is often supposed, a military Government, but rather a Government carrying out the ordinary principles of civil administration through the agency of military officers. The chief disadvantage of this system is its want of stability, as the officers are liable to be removed at the moment when their services are of the greatest value. The first steps have already been taken for the formation of a permanent Soudan Civil Service, and in process of time it will be desirable that the military should gradually yield to the civil element.

There is no more certain sign of the direction in which a country is progressing than that afforded by the condition of its finances. The following table shows the record of the Soudan during its brief existence as a respectable community:

	Soudan Revenue.	Soudan Ordinary Expenditure (Civil and Military).	Deficit met by Egyptian Government.	Extraordinary Credits granted by Egyptian Government.	Total Expenditure supported by Egypt.
	£E	£E	£E	£E	£E
1899 ...	127,000	509,000	382,000	375,000	757,000
1900 ...	157,000	599,000	442,000	116,000	558,000
1901 ...	242,000	626,000	384,000	528,000	912,000
1902 ...	270,000	640,000	370,000	61,000	431,000
1903 ...	336,000	686,000	350,000	47,000	397,000

The satisfactory side of these figures is the steady progression of the revenue, which has wisely been employed in furthering the development of the country and introducing much-needed administrative reforms, rather than in reducing the Egyptian Contribution.

It will be observed that the total cost to Egypt of the Soudan during these five years amounted to over three millions. On the other hand, the Egyptian Customs collect some £E60,000 a year on goods destined for the Soudan, which amount is included in the receipts of the Egyptian Treasury. An annual charge of more than half a million a year may seem a heavy burden for so small a country as Egypt, but in return she not only obtains security from Dervish invasion, but is assured that the course of the Upper Nile, upon which her prosperity depends, can never fall into hostile hands. Further, it cannot be doubted that, if the judicious policy of allowing the increasing receipts of the Soudan to be applied to Soudanese purposes, and of granting considerable sums for capital expenditure in that country be continued, the deficit of the Soudan budget will, in a comparatively few years, disappear. For the moment what the country most requires is capital, and the direction in which that capital is most profitably expended is in improving the means of communication. Much has already been done. The railway line has been completed as far as Khartoum. By the cutting of the sudd that blocked the channel of the Upper Nile, free navigation is assured as far as Gondokoro, and a regular tourist service to that place from Cairo by rail and river is now in full working order. The Egyptian Government have recently approved the proposal for a railway between the Upper Nile and the Red Sea, and have voted the necessary funds—the estimated cost is £E1,770,000—for its construction. Until there is direct communication with the Red Sea the material development of the Soudan will not make any very rapid progress. At present the long and expensive journey up the Nile Valley stifles not only the export, but also the import trade. The fact that a ton of coal at Khartoum costs £4 speaks for itself. When once cheap communication with the outer world has been established, it will become possible to encourage irrigation projects and the production of staple articles of general consumption, such as cotton.

While the material resources of the Soudan are thus in a fair way to multiply, the first steps for the raising of the moral standard of the people have been taken. The Gordon College, which owes its creation to the generous response made by the British public to Lord Kitchener's appeal, is now an accomplished fact, and already provides a practical and useful course of instruction in the vernacular for the youthful generation of Soudanese. At present it is in its first stage of being a primary school, but as the students become capable of learning higher things the institution will gradually develop into a college in the true sense of the word. In addition to the Gordon College, primary schools have also been established at Khartoum,

Omdurman, Wadi Halfa, Suakin, and Berber. These schools are attended by about 600 pupils, and eventually they will be able to supply the subordinate employés of the Soudan Government Service. A small industrial school has been established in connection with the dockyard works at Omdurman, and workshops in which boys are taught carpentry, smith and foundry work and cotton-ginning are attached to the Gordon College. In a word, the schoolmaster is abroad, and it may be hoped that he is laying a solid foundation on which the future legislators of the Soudan may build.

In 1884 General Gordon wrote: 'The Soudan is a useless possession, ever was so, and ever will be so.' The foregoing sketch of the first five years of Anglo-Egyptian administration in the Soudan, under the inspiration of the guiding spirit, who has already brought about the regeneration of Egypt by the same sober and statesmanlike policy, proves that General Gordon's prophecy was unduly pessimistic.

A few words may be added on the future that lies before Egypt, now that the political situation resulting from the occupation has been recognised by Europe, and the veil, which had already become very thin, has been removed from what Lord Milner described as the veiled Protectorate. It is true that the capitulations, and all the intricate judicial machinery, such as the mixed Courts and Consular jurisdiction, that result from them, still survive. But they survive because England wishes it so for the moment. The time has not yet come for the introduction of a judicial system, such as exists in European countries, applicable to all the inhabitants of Egypt alike, whether native or foreign. Whenever it does come—and that will depend largely upon the progress made by the existing native tribunals—we have no longer to fear external opposition in abolishing a privilege which will have become an abuse. The Egyptian question is, in fact, no longer one of the principal pieces of the diplomatic game of chess, and the problem has become purely administrative. If, however, Great Britain's hands are thus freed in dealing with Egypt, her responsibilities have also become greater, and she can no longer plead political complications in the event of failure.

What use, then, will she make of this trust that has devolved upon her? In the way of material progress it is all more or less plain sailing. What the country most needs is further capital expenditure on remunerative works both in Egypt and the Soudan. For this purpose there will be some ten and a half millions available within the next few years; five and a half millions from the Conversion Economies Fund, three millions from the liquidation of the Daïra property, and two millions from the Domains liquidation. Should these sums prove insufficient, the means for raising further funds easily and cheaply are now secured.

In Egypt—and doubtless the Soudan will tell the same tale—there is one form of profitable investment that appears inexhaustible, and that is the execution of vast irrigation projects, whether they consist of reservoirs for storing water until the cultivator requires it, or of canals to bring it automatically to the fields. Since the recovery of the Soudan the Upper Nile regions, including the great lakes and all their irrigation possibilities, have been thoroughly studied by Sir William Garstin, the greatest living authority on the subject. He has recommended a programme based on the principle of utilizing the waters of the White Nile for the benefit of Egypt, and those of the Blue Nile for the benefit of the Soudan. The total cost of the works comes to about twenty-one millions, and their execution would take from ten to fifteen years under the most favourable circumstances. In addition to this vast scheme, about three millions are required to place the Egyptian railways in thorough order, and further sums for improving the railway communications of the Soudan. The Egyptian Government will, therefore, find no difficulty in disposing of their surplus funds.

A problem of much greater complexity, which will require more and more careful handling as time goes on, is presented by the development of the Egyptians as a race, and the changes that must inevitably ensue in their relations with the predominant Englishman. The introduction of the principles of good government, the enjoyment of material prosperity, the spread of education, are good things in themselves, but the Egyptian is obtaining them too easily, without going through the stress and strife that enable a people to extract from them the greatest amount of benefit. The effect on the Egyptian national character is not wholly good, and there is a danger that the fruit will be rotten before it is ripe. To discuss this question in all its bearings would require more space than is here available, but it may be briefly said that the solution will be found rather in the development of the instincts of the people in the direction of local self-government than in the introduction of European institutions unsuited to the genius of the Oriental character.

Whatever difficulties the future may have in store in this connection, it is a pleasant task to be able to chronicle that the relations between English and Egyptians have never been more cordial than in the last six years. In the former editions of this work, the influence of the Palace and its surroundings was considered the dark cloud on the horizon which might portend future trouble. Happily, these forebodings have not been realized. During all these years, though, of course, divergencies of opinion on minor matters have from time to time arisen, no serious misunderstanding has occurred between the Khedive and his English advisers, and His Highness has become convinced that the end to which all parties are working is the same—namely, the welfare of his country. The Egyptian Ministry, under the Presidency of Moustafa Pasha Fehmy, have remained unchanged and united since 1895, and have continuously and cordially co-operated with their English collaborators to the great advantage of their countrymen. In non-official circles also a change has come over the attitude taken up towards the British occupation. Readers of the previous pages will be acquainted with the name of Riaz Pasha, and the considerable rôle which he has played in Egyptian history. He is the last survivor of the old Egyptian statesmen who enjoyed power before the days of the occupation. In temperament and character he is a conservative of the conservatives, an Egyptian of the Egyptians, and may be said to represent all that is worthy of representation in the party whose cry is 'Egypt for the Egyptians.' One quality Riaz Pasha has always possessed, and that is the quality of saying straight out exactly what he thinks. He has never been a respecter of persons, and has always had the courage of his convictions. Such being the man, the following words spoken by him at the opening of an industrial school founded by the Mohammedan Benevolent Society, of which he is President, and which, by the way, is suspected of Anglophobe tendencies, are full of significance.

After a cordial acknowledgment of their indebtedness to Lord Cromer for his support and encouragement, Riaz Pasha continued: 'Allow me to say what I think. If we cast a glance on the past, and if we compare it to the present, we see that our ideas have taken a new development in the direction of science and progress. These indigenous charitable institutions, which are increasing in number, are an indication of this change. When we reflect on the past we must congratulate ourselves on what the present brings us, and on what we may still further hope for in the future.'

Such words from the mouth of one who has often been a severe critic of our Egyptian policy are full of hope as regards the future relations between English and Egyptians, and with them this brief summary may fitly end.

E. G.

July, 1904.

INDEX

THE END